Perfecting Perfection

Perfecting Perfection

Essays in Honor of
Henry D. Rack

Edited by
Robert Webster

☙PICKWICK *Publications* · Eugene, Oregon

PERFECTING PERFECTION
Essays in Honor of Henry D. Rack

Copyright © 2015 Robert Webster. All rights reserved. Except for brief quotations in critical publications or reviews, no part of this book may be reproduced in any manner without prior written permission from the publisher. Write: Permissions. Wipf and Stock Publishers, 199 W. 8th Ave., Suite 3, Eugene, OR 97401.

Pickwick Publications
An Imprint of Wipf and Stock Publishers
199 W. 8th Ave., Suite 3
Eugene, OR 97401

www.wipfandstock.com

ISBN 13: 978-1-61097-849-1

Cataloguing-in-Publication Data

Perfecting perfection : essays in honor of Henry D. Rack / edited by Robert Webster.

xiv + 298 p. ; 23 cm. Includes bibliographical references and index(es).

ISBN 13: 978-1-61097-849-1

1. Rack, Henry D. 2. Wesley, John, 1703–1791. 3. Methodist Church—History—18th century. I. Webster, Robert, 1956–. II. Title.

BX8495.W5 P47 2015

Manufactured in the U.S.A.   11/11/2015

A portion of John Wigger's essay "John Wesley and Francis Asbury" appeared previously in his book, *American Saint: Francis Asbury & The Methodists* (Oxford University Press, 2009). Used by permission.

For Henry D. Rack
Friend, Teacher, Mentor

Contents

Abbreviations | ix

Contributors | xi

Introduction | 1
—Robert Webster

1 From Arminius (d. 1609) to the Synod of Dort (1618–1619) | 8
 —W. Stephen Gunter

2 Robert Barnes and John Wesley's Reformation Heritage | 29
 —David Lowes Watson

3 The Exercise of the Presence of God: Holy Conferencing as a Means of Grace | 61
 —Richard P. Heitzenrater

4 Perfecting Plain Truth for Plain People: John Wesley's Sermons | 81
 —Patrick Streiff

5 Mission Spirituality in the Early Methodist Preachers | 103
 —Philip R. Meadows

CONTENTS

6 Medicine on Demand: John Wesley's Enlightened Treatment of the Sick | 130
—Deborah Madden

7 Wesley's Invisible World: Witchcraft and the Temperature of Preternatural Belief | 147
—Owen Davies

8 John Wesley and Francis Asbury | 173
—John Wigger

9 Echoes of Wesley on the US Southwestern Frontier: The *Autobiography* of William Stevenson | 189
—Ted A. Campbell

10 "Did God Do That?": Common and Separating Factors of Eighteenth-Century Methodism and Contemporary Pentecostal and Charismatic Renewal | 208
—Robert Webster

11 The Oxford Movement and Evangelicalism: Parallels and Contrasts in Two Nineteenth-Century Movements of Religious Revival | 233
—Peter B. Nockles

12 From *The Soul of Dominic Wildthorne* to the Wesleyan Guild of Divine Service: Some Methodist Responses to Anglo-Catholicism in Victorian and Edwardian England | 260
—Martin Wellings

13 Bibliography of the Principal Published Writings of Henry Denman Rack | 280
—Clive D. Field

Index | 285

Abbreviations

AM	*Arminian Magazine*
BEW	*The Bicentennial Edition of the Works of John Wesley.* Edited by Richard P. Heitzenrater. 19 vols. Nashville: Abingdon, 1975– .
BJRULM	*Bulletin of the John Rylands University Library of Manchester*
EMP	*The Lives of Early Methodist Preachers: Chiefly Written by Themselves.* Edited by Thomas Jackson. 4th ed. 6 vols. London: Wesleyan Conference Office, 1871.
JEH	*The Journal of Ecclesiastical History*
JLFA	*The Journal and Letters of Francis Asbury.* Edited by Elmer T. Clark, J. Manning Potts, and Jacob S. Payton. 3 vols. London: Epworth, 1958.
JWJW	*The Works of John Wesley.* Edited by Thomas Jackson. 3rd ed. 14 vols. 1872. Reprinted in 7 vols. Grand Rapids: Baker, 2007.
LJWT	*The Letters of the Rev. John Wesley, A. M.* Edited by John Telford. 8 vols. 1931. Reprint, London: Epworth, 1960.
MH	*Methodist History*
PWHS	*Proceedings of the Wesleyan Historical Society*
WTJ	*Wesleyan Theological Journal*

Contributors

Ted A. Campbell serves as Professor of Church History at Perkins School of Theology, Southern Methodist University, in Dallas, Texas. His principal area of research has been on Methodist founder John Wesley, and he has authored a number of books and articles on Wesley and early Methodist history. In addition, he has written on ecumenical consensus in Christian teachings and on the history of the southwestern United States. He served for two years as a Landmark Commissioner for the city of Dallas, Texas.

Owen Davies is Professor of Social History at the University of Hertfordshire. His research covers the history of witchcraft, magic, and ghosts, and the broader related areas of popular religion and popular medicine. His latest book is *America Bewitched: The Story of Witchcraft after Salem* (2013).

Clive D. Field is Honorary Research Fellow in the School of History and Cultures, University of Birmingham and a former Director of Scholarship and Collections at The British Library. He has written extensively on the social history of British Methodism (most recently on its demographic aspects and the history of the Allan Library) and has been bibliography editor for the Wesley Historical Society since 1974. He is also an authority on British religious statistics and co-directs the British Religion in Numbers project at the University of Manchester.

W. Stephen Gunter is Associate Dean for Methodist Studies and Research Professor at Duke Divinity School. His most recent book is *Arminius and His "Declaration of Sentiments": An Annotated Translation with Introduction and Theological Commentary* (2012).

Richard P. Heitzenrater is William Kellon Quick Professor Emeritus of Church History and Wesley Studies at the Divinity School, Duke University. From 1987 through 2014 he served as the General Editor of the Wesley Works Editorial Project producing the thirty-four-volume Bicentennial Edition of the Works of John Wesley. In addition to the seven volumes of John Wesley's *Journal & Diaries,* he has published over a dozen books, including *Wesley and the People Called Methodist* (2nd ed.), now in seven languages; *The Elusive Mr. Wesley* (2nd ed.); *Mirror and Memory*; as well as five dozen other scholarly articles and chapters of books. A retired elder in the Western Pennsylvania Annual Conference of the United Methodist Church, he chaired the committee that wrote the present doctrinal statement (Part II) of *The Book of Discipline.*

Deborah Madden is a Senior Lecturer at the University of Brighton. She has published books and articles on Wesley's medical activity, as well as the relationship of dissenting religion to Enlightenment intellectual culture. She is currently writing a book about Victorian life writings and autobiographies as historical sources.

Philip Meadows is Senior Research Fellow at Nazarene Theological College (UK) and Director of the Inspire Movement, an ecumenical and international network that equips the church for disciple-making ministry in the Wesleyan spirit. He is a past president of the Wesleyan Theological Society, and has served on the faculties of Cliff College (UK), Garrett-Evangelical Theological Seminary (USA), and Westminster College, Oxford (UK). His current research and publication interests seek to combine theology and spirituality in the Wesleyan tradition with the challenges of discipleship, leadership, and mission in the contemporary church. His recent work includes "Mission and Discipleship in a Digital Culture," *Mission Studies* 29 (2012), and *The DNA of Wesleyan Discipleship* (2013).

Peter Nockles is a librarian and curator in the Department of Rare Books & Maps, Special Collections, in the John Rylands Library, University of Manchester, and an Honorary Research in the School of Arts, Languages & Cultures, University of Manchester. He has also been a Visiting Fellow at Oriel College, Oxford, 2006–11, and was a major contributor to *Oriel College: A History* (2013); *The Oxford Movement in Context* (1994; paperback 1997); the co-editor of *The Oxford Movement, Europe and the Wider World, 1833–1930* (2012) and contributed to the nineteenth-century volume (6) of the *History of the University of Oxford* (1997). Recently, he has edited and contributed to a volume of essays titled *Reinventing the Reformation in the*

Nineteenth Century in a themed issue of the *Bulletin of the John Rylands Library* (vol. 90, no. 1, Spring 2014). He is also one of the three editors of a forthcoming Oxford University Press *Handbook of the Oxford Movement* and has contributed to a forthcoming volume *Receptions of Newman* to be published by Oxford University Press and to the *Oxford Handbook of John Henry Newman*, also to be published by Oxford University Press.

Patrick Streiff is Bishop of the United Methodist Church for Central and Southern Europe. He has published *Reluctant Saint? A Theological Biography of Fletcher of Madley* (2001) and *Methodism in Europe: 19th and 20th Century* (2003). He has most recently published a book in French about John Wesley's theology.

David Lowes Watson is a member of the Order of Elders in the Tennessee Conference of The United Methodist Church. Prior to his retirement in 2005 he served pastoral appointments in the Southern Illinois and North Carolina Conferences, taught at Perkins School of Theology and Wesley Theological Seminary, and was on staff at the General Board of Discipleship of The United Methodist Church where he introduced Covenant Discipleship groups as a connectional ministry. He has written extensively in Methodist studies and practical theology, including *The Early Methodist Class Meeting* (1985), *God Does Not Foreclose* (1990), and *Forming Christian Disciples* (1991).

Robert Webster is Senior Pastor of Fort Donelson Memorial United Methodist Church in Tennessee and former Professor of Methodist Studies in the School of Theology at the University of South (Sewanee, Tennessee). In addition to being the editor of this collection of essays, he has also co-edited, with Clive D. Field, a collection of essays devoted to Charles Wesley in the *Bulletin of the John Rylands University Library* (2006), authored a book on John Wesley's rhetoric of the supernatural, *Methodism and the Miraculous: John Wesley's Idea of the Supernatural and the Identification of Methodists in the Eighteenth Century* (2013) and several articles in the area of Methodist history and theology. He is currently working on research that addresses the importance of dreams and visions among Methodists and other evangelicals in the Enlightenment.

Martin Wellings is Superintendent Minister of the Oxford Methodist Circuit and Past President of the World Methodist Historical Society. He has written widely on Methodist and evangelical history, co-editing *The Ashgate Research Companion to World Methodism* (2013).

John Wigger is Professor and Chair of the Department of History at the University of Missouri. His research focuses on American religious and cultural history. Professor Wigger's books include *American Saint: Francis Asbury and the Methodists* (2009), *Taking Heaven by Storm: Methodism and the Rise of Popular Christianity in America* (1998; paperback 2001), and *Methodism and the Shaping of American Culture*, co-edited with Nathan Hatch (2001). He earned a BS from West Virginia University and a PhD from the University of Notre Dame.

Introduction

Robert Webster

WHEN HENRY D. RACK published his celebrated volume on John Wesley in 1989, *Reasonable Enthusiast: John Wesley and the Rise of Methodism*, it was recognized as a *tour de force* in the field of Methodist and Wesleyan thought. In artistic fashion, Rack painted a life of John Wesley and the rise of the Methodist movement in the eighteenth century. The depth and precision of Rack's work has yet to be surpassed by other scholars in the field. If Dr Rack's contribution to the study of Methodism had been confined to *Reasonable Enthusiast* it would have been admirable. However, throughout his career he has written on Methodism and its intersection with such issues as religious enthusiasm, class meetings, women in the movement, deathbed experiences, and a vast array of individuals who went on to make their own stamp on the movement. Most recently, he has made another contribution to the study of Methodism by editing the *Minutes* of the Methodist Conference from its inception in 1744 to Wesley's death in 1791. A work that will be a resource for scholars and generations to come.

The life and career of Henry D. Rack is unquestionably one of international distinction and the contributions in this Festschrift highlight the influence of his reading of John Wesley as an important religious individual of the eighteenth century and the movement that has been extended into the modern world. Additionally, the scholars collected here take into account the rich historical background of John Wesley's life, which spanned the eighteenth century, but converse with Rack's creative and instrumental interpretation of the movement that John Wesley inspired.

In the first two chapters W. Stephen Gunter and David Lowes Watson open an understanding of John Wesley's theological programme by looking at two linchpins in ecclesiastical history and reformation thought. Professor

Gunter in his chapter delves into the rich but complicated transition from Arminus's thought to the significance of Arminianism in the seventeenth century. Gunter reminds us that from 1610 to 1620 there was an incredible amount of publications that "was nothing less than rhetorical and theological warfare." His contribution here has incisively traced the loss of a pure Arminian theology to one that jacked up the Synod of Dort (1618–1619) with an increased passion concerning the issues that the Arminians considered essential to theological orthodoxy. For David Lowes Watson's part, a return to Robert Barnes's understanding of the doctrine of Justification by Faith illuminates Wesley's own captivity to the doctrine. Watson points out that after preaching to prisoners in Oxford (1738) John Wesley began to consider the *Homilies* of the Church of England and extracted all that he could find on justification. The following year, Wesley published two more extracts by Barnes on the subject. Watson's detailed analysis of Barnes and his political, social, and theological developments in the sixteenth century is instructive for ascertaining both Barnes's and Wesley's attraction to the doctrine of justification. The intensity of evangelical faith is highlighted among Barnes and Wesley who lived in separate centuries but also faced opposition in remarkably similar ways. Despite neither being considered major theologians, both were both instrumental in igniting the fire of justification in the hearts of men and women in their respective generations. As with Barnes, so also was the case with Wesley, Watson maintains that the fundamental instruction gained for contemporary believers is how can the church avoid a sectarianism that is caused by a spirit of Protestantism while being open to the fundamental truth of justification by faith. For Watson, the doctrine is not a "personalized soteriological antipasto," but a movement of the Holy Spirit that initiates a radical and intimate reconciliation with God. Watson's reading of Barnes provides insightful resources for examining John Wesley and his excitement about justification by faith in its theological sense and in its social and political ramifications—which is at the root of reformation thought.

In the next group of essays important and insightful treatments are offered for understanding John Wesley's theology and its implication for accurately observing the rise of Methodism in the eighteenth century. In chapter 3, Richard P. Heitzenrater examines an often-neglected part of John Wesley's idea of the means of grace: Holy Conferencing. In so doing, Heitzenrater analyzes the idea of Christian Conference in the "Large" *Minutes* and maintains that Wesley valued religious conversation in special and unique ways. Religious talk, Heitzenrater insists, has the qualitative characteristic of holiness which fundamentally means that the Christian must emulate Jesus Christ. Therefore, justification is not a sufficient resting place in Christian conversation for Wesley. By necessity there must be a movement toward sanctification and a full understanding of grace. Heitzenrater warns, however, that we should forget anything we have been told about grace. Instead of being understood as a means to pious living grace should be formulated so as to reveal both its passive and active components. Therefore, the grace (transforming presence) of God that is communicated to the believer through the Holy Spirit offers a transformation both in our relationship with God and one another. The opportunities for this transformation are what Wesley, and other evangelicals, termed the means of grace. And while Wesleyans have traditionally seen divine grace in terms of three movements; i.e., prevenient, justifying, and sanctifying; Heitzenrater contends that there are many movement to God's grace that should not be limited to three movements but instead be seen as infinite and multi-faceted. In chapter 4, Bishop Patrick Streiff builds upon his foundational study of John Fletcher and uncovers the ways that Fletcher influenced Wesley in his sermons. In analyzing Wesley's sermons, Streiff notes that after 1760 there occurred a shift in Wesley's emphasis. With the first three volumes of the Standard sermons there had been a focus on the beginning of salvation: sin, repentance, and the new birth. However, with volume four of the sermons in 1760, the focus changes to sanctification. Streiff maintains that both the Perfectionist controversies of the 1760s and Fletcher's understanding of the doctrine of Sanctification were looming in the mind of Wesley as he wrestled with the teaching. In distinction from traditional understandings of the Baptism of the Holy Spirit, including the one I propose in my own contribution to this volume, Streiff asserts that Fletcher contributed to a shift in Wesley's thinking where the experience of sanctification should correctly be seen as an "ongoing process of love" and not rest in a "Second Blessing" *per se*. This, contends Streiff, would have benefited both the holiness preachers of the nineteenth century and the Pentecostal ones in the twentieth. In chapter 5, Philip Meadows enters into the subject of Methodists preachers and their autobiographical accounts of mission and ministry. With various accounts, from the early Methodist preachers, Meadows argues that these followers of Wesley considered themselves to be fundamentally "co-working with God." In an interesting and provocative treatment of the autobiographies, the self-understanding of the Methodist preachers is evaluated. Quite distinct from contemporary preaching styles the early Methodists often preached several times a day and were fond of interjecting their own experiences into the sermon as a key hermeneutical device. With insightful analysis, Meadows offers a glimpse into the commitment and conviction of the early Methodist preachers and the spiritual lives they extended in their witness of the gospel. Often they were disturbed about the condition of souls, including their own, and were not afraid of recording their own despair and resolve in reaching a resting place in Christ. Furthermore, Meadows argues that the resolve demonstrated by Wesley's co-labours in mission and ministry was fleshed out in their belief of the importance of completing their task against unruly and unholy forces of spiritual warfare. On many occasions the work of a Methodist preacher caused such opposition that they were often faced with violence and death. In this turbulent ambiance, "these narratives of persecution" often ended with signs of divine providence and confirmation that their mission and ministry was a divine one. With Meadows treatment of these important documents the reader is reminded not only of the importance of evangelism and discipleship but also the validity of their pursuit in each and every generation. Deborah Madden in her essay for this volume explores the interesting but complex issue of John Wesley's knowledge of medicine and his commitment to healing. Placing Wesley's understanding of natural corruption against the background of his theology of sin, Madden explores a rich means of understanding John Wesley's concept of sin and salvation. The pride of Adam in the Garden is the beginning point in Wesley's mind, Madden correctly argues, "for all of the inconsistencies of human nature." From this departing point Madden follows John Wesley's understanding of medicine and faith as important remedies for the treatment of body and soul. Key to Madden's examination of Wesley is her treatment of the *Primitive Physic* and its popularity in the eighteenth century. Taking up Rack's metaphor of Wesley as "cultural mediator," Madden convincingly argues that the phrase is best seen in the way the *Primitive Physic* distilled the often complicated medical theories of the day and how they were beneficial for the Methodists who were interested in healing for both body and soul. Often Wesley interjected medical imagery into his sermons and Madden shows how his understandings of both natural and supernatural healing were embraced by Methodists. In Owen Davies's chapter 7 in this collection of essays, we have a splendid treatment of John Wesley's understanding of witchcraft and exorcism. For a long time it was an assumption in eighteenth-century historiography that after the emergence of mechanical philosophy that individuals living in the Enlightenment abandoned a belief in the invisible world. In his commanding analysis of the sources, Davies demonstrates how seriously Wesley viewed witchcraft and demonology and in what manner that belief became a central aspect of Methodists living in the Enlightenment. Key to this development was Wesley's editorial supervision of the *Arminian Magazine* and the popularity that it enjoyed in Methodist households but also for broader evangelical circles as well. With the *Arminian Magazine* and treatments of the cases like the Yatton possession case, there emerged "a boon in public debates about the invisible world." Certainly there were many detractors that Wesley had to defend the

Methodists against but, at a more important level, there emerged in Wesley's mind an opportunity to create a rhetoric that treated such experiences seriously. And though the passion for such treatments diminished after John Wesley's death, they were not extinguished. Davies's contribution examines several nineteenth century examples of belief in the existence of witchcraft and exorcism among Methodists and though these and other instances indicate that continual belief in the supernatural was still deeply ingrained in the Methodist spirit and mind.

In chapter 8 John Wigger provides a turning point in our understanding of Methodism and provides a comparative analysis of the lives of John Wesley and Francis ("Frank") Asbury. In so doing we look to Asbury as one of the driving forces of the Methodist witness in America. Wigger, who points to different levels of similarity between the two men, focuses his treatment on Asbury and what was distinct about his life which enabled and empowered the Methodists in North America. While Wesley was highly educated and spent a good deal of time managing a proficient publishing career, Asbury never published anything outside of some letters and his own *Journal*. What became the definitive dividing mark, however, was the American Revolution. A good many of the Methodists in England condemned the Americans as schismatics. John Wesley, John Fletcher, and Charles Wesley all wrote critically about the separation of the American colonies from the authority of British rule. Charles's poetry was particular invective when, for example, he described the patriots as "fiends of hell." For Asbury's part, Wesley had made a grave mistake in delving into American politics and should have kept to his evangelical thrust of winning souls. Despite this deep divide Wigger sees a lot of spiritual similarities between the two leaders of Methodism. Both had a core understanding of the importance of personal piety, discipline, and sacrificial living. Like Wesley, Asbury gave away most of the money that he earned and saw Christ in the poor in profound and meaningful ways. Wigger's analysis of both John Wesley and Francis Asbury provides much to contemplate as the history of Methodism unfolded at the turn of the century in American history. In chapter 9, noted historian Ted A. Campbell explores Methodism in the southwestern frontier by analyzing the *Autobiography* of William Stevenson. The *Autobiography* written first in 1841 was later serialized (1858) in the *New Orleans Christian Advocate*. In a clear and determined manner Campbell shows how Methodism, represented by Stevenson, adapted to a vastly changing culture in North America. Stevenson was often confronted by various denominational cultures and responded with a decidedly open and catholic attitude. The way of salvation was not decreed before the creation of time but involved human participation in repentance, faith, and holiness. Campbell demonstrates that Stevenson's work was "infused with a consistent confidence that God was at work in the events of his life, revealed in a variety of religious experiences and in occasional miraculous occurrences." This is fleshed out in a variety of ways but finds its ultimate resting place in the cherished doctrine of "Entire Sanctification." Campbell's treatment of Stevenson's work suggest that the Methodists of the nineteenth century fleshed out their existence in the new frontier in ways that the John Wesley would not have understood or appreciated. In chapter 10 my own contribution to this volume seeks to unravel the historical link between eighteenth-century Methodism (British) and twentieth-century Pentecostalism (American). Drawing on David Hempton's suggestion from his *Methodism: Empire of Spirit* that the unique inheritors of Methodists in the Enlightenment is not contemporary Methodism but the Pentecostal and Charismatic Christians of the modern world, I note that just as Methodism grew at a phenomenal rate in the nineteenth-century so has the assortment of Pentecostal families seen profound growth in the modern world. What is significant about Hempton's thesis is that both Methodist and Pentecostal growth was predicated on points of "abandonment" by their predecessors. Issues like mobility, empowerment of women, organizational acumen, and the interfacing of religion and politics all proved to be advantageous to one while detrimental to the other. I begin to uncover this social dynamic by considering how both Methodists and Pentecostals have made "room for the Spirit." Building upon my previous work that discusses John Wesley's development of a "rhetoric of the supernatural" as a self-identifying mark of Methodists living in the eighteenth century, I note too how strong a "supernatural consciousness" is to the mission and ministry of Pentecostals in the modern world. Digging deeper into the fabric of both of these renewing movements I explore the idea of a "Second Blessing" and how members of the Holiness movement, mainly Pentecostals and Charismatics, have firmly held on to this teaching in the modern world. Despite its obvious treatment in various denominations it has been Pentecostals that have given it creative expression in the twentieth and twenty-first centuries. My treatment here stands in a different light than the one present by Patrick Streiff in his excellent essay in this collection. I look at it fundamentally as a meaningful experience that is encouraged and inculcated in the spiritual life of votaries. Then my essay looks in a broader fashion at the "supernatural rhetoric" of both Methodists and Pentecostals and what that meant for their respective religious "identities."

With the next two chapters Peter B. Nockles and Martin Welling take us back to Methodism and its relationship with the Church of England in the nineteenth century. In chapter 11 Nockles considers the evangelical category of "revivalism" and applies it to the Tractarian movement. Building on

Yngve Brilioth's *Anglican Revival: Studies in the Oxford Movement*, Nockles asserts that the Tractarians have fundamentally been overlooked in the history of revivalism because of the erroneous thesis of the "undermining of the Protestant credentials of the Church of England." To get beyond the polemics between Tractarians and Evangelicals, Nockles plays out the affinities of the two movements with precision and insight. For example, it is pointed out that not only did the Evangelicals find certain *Tracts for the Times* very appealing, for example Number Nine, "The Gospel a Law of Liberty," but indeed it was designed to be so from the Tractarian point of view. In laying the levels of similarity between Evangelism and Tractarianism, all without eschewing their differences, Nockles has opened the door for a fresh evaluation of Methodism as it moved into a wider audience in the nineteenth century. His analysis provides ample evidence that the Oxford Movement was not only an intellectual movement but a spiritual revival in its own right. With chapter 12, readers of this volume are offered a mapping of Methodist reactions to Anglo-Catholicism in Victorian and Edwardian England by Martin Wellings. After a brief but important historical development of Methodism in nineteenth-century England, Wellings draws out the important distinctions between Tractarians and Methodists surrounding the theme of ritualism. From the Methodist side of things there was grave concern over "Puseyism" and criticism of their ministry by the Tractarians. This contributed in small and large ways to the Methodist ethos of seeing Anglo-Catholicism as a fundamental distortion of the Christian faith, especially with their perception that their theological opponents had distorted their cherished belief in justification by faith. After discussing four specific Methodist responses to ritualism, Wellings contends that the Methodist and Anglo-Catholic positions still remain strained today and this tension provides us with a fundamental ecumenical lesson on the problems of polemical discourse.

With a final summary of Henry D. Rack's work, Clive D. Field has provided a bibliography of Dr Rack's published work for chapter 13. It is not an exhaustive bibliography since Rack has published over two hundred book reviews but it does include his major publications along with less lengthy ones too. For those interested not only in Professor Rack's work but the importance and significance of Methodism, Field's chapter will serve as an important reference.

In conclusion, I want to thank all the contributors of this volume. Their continual patience has been exhibited with my perpetual observations, questions, and clarifications of their essays. In the end, it is our hope that the work presented here would offer an appreciation to Henry D. Rack for his scholarship and friendship. It is also offered with a spirit of being helpful to both those in the academy and the church.

1

From Arminius (d. 1609) to the Synod of Dort (1618–1619)

W. Stephen Gunter

FOR THE BETTER PART of two centuries, it was common to refer to Wesley's theological heirs under the rubric Wesleyan-Arminian theology. Wesley himself was responsible in a sense for this nomenclature, because *The Arminian Magazine* is the periodical he initiated in 1778 to distinguish the Wesleyan wing of the revival movement from his more Calvinist friends (and theological adversaries).[1] In the latter part of the twentieth century, this Wesleyan-Arminian language almost completely disappeared as a descriptor. The reasons for this are many, but I have argued elsewhere that the loss of original distinctives has had significant implications for the evolution of soteriology in the movement.[2]

---

1. For a comprehensive annotated index, see W. Stephen Gunter, *The Arminian Magazine, 1778–1797* at Divinity.Duke.edu/initiatives-centers/cswt/research-resources/Methodist-studies-resources.

2. W. Stephen Gunter, "The Loss of Arminius in Wesleyan-Arminian Theology," in *Reconsidering Arminius: Beyond the Reformed and Wesleyan Divide*, eds. Keith Stanglin, Mark G. Bilby, and Mark H. Mann (Nashville: Kingswood Books, 2014), 71–90. That essay and this chapter were researched and written in tandem. The opening pages of this essay repeat some of that material, but, in fact, the findings in the pages that follow trace out, in some detail, the reasons I assert (in "The Absence of Arminius") that there are doctrinal divergences between Arminius and later Arminians. For this reason, I assert in this essay that it was an altered form of Arminius's theology that we find on trial at Dort. Already a decade after his death, Arminianism was rapidly becoming something with which Arminius would have been less than comfortable. Please note: Throughout the essay, unless otherwise cited, the Latin translations are courtesy of Ms. Jennifer Benedict, a Duke doctoral student in theology and classicist of considerable expertise.

The year after Arminius's death in 1609, his widow and children published his *Declaration of Sentiments*. The publication of this *Verclaringhe* in 1610 was an attempt to honor him, but it was also a literary step toward vindicating him. No one could have anticipated that the decade of 1610–1620 would endure a barrage of publications that was nothing less than rhetorical and theological warfare. Think of it as a presidential election primary debate that lasted almost ten years, with the decision on election finally coming at the Synod at Dort in 1618–1619—in this case an eternal election. Precise and carefully worded truth assertions get lost in the rhetoric needed to score points and win followers.

This decade of pamphleteering resulted in a first phase of losing Arminius from sight so that, by the time the Synod of Dort convened in November 1618, it was in fact a form of altered Arminianism that was on trial, and it was an Arminianism altered in ways that Arminius likely would not have approved. If we have lost a true Arminianism, i.e., an actual reflection of his theological sentiments, then that process of loss began very early on. If one may speak of guilt in this process of loss, then blame may be laid at the feet of both the Arminians known as Remonstrants and the Calvinists known as Contra-Remonstrants. Put simplistically, the Remonstrants protested against a strict doctrine of double predestination and the Contra-Remonstrants to a certain extent (Franciscus Gomarus chief among them) upheld and defended the dogma. Behind the scenes there is an additional doctrinal subtext at play regarding assumptions about sin and the interplay between faith and works. These theological disputes are carried on amid a highly complex set of social, political, and religious issues at work in the Netherlands:

1. The role of civil officials in ordering the life of the church;
2. The nature of the church as an inclusive or exclusive body;
3. The relationship of the confessional standards to church life;
4. The authority of scripture and the authority of creeds;
5. The relationship between human freedom and divine sovereignty.[3]

The Political Situation Leading to Dort

To be sure, the issues are complex, and the Reformed Faith that to an extent held the Republic of the Lowlands together after a successful liberating of

---

3. Douglas Nobbs, *Theocracy and Toleration, A Study of the Disputes in Dutch Calvinism from 1600–1650* (Cambridge: Cambridge University Press, 1938), 25–212.

the country from Spain was a fragile one. Michael Hakkenberg has noted, "The Dutch Republic . . . did not yet have a strong central government, and it was constantly threatened by particularism and political fragmentation."[4] The comprehensive volatility in the Dutch context was not merely a difference over dogma inside the church, it was a complex set of differences that threatened the unity of the nation. Put another way, it was more than the reputation of Arminius that was on the line. He was a casualty on the way to redefining the boundaries of political and religious authority. If one looks only at the formal doctrinally contested points of the warring parties, one misses the volatile republican nature of the rhetorical warfare; and it was this pamphlet warfare—somewhat the equivalent of political action committee advertisements—that drove the agenda in the first decade after Arminius's death when the distinctive emphases of his soteriology began to be lost from view.

Ever since The Synod at Dort, even well-versed historians and theologians have tended to view the theological scene in the Netherlands through the lens of that great synod and see the country as essentially Calvinian. While this was slowly but increasingly true after 1620, it certainly was not the case in prior decades. The Lowlands were religiously and theologically eclectic, and Arminius's teachings were not far out of step with the perspective of many leading voices, especially at the national leadership level. Even by the time of The Synod of Dort, barely one third of the general Dutch population was Protestant, and not all these were strict Calvinists. The general population moved very slowly away from their traditional Roman Catholic beliefs.[5] The Anabaptists (especially Mennonites) were present and active, although they never organized in ways that made them politically powerful. Nevertheless, their doctrinal inclinations permeated the theological climate. They were not doctrinaire in any exclusive way, and they certainly were not strict predestinarians.

It is not an exaggeration to say that toleration (officially affirmed at the Union of Utrecht in 1559) and eclecticism were prevailing inclinations. When forty-three ministers gathered in 1610 at The Hague under the supervision of the Court Preacher, Johannes Uytenbogaert, to formulate their theological opinions in a formal petition for recognition known as The Remonstrance, they were not necessarily doing anything subversive or revolutionary. Theirs was a formal petition to the States of Holland for official

---

4. Michael Adam Hakkenberg, "The Predestinarian Controversy in the Netherlands, 1600–1620" (PhD dissertation, University of California, Berkeley, 1989), 4.

5. Cf. Alastair Duke, "The Ambivalent Face of Calvinism in the Netherlands, 1561–1618," in *International Calvinism, 1541–1715*, ed. Menna Prestwich (Oxford: Clarendon Press, 1985), 109.

recognition and, where necessary, protection against the intolerance and attacks of the strict Calvinists. Interesting to note is that these Arminians, although perhaps a minority in the Dutch Reformed Church as a whole, were actually in a majority among the magistrates in many larger cities. So, the magistrates in those cities took care to appoint Arminian ministers.

In the Five Points of the Remonstrance of 1610, Arminius's influence is clear: phrasing of key points were taken directly from the theological affirmations in his *Declaration of Sentiments*.[6] This formal request for protection stirred the political and ecclesial waters to such an extent that at the end of the year (December, 1610) the States of Holland called for a conference in The Hague. Rather than cooling the temperatures of the opposing parties, the conflict between the Remonstrants and the Contra-Remonstrants intensified. The five points of the Remonstrance were answered with the Five Points of Calvinism, and the controversy was now "on" in the public arena with an open division of parties. From this point on we begin to lose sight of Arminius himself as well as certain important points in his theological affirmations.

Rather quickly, cities across the Republic came to identify themselves with one party or the other, and some cities or towns were divided internally—part Remonstrant and part Contra-Remonstrant. With astonishing speed, the driving issues became territorial, centering on positions of power and influence in pulpits and in positions of civil governing. In 1614 the States of Holland, *without* the support of Amsterdam and other Contra-Remonstrant inclined cities, adopted the "Resolution for Peace in the Churches." This Resolution condemned the extreme positions on either side of the issue:

1. That God "created any man unto damnation," or
2. That man "of his own natural powers or deeds can achieve salvation."[7]

This further stipulated, in an attempt to protect the Remonstrants, that those who refused to affirm the Five Points of Calvinism were not to be subject to slander and attacks, but were, indeed, to be tolerated in the churches.

The Resolution for Peace was anything but, as it failed to satisfy either side of the squabble. At this point the story gets complicated by scenarios of unintended consequences. The Amsterdam *classis* (local council of

---

6. Cf. W. Stephen Gunter, *Arminius and His Declaration of Sentiments. An Annotated Translation with Introduction and Theological Commentary* (Waco: Baylor University Press, 2012), esp. 135–36, 180, 190–91.

7. Pieter Geyl, *The Netherlands Divided (1609–1648)*, trans. S. T. Bindoff (London: Williams and Norgate, 1936), 52.

ministers), dominated now by anti-Arminian sentiment, blatantly refused to follow the directives of the Resolution for Peace and began openly to support Contra-Remonstrant "strict Calvinist" groups who wished to hold separate worship services in towns where Remonstrant ministers were appointed. The Resolution for Peace was increasingly interpreted as an instrument in support of the Arminians, and when powerful church leaders openly defied the intent of the Resolution, the government was faced with a difficult decision: to enforce or not to enforce. The Advocate General, Oldenbarnevelt, chose to enforce the State's authority "to use their supreme power to dismiss, or make the towns dismiss, any ministers infringing the resolution."[8] In principle, this meant that action could be taken against both Remonstrants and Contra-Remonstrants, but it was in practice the Contras who suffered the most. In a majority or at least a significant plurality of towns, the civil magistrates were Arminians, thus it was the Contra-Remonstrant ministers, often against the wishes of the local congregation itself, who were dismissed for violating the Resolution for Peace. The controversy was so heated that, in 1616 in The Hague, Rev. Henricus Rosaeus refused to celebrate communion with his Remonstrant colleague, Uytenbogart, who was chaplain to the Senate. When Rosaeus was dismissed from his ministerial office, he went to the neighboring village of Rijswijk, and every Sunday a large group of his supporters walked from The Hague to Rijswijk (a distance of several kilometers) to hear him preach. In numerous other towns and villages, Contra-Remonstrant ministers were dismissed and replaced with Remonstrant ministers, almost always against the wishes of their congregations. Even in situations where local sentiment was pro-Arminian, civil magistrates forcing out their minister was not a welcomed act.[9] The Contra-Remonstrants began to separate from the public churches and to establish their own churches, calling their own ministers without the "interference" of civil magistrates.

By 1617 the situation in the Lowlands had devolved into what the poet Jacob Cats described as "the year of violence."[10] The policy of "mutual toleration" had resulted in almost comprehensive "mutual condemnation and reprisal." Both sides struggled to turn popular opinion in their favor, but the struggle was increasingly characterized by violence:

> In the pulpits and the taverns, on the streets, . . . in high places and low, were heard the violent discussions in which no bitter

---

8. Jan Den Tex, *Oldenbarnevelt*, trans. R. B. Powell (Cambridge: Cambridge University Press, 1973) 2:554.

9. Den Tex, *Oldenbarnevelt*, 2:680.

10. Quoted in Den Tex, *Oldenbarnevelt*, 2:566.

term was spared. The quarrel threatened the existence of the young nation. The academic discussion of Gomarus and Arminius had become [the] bone of contention that divided Holland into two hostile camps.[11]

We do not need to get bogged down in too much historical detail here, but one cluster of events stands out in its symbolic importance. It was mentioned previously that the Contra-Remonstrants in The Hague were walking to an adjacent village to hear their preacher, who had been forced out of his pulpit in The Hague. Prince Maurits had heretofore remained aloof from the fray in the sense that he supported the official government decision of "mutual" toleration. That changed in 1617. In January, the Contra-Remonstrants of The Hague returned to the city for worship in the home of a layman. The States of Holland formally requested Prince Maurits, as commander of the army, to enforce government policy, but the Prince refused, saying that his actual responsibility was not to enforce policy but to defend true religion, the implication being that the Contra-Remonstrants were the orthodox party in the dispute. Maurits's support emboldened the Contra-Remonstrants, and on July 19, 1617, they broke into the Cloister Church (*Kloosterkerk*) in The Hague and began holding worship services there—clearly in violation of the edicts passed by the States of Holland. On July 23, Maurits himself joined them to worship in the Cloister Church.

Led by Advocate General Oldenbarneveldt, the States of Holland took decisive action, passing on August 4 the "Scherpe Resolutie" (Sharp Resolution). The province of Holland had formally called in May for a National Synod to resolve the religious dispute, but the States of Holland's "sharp resolution" asserted that no regional provincial government had the power to convene a National Synod. That power resided solely with the national government of the States. Furthermore, the "sharp resolution" provided for the raising of a national guard (*waardgelders*) to maintain order in the municipalities, i.e., enforce national law. In effect this set up a power struggle between the Advocate General Oldenbarnevelt and Prince Maurits. The country was literally on the brink of civil war. The National Guard was being raised in cities led by Remonstrant Councils, so Prince Maurits began a process of dismantling the city councils: he dismissed Remonstrant council members and appointing all Contra-Remonstrant councils. At that point, all support for Advocate General Oldenbarneveldt evaporated. He was arrested on August 29, 1618. After being tried on trumped-up charges of

---

11. Hakkenberg, "Predestinarian Controversy," 48, quoting Petrus Blok, *History of the People of the Netherlands*, trans. Ruth Putnam (New York: G. Putnam's Sons, 1900), 3:438. [I could not locate this citation in Blok.]

treason, he was condemned as a traitor, and on May 13, 1619, the former Advocate General was beheaded.

His arrest in late August paved the way for the Synod of Dort to convene in November, 1618. So finally this brings me to the point of this history lesson. In the months leading up to the Dort Synod, a book appeared that was evidently read by most every delegate to the Synod, *Specimen controversarium Beligarum*. The author was Arminius's long-time ecclesial adversary Festus Hommius. The book caricatures Arminius's anthropology as highly optimistic regarding human capacity: human beings are "not slaves of sin, but free to will good and evil." This type of caricature had been playing out for a decade in the pamphlet and civil warfare that we have noted. The actual theology of Arminius is now lost beyond the horizon of struggles for political dominance.

Aza Goudriaan has pointed out that these assertions do not "fit especially well into the text of Articles three and four of the Remonstrance of 1610, which insisted that the human being cannot 'think, will or do anything that is good' except by the grace of God."[12] This anthropology is taken directly from Arminius's 1608 *Declaration of Sentiments*. Excepting their appearance in caricature as scapegoats in the rhetorical warfare, Arminius's actual teachings have already and to a large extent been lost from sight by the time The Synod of Dort convened, especially the seriousness with which Arminius took Augustinian teachings on fallen humanity and humanity's utter inability to make a contribution in any way to God's saving initiative in Christ.

This slow disappearing act was accelerated by Arminius's own student, Simon Episcopius, who was the leading spokesman for the Remonstrants at The Synod of Dort, as well as by Arminius's life-long friend, Peter Bertius. Even their nuanced doctrinal shifts must, however, not be seen as isolated doctrinal difference. Theology and politics are inextricably intertwined, so our familiarity with the political landscape is essential to understanding how the eventual pronouncements at Dort could have had such a pervasive and far-reaching impact. We know that, for example, Arminius and Franciscus Gomarus had sharp disagreements over theological dogma, and these doctrinal differences are often understood to be the fundamental wedge that split the Reformed Church. Without underestimating the importance of the dogmatic conflict, we will also see that this difference was markedly exacerbated by their oppositional perspectives on how issues of church and state were to be resolved.

---

12. Aza Goudriaan, "The Synod of Dort on Arminian Anthropology," in Aza Goudriaan, ed., *Revisiting the Synod of Dort, 1618–1619* (Leiden: Brill, 2011), 82.

The States of Holland and Ecclesial Polity

Although the Synod of Dort "officially" settled the dogmatic dispute over predestination by siding with the strict Calvinists over against the Arminians, the complex issues related to governing church and state could not be resolved by dogmatic pronouncement. The charges that led to the execution of Oldenbarneveldt in 1619 had little to do with his apparent sympathy for Arminian theological dogma. The charges against him were designed to rid the public arena of his position on how the national government should function in both church affairs and provincial decision-making. On these points, Oldenbarneveldt was much closer to Arminius than to Gomarus. It should also be pointed out that the vexing issue of church-state relations was not solved at Dort. As Douglas Nobbs has noted, "The Synod of Dort in 1618, the only national synod acknowledged by provinces and states, failed to settle the relationship of church and state upon Calvinist principles."[13] Nobbs's phrase "upon Calvinist principles" reflects the fault lines of difference between the respective positions of Arminius and Gomarus.

Serious students of church history know that sorting out theological differences is a messy affair, but the process is even more intractable when it is unclear who has the final authority to separate "right" from "wrong." In the Netherlands, three alternatives were on the table: (1) A pure Erastianism—the church is dependent on the state, so that its doctrine as well as organization is in the hands of the state's governing body; (2) The church is independent of the state—the church is a self-sufficient body. The state has neither dependence upon nor formal governing connection to the church; (3) The third alternative was essentially an Anabaptist perspective: politics and true Christianity are incompatible. Any connection between the two must be viewed as heretical.

To the twenty-first-century reader, the formal separation of church and state into independent entities is so normal that it is difficult to imagine a society with an entirely different norm; however, a different normative situation is what must be envisioned. The States of Holland, using the authority that resided with them, convened the Synod of Dort—with the explicit proviso that the rights of the local provinces that comprised the Netherlands would not be infringed upon, with the explicit provision that patronage would not be abolished. The States also set the number of delegates to the Synod from within the Netherlands and invited specific international representatives. The States sent "deputies" to assure that doctrinal discussions remained with Scriptural limits. The proviso protecting political

---

13. Nobbs, *Theocracy and Toleration*, xii.

patronage was short-lived, but in some ways ministerial appointments became even more circumscribed than before. A person's "call" to the ministry came to be routed through the municipality. This did not represent a formal change of due process, but in practice the local decision was revised. Previously, the municipal purview was limited to the "civil conduct" of the candidate—whether he was an upstanding citizen. If the legal slate was clean, then the person recommended to them was approved. After Dort, local approval included confessional domains, and the States could commission two "deputies" to attend the municipal approval process in an advisory capacity. The practical results of these changes meant that, for example, when the Remonstrant clergy were relieved of their post after the Synod of Dort, the efficient means to accomplish these removals was in place. Municipal approval was required to call as well as to re-appoint clergy. After 1618 the policy of local governments toward the church was in many cases more oppressive than before.[14]

Nobbs's assertion about Dort's failure along Calvinist lines requires that we look at how Arminius differs from the strict Calvinists about governance. Arminius was fundamentally an Erastian in his assumptions about church and state, assuming the validity of Erastus's assumption denying independent ecclesial jurisdiction. Arminius seems to have agreed with his Stadholder (Grand Pensionary), Johannes Uytenbogaert, that this established order was *revealed*.[15] There is an evolution in the "Arminian position" that moves along a path from assertions regarding the divine right of the ruler (Arminius) to a larger framed legal theory of sovereignty (Hugo Grotius), and finally, on the eve of Dort, to a theory of toleration for private churches alongside the state established church.[16] Arminius would have cared greatly about these issues because, in the final analysis, doctrinal orthodoxy in the Lowlands was decided in this political domain. In his disagreements with Gomarus, differences of opinion on governance were continually in play. In his *Declaration of Sentiments*, when we read Arminius asserting that he is not obliged to answer the requests of certain ecclesial deputies at his door demanding doctrinal clarification, he was doing much more than avoiding interpersonal conflict. He was following his and Uytenbogaert's Erastian assumptions about to whom an answer is actually due. Arminius and

---

14. Cf. Nobbs, *Theocracy and Toleration*, xii–xiv; H. W. Ter Haar, *Jacobus Trigland* ('s Gravenhage: Nijhoff, 1891), 63–66; H. C. Rogge, *Johannes Uytenbogaert in zijn gevoelen aangaande de Magt den Overheden in Kerkelijke zaken, tegenover zijne bestridjers* (Utrecht: Kemink en Zoon, 1858–1863), esp. vol. 3.

15. J. Uytenbogaert, *Tractaet van't Ampt ende Authoriteyt een hooger Christelijcker Overheyt in Kerckelycke Saecken*, 3rd ed. (Rotterdam, 1647), esp. vols. 1 and 2.

16. Cf. Nobbs, *Theocracy and Toleration*, 25–107.

Uytenbogaert regarded such a position not only as established by precedent and practice, but also as revealed by God as the right order of things.

The Arminian theory attempted to protect simultaneously both the function of the church and the duty of the ruler. It did so by distinguishing the acts of religion from the organizational polity of the church. One might say that the Arminian ideal was state oversight without operational control—not direct control of the church by the state, but through ecclesial structures a state inspection and supervision of the church's due processes. While the state had a share in overseeing the church's due process, it had neither the power nor the right to usurp the spiritual dimensions, to override the divine mandate that gives the church its identity, or to violate the individual conscience of believers. While it may not have been simple, it is important to point out that (following Uytenbogaert), the Arminian theory was a straightforward attempt to address one side of the two-dimensional issue by answering a single question:

> What Authority, Command, Power and Jurisdiction [does] a chief sovereign Magistrate (be it Emperor, King, Prince or State) have according to God's word, in matters concerning religion: with the Lands and Dominions, over which those magistrates are supreme governours.[17]

The practical implication of the Arminian position is that the power of the church was a matter of incidental discussion consequent upon an independent settlement of the sovereign's power in religion. Put another way, the power of the church was defined negatively by establishing what a sovereign ruler might and might not command. Uytenbogaert's position, adopted by Arminius, was coherent and organic to the extent that it determined one issue (sovereign right), while indirectly addressing the second issue (ecclesial rights). Nobbs concludes, "Uytenbogaert preserved a simplicity of design which gave plausibility, consistency and integrity to his particular interpretation of divine right."[18]

For the Calvinian party of Gomarus, this position was untenable, if for no other reason than that it failed to preserve the guarantee of a Christian sovereign that ruled from within biblical and orthodox Christian assumptions. Throughout his theological debates with Arminius, Gomarus was operating with a different theory of church and state, which he set out in published form alongside his theological points in the same year as

---

17. Here Nobbs, *Theocracy and Toleration*, 27, is citing the MS translation (British Museum Reg. 17B. XLIV) of Uytenbogaert's "Tractaet," ms. 18, *Tractaet*, 7.

18. Ibid., 28.

Arminius's death.[19] Gomarus's (and the Contra-Remonstrants's) approach, unlike Uytenbogaert's, was designed to establish simultaneously two authorial centers—the church and government; but it was the "one true Church." This true church was to be the only public church, and it would be actively supported by the ruling governor. There was, to be sure, a separation of domains: the ruler was the organ of power to enforce ecclesial decisions. Simply put, the domain of the governor was the domain of enforcing power. The domain of the church resided in the realm of "the spiritual," the church being led by the grace of God, which alone could move the heart to good. The political ruler had neither the right nor the capacity to move in the spiritual domain, and the church was required to refrain from employing the powers of enforcement granted to the sovereign ruler. Each was supreme in its own sphere.

It is at this dialectical juncture that Gomarus's logic comes most evidently into play. What he and the opponents of the Arminian theory could not abide was that Uytenbogaert's political theory did nothing to guarantee that the governing leader would be Christian. This was assumed but left unstated. So Gomarus takes a step proactively to preserve Christian governance: loyalty to the ruler was loyalty to God, so long as the sovereign followed the divine will—as it had been interpreted to be the case spiritually by the church. Gomarus insisted that the ruler's individual power was ultimately subordinate to God's law, therefore, neither unlimited nor absolute. Furthermore, the governed subjects were to obey an oppressive governor only so long as that obedience did not entail sinning against God: render unto Caesar.[20] If the Arminians saw divine order in the providentially established priority of the governing structure, the Contra-Remonstrants vested the power in God's very self—as interpreted and established by the church. The offices of the church were created by God through divine law. The church's ministers were divinely led envoys who represented and interpreted to its membership divine insights and commands. Nobbs sums this interlocking set of assumptions up nicely:

> So long as they followed His Will, they were endowed with the authority of God Himself, and directly empowered to undertake their [ministerial] function.... The true sovereignty was with God.... Neither the state nor the ruler, neither the church nor

---

19. Franciscus Gomarus, *Waerschouwinghe over de Vermaninghe aen R. Donteclock* ... (Leyden, 1609).
20. Gomarus, *Waerschouwinghe*, 14.

its ministers, nor even the Holy Community, held the sovereign power, but God in them.²¹

Such a notion was obviously a complicated dialectic. Gomarus confessed that not all rulers were equal, nor were all ministers similarly gifted. Some rulers have spiritual gifts useful and necessary for spiritual worship, and some ecclesial leaders were fit to serve on the councils of state. But God demands that each serve to the utmost of his capacity. To these church ministers were entrusted the "things of the Lord"; the civil rulers were entrusted with the "things of the world."²² In the specific situation we are considering, where Prince Maurits was trying to hold a fragile republic together, Gomarus's dialectic of two realms suited Maurits's purposes splendidly. Maurits quite willingly affirmed that ecclesial self-sufficiency was complete and inherent in the church so long as he, the ruler, was treated as the divinely ordained collaborator with the church, albeit with religious obligations. As Nobbs has pointed out, "The *corpus cristianum* was still the objective of Contra-Remonstrant theory, and no Christian society was [deemed] possible whenever church and state were opposed."²³ So, when some were inclined to chastise Prince Maurits for attending the illegally convened congregation led by Rev. Rosaeus at The Kloosterkerk in The Hague (July 1617), Maurits responded that it was his duty to uphold and defend spiritual truth. Within the theory of governance propagated by the Contra-Remonstrants that was slowly gaining ascendancy, the theory he had also chosen to support, his *not* "defending spiritual truth" would have meant that he was not properly fit to rule. The die was publicly cast the day Maurits walked into The Kloosterkerk. This was the new reality of governance that came to define the political and religious reality of the decade after Arminius death, the reality that voted against the probability that the Arminians could carve out a place for themselves in the Dutch church. Arminius's (and Grotius's) political theory loses in the battle for civil governing, and, as we shall now see, the distinctiveness of Arminius's theological lines of thought get blurred as well in the hands of his well-meaning disciples and successors. This emerging loss may be discerned in the thought of his lifelong friend and colleague, Peter Bertius, especially in his teachings on justification by faith. The same loss of distinctiveness may also be discerned in the formulations of his student and successor at Leiden, Simon Episcopius, especially those on the doctrines of sin, grace, and human freedom.

21. Nobbs, *Theocracy and Toleration*, 9.
22. Gomarus, *Waerschouwinghe*, 19, 21–24.
23. Nobbs, *Theocracy and Toleration*, 17.

Bertius on Justification by Faith

The life journey of Peter Bertius is a twisted path. As Carl Bangs has noted: "The last history of Bertius is not pleasant ... He became a troublemaker within Remonstrant circles ... drawing the censure of Uytenbogaert. He then went over to the Contra-Remonstrants, who did not receive him warmly. Finally, he went to Paris, returned to the Roman Catholic fold, and died in 1629."[24] An examination of Bertius's thoughts on faith and justification helps explain why the Contras did not receive him warmly. We discover as well some clues as to why this life-long Protestant ended up back in the Roman fold toward the end of his life.

In their recent systematic theology, G. van den Brink and C. van der Kooi touch a central nerve in the Arminian system when they note that, although more in his disciples than in Arminius himself, "his disciples were so fearful that the doctrine of perseverance [of the saints] did not take the human factor with enough seriousness to avoid the danger of immoral behavior that they increasingly underscored the necessity of human cooperation with God's grace."[25] The authors are cognizant that both Arminius and the original framers of the *Remonstrantie* of 1610, who borrowed explicitly from Arminius, were less inclined than their successors to overemphasize the factor of human cooperation.[26] Arminius and the original Remonstrants hewed closer to the line of sovereign grace than their heirs. At Leiden Arminius was kept mindful of this point by Gomarus, and from the University of Franeker in Friesland the rejoinders came from Sibrandus Lubbertus, who went so far as to spread unfounded theological libel against Arminius on this and other points.[27] Beginning in 1608, Lubbertus carried on an exchange with Bertius (Arminius's only theological friend and ally at Leiden) with regard to whether faith was a gift or a "work." Lubbertus makes some crucial distinctions about faith that later Arminians were not very careful to keep in view.[28]

---

24. Carl Bangs, *Arminius. A Study in the Dutch Reformation* (Nashville: Abingdon, 1971), 357.

25. G. van den Brink and C. van der Kooi, *Christelijke dogmatiek. Een inleiding* (Zoetermeer: Boekencentrum, 2012), 628. (My translation of the Dutch).

26. Cf. Gunter, *Arminius and His "Declaration of Sentiments,"* 130–31.

27. Gunter, *Arminius and His "Declaration of Sentiments,"* 84–86.

28. Cf. Aza Goudriaan, "Justification by Faith and the Early Arminian Controversy," 155–78, in Maarten Wisse, Marcel Sarot, and Willemien Otten, eds. *Scholasticism Reformed. Essays in Honour of Willem J. van Asselt* (Leiden: Brill, 2010). I follow Goudriaan in the examination of the primary sources that reflect this exchange. In some cases I have silently "improved" Goudriaan's translation of the Latin original. For example, recognizing that his translation is the literal rendering of Lubbertus's phrasing, I prefer

Lubbertus reminds Bertius, "The specific difference between justification by faith and justification by works is this, as I said before, that in justification by works we do something for God, but in justification by faith we receive something from God."[29] This exchange of letters across several years between Bertius and Lubbertus is of more than passing consequence, as it seems to demonstrate an evolution of Arminianism. In the opening page of his essay, Goudriaan posits, "Arminius' vacillates between two positions on imputed righteousness," whereas Bertius makes a "more deliberate attempt to combine two viewpoints"—the two viewpoints being faith as a gift *from* God versus faith as our gift *to* God.[30] If I may be so bold, rather than interpreting Arminius on this point as vacillating, perhaps Goudriaan should consider that Arminius's vacillation is not indecision so much as it is his trying to hold both imputation and impartation to be equally gifts from God to—a theological dialectic between equally important poles—with God consistently remaining the sovereign initiator. For Arminius, the issue was not so much human involvement as much as it is the nature of God's saving initiative. In order to avoid determinism (thereby making God the author of sin), the human response must take place *non necessitas* (in a "non-necessitated" way).[31] The important point to be discerned here is that Bertius's move was actually a move away from Arminius on justifying faith.

Goudriaan, rather than examining Arminius's writings, takes the methodological approach of reconstructing Arminius's thought by taking to a large extent at face value what Gomarus represents as Arminius's teaching. I will pass on the temptation to criticize Goudriaan's decision to take one's opponent as a reliable resource, but choose rather to acknowledge where I can agree that Gomarus (and Goudriaan) get Arminius right. The most important place is the one where Bertius himself begins: the Arminian emphasis is on justification in relation to an act of faith on the part of the believer, simultaneously holding firmly to the imputation of Christ's righteousness to believers. Indeed, this point constitutes the fundamental debate between Lubbertus and Bertius, reflected in seven letters by Lubbertus and six letters

---

"justification *by* faith" versus "justification *by* works" where Goudriaan has "justification of faith" and "justification of works."

29. Goudriaan, "Justification by Faith and the Early Arminian Controversy," 166, citing S. Lubbertus, *Epistolica disceptatio de fide iustificante deque nostra coram Deo iustificatione* ... (Delft, 1612), 136.

30. Goudriaan, "Justification by Faith and the Early Arminian Controversy," 164.

31. Cf. Arminius' *Verklaringhe* in Gunter, *Arminius and His "Declaration,"* 124, 141, 174, 176. The driving issue for Arminius was the doctrine of God, not human involvement.

from the hand of Bertius.³² Bertius maintains that faith is justifying "because it is considered by the gracious acceptation of God in Christ as the whole righteousness of the law that we were held to accomplish. And because only this apprehends the righteousness of Christ that is ours by imputation."³³

Bertius admits that he cannot explain exactly how this duality can be logically reconciled, but he insists that both tenets are scripturally supported.³⁴ He then proceeds to try out different options. (1) Perhaps God considers human faith both as the instrument "apprehending the righteousness of Christ" as well as simultaneously "obedience . . . to the Gospel."³⁵ I would suggest that this ascription is very close to Arminius's dialectic of faith, but as Goudriaan points out, this is not Bertius's favored line of interpretation. Bertius suggests also (2) that to those persons "whose faith has been accepted as the whole fulfillment of the law, He subsequently imputes the righteousness of His Son."³⁶ In phrasing it this way, Bertius seemed to assert that the act of faith is a meritorious act. Indeed, it would seem that placing the emphasis on human volition is his preferred alternative.³⁷ When we look at other places in the *Epistolica*, we become increasingly convinced that faith defined fundamentally as a human act has for Bertius, and also for later Arminians who were less careful than Arminius on this point, become the default position. In some assertions, the volitional act of faith has become the condition to be fulfilled, followed "after the fact" by an attribution of Christ's righteousness.³⁸

---

32. Cf. C. van der Woude, *Sibrandus Lubbertus: Leven en werken, in het bijzonder naar zijn "correspondentie"* (PhD dissertaion, Free University of Amsterdam, 1963), esp. 185–97, and L. J. M. Bosch, "Petrus Bertius, 1565–1629" (PhD dissertation, Catholic University of Nijmegen, 1979), esp. 180–82., 116–18.

33. Goudriaan, "Justification by Faith and the Early Arminian Controversy," 164; *Epistolica disceptatio*, 6; van der Woude, *Lubbertus*, 186.

34. *Epistolica disceptatio*, 104.

35. "But, in justifying us, God looks at faith not merely as an instrument, apprehending the righteousness of Christ, but also as the obedience which is presented by us to the Gospel. Therefore, I think these things can be reconciled in this way, so that things which seem to be opposed and to fight one another may at the same time be consistent and harmonize smoothly." Ibid., 108.

36. "Let us also explore another way: that God imputes the righteousness of His son to those whose faith he has taken and accepted in place of complete fulfillment of the law." Ibid., 109.

37. "You have two ways of reconciling [these alternatives], the latter of which pleases me more." Ibid., 113.

38. "If the righteousness of faith accedes to the place of the righteousness of the law, it follows that the condition of faith and the acceptance of it [faith] has acceded to the place of the full and strict fulfillment of all commandments; but the former is true, therefore the latter is as well." Ibid., 46. See also 139 for a similar assertion.

To the modern reader these distinctions might seem arcane, but this move is the "inch that becomes a mile" in Arminian soteriology. Bertius makes the formal move that both Gomarus and Lubbertus accused, namely, rendering faith as a work we do to earn favor from God, rather than the gift we receive from God. Arminius would not approve. To make this move, Bertius had to either implicitly or explicitly play down the pervasive nature of sin. Implicitly, he certainly made this move when he assumed that the capacity for faith is an inherent human quality on which the believer must simply act.[39] It is clearly a *non sequitur*, but Bertius seemed to assert that Biblical admonitions to believe and be saved warranted the conclusion that faith and believing were inherent human capacities. Surely, Augustine and Arminius alike would have queried Bertius whether he had forgotten all the other texts about *all* being sinners and falling short of the glory of God. Indeed, what does become of sin in the Arminian tradition the decade after Arminius's death? In order to answer this question, we look at the most influential Arminian theologian in that decade, Simon Episcopius. What we discern are some subtle but important shifts of emphasis. These are not so much contradictions of Arminius as they are slight changes of emphasis that shift the Arminian trajectory. They are, however, changes that did not go unnoticed, not only among Arminius's theological adversaries, but also among Remonstrant theologians themselves.

Episcopius on Grace, Freedom and Sin

To address these changes, we look at the most influential Remonstrant theologian during the decade after Arminius's death, Simon Episcopius. What we discern are some subtle but important shifts of emphasis. They are not so much contradictions of Arminius as they are, in most cases, slight changes that shift the Arminian trajectory soteriologically—changes that were noted by Arminius's theological adversaries as well as by his Remonstrant heirs. In Goudriaan's discussion of the exchange between Lubbertus and Bertius on justification by faith, it is noteworthy that the doctrines of sin and grace are conspicuously absent. In contrast, Arminius was consistently disinclined to visit the subject of justification without considering the disability of sinfulness and the absolute necessity of a proactive divine gracious enabling of humanity to counter the effects of sin. This is Arminius the pastor-theologian at work, someone who knows that weaving a purely mental vision of doctrine is inadequate to the lived life of faith. We do indeed encounter

---

39. "Through his word, or, through a quality inhering in him." Ibid., 69.

these important discussions in Episcopius, but they are much altered in key areas when compared to corresponding strains of thought in Arminius.[40]

Unlike Arminius, Episcopius was silent about the effects of Adam's sin—the concepts of *reatus* and *privation*—seminal presence in Adam and whether Adam's descendants shared in his punishment for that sin. Arminius had asserted:

> The whole of this sin, however is not peculiar to our first parents, but is common to the entire race and to all their posterity, who, at the time when this sin was committed, were in their loins, and who have since descended from them by the natural mode of propagation, according to the primitive benediction: For in Adam "all have sinned." (Rom. 5:12.) Wherefore, whatever punishment was brought down upon our first parents, has likewise pervaded and yet pursues all their posterity: So that all men "are by nature the children of wrath," (Eph. 2:3) obnoxious to condemnation, and to temporal as well as to eternal death; they are also devoid of that original righteousness and holiness. (Rom. 5:12,18,19) With these evils they would remain oppressed forever, unless they were liberated by Christ Jesus; to whom be glory forever.[41]

In sharp contrast to Arminius's Augustinian notions, the only source Episcopius explicitly mentioned as the reason for sinful disobedience is free will:

> When we speak of actual sins, we wish that to be taken to mean those that we ourselves perpetrate of our own accord and of our own absolutely free will, against the divine will or the law. I say, "by [our] own will," not by that of another; "absolutely free," which excludes not only coercion (although the will cannot be recognized through any potency) but also any sort of necessity or determinism at all.[42]

Mark Ellis is of the opinion that Episcopius makes no mention of sin as corruption, and this is noteworthy because Episcopius otherwise follows Arminius closely, borrowing heavily from him.[43] This changes, however, when we get to the treatment of the Mosaic Law, to which Arminius dedi-

---

40. Here I am following Mark A. Ellis, *Simon Episcopius' Doctrine of Original Sin* (New York: Peter Lang, 2006), esp. 107–130.

41. James Arminius, Public Diputation VII, "On the First Sin of the First Man," in *The Works of Arminius*. London Edition (Kansas City: Beacon Hill, 1986), 2:156–57.

42. Simon Episcopius, *Disputationes Theologiae Tripartae* (Amsterdam, 1644), 1:10.

43. Mark A. Ellis, *Episcopius*, 107, 108–10.

cated his entire Public Disputation XII, "On the Law of God." Taking up the three uses that Calvin identified (moral, ceremonial, and judicial), Arminius analyzed the degree to which they were abrogated by the new Covenant in Christ.[44] Episcopius provides no separate treatment of the Law, and Ellis sees this as a consequential omission: "We cannot overemphasize his perception of Law as only a type and shadow of grace."[45] In Episcopius we encounter statements abrogating the Law in ways quite alien to Arminius: Finally (so that we might comprehend the entire matter in brief), we should judge whatever was contained by the old covenant to have been clearly a type and to have held "a shadow of the things to come; but the substance belongs to Christ." [Col 2:17][46]

For all practical purposes, in the hands of Episcopius, the entirety of the Law was abrogated with respect to the believer—applicable only to the Jews and not the rest of humanity. The Law is a *paidagogos* to bring us to Christ (Gal 3:24), but it seems to have no normative character. Because Arminius considered sin so seriously, he understood that the Law revealed the righteousness of God in stark contrast to human sinfulness. Episcopius appeared only to see that the Law reveals human disobedience, that being conceived purely as a volitional act. Within this volitional frame of reference, he seems to have feared that a strong emphasis on Law could lead to a moralism that would do grave injury to Christ and his grace. It might even risk the loss of a distinctively Christian soteriology.[47] This trajectory of reasoning leads to Episcopius's most striking deviations from Arminius:

> Episcopius did not give separate disputations on predestination, calling, free will or grace. All one needed to understand the Gospel of grace was that, although people are sinners, Christ provided forgiveness for sins, sanctification and eternal life for all who believe.[48]

These omissions did not go unnoticed by Episcopius's contemporaries, and they concluded that he was following a line (initiated by Bertius) that was taking Remonstrant theology in an un-Arminian direction—in the sense that it takes the theology in directions Arminius would not likely have chosen.

---

44. Arminius, *Works*, 2:196–203.
45. Ellis, *Episcopius*, 1:10.
46. Episcopius, *Disputationes*, 1.22 and similarly 24. Emphasis added.
47. Cf. Ellis, *Episcopius*, 110, referencing *Disputationes*, 1.11.7, 15, 16.
48. Ellis, *Episcopius*, 111.

In the aftermath of the Synod of Dort, Episcopius played the key role in formulating the Remonstrant "Confession of Faith" in 1621.[49] Ellis points out that, in contrast to Episcopius's own theological treatises, the Confession of 1621 "provides a clear indication that the other Remonstrants demanded that the *Confessio* be more reflective of Arminius . . . . Episcopius' colleagues were not supportive of his departure from Arminius on several of the key issues . . . . They demanded a return to Arminius."[50] Even so, Episcopius still manages in the Confession to shift the theological moorings of Arminianism. Arminius had taught that in Christ universal provision for salvation was made, but he did not teach that humanity was intrinsically capable (without the aid of divine grace) of freely participating in this provision. He was simply too Augustinian to make such a move, and his assumptions about the sovereignty of God prohibited such a move as well. It is clear that not all believe, and the fact that some are condemned has to be accounted for. It is at this specific juncture that Episcopius contravenes his mentor. Arminius taught that God's prevenient grace is reaching out to all of humanity; but because some do not believe, we are left with the mystery of why this is so.[51] The freedom to decide is due to proactive divine enabling; there is no mention in Arminius of human ability to decide *for* God apart from intervening grace. Arminius was content to live in the tension of this soteriological dialectic.

This seems to have been a dialectic that Episcopius felt necessary to resolve. He gave a polite nod to Arminius, but then proceeded to set out a rather different course for subsequent Arminian soteriology. Episcopius takes a step on prevenient grace that I have not been able to discern in Arminius. In the *Confessio*, 17:8, we read:

> And even if there truly is the greatest disparity of grace (Rom. 12:6f, 1 Pet. 4:10), clearly according to the most free dispensation of the divine will, still the Holy Spirit confers such grace to all (Matt. 11:21, Tit. 3:4f, 1 Pet 1: 23 & 2:9, Ja. 1:18, 2 Cor. 3:6, Heb. 4:12), both in general and in particular, to whom the Word

---

49. CONFESSIO, SIVE DECLARATIO, Sentententiae Pastorum, qui in Foederato Belgio REMONSTRANTES vocantur, Super praecipius articulis Religionis Christianae. [*The Confession or Declaration of the Pastors which in the Belgian Federation are called the Remonstrants, on the principle articles of the Christian Religion*]. Mark A. Ellis, trans. and ed. *The Arminian Confession of 1621* (Eugene, OR: Pickwick, 2005), 51.

50. Ellis, *Episcopius on Original Sin*, 127.

51. Ellis asserts on this point, "Arminius denied that sufficient grace was given to all men." Ibid., 127. I am not aware that Arminius makes this an explicit assertion, although it is logically consistent. To assert that God purposefully withholds sufficient grace is to assert that God has chosen specifically to damn specified individuals. Arminius entire *Declaration of Sentiments* is a polemic against this logic.

of faith is ordinarily preached, as is sufficient for begetting faith in them, and for gradually carrying on their saving conversion. And therefore sufficient grace for faith and conversion not only comes to those who actually believe and are converted, but also to those who do not believe and are not really converted (Is. 62:2, Ez. 18:11, Prov. 1:24f, Matt. 23:37, Lk. 8:12).[52]

There can be little doubt that this statement reflects what turns out to be Arminian sentiment for subsequent generations, but it is not exactly how Arminius would have expressed the dialectic of grace and human freedom. Episcopius and subsequent Arminians describe this sufficient grace, also known as prevenient grace, as a universal endowment that becomes for all practical purposes a "divine spark" intrinsic to the status of being human. In this way, free will enjoys pride of place in the interplay among sin, grace and freedom. The sovereign God has been replaced with the sovereign human. As Richard Mueller has pointed out:

> The fall [of humanity] does not appear as an element either structural or doctrinal in Episcopius.... [Humanity] has a natural inclination toward God, and the right reason (*ratio recta*) with which he is endowed enables his mind to apprehend the good and the just.... This *recta ratio*, moreover, proscribes the love and worship of God.[53]

The practical implications of this have far-reaching implications for evangelical soteriology. An entire essay would be required to spell out just how far-reaching and the extent to which this move changed the trajectory of Arminian (and later Wesleyan) soteriology.[54]

---

52. Ellis, *Arminian Confession*, 109–110.

53. Richard Muller, "The Federal Motif in Seventeenth Century Arminian Theology," *Nederlands Archief voor Kerkgeschiedenis* 68 (1988) 110.

54. This has, indeed, proved to be the case in the evolution of Wesleyan-Arminian theology: (1) As an operating assumption, free will as a natural endowment has replaced "the will graciously set free." (2) The notion of God as salvific sovereign has been replaced with God as the one who affirms our innate liberty to choose. (3) Sin as a fundamental debilitating factor that can be overcome *only* by gracious intervention has virtually disappeared from the theological horizon. Lip service is paid to sin's debilitating force, but soteriologically *ratio recta* reigns. (4) In a system where human beings are sovereign, any notion of a sovereign God that "predestines" (conditionally or otherwise) is ludicrous – never mentioned.

Conclusion

The decade after Arminius's death in 1609 proved to be a telling one. The church he had pastored in Amsterdam became the veritable center of an Anti-Arminian sentiment that eventually drove the Arminians out of all the pulpits in the Netherlands. The Erastian theory of church-state governance espoused by Arminius and Hugo Grotius was undermined to the extent that it was no longer practically viable. At the hands of his closest friends and most famous student, Arminius's soteriology was changed in subtle ways that determined its trajectory in some rather un-Arminian ways. Even though the Arminian theology that was judged and found wanting at the Synod of Dort in 1618–1619 did not faithfully reflect Arminius, he was inferentially condemned as heretical at the great synod. If the Contra-Remonstrants at Dort closed the coffin on Arminius, the Remonstrants themselves lowered him into the ground and covered him over with Pelagian sentiment. Even as we contemplate the more recent absence of Arminius in Wesleyan-Arminian theology, history teaches us that Arminius's actual teachings were already much obscured a century prior to Wesleyan-Arminian theology's coming into being. Twentieth-century Wesleyans lost Arminius from view, and we in this new century would be well served to recover the soteriological distinctives that he set out.

— 2 —

Robert Barnes and John Wesley's Reformation Heritage

David Lowes Watson

Introduction

IN THE EXTRACT OF John Wesley's *Journal* published in 1742 we find the following entry for Sunday, November 12, 1738: "I preached twice at the Castle. In the following week I began more narrowly to inquire what the doctrine of the Church of England is concerning the much-controverted point of justification by FAITH. And the sum of what I found in the Homilies I extracted and printed for the use of others."[1] Since this publication went through multiple editions in Wesley's lifetime, and several further editions following his death, it was clearly a foundational document for the early Methodist societies.[2]

The *Extract* drew from Thomas Cranmer's *Homily of Salvation, Homily of Faith,* and *Homily of Good Works annexed unto Faith,* the third, fourth and fifth of the twelve Homilies published in July, 1547.[3] These provided

---

1. John Wesley, *Journal and Diaries II (1738-1743)*, eds. W. Reginald Ward and Richard P. Heitzenrater, *BEW*, 19:21.

2. John Wesley, *The Doctrine of Salvation, Faith, and Good Works, Extracted from The Homilies of the Church of England* (Oxford, 1738), in *Doctrinal and Controversial Treatises I*, ed. Randy L. Maddox, *BEW*, 12: 31–43. Albert C. Outler described this as Wesley's "first published doctrinal manifesto" in his *John Wesley* (New York: Oxford University Press, 1964), 121.

3. Thomas Cranmer, *Miscellaneous Writings and Letters of Thomas Cranmer, Archbishop of Canterbury, Martyr, 1556*, edited for The Parker Society by The Rev. John

a critical compass heading for the emerging Anglican *via media*, and the opening section in Wesley's *Extract* consists of Cranmer's exposition of the doctrine of justification. We are all sinners against God, and cannot be justified or made righteous by our own works. Accordingly, three things must go together for our justification: on God's part, mercy and grace; on Christ's part, the satisfaction of God's justice by his passion and death; and on our part, a true and lively faith in the merits of Jesus Christ. Our justification is not a thing that we render unto God, but rather that we receive from God. Furthermore, it is not our own act to believe in Christ, nor yet is it our faith that justifies us. Indeed, we must renounce the merit of faith, hope, charity, and all other virtues and good works, as too weak to deserve our justification. For this we must trust only in God's mercy, and the sacrifice which Christ offered for us on the cross.

The *Extract* goes on to identify two kinds of faith. There is what the Scriptures call a dead faith, compared in the Epistle of James to "the faith of devils, who believe and tremble yet do nothing well," and likewise compared to the faith of "wicked Christians" who profess they know God, but in works deny this knowledge. Even a belief in the truth of the Word of God is not faith, properly so called, inasmuch as faith without works is dead, and as such is not faith, just as a dead man is not a man. We must therefore declare our living Christian faith by our works, rejoicing in it, diligently maintaining it, and letting it "be daily increasing more and more by good works" to the end of our faith, even the salvation of our souls.[4] The wording of Wesley's first sub-heading for the *Extract* is significant: "Of the Salvation of Mankind," pointing to Cranmer's eloquent affirmation of universal grace: "First, you must have an assured faith in God, and give yourselves wholly unto him. Love him in prosperity and adversity, and dread to offend him evermore. Then for his sake love all men, friends and foes, because they are his creatures and image, and redeemed by Christ as ye are."[5]

The following year Wesley published another *Extract* from two theological treatises by Robert Barnes (1495–1540), the sixteenth century Cambridge Reformer.[6] This was published only once, but it is noteworthy

---

Edmund Cox (Cambridge: Cambridge University Press, 1846), 128–49. See ibid., 128n1 for a discussion of Cranmer's authorship. For the context of the *Homilies*, published some six months after the death of Henry VIII, see Diarmaid MacCulloch, *Thomas Cranmer: A Life* (New Haven: Yale University Press, 1996), 372–75.

4. Wesley, *The Doctrine of Salvation, Faith, and Good Works*, BEW, 12:41.

5. Ibid., 43.

6. John Wesley, *Two treatises. The First, on Justification by Faith Only; the Second, On the Sinfulness of Man's Natural Will. With Some Account of the Life and Death of Dr. Barnes: Extracted from the Book of Martyrs* (London, 1739).

because Barnes emerged as the most Lutheran of the Cambridge scholars who were discussing and disseminating the teachings infiltrating from the continent of Europe. Barnes was an acknowledged leader of these scholars, and provides a window into the genesis of the English Reformation on which Wesley was to draw time and again for the theological and ecclesiological vindication of his ministry.[7]

Barnes was not a major theologian, though his early years showed much promise, and his scholarship certainly stimulated a revival of learning at the Augustinian House in Cambridge. But rather than his publications, it was his witness and ultimately his martyrdom that made Barnes a significant Reformation figure. Wesley acknowledged as much in "The Principles of a Methodist,"[8] perhaps recognizing a kindred spirit in this scholar and preacher, and while much of our information about Barnes is still dependent on the seminal sixteenth-century work of John Foxe,[9] interest in his role as reformer, theologian, and diplomat continues to foster important research.[10] It is encouraging to note that he also attracts the interest of younger scholars.[11]

---

7. For example, John Wesley, *Sermons I 1-33*, ed. Albert C. Outler, *BEW*, 1:158; *Sermons II 34-70*, ed. Albert C. Outler, *BEW*, 2:86 and n18; *Journal and Diaries IV (1755-1765)*, eds. W. Reginald Ward and Richard P. Heitzenrater, *BEW*, 21:299; *Journal and Diaries V (1765-1775)*, eds. W. Reginald Ward and Richard P. Heitzenrater, *BEW*, 22:46; and *Letters II (1740-1755)*, ed. Frank Baker, *BEW*, 26:161.

8. John Wesley, *The Principles of a Methodist in The Methodist Societies, History, Nature, and Design*, ed. Rupert E. Davies, *BEW*, 9:56. See ibid., 47-48 for the background to this treatise, largely consisting of a response to Josiah Tucker's pamphlet, *A Brief History of the Principles of Methodism*, in which Tucker refers to Wesley's Extract from Barnes, but wrongly identifies not only Barnes's religious order, but also his theological pedigree.

9. John Foxe, *Actes and Monuments of these latter and perillous dayes, touching matters of the Church*, eds. George Townsend and Stephen Reed Cattley (1563; repr., London: Seeley & Burnside, 1837-41). Barnes himself provides details of parts of his career in his own writings, also published by John Foxe: *The Whole Workes of W. Tyndall, John Frith and Doct. Barnes*. (London, 1573).

10. Noteworthy is the recent volume by Korey D. Maas, *The Reformation and Robert Barnes: History, Theology and Polemic in Early Modern England* (Woodbridge: Boydell, 2010). This includes a detailed biography, theological and historical commentary, and extensive bibliography. See also Neelak Serawlook Tjernagel, *Henry VIII and the Lutherans: A Study in Anglo-Lutheran Relations from 1521 to 1547* (Saint Louis: Concordia, 1965), with informative sections on the life and work of Barnes. The two treatises excerpted by Wesley are included in Tjernagel's edited transcription, *The Reformation Essays of Dr. Robert Barnes, Chaplain to Henry VIII* (Eugene, OR: Wipf & Stock, 2007), 20-36, 62-76.

11. For example, in 2009 Barnes was the subject of a presentation to the Hemel Hempstead Local History and Museum Society: "Dr. Robert Barnes: English Reformer and Martyr," by three Sixth Form A Level students, Ed Gardner, Rosie Hutton, and Huw Wales, tutored by John Ross.

Henry VIII: Fidei Defensor; Supreme Head

No study of the English Reformation can fail to take into account the overwhelming presence of Henry VIII and the theological implications of his title, Supreme Head of the Church in England.[12] Henry has been described as brutal, crafty, selfish and ungenerous, eaten up by his all-devouring egoism, and a king who would ride roughshod over the bodies of his broken servants.[13] Yet his reign was also marked by respect, even popularity among the people, by undivided loyalty from those who served him, and by admiration from men of learning. In the early years of his reign "the life-giving airs of the Renaissance seemed to be blowing upon England,"[14] and in 1519 Erasmus wrote that literature would flourish if only there were kings such as Henry. Describing him as no inconsiderable scholar, Erasmus observed that there were more men of learning to be found in Henry's court than in any university.[15]

A powerful and unpredictable combination of charisma, craft, largesse, and ruthlessness guided Henry through a reign which, at thirty-eight years, was among the longest of any English monarch, and also one of the most turbulent. Of paramount concern for the Tudor dynasty was the danger of a reversion to the struggles of the preceding century when the Plantagenets had pursued their own self-destruction.[16] At all costs law and order were to

---

12. " Let the king therefore be called Supreme Head . . . . What other thing then is it, to condemn and despise the word of God, not to obey the king, which is God's minister, and God's vicar? I mean not, by this vicar of God, that Bishop of Rome, which by his proper right hath nothing to do without his province. He is the Bishop of Rome: let him play the Bishop of Rome. For in England he hath no more power than the Archbishop of Canterbury hath at Rome." Richard Sampson in an oration toward the end of 1533. See John Strype, *Ecclesiastical Memorials; relating chiefly to Religion, and its Reformation, under the reigns of King Henry VIII, King Edward VI and Queen Mary the First,* 7 vols. (London: printed for Samuel Bagster, 1816), 1:245. See also, "[Henry] had no intention of remaining a mere secular protector of the national Church. He meant to exercise certain spiritual functions hitherto pertaining to the Papacy . . . . [His] theological knowledge and self-righteousness gave his Supremacy a dangerously personal character." A. G. Dickens, *The English Reformation* (New York: Schocken, 1964), 119.

13. J. D. Mackie, *The Earlier Tudors 1485-1558* (Oxford: at the Clarendon Press, 1952), 442. See however, "Maybe Henry was no more unaware and irresponsible than many kings have been; but rarely, if ever, have the unawareness and irresponsibility of a king proved more costly of material benefit to his people." J. J. Scarisbrick, *Henry VIII* (Berkeley: University of California Press, 1968), 526.

14. Mackie, *The Early Tudors,* 235.

15. J. S. Brewer, James Gairdner, and R. H. Brodie, eds. *Letters and Papers, Foreign and Domestic, of the Reign of Henry VIII, 1509-47,* 21 vols. and 2 vols. Addenda (London: H. M. S. O., 1862-1932), 3: no. 251.

16. "His instinct for rule carried his country through a perilous time of change, and

be maintained, and since religious differences were a ready source of civil strife, the publication in October 1520 of Luther's *The Babylonian Captivity of the Church*, even though it was primarily an attack on the sacramental system of the medieval Church, was a cause for alarm.[17]

From Henry's standpoint Luther presented a threat to the social and political order with which, in the sixteenth century, religion was inextricably involved and accordingly the English government had been concerned about Lutheran influences from the outset. There was a deliberate attempt not to over-estimate the threat of the new doctrines, but even so, within two years of the promulgation of the Ninety-five Theses at Wittenberg in 1517 Lutheran books were condemned, and by 1521 Cardinal Wolsey, Henry's Lord Chancellor, regarded their circulation as a serious menace. There was the additional motivation on the part of Wolsey and Henry to enlarge their personal prestige in European politics, and the encouragement of the Pope toward their anti-Lutheran policy was undoubtedly a factor in Henry's taking pen to paper personally to refute Luther.[18] He dedicated his treatise, *Assertio Septem Sacramentorum*, to Leo X and in return received the title *Defensor Fidei*, a title which oddly still remains on the head of British coinage.[19]

Henry's affirmation of the seven sacraments showed a creditable knowledge of the Bible and the Church Fathers, though it is impossible to say how much of it he actually wrote.[20] While it was primarily a sacramental

---

his very arrogance saved his people from the wars which afflicted other lands. Dimly remembering the Wars of the Roses, vaguely informed as to the slaughters and sufferings in Europe, the people of England knew that in Henry they had a great king." Mackie, *Earlier Tudors*, 442–43.

17. Martin Luther, *Word and Sacrament II*, ed. Ardel Ross Wentz in *Luther's Works* (Philadephia: Fortress, 1959), 36:3–126.

18. Henry VIII, *Assertio Septem Sacramentorum*, ed. Louis O'Donovan (New York: Benziger Brothers, 1908). It seems that Henry's concern from an early date in his reign was to acquire from the Pope some sort of Christian assignation. Legatine correspondence indicates that the title of *Defender* had already been considered in 1515, but rejected because it had already been given to the Swiss. Among other possibilities were *King Apostolic* and *Orthodox*, neither of which the Pope found to be satisfactory. See Brewer and Gairdner, *Letters and Papers*, 2: 967.

19. The Roman edition of the *Assertio*, dated 1521, includes a letter from Leo X in which he indicates his granting of the title. The original publication has been reproduced by The Gregg Press, Inc. (Ridgewood, NJ, 1966). See also Scarisbrick, *Henry VIII*, 110–15.

20. Gordon Rupp suggested that he probably had considerable assistance from More and Fisher, especially with the Greek and Hebrew references. E. Gordon Rupp, *Studies in the Making of the English Protestant Tradition, Mainly in the Reign of Henry VIII* (Cambridge: Cambridge University Press, 1949), 90.

treatise, the *Assertio* showed that Henry's real concern was the unsettling effect the *Babylonian Captivity* would have on the people of his realm.[21] The extent to which he was unable or unwilling to enter into Luther's spiritual struggle is indicated by his failure to grasp the underlying argument of the treatise, and in the final analysis the importance of the *Assertio* was political rather than theological. Likewise Luther's reply, published in 1522 and bristling with invective, was primarily of significance in making personal or even diplomatic contact between the two men all but impossible.[22] In a long letter to the Saxon dukes, Henry urged them to restrain the Lutheran faction in Germany which, he warned, would do the greatest mischief if not controlled.[23]

Notwithstanding Luther's subsequent apology,[24] Henry had publicly committed himself to certain doctrinal statements which he could not retract without losing face. Prolonged attempts during the following decade to reach an agreement with the Lutheran princes foundered on Henry's refusal to accept the doctrines of the Augsburg Confession, against which his *Assertio* continued to be a royal pronouncement. Influences from Wittenberg on the early English Reformation must therefore be viewed in light of this mutual distrust, which has tended to obscure the fact that Lutheranism did makes its mark on English religious life, especially in the emerging articles of belief.

Initially it was Renaissance humanism rather than religious protest that created a climate for reform in England, not least because the Tudors proved to be active and generous patrons of the new learning. Lady Margaret Beaufort, mother of Henry VII, created professorships at Oxford and Cambridge, endowed St. John's College at Cambridge, and provided many

21. Henry was especially forceful in his attack on Luther's view of holy orders, saying that he was substituting anarchy for the authority of the priesthood, the very essence of order so important to a king. See *Assertio*, 394–95.

22. "The King of England, wretched scribbler, suffering from a lack of matter, clearly lies, and with his lies acts the part of a comic jester rather than that of a king . . . Let him blame himself and his lies if he is compelled to hear things unworthy of his kingly name. His wicked mouth has deserved this; for he has blasphemed my king, who is the King of Glory." Cited in Tjernagel, *Henry VIII*, 19.

23. "No faction was ever so universally pernicious as this Luther conspiracy, which profanes sacred things, preaches Christ so as to trample on his sacraments, boasts of the grace of God so as to destroy free will, extols faith so as to give license to sin, and places the inevitable cause of evils in the only good God. The poison is producing dissension in the church, weakening the power of the laws, and of the magistrates, exciting the laity against the clergy, and both against the People, and has no other end than to instigate the people to make war on the nobles while the enemies of Christ look on with laughter." Brewer and Gairdner, *Letters & Papers*, 4:40.

24. See Tjernagel, *Henry VIII*, 26–33.

other benefactions. For four years Erasmus was Lady Margaret Professor of Divinity and Lecturer in Greek at Queen's College, Cambridge, and when she died in 1509 it was he who composed her epitaph, Skelton who sang, and Fisher who preached at her funeral.[25]

The combination of humanism and religious revival engendered a sympathetic atmosphere in which Luther's teachings rapidly spread. This was especially true at Cambridge, which produced twenty-five martyrs in as many years.[26] Those devoted to the new learning made up an informal company whose excitement at the revelations from new scriptural texts drew them together for meetings at the White Horse Tavern.[27] Even Stephen Gardiner, who later as Bishop of Winchester became a staunch ecclesiastical conservative, described them as being without malice and "having some savor of learning."[28]

Robert Barnes at Cambridge

Robert Barnes was a notable recruit to this fellowship. Born at King's Lynn in 1485, a decade after the Tudors came to power, he entered the House of the Augustinian Friars at Cambridge in 1514, where he quickly showed outstanding scholastic promise. He was sent to Louvain to continue his studies, and on his return was made head of the House, receiving the degree of Doctor of Divinity in 1523 and fostering classical study among the friars.[29] Gar-

---

25. James Bass Mullinger, *The University of Cambridge: from the earliest times to the Royal Injunctions of 1535* (Cambridge: Cambridge University Press, 1873), 463. See chapters 5 and 6 for a detailed account of Cambridge humanism. See also Dickens, *English Reformation*, 63–67.

26. These included Thomas Bilney, William Roye, John Frith, John Lambert, John Rogers, John Bradford, Hugh Latimer, Nicholas Ridley, and Thomas Cranmer. See H. C. Porter, *Reformation and Reaction in Tudor Cambridge* (Cambridge: Cambridge University Press, 1958), 58–73.

27. "The house that they resorted most commonly unto was the White Horse which, for despite of them, to bring God's word into contempt, was called Germany. This house especially was chosen because many of them of St. John's, the King's College and the Queen's College, came in on the back side." Foxe, *Actes*, 5:415. Dickens, *English Reformation*, 91, suggested that the White Horse meetings might well have begun prior to 1520.

28. Cited in Rupp, *Studies,* 18.

29. "[So that] what with his industry, pains and labour, and with the help of Thomas Parnell, his scholar, whom he brought from Louvain with him, reading 'copia verborum et rerum,' he caused the house shortly to flourish with good letters, and made a great part of the house learned (who before were drowned in barbarous rudeness), as Master Cambridge, Master Field, Master Coleman, Master Burley, Master Coverdale, with divers others of the university, that sojourned there for learning's sake." Foxe, *Actes*, 5:415

diner described him as "a trymme minion frer Augustine, one of a merye skoffynge witte frerelike, and as a good felowe in company, was beloved of many."[30] As the most promising figure among the Cambridge humanists, and increasingly noted for his anti-clericalism, Barnes found himself drawn into the growing circle of adherents to the teachings of Luther.

It seems to have been Bilney who converted him to the new theology, and the two, along with Latimer, became leaders of the White Horse circle.[31] Increasingly they began to occupy themselves with matters of ecclesiastical practice which those in authority in the university could not ignore. Their strong anti-clericalism was a mixture of new scholarship, new access to the Scriptures, and new interpretations suggested by Luther's writings, though all of this was still in ferment and had yet to find a clear formulation. What was indisputable, however, was the intensity of the evangelical faith that strongly influenced the group, expressed convincingly in a letter which Bilney wrote to Cuthbert Tunstal, Bishop of London, describing his conversion:

> But at last I heard speak of Jesus, even then when the New Testament was first set forth by Erasmus; which when I understood to be eloquently done by him, being allured rather by the Latin than by the word of God (for I knew not what it meant), ... and at the first reading (as I well remember) I chanced upon the sentence of St. Paul (O most sweet and comfortable sentence to my soul!) in I Tim.1, "It is a true saying and worthy of all men to be embraced, that Christ Jesus came into the world to save sinners; of whom I am the chief and principal." This one sentence, through God's instruction and inward working, which I did not then perceive, did so exhilarate my heart, being before wounded with the guilt of my sins, and being almost in despair,

---

30. Cited in S. R. Maitland, *Essays in Subjects Connected with the Reformation in England* (London: Francis & John Rivington, 1849), 346. The assessment of H. Maynard Smith is more functional: "Wherever men congregate regularly in a club or a public-house there is sure to be one who takes the lead. It is generally the man with the readiest tongue, the loudest voice and the best conceit of himself. If men don't like him, they go elsewhere. They did like Friar Barnes." *Henry VIII and the Reformation* (London: Macmillan, 1962), 255. Another Tudor biographer has described Barnes as "gregarious, witty, talkative, likeable, and as shallow as a saucer." Richard Marius, *Thomas More: A Biography* (New York: Alfred A. Knopf, 1985), 314.

31. "Thus Barnes ... became famous and mighty in the Scriptures, preaching ever against bishops and hypocrites; and yet did not see his inward and outward idiolatry, which he both taught and maintained, till that good Master Bilney with others ... converted him wholly to Christ," Foxe, *Actes*, 4:635; 5:415.

that immediately I felt a marvelous comfort and quietness, insomuch "that my bruised bones leaped for joy."[32]

The group became sufficiently convinced of this new theology to seek an occasion for open declaration of their convictions, and Barnes was their spokesman in a sermon preached on Christmas Eve, 1525. The church of St. Edward at Trinity College was filled to hear what was expected to be a controversial sermon, and Foxe tells us that Barnes "postilled the whole epistle, following the Scriptures and Luther's Postil."[33] But then he went on to make a pointed attack on ecclesiastical litigiousnness.[34] A poor man in Cambridge had died, leaving a kettle to the church, but his executor was in hard circumstances and had withheld the kettle from the churchwarden, begging some latitude. Instead, the warden sued him and had him thrown in prison, where he could neither pay the debt nor support his family. Seeing the warden in the congregation, Barnes was nothing if not direct:

> Wherefore I will be judged by all Christen men, if I ought not in this to give my frende counsell, not for to sue. Or whether I be worthy to be condemned for an hereticke, because I counsell my frende and brother, rather to suffer wrong, than for to undoe a whole household for a naughtie leude kettel.[35]

Barnes continued with a diatribe aimed at the pretensions and shortcomings of the clergy in general and Cardinal Wolsey in particular, providing the confrontation which had been building up for some time between the university authorities and the White Horse circle. At a preliminary hearing held behind closed doors he was cited for statements alleged to be heretical, seditious, contentious and blasphemous, and a subsequent session was broken up by student demonstrations. To avoid further unrest Barnes was tricked into meeting with the authorities informally to discuss his views, but instead the session was officially recorded and used to give the impression that Barnes had agreed to revoke his heretical statements.

Barnes denied this revocation, and the matter was quickly placed in the hands of Wolsey, who at the time was planning a burning of heretical literature similar to one that he had organized in 1521. Men were sent to Cambridge to arrest Barnes and search for literature, though they were

---

32. Foxe, *Actes*, 4:635

33. For the fourth Sunday in Advent, Phil 4:4–7. Foxe, *Actes* 5:415. See also Charles H. Cooper, *The Annals of Cambridge (1574–1798)*. 3 vols. (Cambridge: Cambridge University Press, 1842–1845), 1:312.

34. Barnes, *Works*, 205–7.

35. Barnes, *Works*, 209.

successful in finding only Barnes. He was charged with twenty-five heretical articles, of which eighteen were related to his criticisms of the ecclesiastical hierarchy. While Foxe's account of the subsequent trial is emotionally weighted toward the threat of being burned at the stake if he did not abjure, it was clear that Wolsey and the bishops did not intend for this to be the outcome, since Barnes was released to the custody of two of his former Cambridge friends. The offence was not so much with Barnes's sermon as with his having preached it before a university congregation, and Wolsey made clear that the issue was ecclesiastical impertinence rather than heresy:

> What, Master Doctor, had you not a sufficient scope in the Scriptures to teach the people, but that my golden shoes, my pole-axes, my pillars, my golden cushions, my crosses did so sore offend you, that you must make us "ridiculum caput" among the people? We were jollily that day laughed to scorn. Verily it was a sermon more fit to be preached on a stage than in a pulpit; for at the last you said, I wear a pair of red gloves (I should say bloody gloves, quoth you), that I should not be cold in the midst of my ceremonials. And Barnes answered, "I spake nothing but the truth out of the Scriptures, according to my conscience, and according to the old doctors."[36]

While the full weight of the law was severe concerning heresy, considerable leniency was exercised in dealing with younger scholars of promise, who were expected to step out of line as they flexed their intellectual muscle. But in his arraignment before the bishops, Barnes quickly took up any slack that might have been extended. The description given by Foxe is supplemented by Barnes's own account.[37] He was first accused of denouncing the holy days of the Church, to which he replied that for faithful Christians every day should be Christmas day, since "Christ is every day borne, every day risen, every day ascended."[38] But he then went on to affirm the right of a preacher to speak the truth:

> There be certain men like conditioned to dogges. If there be any man, that is not theyr countryman, or that they love not, or know not, say anything agaynst them. Then cry they, an hereticke, an hereticke, *ad ignem, ad ignem*. These be the dogges that feare

---

36. Foxe, *Actes*, 5:416

37. Barnes, *Works*, 205–226. This was the second of ten treatises that comprised *A Supplication to King Henry VIII*, published after he had fled England and joined the theological community at Wittenberg. For the new definitive edition of the *Supplication*, see below, n52.

38. Ibid., 205–6.

true preachers. . . . We make nowe a dayes many Martyrs, I trust we shall have many more shortly. For the viritie coulde never be preached playnely but persecution did follow.[39]

In this exchange can be found the basis for the Protestant rejection of much of the traditional teaching of the Church. Not only was the authority of custom and practice open to question; if it was contrary to Scripture it was no longer acceptable at all. Barnes's diatribe was not only anti-clerical, but an argument against the larger issue of ecclesiastical authority, and he argued well on this point. The relationship between canon and civil law was tempered by the fact that most of Henry's bishops had been trained in law rather than theology, and were therefore quickly on the defensive against a challenge to their authority on the basis either of Scripture or of early Christian practice:

> They say they be the successours of Christ and of his Apostles, but I can see them folow none, but Judas. For they beare the purse, and haue all the money. . . . As for this article I will ouercome you with the witnes of all the world, you may well condemne it for heresie, but it is as true as your *Pater noster*. . . . But I graunt that I did offende in caulling you ordinary Byshops, for I shoulde have called you inordinate butchers.[40]

Barnes pressed the point with a litany of ecclesiastical malpractice, evincing a concern for the poor that was characteristic of the White Horse circle: "Wilte thou know what their benedictions is worth? They had rather geeue thee ten benedictions then one half-penny. Is this not a sore heresie? You ryde thorowe streetes and towns, blessing man and stone, but you neuer geeue halfepenye to man, nor childe."[41]

Barnes's response to the articles against him might seem irascible, and it should be noted that a genuine effort was made by Wolsey and the bishops to avoid sending him to the stake. Even if some of the articles against him were falsified, they were drawn up on the basis of a sermon preached before a not unsympathetic university congregation, and such sermons rarely proved to be restrained; indeed, they were expected not to be. Barnes ultimately agreed to do public penance, following which he was committed, with privileges, to the Fleet prison.[42] He was later assigned to the priory of his order in London, effectively under house arrest but with sufficient

---

39. Ibid., 207.
40. Barnes, *Works*, 211.
41. Ibid., 212. See Dickens, *English Reformation*, 43–44.
42. Foxe, *Actes*, 5:418.

freedom to pursue what became his new interest, the sale and distribution of Tyndale's translation of the New Testament.

We have an account of this aspect of Barnes's activities in the confession of John Tayball, a Lollard accused of heresy in 1528, and it gives us an insight into another of the antecedents of the English Reformation. Tayball and fellow Lollard Thomas Hilles paid a visit to Barnes in the spring of 1527, during which Barnes declared that Tyndale's *New Testament* was a great improvement on the old Lollard version, and persuaded them each to purchase a copy at the considerable price of three shillings and two pence, an average weekly wage for a laborer.[43] Since the time of Wycliff, Lollard communities had survived throughout England and evidence continues to come to light of regular persecutions under the early Tudors.[44] Strongly anti-clerical, they lacked both a national organization and a sound theological basis for their teachings, yet this very fact enabled them to avoid the judicial machinery of church and state. Foxe described their heretical doctrines as denial of transubstantiation, reading the Scriptures in English, and a somewhat crude rejection of various ecclesiastical practices.[45] Their simple but abrasive piety can be found in the earthy language of William Bull, a young clothworker from Dewsbury, who said he would "rather be christened in the running river" than in the font in his church, "standing stinking by half a year." And he would rather confess to a layman than a priest, since if he confessed to a priest that he had "japed a fair woman, or such like offence, the priest would be as ready within two or three days after to use her as he."[46]

The transition from Lollardy to Protestantism provides one of the most fascinating aspects of the English Reformation, and the link with Barnes imparts a sense of the baton being handed to the next runner. His promotion of the Tyndale *New Testament* once again brought him to the attention of the authorities, and hearing that his life was in danger, Barnes fled England in 1528, leaving evidence behind to suggest a suicide by drowning.[47] By way of the Low Countries he arrived at Wittenberg, where he was warmly welcomed by the theological community, in particular by Bugenhagen, and he

---

43. Strype, *Memorials*, 5:368–69.

44. See A. G. Dickens, *Lollards and Protestants in the Diocese of York, 1509–1558* (London: Oxford University Press, 1959). See also Joseph W. Martin, *Religious Radicals in Tudor England* (London: Hambledon, 2003), and Peter Marshall, "The Reformation, Lollardy, and Catholicism" in *A Companion to Tudor Literature*, ed. Kent Cartwright (Chichester, Wiley-Blackwell, 2010).

45. Foxe, *Actes*, 4:457–59.

46. Cited in Dickens, *English Reformation*, 31.

47. Foxe, *Actes*, 5:419; Maas, *Barnes*, 21–22.

began to write under the name of *Antonius Anglus*.[48] It was clear from the articles to which Barnes answered before the bishops that he had not, at the time of his flight, arrived at a definitive theological position, still less a Lutheran understanding of the faith, something that he himself admitted in describing his penance:

> And that the worlde shoulde thynke I was a marueylous haynous heretyke, the Cardinall came the next day with all ye pompe and pride that he could make to Paules church . . . . And moreover were there commaunded to come all ye bishops . . And to set the matter more forth . . . the byshop of Rochester must preach there the same day, and all his sermon was agaynst Lutherians, as though they had counted me for one: The which of truth, and afore God, was as farre from these thinges as any man could be.[49]

But not for long. In England the ground was fertile, the scholarship was available, as were the newly-translated Scriptures. With the fall of Cardinal Wolsey in 1530, and the question of the royal divorce now the defining issue between Henry VIII and Rome, the climate in England became more receptive to the new theology. Under the influence of the reformers at Wittenberg Barnes was to publish a series of essays that paved the way for him to become a Lutheran theologian as well as an Anglo-German diplomat.

Robert Barnes, Theologian

It is important to remember that Barnes was only one of a distinguished group of English exiles during this period, most of whom were associated in one way or another with the work of Bible translation. Lambert and Frith were close friends of Tyndale at Antwerp; George Joye and William Roye were his assistants; Miles Coverdale, Richard Taverner, and John Rogers were later to complete his work with their own editions of the whole Bible. In addition, John Rogers served a congregation at Wittenberg, and Taverner translated the Augsburg Confession in 1536. Yet it was Barnes who came closest to an understanding of Luther's theology at its source. His first published work in 1530 was the *Sententiae ex doctoribus collectae, quas papistae valde impudenter hodie damnant*, translated into German by Bugenhagen

---

48. Johann Bugenhagen had come to Wittenberg in 1521 after reading Luther's *Babylonian Captivity*, and emerged as a leading organizer of Lutheran churches, as well as spiritual adviser to Luther and his family. He was appointed superintendent general of Saxony in 1539. Barnes was affectionately known as Dr. Anthony among the Lutherans in Germany.

49. Barnes, *Works*, 225.

the following year. Essentially it was a collection of proof texts from the Scriptures with supportive passages from patristic sources, and the headings in the volume point to the theological agenda that Barnes was already developing in the collegial climate of Wittenberg. There are nineteen captions in all,[50] and while the some of the well-worn criticisms of the Church from Barnes's earlier career are present, and while the primacy of Scripture does not yet appear as a doctrinal issue, the change in emphasis is marked.[51] The priority now is justification by faith and its radical implications.

From this preliminary effort, Barnes went on to publish his major work the following year, the *Supplication to Henry VIII*, initially printed at Antwerp.[52] Identified by the title of the first treatise in the volume, it included an account of his defense before the bishops in 1526 and a collection of essays that defined him as "thoroughly seasoned in the Wittenberg theology."[53] The most distinctively Lutheran treatise is titled *Onely faythe iustifieth before God*.[54] Christ is affirmed as our only mediator and justification is given freely by grace:

---

50. The captions are: 1. Only faith justifies. 2. Christ's death has made satisfaction for all sins and not only for original sin. 3. God's commandments cannot possibly be kept in our own strength. 4. Freewill by its own nature is only able to sin. 5. The just sin in all good works. 6. What is the true Church and how she may be told. 7. God's Word, not men's powers, is the keys of the Church. 8. Councils may err. 9. All should receive the sacrament in both kinds. 10. Priests may marry. 11. Human ordinances cannot free sinners. 12. Auricular confession is not necessary for salvation. 13. Monks are not more holy than lay people on account of cowls and monasteries. 14. Christian fasting does not consist in discrimination between foods. 15. For the Christian every day is a Sabbath day and a festal day and not only the seventh day. 16. Unjust banning by the Pope does not disgrace the banned. 17. In the Sacrament of the Altar is truly the Body of Christ. 18. Saints may not be appealed to as mediators. 19. Of the origins and parts of the Mass. From the Latin in the 1536 edition housed in the Rare Book Room at Duke University Library. I am indebted to Roger Loyd, Librarian at Duke Divinity School, for access to this and other pertinent volumes and documents.

51. What had been the first article brought against him for his 1525 sermon is fifteenth in this list.

52. A definitive text is now available, edited by Douglas H. Parker: *A Critical Edition of Robert Barnes's "A Supplication Vnto the Most Gracyous Prince Kynge Henry The. VIII.1534."* (Toronto: University of Toronto Press, 2008). Parker provides both the 1531 and 1534 editions with detailed commentary.

53. Tjernagel, *Henry VIII*, 59. See also Gordon Rupp, *The Righteousness of God* (London: Hodder & Stoughton, 1953), 39.

54. Barnes, *Works*, 226–42; Barnes, *Supplication*, 214–46, 529–56. The original Antwerp edition has an introduction dealing with ancient authorities that was omitted in later editions, as was a deprecating reference to Henry's title *Defensor Fidei*, in which Barnes declared that the English bishops not only purchased the title for Henry, but never took the trouble to spell out exactly what was the faith he supposedly had defended. Ibid., 498.

> Nowe yf we wyll truely confesse Christ, than we must graunt with our hertes, that Christ is all our iustice, all our redemption, all our wysdome, all our holynes, all alonly the purchaser of grace, alonly the peace maker betwene God and man. Breuely all goodnes that we haue, that it is of hym, by hym, and for his sake onely. And that we haue nede of nothyng towardes our saluacyon, but of hym onely.[55]
>
> Here can be none euasion, the wordes be so playne. Yf you brynge in any helpe of workes, than for so moche is not our redemption freely, nor yet is it of grace, as concernynge the parte, that commeth of workes, but partly of workes, and than do you destroye all saynt Paul and his holle disputacion.[56]

The implications of this are then developed. Righteousness is imputed to those who believe, and no works of penance are required for the forgiveness of sins. Not even faith is a prerequisite, since the faith which justifies is itself a gift from God, and not the result of human reasoning:

> The very trewe way of iustificacion is this. Fyrst cometh God, for the loue of Christ Iesus, alonely of his mere mercye, and gyueth us freely the gyfte of faythe, wherby we do beleue God, and his holy worde, and stycke faste vnto the promyses of God ... This is not suche a fayth, as men dreme, whan they beleue that there is one God, and beleue, that he is eternall ... But the faythe, that shall iustifie vs, must be of an other maner strength, for it must come from heuen, and not from the strength of reason. It must also make me beleue, that God the maker of heuen, and erthe, is not alonely a father, but also my father.[57]

The nature of the good works which follow from this are then clarified, and some objections raised by John Fisher, Bishop of Rochester, are answered. Fisher had stated that while faith begins justification in us, works perform and make it perfect. Barnes dismisses the argument, and answers the objection that *sola fide* destroys good works by quoting the Pauline text that the law is in fact fulfilled through faith.[58] The remainder of the essay deals with further textual objections, and concludes with an appeal to Henry VIII in which he is careful to affirm orderly living:

---

55. Barnes, *Works*, 226; Barnes, *Supplication*, 215; Wesley, *Treatises*, 26–27.
56. Barnes, *Works*, 228; Barnes, *Supplication*, 218; Wesley, *Treatises*, 32.
57. Barnes, *Works*, 235; Barnes, *Supplication*, 232; Wesley, *Treatises*, 57–58.
58. Barnes, *Works*, 236–39.; Barnes, *Supplication*, 235–38; Wesley, *Treatises*, 63–66. Barnes comments on Fisher's argument: "What Christened man would think, that a Bishop would thus trifle and play with God's holy word?"

> Now most honorable, and gracyoust prynce, I haue declared vnto your hyghnes, what faythe it is that dothe iustifie vs before God ... that your grace myght se, that I am not moued to this opinion of a lyghte cause, nor that this doctryne of myne is so newe, as men hath noted it. Moreouer, I haue declared vnto your grace, howe that I wolde haue good workes done, and wolde not haue a christen mans lyfe to be an ydle thynge, or elles a lyfe of vnclenness, But I wolde haue them to be chaunged in to all vertue, and goodnes, and to lyue in good workes, after the commaundment, and wyll of God.[59]

In the treatise, *Free wyll of man, after the falle of Adam, of his naturall strengthe, can do nothynge but synne, afore God,* Barnes argues that sin has deprived humanity of any capacity even to believe in God, still less know and love a God who is parental:

> In this article wyll we not dispute, what man may do, by the common influence gyuen hym of God, ouer these inferior, and worldly thynges, as what power he hath in eatynge, and drynkynge, in slepyng ... and in all other suche naturall thunges, that be gyuen of God, indifferently to all men, bothe to good, and bad. But here wyll we serche, what strength is in man, of his naturall power, without the spirite of God, for to wyll, or to do those thynges, that be acceptable afore God, vnto the fulfyllyng of the wyll of God, as to beleue in God, to loue God after his commaundementes, to loue iustice for it selfe, to take God for his father.[60]

> Here it is open, that the Pelagions graunt as moche of grace, as my lorde of Rochester dothe, and all his Duns men, whiche lerneth, that man may haue a good purpose, *bonum studium*, and a good mynde, and a loue to grace, of his owne naturall strength, the Pelagions graunt euen the same. But here you se, howe saynt Augustyne is clere agaynst them.[61]

---

59. Barnes, *Works*, 242; Barnes, *Supplication*, 245–46; Wesley, *Treatises*, 75–76. Wesley's edited title of this treatise has a different emphasis: "On the Sinfulness of Man's natural Will, and his utter Inability to do Works acceptable to God, until he be justified and born again of the Spirit of God, according to the Doctrine of the Ninth Tenth, Twelfth and Thirteenth Articles of the Church of England."

60. Barnes, *Supplication*, 255–56; Wesley, *Treatises*, 77–78.

61. *Supplication*, 267–68; *Treatises*, 98. At this point Wesley breaks off his transcript of the essay, and brings the *Extract* to a conclusion, omitting Barnes's detailed refutation of the Scotist doctrine of attrition.

The other treatises in the *Supplication* are essentially an elaboration of Barnes's theological agenda laid out in the *Sententiae ex doctoribus collectae*.[62] Since he had addressed the *Supplication* to Henry VIII, it was to be expected that the authority of the crown should be affirmed, but it is a mark of his writing, and of the English reformers in general, that the power of princes and the laws of the realm were not also, but primarily, ordained of God. They were concerned to refute the charge, not infrequently brought against them, that their new doctrines led to anarchy. Anabaptism in particular had made Protestantism suspect in England, and the revolt of the German peasants in 1524–1525 provided conservatives with supportive evidence for their case.[63]

The *Supplication* and the accompanying essays were published at the beginning of an intensive period of parliamentary legislation officially severing ties with Rome, and by 1534 the writings of Barnes and other English exiles were being seen in a new light. Thomas Cromwell in particular was not slow to see the advantage of a Protestantism that Henry might be persuaded to accept because the writers were loyal to him, and repudiated anarchy, disorder and revolution.[64] Accordingly, Cromwell's agent in Antwerp, Stephen Vaughan, was active in locating the exiles and soliciting their return to England. Such a step was not without danger, since the king was by no means convinced of their doctrine. Moreover, the conservative element in the Church continued to lean toward Rome, and while lacking original ideas on church or government, they did possess the political talent to utilize the king's suspicion of doctrinal change to their own advantage. Led by the Duke of Norfolk and by Stephen Gardiner, now Bishop of Winchester, they had the sympathy of most of the bishops who, while theologically conventional, were utterly loyal to the king.

---

62. Above, n50.

63. For example, on February 28, 1528, Erasmus wrote to More, stating that he had received great consolation from the king's invitation to come to England. Things were now in such a state that he felt he must look out for a grave where he could rest in quiet after his death since that was no longer possible in this life. The heresy of the Anabaptists was everywhere, he noted, and far more widely diffused than any one expected. Brewer and Gairdner, *Letters and Papers*, 4:3983.

64. From humble beginnings, Thomas Cromwell began his political career in service to Cardinal Wolsey, advanced as secretary to the king in 1533, master of the rolls in 1534, keeper of the privy seal in 1536, and as vicar-general he supervised the dissolution of the monasteries. In many ways he was the progenitor of the modern bureaucratic state, and during his relatively short time in office made possible the realization of the English Reformation. See Geoffrey R. Elton, *Reform and Renewal: Thomas Cromwell and the Common Weal* (New York: Cambridge University Press, 1973). Typically he was rewarded by his king with disgrace and execution in 1540.

Robert Barnes, Diplomat

Meanwhile negotiations continued with the Protestant German Princes. Through Cromwell's influence Barnes had already been back in England for a brief visit as early as 1531, and for the greater part of the decade he was to play an active role in the attempts to reach an agreement with the Lutherans. When his *Supplication* was printed in Antwerp in 1531, Vaughan obtained copies immediately for the king and Cromwell,[65] and while certain of the essays were not likely to please Henry, his reaction in general seems to have been sufficiently favorable to grant Barnes a safe-conduct to England.

His stay was short, however, because he had also acted as messenger for Luther, bringing to Henry the unfavorable Wittenberg position on the royal divorce. Having failed to get support from Catholic universities on the issue, Henry had turned to the Lutherans, only to be further disappointed. Whether Barnes acted on his own or on Cromwell's initiative in this is unclear, though Luther's letter to him dated September 3, 1531 indicates that he was fully involved.[66] Luther rejected the argument that the king had either the duty or the privilege to divorce the queen. Since matrimony is a matter of divine law, according to which it is indissoluble, then the divorce could not be sanctioned, divine law taking precedence over all other statements of law.[67]

By January of 1532 Barnes was back in Germany, his short visit to England indicative of the role he was to play in the complicated and ultimately abortive negotiations with the German princes and theologians. England may have moved inexorably toward Protestantism during Henry's reign, but at no time did he allow the reformers or the conservatives to have the advantage. Tension was maintained through a masterful employment of *realpolitik*, and while the Protestants were able to advance their cause significantly under the patronage of Cromwell, they suffered reverses as the failure of the German negotiations led to his downfall. As with so many of Henry's loyal servants, Cromwell found himself caught in a tide of reform that was always subject to the unpredictability of a monarch whose theological acumen and political instincts made royal service fraught with risk. Cromwell's reputation has tended to that of ruthless tactician in the dissolution of the

---

65. On November 14, 1531, he wrote: "Look well upon Dr. Barnes' book. It is such a piece of work as I have not yet seen any like it. I think he shall seal it with his blood." Brewer and Gairdner, *Letters and Papers*, 5:533.

66. "My Antony: here you finally have also my opinion on the case of the King of England, since you insist on it with great perseverance." Luther, *Luther's Works*, 50:31.

67. Ibid., 40.

monasteries, albeit tempered by his pioneering of the bureaucratic state, yet A. G. Dickens pays him a signal compliment:

> One who reads without prejudice his letters, his injunctions, his final parliamentary speech of 12 April 1540, cannot doubt his positive desire to establish a religion based upon the Bible, a religion eschewing on the one hand blind trust in ecclesiastical tradition, and on the other the brawling of self appointed expositors.[68]

It was Barnes's fate also to be caught in these tensions, advocating a Lutheran theology when Henry's real concern was a political alliance that would consolidate his divorce from Queen Catherine. Even so, the period after his return to Germany was congenial for Barnes. He served as assistant pastor to John Aepinus in Hamburg for a time, and then returned to Wittenberg where he researched his history of the papacy.[69] His next visit to England was in 1534, as part of an embassy which Henry invited from Hamburg and Lubeck for exploratory negotiations.[70] The divorce had left the king exposed to the possibilities of hostile European coalitions with the Emperor,[71] and a rapprochement between the German reformers and the Roman Church was a real possibility during the 1530s. Overtures were therefore extended to the German theologians, Melanchthon being repeatedly invited to come to England,[72] and to this end Barnes was sent on an informal visit to Wittenberg in March of 1535. As a result of this visit Melanchthon wrote a tactful letter to Henry, making the position of the reformers clear, and indicating to Henry that religious controversy might be avoided "if your Majesty would lend his authority to incline other monarchs to moderation: if indeed he would deliberate with learned men about a form of doctrine."[73]

Barnes was enthusiastic about the possibilities of an English acceptance of Lutheran teachings, even to the point of discerning signs and

---

68. Dickens, *English Reformation*, 135.

69. Robert Barnes, *Vitae Romanorum Pontificum*, published in 1536. This was a history of the papacy from the apostle Peter to the end of the pontificate of Alexander III in 1181, and was the last published work of Barnes, for which Luther himself wrote a preface. For a critical assessment of the text and secondary literature, see Maas, *Barnes*, 107–36.

70. Brewer and Gairdner, *Letters and Papers*, 7:710, 737, 871, 926, 957.

71. Charles V, Holy Roman Emperor of the Hapsburg Spanish and Austrian territories, 1519–1556.

72. Brewer and Gairdner, *Letters and Papers*, 8:385.

73. Cited in Rupp, *Studies*, 93.

wonders,[74] though the progress he had made received a setback when Fisher and More were executed.[75] There was such an outcry in Europe over these executions that Henry and Cromwell furnished their ambassadors with a vindication of what were widely seen as extreme acts of political retribution. To keep the negotiations with the German prince alive, Henry dispatched a formal mission with a view to his admission to the Schmalkaldic League.[76] Barnes was once again commissioned to prepare the ground, and arrived at Wittenberg in August 1535 with a letter designating him "our beloved and faithful chaplain." On Luther's recommendation he was given an audience with John Frederick, Elector of Saxony, who agreed to receive a formal embassy from Henry, but made clear that he would have to subscribe to the Augsburg Confession if he wished to join the League. John Frederick cautiously pointed out that he would have to consult with his fellow members about admitting Henry, since the League had been founded for the defense of "the pious and pure doctrine of the Gospel."[77]

The official deputation arrived in November, and on Christmas Day, 1535, thirteen articles were drawn up as a tentative basis for negotiation, the first of which set the tone:

> *Imprimis*, That it may please the king's majesty to promote the doctrine of the gospel, as the confession of the Germans at Augsburg & the apologies thereupon to import: unless his grace will change or reform any thing according to the word of God.[78]

As negotiations proceeded the English and the Germans revealed different concerns and objectives. Henry in no way intended to reform English doctrine along the lines of the Augsburg Confession, yet this was precisely what held the interest of the Germans through the interminable sessions. Barnes, though by now in a subordinate position to the official delegation, continued to send hopeful signals in his correspondence to England.[79] Gar-

---

74. In a letter to Cranmer, Brewer and Gairdner, *Letters and Papers*, 8:385

75. John Fisher, Bishop of Rochester, was beheaded on June 22, 1535, shortly after he had been made a Cardinal by Pope Paul III. Thomas More, former Lord Chancellor, was beheaded on July 6, 1535. Both men had refused to take the oath to uphold the 1534 Act of Succession which declared Henry's first marriage unlawful and had changed the royal succession to the progeny of his marriage to Ann Boleyn.

76. The political and religious alliance of the Lutheran princes formed in 1531.

77. Tjernagel, *Henry VIII*, 149–52; Maas, *Barnes*, 30–32.

78. The Articles are reproduced in full in Strype, *Memorials*, 5:559–61.. See also Brewer and Gairdner, *Letters and Papers*, 9:1016–18; Tjernagel, *Henry VIII*, 184–89; Maas, *Barnes*, 60–67.

79. For example, Barnes to Cromwell, December 28, 1535, concerning the attitude of the Germans toward Henry's divorce. See Brewer and Gairdner, *Letters and Papers*, 9:1030.

diner, by contrast, made every effort to sabotage the venture, and when the Germans would not agree to condone the royal divorce, Henry made clear that he would not accept the Augsburg Confession without modifications.

In April, 1536, the English delegation returned with the draft of what became known as the Wittenberg Articles.[80] Seventeen in all, they seem to have been chiefly the work of Melanchthon, and while drawing heavily on the Augsburg Confession, they also represent an attempt to make concessions to the English without sacrificing any major theological positions. Of particular interest is Article 5, concerning good works which "ought necessarily to follow on our part" after reconciliation with God: "It is necessary that the church be often admonished to put this doctrine concerning good works out into the clear light of day. It must teach clearly what kinds of works are demanded . . . how they please God . . . and that these commanded works are not only external, civil work, but also spiritual activities."[81]

Even though Luther himself was quite firm on how far such concessions could go,[82] following the return of the delegation to England a new formula of faith, the *Ten Articles*, was approved by Convocation on June 9, 1536, evincing considerable agreement with Wittenberg.[83] With a preamble from the King, they dealt with doctrine and church ceremonies in equal measure, though the title reflected the challenges presented by the spread of Protestant reforms:

> *Articles devised by The Kinges Highnes Majestie, to stablyshe Christen quietnes and unities among us, and to avoyde contentious opinions, which articles be also approved by the consent and determination of the hole clergie of this realme, Anno M.D.XXXVI.*[84]

Of the five articles on doctrine, the fifth, on Justification, made clear the ongoing theological tension:

---

80. Reproduced in Tjernagel, *Henry VIII*, 255–86.

81. Ibid., 262.

82. "Since my Most Gracious Lord [Elector John Frederick] has requested an answer to the question of how far one could go in making concessions to the King of England regarding the articles, it is my judgment, dear Mr. Vice-Chancellor, than in this matter we are unable to concede anything beyond what has been already conceded . . . [It] would be a disgrace for us not to be willing to concede to the Emperor and to the Pope what we would now concede to the King." Martin Luther to Francis Burkhardt, Vice Chancellor of Saxony, April 20, 1536, in Luther, *Luther's Works*: 50:140–41.

83. The Act for the Submission of the Clergy in 1534 decreed that Convocation, the assembly of the clergy in the provinces of Canterbury and York for the governance of the English Church, was now to be convened by royal edict.

84. *Formularies of Faith*, ed. Charles Lloyd (Oxford: at the Clarendon Press, 1825), 3–20. See also MacCulloch, *Cranmer*, 160–66.

> That sinners attain this justification by contrition and faith joined with charity ... not as though our contrition, or faith, or any works proceeding thereof, can worthily merit or deserve to attain the said justification; for the only mercy and grace of the Father, promised freely unto us for his Son's sake Jesus Christ, and the merits of his blood and his passion, be the only sufficient and worthy causes thereof; and yet that notwithstanding, to the attaining of the said justification, God requireth to be in us not only inward contrition, perfect faith, and charity ... but also he requireth and commandeth us, that after we be justified we must also have good works of charity, and obedience towards God, in the observing and fulfilling outwardly of his laws and commandments: for although acceptation to everlasting life be conjoined with justification, yet our good works be necessarily required to the attaining of everlasting life.[85]

As with all issues arbitrated by Henry, this tension was not without political significance. The execution of Ann Boleyn, his second wife, had given new vigor to the conservatives, and a northern uprising later in the year indicated that popular opinion could not be forced into reform as readily as the Protestant protagonists might have hoped or imagined.[86] Known as the Pilgrimage of Grace, it was perhaps the most serious threat to civil order during Henry's reign, and its impact on the government was considerable.[87] The demands of the rebels included the censure of the heresies of Huss, Luther, Melanchthon, Bucer, Barnes, Tyndale and others, and the consecration of bishops was to be reserved to the See of Rome. Thus, shortly after approving the *Ten Articles* incorporating significant Protestant advances, Convocation published in June 1536 a list of fifty-nine heretical opinions then current in the realm. Of these, forty-four were doctrines representing positions of the Wittenberg theologians which were, according to the English bishops, "preached and discoursed to the slander of this noble realm, the disquiet of the people, and to the hindrance of their salvation."[88]

By the same token, one of the major works in support of the royal supremacy, *De Vera Obedentia*, was written by the conservative Bishop of Winchester, Stephen Gardiner, and published in the weeks following the

---

85. Lloyd, *Formularies*, 12.

86. A point acknowledged by Luther in his letter of April 20, 1536 to Burkhardt, above n82. See also Maas, *Barnes*, 33.

87. The historical novel by H. F. M. Prescott, *The Man on a Donkey* (London: Eyre & Spottiswoode, 1953), provides many poignant insights into this abortive and tragic rebellion.

88. Tjernagel, *Henry VIII*, 163-64.

executions of Fisher and More. Gardiner defined the Church as "that multitude of people united in Christian belief. The true Christian never fails in obedience to God, and since God is not visibly present, men are set in place to be his vicars. Such vicars are princes, placed by God at the summit of the hierarchy of his earthly representatives."[89]

There was a further attempt in 1537 to establish religious norms for the country in response to the Pilgrimage of Grace and other disturbances: *The Institution of a Christian Man*.[90] Popularly known as the *Bishops' Book*, its title indicates that it too was a compromise between the old and new doctrines, with Edward Fox and Thomas Cranmer largely responsible for its contents. There were two more attempts in 1538 to reach agreement with the Germans: a set of Thirteen Articles in which the Wittenberg Articles again figured prominently,[91] and a German delegation that came to England to continue discussions. During this period there was a relaxation of the restrictions against Protestants and a new freedom of religious expression. Barnes was preaching regularly, and confessional literature did much to disseminate Lutheran doctrine. Cromwell's *Ecclesiastical Injunctions* of 1536 and 1538 were likewise an effort at religious reform directed toward the parish clergy, in which the sharp distinctions between the real doctrines of salvation and the rites and ceremonies of the church had a definite Lutheran flavor.[92]

By mid-1539, however, the German negotiations were more or less exhausted. It became clear that Henry had been motivated throughout by political considerations, as he endeavored to avoid being isolated by alliances which might be formed between the Germans and the French, or the French and the Emperor; or worst of all, between the Emperor and the Protestants. This actually came to pass during the spring of 1539, when the Emperor and the Protestants reached an agreement precluding the admission of new members to the Schmalkaldic League, and when word of this reached England, Henry responded with the *Act of Six Articles*, which became law in June of that year.[93] Described as "a device in Parliament for unity in re-

---

89. See Philip Hughes, *The Reformation in England*, 3 vols. (New York: Macmillan, 1963), 1:337-41. See also Dickens, *English Reformation*, 172-74.

90. *The Institution of a Christian Man.; containing the exposition or interpretation of the Common Creed, of the Seven Sacraments, of the Ten Commandments, and of the Pater Noster, and the Ave Maria, Justification, and Purgatory*. Lloyd, *Formularies*, 21-211.

91. Reproduced in Cranmer, *Writings*, 472-80.

92. MacCulloch, *Cranmer*, 226-28.

93. Brewer and Gairdner, *Letters and Papers*, 14, pt.1: 655. For the text of the Act, see David Wilkins, *Concilia Magnae Britanniae et Hiberniae*, 4 vols. (London, 1737), 3:848.

ligion," it affirmed transubstantiation, rejected communion in both kinds, forbade the marriage of priests, affirmed monastic vows, continued private masses and retained auricular confession. The penalty clauses were severe, gaining it a reputation as "the whip with six strings." For any heresy against five of the articles there was loss of goods and imprisonment, with death for a repeat offense, and anyone speaking against transubstantiation was to be burned with no abjuration possible.

There was strong reaction to the *Act*, from overseas and at home. Melanchthon in particular protested vehemently in a letter to Henry, which Foxe reproduced in full so as not to "defraud the reader of the fruit thereof, for his better understanding and instruction."[94] Henry was faced with resignations from Bishops Saxton and Latimer, and Cranmer even sent his wife back to Germany to avoid the possibility of penalties.[95] To what extent this was an attempt by Henry to convince Catholic Europe of his orthodoxy and thereby remove any threat of hostility, or to what extent it was an act of petulance, remains an enigma, as with so much of this monarch's rule. Yet Henry was genuinely concerned about England's political isolation and relative weakness, and Cromwell noted in March of 1539 that, along with the "device in Parliament for unity in religion," there was also to be "a device for the defence of the realm in time of invasion."[96] No fewer than twenty-six places were listed to be fortified, along with Calais, Guisnes, and Hammes "on the other side," and by virtue of a royal commission issued on March 1, 1539, military musters were held throughout the country. These were meticulously recorded, listed by county, town, village, and the exact numbers of men mustered.[97]

As things transpired, the "whip with six strings" was used sparingly. Some five hundred persons were rounded up fairly quickly, but the following year there was amnesty. Richard Hilles, a cloth merchant whose business took him often to the continent where he was on familiar terms with some of the leading Protestants, wrote to Bullinger in 1541 that the king had published a general pardon by which he forgave the nobility and others of his subjects all heresies, treasons, felonies, and other offences committed before July 1, 1540, and that no further persecution should take place on

---

94. Foxe, *Actes*, 5:350–58.

95. During a visit to Nuremberg in 1532, Cranmer had married Margerite, niece of the wife of Andreas Osiander, who reportedly officiated at the wedding. Osiander, who became good friends with Cranmer, was the only major Lutheran theologian to support Henry's arguments for the annulment of his marriage to Catherine. See MacCulloch, *Cranmer*, 69–72.

96. Brewer and Gairdner, *Letters and Papers*, 14, Pt.1: 655.

97. Ibid., 14, Pt.1: 652–54.

account of religion.[98] And on the return of the German embassy following the termination of the negotiations, Burkhardt, who had been a member of the delegation, reported to Melanchthon that "nothing is done as yet, for all execution is suspended, and the King already seems displeased at the promulgation of the decree."[99]

For Luther, however, it was the last straw. On October 23, 1539, he wrote to Elector John Frederick:

> Martin Bucer has previously also written to me . . . requesting my assistance on urging that a legation, especially Master Philip, be sent to England. For the time being I have answered him suggesting that he abandon such hope . . . .The king is a dilettante and has no serious intentions. This we have certainly found out from the English who have been here, although at the time out of Christian love we had to believe that he was serious. But finally, when we had debated *ad nauseam*—at great expense to Your Electoral Grace—everything was sealed with a sausage and left to the King's pleasure. The English themselves said: "Our King vacillates," and Doctor Anthony said several times: "Our King in no way respects religion and the gospel."[100]

Luther's reference to "Doctor Anthony" reminds us that Barnes throughout this period was a participant in the various efforts to reach an agreement, but with declining fortunes. Never high in the esteem of the king following his visit to England in 1531, when he had relayed the Wittenberg position on Henry's divorce, his status now decreased from "royal chaplain" to "household servant," and in 1536 he was sufficiently impecunious to be asking Cromwell for financial assistance.[101] Cranmer tried to get him the deanery of Tamworth College,[102] and Latimer also made efforts on his behalf, reminding Cromwell of his quality as a theologian.[103] But eventually he

---

98. *Original Letters Relative to the English Reformation, written during the reigns of King Henry VIII, King Edward VI, and Queen Mary: Chiefly from the Archives of Zurich*, edited for The Parker Society by Hastings Robinson, 2 vols. (Cambridge: Cambridge University Press, 1846-47), 1:208.

99. Brewer and Gairdner, *Letters and Papers*, 14, Pt. 2: 423.

100. Luther, *Luther's Works*, 50:189-90, 205-206.

101. Brewer and Gairdner, *Letters and Papers*, 10:880.

102. Cranmer, *Writings*, 380.

103. "Mr. Doctor Barns hath preached here with me a Hartlebury [on Christmas Day, 1537] and at my request at Winchester, and also at Evesham. Surely he is alone in handling a piece of scripture, and in setting forth of Christ he hath no fellow. I would wish that the king's grace might once hear him." *Sermons and Remains of Hugh Latimer*, edited for The Parker Society by George E. Corrie, vol. 28. (Cambridge: Cambridge University Press, 1845), 378, 389.

had to be satisfied with a Welsh prebend worth only eighteen pounds a year, an amount slightly more than half what was considered to be an adequate annual income.[104]

One last opportunity seemed to present itself when Henry opened negotiations with the King of Denmark in 1539. Barnes was sent with full diplomatic status, and wrote enthusiastically about the possibilities of an alliance.[105] But Henry, irritated by Danish references to his lack of agreement with the Augsburg Confession, did not proceed. Barnes, having delayed his return to England on hearing about the *Act of Six Articles*, eventually came back in considerable apprehension. Cromwell's German policy was already close to failure, and his negotiations for Henry's marriage with Ann of Cleves proved to be the disappointment to the king that inevitably led to royal disfavor. Moreover, Barnes himself was firmly identified with the German theologians, and the frustrations of the past ten years had taken their toll. He probably sensed that his time was running out, so when Gardiner and the conservatives engineered a confrontation, Barnes decided to stand his ground and be "counted for a Lutheran," this time by conviction as well as repute.

Robert Barnes, Martyr

Further invigorated by the *Act of Six Articles*, the conservatives had resumed the offensive against the Protestant cause in 1540. Knowing that Barnes and two other abjured heretics, Thomas Garrett and William Jerome, had been designated to preach the Sunday sermons at St. Paul's Cross during Lent, Gardiner himself preached a sermon directed against Barnes on the first Friday, choosing for his attack the doctrine of justification by faith. Although this had been included in the *Ten Articles* and the *Bishops' Book*, the full significance of the doctrine had not been fully perceived by the king or the English bishops, whose attention had been focused on ecclesiastical rites and the eucharist. But Gardiner sensed that, for a convinced Lutheran, this was the core of his convictions.[106]

Barnes's response, preached two weeks later, was favorably judged by at least one observer,[107] but Gardiner's reaction was predictably belligerent:

---

104. Though still in the top 20% of livings at that time. Dickens, *English Reformation*, 48–49.

105. Brewer and Gairdner, *Letters and Papers*, 14, Pt.1: 1273, and Pt. 2: 400.

106. For the course of this dispute, see Maas, *Barnes*, 37–41 and Tjernagel, *Henry VIII*, 214–18.

107. "I must not omit to tell you that the bishop of Winchester preached a very popish sermon, to the great discontent of the people, on the first Sunday in Lent, and

> There he beganne to call for me to comme forth to aunswer him; he termed me to be a fightynge cocke . . . and, not content therwith, he . . . opposed me in my grammar rules, and sayde if I had aunswered him in the scoole as I had there preached at the Crosse, he wolde have given me syxe strypes . . . as he rayled of me by name, alludynge to my name, Gardener, what evell herbes I sette in the garden of Scripture, so farre beyonde the termes of honestie as all men wondered at it, to here a bysshop of the realme as I was, so reviled, and by such one, openly.[108]

In a letter to John Aepinus, his superior when he was at Hamburg, Barnes made clear that the real issue was the theological tension between faith and works:

> A fierce controversy is going on between the bishop of London, Gardiner, and myself respecting justification by faith and purgatory. He holds that the blood of Christ cleanseth only from past sins previous to baptism, but that those committed since are blotted out partly by the merits of Christ, and partly by our own satisfactions, He adds too, that voluntary works are more excellent than the works of the ten commandments.[109]

Not unexpectedly, the conflict came to the attention of the king, who commanded Barnes and Gardiner to debate in front of him. According to Foxe, Barnes was ordered to receive instruction from Gardiner, since the king was "earnestly incensed" against him.[110] Barnes refused, and was thereupon ordered by the king to apologize to Gardiner and to recant in an Easter sermon.

At this point Barnes yielded, and had he followed custom he would have preached a routine recantation sermon. It was nothing new to make a statement which satisfied the authorities without conceding major doctrines.[111] But instead of merely retracting his Lutheran opinions, he asked Gardiner to indicate acceptance of his apology by raising his hand. The embarrassed Gardiner raised an uncertain finger, upon which Barnes launched

---

that he was ably answered by Dr. Barnes on the following Lord's Day with the most gratifying and all but universal applause." Bartholomew Traheron to Heinrich Bullinger, February 20, 1540, *Original Letters*, 1:317.

108. Stephen Gardiner, *The Letters of Stephen Gardiner*, ed. James A. Muller (Cambridge: Cambridge University Press, 1933), 170.

109. *Original Letters*, 2:616–17.

110. Foxe, *Actes*, 5:431. Foxe implicates Gardiner as having complained personally to the king about Barnes's sermon, which had caused him to be "tickeld in the spleen."

111. As Gordon Rupp observed, some had made it a fine art. See Rupp, *Studies*, 45.

into a further sermon, effectively negating his apology and affirming his Lutheran theology. He was condemned by act of attainder, imprisoned for four months and, along with his fellow reformers, Jerome and Garrett, burned on July 30, 1540. Two days before, Cromwell had been beheaded. On the same day that Barnes died, three Catholics were executed for treasonable beliefs.

While Barnes's Easter confrontation with Gardiner can be viewed as one more example of his feisty nature, he must also have become increasingly frustrated that his attempts to forge a diplomatic liaison with Wittenberg had been abused by Henry time and again. And if he had been hesitant to malign his prince, he must have seen in Gardiner an opponent whose persistent efforts to sabotage the Lutheran negotiations seemed finally to have succeeded. More important, Barnes was by then sincerely committed to the centrality of *sola fide*, as his protestation at the stake affirmed: "And I believe ... that no work of man did deserve any thing of God, but only [Christ's] passion as touching our justification: for I know the best work I ever did is impure and unperfect."[112] George Joye's outcry against Gardiner was a fitting epitaph for Barnes: "Dare he claim (think ye) any part of his justification for burning of Doctor Barnes and his fellows for preaching against these wickedly armed articles? Tell us, Win[chester], didn't thou burn them so cruelly of love and not of hatred or envy? Truly love burneth no man for preaching the truth—charity envyeth not."[113]

Epilogue and Prologue

Barnes's prince, King Henry VIII, lived for seven more years, dominating the religious life of his people at the close of his reign as he had throughout, and exercising his royal office as Supreme Head of the Church in England with an astute understanding of the political power held by the Church and its teachings. Thus, when the *Bishops' Book* was revised and re-issued in 1543 as the *King's Book*, we find the doctrine of justification qualified not only by the necessity of consequent good works, but also by the dynamics of prevenient grace:

> And albeit God is the principal cause and chief worker of this justification in us, without whose grace no man can do no good thing. . . . yet it so pleaseth the high wisdom of God, that man,

---

112. Foxe, *Actes*, 5:434.

113. Cited in Charles C. Butterworth & Allan G. Chester, *George Joye, c 1495–1553: A Chapter in the History of the English Bible and the English Reformation* (Philadelphia: University of Philadelphia Press, 1962), 210.

prevented by his grace (which being offered, man may refuse or receive), shall be also a worker by his free consent and obedience to the same, in the attaining of his own justification.... And therefore it is plain, that not only faith, as it is a distinct virtue or gift by itself, is required to our justification, but also the other gifts of the grace of God, with a desire to do good works, proceeding of the same grace.[114]

That Henry should remain an enigma is perhaps just as well, but a reminiscence of Cranmer, recorded by Foxe, leaves us with the impression that Barnes and his fellow martyrs were indeed at the vanguard of reform:

I am sure you were at Hampton Court, quoth the archbishop, when the French king's ambassador was entertained there at those solemn banqueting houses, not long before the king's death: namely, when, after the banquet was done the first night, the king leaning upon the ambassador and upon me, if I should tell what communication between the king's highness and the said ambassador was had, concerning the establishing of sincere religion then, a man would hardly have believed it. Nor I myself had thought the king's highness had been so forward in those matters as then appeared. I may tell you, it passed the pulling down of roods and the suppressing the ringing of bells.[115]

All of which brings us back to the *Extracts* that John Wesley drew from Cranmer and Barnes as he inquired more narrowly into the doctrine of the Church of England concerning the much controverted point of justification by faith.[116] While he further developed his exposition of the doctrine in his preaching, teaching and writing,[117] and just as important in his polity,[118] it was clearly a priority at the outset of his evangelical ministry.[119] Under the

---

114. Lloyd, *Formularies*, 365, 368.

115. Cranmer, *Writings*, 416n.

116. See Albert C. Outler's Introduction to "The Lord Our Righteousness," *Sermons 1–33*, *BEW*, 1:444–46.

117. For example, in his 1739 sermon, "Free Grace," *Sermons III:71-11*, *BEW*, 3:542–63 and in the controversy following the 1770 Conference, *The Methodist Societies: The Minutes of Conference*, ed. Henry D. Rack, *BEW*, 10:392–94. See also the excellent biography by Henry D. Rack, *Reasonable Enthusiast: John Wesley and the Rise of Methodism*, 3rd. ed. (Peterborough: Epworth Press, 2002), 388–93, 454–61 and Frank Baker, *John Wesley and the Church of England*, 2nd ed. (Peterborough: Epworth Press, 2000), 92–94.

118. For example, see David Lowes Watson, *The Early Methodist Class Meeting: Its Origins and Significance* (1985; repr., Eugene, OR: Wipf and Stock, 2002), 39–65.

119. *The Minutes of Conference*, *BEW*, 10:29–30, 120–21.

general, and all too often polemical heading of "Faith and Works," the issue continues to challenge the witness and mission of the church in the twenty-first no less than in the eighteenth and sixteenth centuries.

It is a question of historiography and theology alike, the inter-disciplinary challenge that the Bicentennial Edition of *The Works of John Wesley* has brought to the fore.[120] The laudable concern of the editors of these volumes has been to establish clear criteria for what is now a major field of church history and historical theology, with its own rich lode of research and writing. Dimensions of Wesley's life and work that have long been cloistered by legend and folklore are emerging in their proper context,[121] and at the same time there are fresh assessments of his theology, ecclesiology, and polity, acknowledging his distinctive contribution to the ongoing life and work of the church.[122]

The particular challenge raised by Wesley's, Cranmer's, and Barnes's *Extracts* is how Christian tradition can accommodate, indeed celebrate, the evangelical spirit that caused Thomas Bilney's "bruised bones to leap with joy" and John Wesley's heart to be "strangely warmed" without succumbing to the sectarianism implicit in the very word *Protestant*. We would do well to pursue the same narrow inquiry that Wesley undertook in late 1738, and to labor, as did he, toward keeping a balance between a faith that, *coram Deo*, brings sinful human beings to an absolute surrender of self-sufficiency through the grace of God in Jesus Christ, and the concomitant obligation to walk as Christ walked in the world. Wesley affirmed this twofold work of grace in his *Extract* from the *Homilies* of Thomas Cranmer, but he also sensed in the Lutheran *Treatises* of Robert Barnes the radical evangelical

---

120. See Kenneth E. Rowe, ed. *The Place of Wesley in the Christian Tradition: Essays delivered at Drew University in celebration of the commencement of the publication of the Oxford Edition of the Works of John Wesley* (Metuchen N.J.: Scarecrow, 1976), especially the lead essay by Albert C. Outler which is also the title of the volume, and his reference (p.22) to Wesley's *Journal* entry for November 12, 1738 (above, n1) See also *A History of the Methodist Church in Great Britain,* ed. Rupert Davies, A. Raymond George, and Gordon Rupp, vol. 1. (London: Epworth, 1965), and the extensive bibliography in 4:650–830.

121. As general editor of *BEW*, a position first held by the late Frank Baker, a major contribution of Richard P. Heitzenrater has been the enrichment and illumination of the seven volumes of Wesley's *Journal*, edited by W. Reginald Ward, with the definitive text of his *Diaries, BEW*, vols. 18–24.

122. For example, Randy L. Maddox, *Responsible Grace: John Wesley's Practical Theology* (Nashville: Kingswood, 1994); Theodore Runyon, *The New Creation: John Wesley's Theology Today* (Nashville: Abingdon, 1998); Brian E. Beck, *Exploring Methodism's Heritage: The Story of the Oxford Institute of Methodist Theological Studies* (Nashville: General Board of Higher Education and Ministry of The United Methodist Church, 2004).

doctrine that the grace of God is absolutely everything and human striving absolutely nothing in the redemption accomplished for us by Jesus Christ.

On the one hand, the Cranmer *Extract* declared that God's preventing grace is universal, not a personalized soteriological antipasto, and that the obligation of forgiven sinners is "truly to live upon Christ by faith, not only as our Priest, but as our King . . . to 'make him a whole Christ, an entire Saviour,' and truly to 'set the crown upon his head'. . . so that 'every high thing which exalted itself against' him, every temper, and thought, and word, and work is 'brought to the obedience of Christ.'"[123] The regular publication of this pamphlet indicates that it was a basic doctrinal perspective that Wesley sought to enjoin on the early Methodist societies, and it is noteworthy that there were two editions in 1770, the year in which "the storm broke . . . with the Calvinists and . . . Wesley stated his position on the disputed points with far less caution."[124]

On the other hand, the Barnes *Extract* went to the heart of the divine initiative that confronts sinful human nature with parental anguish, and imparts the inward witness of the Spirit which, at any given moment, brings a sinner into the most intimate reconciliation with God. The only precondition for this is the inactivation of the human will through despair, well expressed by Charles Wesley:

> His love is mighty to compel;
> His conqu'ring love consent to feel,
> Yield to his love's resistless power,
> And fight against your God no more.[125]

John Wesley's knowledge and understanding of his Reformation heritage makes this *Extract* from Barnes spiritually heartfelt as well as theologically incisive.

We can further find the insights of both Cranmer and Barnes reflected in Wesley's description of the new birth.[126] While the difference between a baby in the womb and one who has just been born is indeed radical (Barnes), it is not the total transformation implied by an overloaded doctrine of justification (Cranmer). A baby about to be born is essentially formed, and needs only the labor of birth provided by the mother, but by the same token the baby's life is threatened if she or he does not show growth, for which

123. Wesley, Sermons I 1–33, *BEW*, 1:352.

124. Rack, *Reasonable Enthusiast*, 454.

125. John Wesley, *A Collection of Hymns for the Use of the People called Methodists*, ed. Franz Hildebrandt and Oliver A. Beckerlegge, asst. James Dale, *BEW*, 7:82.

126. Wesley, "The Great Privilege of those that are Born of God," in *Sermons I 1–33*, *BEW*, 1:432–35.

there are self-evident conditions. The spiritual implications are profound, and Wesley's language is quite remarkable.[127]

While there were many other sources from which Wesley drew his theology and polity, not least being the response to his preaching as he took the gospel "into the highways and hedges, (which none else will),"[128] and while his disputes over justification came to focus on Calvinist rather than Lutheran tenets, these *Extracts* provided two critical compass headings at a formative stage in his evangelical ministry. They declared an assurance in the mercy of God through the merits of Jesus Christ, while avoiding "the practically absolute disjunction between Nature and Grace—that philosophical and theological ineptitude of the Reformation."[129]

---

127. It is noteworthy that Wesley's description of the Church occasionally uses similar maternal imagery. See "Reasons against a Separation from the Church of England" in *The Methodist Societies: History, Nature, and Design*, ed. Rupert E. Davies, BEW, 9:340.

128. "The Large Minutes" *The Minutes of Conference*, ed. Henry D. Rack, BEW, 10:846.

129. Robert E. Cushman, "Salvation for All—John Wesley and Calvinism," in *Faith Seeking Understanding: Essays Theological and Critical* (Durham, North Carolina: Duke University Press, 1982), 74.

3

The Exercise of the Presence of God
Holy Conferencing as a Means of Grace

Richard P. Heitzenrater

THE UNITED METHODIST CHURCH has become enamored of "holy conferencing" as a current practice that is seen as part of our Wesleyan tradition. References (often by bishops) place the source of the practice squarely in the midst of the description of the means of grace in the "Large" *Minutes*, the guidebook of doctrine and discipline that Wesley provided for his people.

Number five under Wesley's listing of the "instituted means of grace" is his enumeration and explanation of "Christian conference."[1] Current parlance often makes a short jump from that term to "holy conferencing," even though Wesley himself never uses the phrase. In fact, his reference to "Christian conference" in the "Large" *Minutes* is the only use of that phrase that can be found in Wesley's writings.

To understand what Wesley means by this term, we must go back to some fundamental concepts that are traditionally left vague and are therefore poorly understood, even though they are basic elements of the Christian faith. The concept under consideration pulls together many common themes that are central to the Wesleyan heritage, as we shall see. The four essential terms or concepts are: conference, holy, grace, and means.

---

1. *The Methodist Societies: The Minutes of Conference*, ed. Henry D. Rack, *BEW*, 10:856–57. This description was included in the 1763 edition and repeated essentially unchanged in the four subsequent editions during Wesley's lifetime.

Conference—Conversation

When Wesley referenced "Christian conference" in the "Large" *Minutes* explanation of the means of grace, he was not drawing attention to the annual conference of ministers that he had begun in the 1740s. Conference, in this context, meant "conversation." The first point to remember, then, is that by "conference" in this context, Wesley was meaning "conversation."

The right ordering of our conversation is something that is not often considered a significant element of the hubbub of one's daily schedule or in the regular contacts between people. Even ministers who are calling on parishioners today would sometimes be hard-pressed to say that their conversations during such visits were important enough to be planned out ahead of time and both preceded and followed by prayer. Yet for Wesley, religious conversation was considered as one of the five means of grace that were instituted by Jesus Christ himself.

The fact that "conference" means "conversation" and that the practice is significant in the life of the believer becomes very clear when the whole entry for Christian Conference in the "Large" *Minutes* is considered:

a. Are we convinced how important and how difficult it is to order our conversation right?

b. Is it always *in grace*? Seasoned with salt? Meet to minister grace to the hearers?

c. Do we not converse too long at a time? Is not an hour at a time commonly enough?

d. Would it not be well to plan our conversation beforehand? To pray before and after it?[2]

In these questions, Wesley first highlighted the *propriety* of proper conversation, then asked if it was always considered as a carrier of *grace*. He also raised the issue of the appropriate *length* of the conversation, and finally stressed that it should not only be pre-planned but also bracketed by *prayer*. The answer to each question should obviously be "Yes," but the question format not only followed the pattern of the *Minutes* but also implied that each preacher should have to answer these questions annually.[3] It is intriguing to think what would happen to the preacher who answered "no" to any of these questions when asked by Wesley.

2. "Large" *Minutes* (1763) in *Minutes, BEW,* 10:856–57.

3. The preachers were, when accepted on trial and then annually after 1768, examined yearly for their fitness on the basis of the questions concerning gifts and grace and the "historic questions" that are still asked of persons being ordained today. See Henry D. Rack's "Introduction: The Conference History and *Minutes," BEW,* 10:77–80.

The question of appropriate limits of length gives a strong hint that Wesley was not talking about the Annual Conference in this section of the *Minutes*. The meetings do indeed often go "too long at a time," but putting the limit of an hour on such gatherings would be unrealistic in Wesley's time, much less today. Religious conversation itself, however, can become taxing to the listener after a time, and the maximum of an hour probably reflects an eighteenth-century limit of tolerance more than a modern one, which would probably be shorter.

Wesley's diary is a good indicator of his own practice in this matter. His daily record, jotted down in cryptic fashion (but much more complete in detail than his narrative *Journal*) contained continual references to "rt" ("religious talk") with individuals and groups. The earlier diary entries, at Oxford in the ten years between 1725 and 1735, contain an average of about five daily references to religious talk with someone. These occasions rarely lasted more than an hour. The subject of the conversation was rarely elucidated, though the importance of it was often underscored by an indication of the "degree of attention."[4]

When Wesley was in Georgia during 1736 and 1737, the daily rate of "religious talk" continued at about the same pace. Upon his return to London, the diary entries decreased to about half the length, but the indications of religious talk still occurred at nearly the same rate, happening about three times per day. This apparently became the lifelong pattern, as the extant diaries from his later years also indicate that he has religious conversation with people at a rate of two to three times per day, every day, all year—up to the week before his death when he discontinued keeping a diary.[5]

Wesley considered a person's conversation to be an important indicator of the bent of their heart. His 1750 sermon, "Catholic Spirit," reiterated the importance of having a "right heart" and spends a good bit of time outlining (again in the form of multiple questions) the prerequisites for claiming a correct inclination of heart.[6] Often overlooked, however, is one of his most pithy statements, in the 1748 discourse on Christ's Sermon on the

---

4. The Wesleyan form of diary can be seen in Benjamin Ingham's daily diary, which was much fuller than Wesley's, often delineating the topic of conversation designated as "religious talk." *Diary of an Oxford Methodist: Benjamin Ingham, 1733–1734*, ed. Richard P. Heitzenrater (Durham, NC: Duke University Press, 1985), 1–3. A comparison of the Ingham and Wesley documents can be seen in Plates 2 and 3, following page 120. Cf. John Wesley, *Journal & Diaries I (1735–1738)*, ed. W. Reginald Ward and Richard P. Heitzenrater, BEW, 18:302–10. In the daily summaries in his diary Wesley does often indicate when people were "affected" by religious talk.

5. See, for example, the last few weeks of his diary in February, 1791 in John Wesley, *Journal and Diaries VII (1787–1791)*, BEW, 24:346–48.

6. John Wesley, *Sermons II 34–70*, ed. Albert C. Outler, BEW, 2:87–89.

Mount, when Wesley said, "Let your words be the genuine picture of your heart."[7] This injunction emphasized the importance that Wesley attached to proper Christian conversation and its role in the life of the person who is striving to be a true believer.[8] He was always stressing the necessary goal of holiness of heart and life, but in this sentence, we see the crucial emphasis that he placed upon the role of religious talk.

So we must start our understanding of Wesley's meaning of this phrase by noting that when he says, "Christian conference," he was concerned with the religious conversations of Christians.

Christian—Holy

A fascinating line of development within Wesley's life was his changing concept of what it means to be a "Christian." The term obviously means "one who follows Christ" or is "holy like Christ." But most theologians attempt to define the term more precisely, spelling out just what is entailed in being a Christian: how they become a Christian, how they know they are a Christian, how they live and think as a Christian, and what happens to Christians after death. Wesley was particularly concerned with the first three of these questions.

Wesley was especially (and early) concerned with the question of how Christians know (are assured) that they are children of God, justified by grace, and pardoned of their sins. He was sure that they should be able to sense this forgiveness of sins, as he explained to his mother in a letter of 1725: "If we dwell in Christ and Christ in us, which he will not do till we are regenerate, certainly we must be sensible of it."[9] The discussion with his mother, which continued for many weeks and raised several theological questions, including this matter of the witness of the Spirit, indicates that his life-long quest for this sensibility that he was indeed a child of God began at a relatively early stage of his career. That his specific position on the necessity of the sense of assurance in order to call oneself a Christian varied throughout his life does not detract from his continual concern with the matter or its centrality to the drama of salvation, as he understood it.[10]

---

7. See John Wesley, "Upon our Lord's Sermon on the Mount, Discourse the Fourth" (1748), IV.3, in *Sermons I 1–33, BEW*, 1:548. See also ibid., 2:289, 425, 573; cf 1:171.

8. See also an example of this lifelong concern expressed in Wesley's sermon, "The More Excellent Way" (1786), IV.3, *Sermons III 71–114, BEW*, 3:271–72.

9. John Wesley to Susanna Wesley, June 18, 1725, *Letters I:1721–1739*, ed. Frank Baker, *BEW*, 25:170.

10. Richard P. Heitzenrater, *Wesley and the People Called Methodist*, 2nd ed. (Nashville: Abingdon, 2013), xiii, 169, 178, 227–28, 293–94.

Another of the related issues that persisted throughout Wesley's own thought during his lifetime was whether holiness of heart and life is a prerequisite for being called a Christian. At times, such as when he wrote the 1740 sermon "The Almost Christian," Wesley indicated that the "real" Christian is one who had experienced the sanctifying presence of God in their lives and moved from the searching mode, which is marked by moments of doubt, fear, and sin, to a life of holiness that expressed the fullness of joy, love, and peace. He later refers to "the almost Christian" as a "servant" of God that was distinguished from a "child" of God. In the earlier iteration of his concern, influenced by the Moravian insistence that one experience the plerophory of assurance (which would result in an absence of doubt, fear, and sin, and the presence of joy, love, and peace), Wesley considered the "almost" Christian not within the bounds of the Christian faith.[11] In later life, as seen in his 1789 sermon, "A More Excellent Way," the wisdom of age and experience brought him to see this distinction of Christian experience falling within the definition of Christian—that both the searching servant of God and the holy child of God are expressing degrees of faith that are evident in the fluctuating life of the Christian. The latter, of course, is more excellent and reflective of what he still termed the "real" Christian.[12]

In the midst of a letter that Wesley wrote to Lady Maxwell in 1765 (shortly after he had published the first major edition of the "Large" *Minutes*), he made the point that holiness of heart and life, whether given gradually or instantaneously, was reflected in her words:

> It may be He that does all things well has wise reasons, though not apparent to us, for working more gradually in you than He has done of late years in most others. It may please Him to give you the consciousness of His favour, the conviction that you are accepted through the Beloved, by almost insensible degrees, like the dawning of the day. And it is all one how it began, so you do but walk in the light. Be this given in an instant or by degrees, hold it fast. Christ is yours; He hath loved you; He hath given Himself for you. Therefore you shall be holy as He is holy, both in heart and in all manner of conversation.[13]

Wesley has here expressed some concern that Lady Maxwell has not experienced the witness of the Spirit instantaneously, but whether it happens gradually (as in her case) or quickly, such knowledge of divine favor should result in holiness of heart and holiness "of all manner of conversation." The

11. John Wesley, *Sermons I 1–33*, *BEW*, 1:130–40.
12. John Wesley, *Sermons III 71–114*, *BEW*, 3:263–77.
13. John Wesley to Lady Maxwell, July 5, 1765, *LJWT*, 4:308–9.

witness of the Holy Spirit with one's own spirit, or a consciousness that one has received the favor of God, is considered a child of God, and has been thus transformed in heart and life, is a work of the divine presence in one's heart and mind that is theologically called "justification." Such knowledge is the result of the enlightening work of the Spirit in one's life, and is thus a way by which the work of Christ, through his life, death, and resurrection, is applied to the believer who exercises the presence of God and has faith (or a sure trust and confidence) that Christ can and has liberated them from their sinful inclinations.

Throughout his long lifetime, then, Wesley was continually adjusting his understanding of what it meant to be a Christian. As a good Anglican from his birth in 1703, he felt that beliefs and practices should coincide in the life of the Christian—right faith was borne out in good works. One's assurance was grounded in one's sincerity. As a young man in grammar school the following decade, he was swayed by Luther and Calvin toward faith as the more important aspect of the two. His assurance became associated with holding the right beliefs. The Moravian (radical Lutherans) told him in the late 1730s that true faith would result in the fullness of love, peace, and joy that would result in the loss of all doubt, fear, and sin. Assurance of one's Christian standing was depending upon having this plerophory of faith. In the following years, Wesley further defined the searching person who is trying to be a Christian as the "almost Christian"—the "servant of God" rather than the "child of God." While he continued throughout his life to examine the nuances of this issue of what is entailed in being a "real" Christian, his mature view (more tolerant than his earlier opinion) is that anyone who fears God and lives righteously (Acts 10:35) is accepted of God, even if as only a "servant."[14]

The goal of being a Christian was, for Wesley, seen as a combination of "having the mind of Christ and walking as he walked" (Phil 2:5). In his parlance, this two-fold emphasis meant exhibiting holiness of heart and mind, the central feature of the holy living tradition over the centuries. For the last sixty years of his long life, he did not shy away from this goal as being too high a divine standard. Two examples make our point. (1) The Scriptures said "Be ye holy, for I am holy" (1 Pet 1:16).[15] Wesley reiterated this prin-

---

14. John Wesley, "On Faith" (1788), I.10 in *Sermons III 71–114, BEW*, 3:397. While the minimum requirements of maintaining membership in the Methodist societies were defined in 1743 by the *General Rules* (avoid evil, do good, attend to the means of grace), from mid-century on Wesley was more comfortable in allowing those who adhered to this minimum threshold to be considered a Christian. See his sermons: "Catholic Spirit," "The More Excellent Way," and the like.

15. Wesley's annotation to the scriptural text, "The Father judgeth according to every man's work," read "[Judgeth] according to the tenor of his life and conversation." John Wesley, *Explanatory Notes Upon the New Testament* (London, 1755), 632.

ciple in his 1744 sermon on "Scriptural Christianity." In that homily, Wesley inquired, "Are we 'holy as he which hath called us is holy, in all manner of conversation?'"[16] (2) And Jesus said, "Be ye perfect, even as your father in heaven is perfect" (Matt 5:48). Such injunctions were seen by Wesley as possible of fulfillment in this lifetime since a divine command must be considered a covered promise—God will help you achieve the goal.[17] To think otherwise is to conceive of God as devious, which is unthinkable. Holiness, even perfect love, must be the goal of one's striving to live the fullness of the Christian life.

For Wesley, conversation was crucial within this whole picture. Six weeks after his Aldersgate experience, Wesley wrote from Germany to his mother, referencing that his experience with the German Moravians has helped him understand the concept that Christians actually love one another and "all who have the faintest desire to love the Lord Jesus Christ in sincerity!" He then prayed that God may "sanctify to us their holy conversation, that we may be partakers of the spirit which is in them—of their faith unfeigned, and meekness of wisdom, and love which never faileth!"[18] Two things are especially important in this comment: (1) Wesley is asking, in fact, that the "holy conversation" of the Early Church might be implemented in their own experience, which might thus be made productive of holiness or piety.[19] And (2) he is prone to stress the *sincerity* of those who desire to be Christian—a lifelong emphasis that began during his Oxford years.[20]

"Holy" in its absolute sense is a concept that distinguishes the divine from the human. Only God is truly holy.[21] Holiness is therefore possible only by participation in the divine being. Wesley may have distanced himself from the mystics of whom he was enamored in the early 1730s, but he never discarded their goal of *deificatio*—a concept that characterized Eastern Christianity in its dynamic understanding of the possibility of becoming one with the holy. Deification, becoming one with God, was a matter of relationship, of coming into and thriving within the divine presence. For

---

16. See John Wesley, Section IV.3 in *Sermons 1–33*, BEW, 1:175.

17. See Albert C. Outler, "Introduction," *Sermons I 1–33*, BEW, 1:76; Sermon 25, "Sermon on the Mount, V" (1748), III.3, ibid., 1:555.

18. John Wesley to Susanna Wesley, July 6, 1738, *Letters I 1721–1739*, BEW, 25:557.

19. s.v. "sanctify," http://www.merriam-webster.com/dictionary/sanctify.

20. See many references to sincerity in Wesley's thought throughout his lifetime.

21. Rudolf Otto reminded us in *The Idea of the Holy: An Inquiry into the Non-Rational Factor in the idea of the Divine and its Relation to the Rational* (1923; repr., New York: Oxford University Press, 1950) that the divine only is truly holy and therefore there will always be a gulf between human (no matter how spiritual) and divine.

Wesley, becoming Christ-like was not only possible, with God's help, but was the expected goal of every true Christian.

Must one be made holy (sanctified) as well as pardoned of sin (justified) to be called a Christian? From an early time, Wesley often pointed out that the person who is holy is truly happy, and to be happy (or whole as a human being) is to be holy.[22] He talked about degrees of faith, degrees of assurance, categories relating to one being considered a "Christian"—almost, fully, servant of God, child of God, searching, real. And although he constantly talked about holiness as the goal and measure of the "altogether Christian," he never disparaged others who were still searching, struggling, and striving in that direction (who have never experienced an assurance of their being a child of God). There may be a difference of opinion among scholars and denominations as to what Wesley actually thought on this matter, but Wesley seems always to give the "servant" of God the benefit of the doubt.

Christian conference, then (or proper religious conversation) is a powerful practice in the Wesleyan heritage. The phrase itself is laden with a host of implicit meanings that are central to his understanding of salvation—an understanding that shifts somewhat during his life, but is always near the center of concern. The same is true with his understanding of grace and the means by which one experiences this powerful divine force.

Grace—God's Presence

Forget anything you have heard or read about "grace." If you heard the term used by a minister or read about the concept in a theological treatise, the usage probably carried an amorphous pietistic ring or suffered from a logical deficiency. What does someone mean when they say, "The grace of our Lord be with you?" Is divine grace something that is given out like an energy bar or carried around like a thermos bottle of Gatorade? Is it something that is dispensed by divine authority like a prescription or medicine and taken by human beings when needed to bolster one's spiritual health? When an author says that grace is the "unmerited favor of God," does that description of a divine attitude pinpoint what *transforms* us, *changes* us, *empowers* us in our spiritual pilgrimage—divine favor or mercy?

What is lost in most discussions of grace is the consideration of just what *Grace* is. People like to reflect on what it *Does*, but seldom press the issue of exactly what it might *Be*. Part of the reason, perhaps, is that the

---

22. John Wesley to Susanna Wesley, June 11 and Nov. 17, 1731, *Letters I 1721–1739*, BEW, 25:283, 321.

term "grace" is used in ways that denote more than one reality (but don't necessarily make logical sense), and sometimes is used in ways that portray no perceived reality at all. "Grace" is an amorphous or mysterious reality. The mystical and pietist use of the term, in some sense beyond meaning and reality, just sounds religious and therefore good.

Recently, the pastoral prayer in a morning service included the petition, "Make us people of grace." However, when asked what that phrase meant, especially what was meant by "grace" in that context, the pastor was unable to respond with any specific meaning. If she had said something like, "Make us Christ-like," that might have been helpful, since Christ and Mary are the only two in the Bible who are specifically described as "full of grace"—that is, filled with the presence and power of God.

But quite honestly, Christians use phrases like that, using the term grace in ambiguous and amorphous ways, mainly because it sounds good, it sounds religious, it sounds pious, it sounds Christian. "May the grace of God be with you." Just what do we mean by that? What is it that we are hoping will be with someone, or go with them?

> What *is* grace? That is quite a different question from "what does grace do?"
>
> What *is* grace? Some will say "we are justified by grace," which is true. But that tells us what grace does; it does not give a hint as to what grace *is*.
>
> What *is* grace? That is quite a different question from "will you describe grace?"
>
> What *is* grace? Some will say, "It is a gift" or "it is free." Right, but those terms are descriptive or adjectival; they do not tell us what grace *is*.

What is grace? Some will way, "It is God's unmerited mercy." That is getting much closer. But such terminology describes a divine attitude more than a divine action. To say that we are saved by God's unmerited mercy is a relatively weak theological phrase that consists of insider vocabulary that is nearly empty of real meaning in common parlance.

In order to understand what grace is, and then derive from that perspective what ways (or means) can be understood as making it possible, let us try to develop a logical explanation of the concept within our Christian perception—that is to say, outline a theological explanation of reality.

If one presses the matter, grace itself must be seen in at least two ways—on the one hand, a passive sense, a divine attitude; and on the other, an active sense, a divine action. But grace is never considered properly as a substance—some *thing* that is given out or distributed by God as a commodity, even in a gift package. It is not a divine prescription, much less a divine cure-all, like a holy medicine that helps solve problems of sin or health or weakness or knowledge. Grace is always to be considered a relational concept, dealing with the connection of the divine/human relationship.

First, grace can be viewed in the *passive* sense as an attitude. In this sense, grace as a human attitude is the favor that one feels toward a person, even though that person does not deserve anyone's favor and has done nothing to earn such a favorable disposition on anyone else's part. In the divine/human relationship, divine grace in this passive sense is the favorable attitude that God has for humans, even when we do not deserve it and have certainly not earned it. Such divine attributes as love, mercy, kindness, and compassion all are indicative of God's positive attitude toward us, in spite of our lack of worthiness. God's actions in and with persons are perceived in tangible ways, in terms of enlightenment, conviction, judgment, forgiveness, pardon, liberation, empowerment, holiness, guidance, comfort, sustenance, perseverance, perfection, and glorification.

God's perceivable active presence in humankind is understood as grounded in a divine *attitude* that, although never completely comprehended, is seen as analogous to the human attitude of unmerited favor or mercy.[23] God's accepting attitude of love does not result from a person's previous good actions. People do not deserve divine mercy *because* they have already earned it. God's favorable inclination toward humankind is a part of the divine nature, not a result of human activity or character. God's attitude is understood to be continually grounded in divine mercy, love, forgiveness, concern, and compassion, which are not dependent upon prior human activities.

Such a divine attitude, however, has no direct effect on us immediately as such, but does set the stage for divine grace as a manifestation of divine energy or power that we can detect in our relationship to God and to which we can respond in our experience of God in our lives. Many Christians have perceived that God acts upon human beings in perceivable ways. This understanding of God acting in history is the basis of the biblical stories, the framework of the New Testament message, and the heart of the Christian faith. God is not just a philosophical phenomenon that exists "out there" beyond time and space but is a reality that humankind can experience in daily life and personal relationship.

23. See, for instance, Wesley's sermons, which throughout his lifetime are full of references to God's free mercy and favor; esp. "Free Grace" (1739), *Sermons III 71–114*, BEW, 3:542–63.

That active divine presence is basic to the beginning and continuance of one's faith and life as a Christian. The divine presence energizes faith itself and is the force that actuates the potential for Christian activity in the world. The divine presence makes faith itself possible and thus transforms human life by actuating a new approach to life itself, characterized by acts of love toward God and neighbor.

Second, then, grace can be viewed in the *active* sense as human or divine *actions* that result from this attitude. Because someone sees us in a favorable view that we do not deserve, that person might do things to us and for us that derive from this attitude, in spite of our lack of deserving it. At Oxford in the eighteenth century, students could "supplicate for their grace" from the Vice-Chancellor of the University (permission to be granted a degree) with a dispensation of having missed two or three terms of their graduation residency requirement simply by showing up on a certain day and asking for it, whether they deserved it or not.[24] In the divine/human relationship, God does things to us and for us in spite of our condition of unworthiness. God enlightens us, judges us, liberates us, strengthens us, guides us, comforts us, and glorifies us—not because we deserve such blessings, but because we have faith that God can transform us by this divine assistance into the fullness of our humanity, even though we do not deserve it. These transformational actions are grounded in God's grace-full attitude toward us (unmerited favor), but are themselves more than just divine dispositions.

Grace in this second sense, which we can perceive and understand, is thus a relational matter—God's presence with us. Wesley's description of both individual and corporate experiences in his *Journal* was regularly punctuated with the phrase, "And God was with us of a truth." God with us—Emmanuel. Grace is grounded in the divine incursion into human history and God's relationship to humankind. Grace is: God's presence in human experience, God's energy transforming human beings, God's power energizing human activities for good—these are all facets of God's presence, energy, and power working in the lives of people. We call this present activity of God the work of the Holy Spirit, but within a Trinitarian understanding, the work of Christ and of the Holy Spirit are one with the work of God the Father.[25]

---

24. John Ayliffe, *The Ancient and Present State of the University of Oxford*, 2 vols. (London, 1723), 2:145. See Ingham, *Diary*, 220, n217.

25. Writing to John Newton, the author of "Amazing Grace," in April 1766, Wesley told his friend that they were essentially proclaiming the same message ("there is a hair's breadth difference between us with regard to the nature of sanctification"), except that they differ in their manner of speaking: Newton uses the words "Christ" and "faith"

God's action in human life is coincident with God's presence in and with the lives of people. Divine presence is perceived in terms of God's active energy (or power) being exerted upon a person. Wesley explains the matter by saying that grace means "that power of God the Holy Ghost, which 'worketh in us both to will and to do of his good pleasure.'"[26] Here he is expanding upon the traditional understanding of grace as "the assisting operations of [God's] Spirit."[27]

The present action of God in history (often expressed in terms of the "Holy Spirit") can be understood in terms of the biblical word that is used for spirit—*ruach* (רוח)—which also means "wind." One can never actually see the wind, but the results of the wind's presence are perceivable: the trees swaying and their leaves moving, the dust devils twirling along the ground, the air moving against one's face, the ripples on the surface of the water, These and many other perceptions of the wind's presence make it a real phenomenon in spite of the fact that we can never actually see the air itself moving. So it is with God's presence also—we can perceive the divine presence by the results of its action in human experience.

God (as a spiritual being) does not have a spatial presence. Medieval thinkers are often seen as wasting their time arguing over how many angels can sit on the head of a pin. The discussion rests on a fine philosophical point, however. As Thomas Aquinas pointed out, spiritual/divine beings manifest their presence through their actions, which is to say their power being exerted upon an object.[28] The question thus has nothing to do with angels taking up space on the head of that pin, but rather is concerned with how many angels can act upon the head of that pin.

In similar fashion, God's presence is evident through divine activity and the transformational power of those divine actions. Such manifestations of the divine presence and power in our lives can be perceived (and

---

more often. Wesley claimed to be more scriptural in his language, implying that he (Wesley) referred more often to "God" and "grace." See John Wesley to John Newton, April 1, 1766, *LJWT*, 5:7–8.

26. John Wesley, "The Witness of Our Own Spirit," at §15, *Sermons I 1–33, BEW*, 1:309. See also his references "the grace or power of the Holy Ghost," which seem to equate the two: "The Spirit of Bondage and of Adoption," III.1; "The Means of Grace," II.6, ibid., *BEW*, 1:260, 383.

27. See, for instance, John Norris, *A Treatise Concerning Christian Prudence; or, The Principles of Practical Wisdom, fitted to use of human life, and designed for the better regulation of it.* (London, 1710), 284.

28. The medieval question of how many angels can sit on the head of a pin is actually, in Thomist terms, a question of how many angels can act upon, or exert power upon, the head of a pin. And since they do not take up space, the answer can be, an infinite number.

received) as transforming actions in our relationship with God. In both these senses, passive and active, grace is a relational concept as exhibited in the divine/human interaction. Grace is grounded in the divine attitude that is then manifest in divine transformative actions, by which divine grace is both perceived and received by humans in terms of gifts (not substantive "things" but relational realities) that we do not deserve or earn.

I refer to grace in this active sense as the presence and power of God in our lives. Grace as an attribute of God (as is divine love, justice, mercy, etc.) is an important theological concept, and we can try to understand the internal stance of God on these matters by analogy from human experience. But we can perceive the presence of God through our awareness of the divine exercise of energy and power, such that God's grace (as exhibited in these transformative actions) actually can be experienced in our lives. Whether or not God's grace is in fact transformative depends in part upon our response to God's presence and activity in our lives.

When we use the concept of grace in our discussions of soteriology, we often use the theological terms "prevenient grace," "justifying grace," and "sanctifying grace," as though they denoted three different realities in the process. What we are really talking about is three ways that God's singular *attitude* of grace is *active* in our lives through a variety of manifestations of the divine presence and power in the drama of salvation. The three manifestations of active divine grace are, in fact, important (if not to say crucial) in the process of salvation. (1) God enlightens us as to the nature of good and evil (before we actually DO anything ourselves; therefore the term "prevenient" indicates that God's grace in action *comes before* any action or response of ours); (2) the term "justifying grace" indicates that God's grace in action *liberates* us or frees us of the guilt of our sin by forgiving us or pardoning us and dispensing with the punishment of sin; and (3) the term "sanctifying grace" simply indicates that God's grace in action *empowers* us by relieving us from the power of sin in our lives. In any of these descriptions, the phrase "God's presence and power" could be substituted for the phrase "God's grace in action." It is the energy of divine presence (power) that transforms us in every step of our spiritual pilgrimage.

But importantly, there are other ways (besides the three outlined above) that God's grace impacts us in the drama of salvation and in our spiritual pilgrimage. God's grace, through divine presence and power, (4) judges and condemns us, once we are enlightened and know the difference between good and evil. This type of divine action could be called "judging grace" or "convincing (convicting) grace" and leads to repentance, which is a necessary response before God can forgive or liberate us from the guilt of sin. So also, (5) God's presence is often felt in times of trial and anxiety as a comforting presence (energy or power), which might be called "comforting grace." Likewise, (6) God's presence and power can be felt at times when a person needs some support and direction in life, which could then be called "guiding grace." And the illustrations could go on and on (7, 8, 9, etc.). There are much more than "three types of grace," a concept which in itself is so limited as to be perverse and degrading to the limitlessness of not only God's attitude of grace but the multitude of ways that the active and transforming nature of the divine presence and power can become manifest and perceived in human experience during one's spiritual pilgrimage toward final salvation.

Theologically, this divine attitude and action are both understood and explained as basic aspects of God's "grace." God's grace thus has both an active and a passive sense: God's active presence and the divine attitude that gives rise to such action. Grace is the term that is used for both—the favorable divine inclination toward humankind and the transforming actions that result from God's actual presence in human life. At times, the term grace is also used to describe the effects of God's action in human life.[29]

Means of Grace—Opportunities to Experience God's Presence

The occasions through which persons are made aware of the gracious presence of God, perceive this divine presence or energy (and its results), and are helped to experience its transforming power[30] are called "means of grace." These means can be experienced as special rites within the church

---

29. "By grace we always understand, as the word of God teacheth, first, his favour and undeserved mercy towards us; secondly, the bestowing of his Holy Spirit which inwardly worketh; thirdly, the effects of that Spirit whatsoever, but especially saving virtues, such as are faith, charity, and hope; lastly, the free and full remission of all our sins." Richard Hooker, *Of the Laws of Ecclesiastical Polity*, 2 vols. (London: Dent, 1964), 2:504: Hooker uses grace in both of these senses. Aquinas ties the meanings more closely together when he speaks of grace as not only a divine disposition and power/action but also a quality that exists in the human soul (grace and "infused virtues" being different aspects of one identical essence); Thomas Aquinas, *Nature and Grace*, trans. and ed. by A. M. Fairweather (Philadelphia: Westminster, 1954), 161. Hooker felt that Thomas went too far in considering grace as an inherent quality or formal habit that causes humankind's virtuous actions to be meritorious, even though Thomas himself was trying to protect the doctrine of sanctification from the charge of Pelagianism. Hooker, *Ecclesiastical Polity*, 2:505.

30. "Transforming power" does not imply that grace is necessarily manifest in dramatic ways like a loud clap of thunder or the roar of an erupting volcano. Power can be manifest in the quietness of angelic singing, in the tenderness of a mother's lullaby, in a furtive but loving glance, or in the soft splendor of a sunset.

or family of God that are especially designed to bring people into the presence of God where they can sense this divine energy and power, or they can be experienced as traditional occasions or exceptional opportunities in the lives of persons or communities when God's transforming presence and power is encountered and actually felt.

The usual understanding of "means of grace" within Christian vocabulary is often limited by seeing it as a phrase that is synonymous with the traditional sacramental rites of the church such as the Lord's Supper and Baptism. Christian groups, however, vary among themselves as to what might be considered sacraments. The usual definition of a sacrament is that it is an outward and visible sign of an inward spiritual grace. Traditionally, the sacraments are understood to be traceable to the life and actions of Jesus and thus instituted by him. Such guidelines, however, do not result in a consensus on the matter, since Christian groups differ widely on what rites can be seen as sacred acts of divine institution.[31]

Wesley, along with some other Christian leaders in the history of Christian thought, tried to broaden the concept of *instituted means of grace* to include other practices that have been associated with the ministry of Christ. His list of five instituted means, as found first in the "Large" *Minutes* of 1763, consisted of prayer, searching the Scriptures, the Lord's Supper, fasting, and Christian conference.[32] These are for him the primary means or ways by which one might experience the transforming power of the divine presence.[33]

In addition to these prevalent and rather obvious means of grace, Wesley added two further categories: prudential and general. The concept of *prudential means of grace* he apparently adopted in 1731 from John Norris's book, *Christian Prudence*.[34] Prudential means of grace are intended to advance our heavenly affections or increase our progress in some particular virtue, so long as we do not press the matter too broadly or strictly.[35]

---

31. Roman Catholic practice includes seven sacraments as instituted by Christ, similar to Eastern Orthodoxies acceptance of the seven "principal mysteries," reduced during the sixteenth century by Luther to three (then two) sacraments or ordinances (a view held by most Protestant denominations). Some groups have added other rites (such as foot-washing or hearing of the Gospel) while others have totally eliminated any sacramental dimension.

32. "Large" *Minutes* (1763), [§§ 40.1–40.5], *Minutes, BEW*, 10:855–57.

33. The absence of Baptism from this list has frequently been noted but never adequately explained.

34. Norris, *Prudence*, 284–85. Wesley wrote to his mother on June 11, the day after he started reading Norris, "collected" (made a summary of) the book during that month, and read it with the Oxford Methodists at their gatherings in December 1731.

35. John Wesley to Susanna Wesley, June 11, 1731, *Letters I 1721-1739, BEW*, 25:283.

The prudential means that he listed are divided into four categories: for all Christians, for Methodists, for preachers, and for Assistants (lead preachers on a circuit). Within the four categories, these include (1) avoiding evil, doing good, (2) attending class and band meetings, (3) meeting with the society weekly, as well as with the leaders of the classes and bands, visiting the sick ("and the well") and instructing the parents; and (4) promoting the sale of books, keeping monthly watch-nights and love-feasts, and sending Wesley an account of preachers who have difficult "defects."[36]

There are, of course, a myriad of other opportunities that can be added to Wesley's list of prudential means of grace, seen as occasions for us to experience the transforming power of God's presence. These activities, if seen as opportunities as such, would include activities within the fellowship of believers such as singing in the choir, teaching church school, participating in social concerns, programs, and projects. They would also include activities that are more individual or "secular," such as registering voters, helping take meals to the elderly, doing homework, or driving carefully. The awareness of God's presence and power can be much more prevalent than we tend to be aware.

An example of what Wesley meant by these activities being a means of God's presence can be seen in letters that he wrote to Miss March in the mid-1770s, encouraging her to visit the sick. He knew that the sick were often poor, and such visits would not be pleasant. But he encouraged skittish followers such as Miss March to "creep in among these in spite of dirt and an hundred disgusting circumstances, and thus put off the gentlewoman." He admitted that he himself would rather spend time with "genteel and elegant people," but he could not do so and imitate the life of Christ.[37] He also pointed out that although in such visits there may be a "thousand circumstances [that will] shock the delicacy of our nature," she will receive a blessing that "will more than balance the cross."[38] The nature and source of that blessing is God's grace. Such visits are a means of grace—an activity through which God's active presence and power is known and felt, not only to the sick person but to the visitor as well. As Wesley told Miss March, "Go and see the poor and sick in their own poor little hovels . . . Jesus went before you, and will go with you."[39]

These "prudential" methods, like the "instituted," might or might not actually turn out to be channels of God's grace. Like baptism, the exercise

---

36. "Large" *Minutes* (1763), [§ 40.6], *Minutes*, BEW, 10:857.
37. John Wesley to Miss March, February 7, 1776, *LJWT*, 6:207.
38. John Wesley to Miss March, February 26, 1776, *LJWT*, 6:209.
39. John Wesley to Miss March, June 9, 1775, *LJWT*, 6:153.

of a rite might or might not result in the transforming work of the Spirit. According to Wesley, baptism by water and the Spirit in adults requires the presence of faith and the evidence of transformation—the practice itself does not automatically result in the hoped-for result.[40] A person might participate in these means and thus have the form of godliness, but without the power. The means of grace might indeed at times be practiced "without fruit," as Wesley says. They do not automatically result in one perceiving the presence of God.

But the list of *general means of grace*, which Wesley listed in more than one place, were *always* accompanied by the benefit of "fruit."[41] These practices include watching, denying ourselves, taking up our cross, and the exercise of the presence of God. This last practice is, for Wesley, the focus of his advice: one should constantly be aware of and make use of the transforming and enabling power provided by God's presence. This focus is the center of his synergistic message—working with God entails opening oneself to God's presence and power, and thus letting the divine energy work in and through oneself.

One of Wesley's most important suggestions, then, is found as the climax of his discussion of the means of grace: the exercise of the presence of God. One should consciously be aware of the nearness of God and be transformed by his power and energy as constantly as possible.

Summary and Conclusion

In Wesley's discussion of the means of grace in the "Large" *Minutes*, he highlighted three categories: instituted, prudential, and general. The first are those practices that were begun by Christ, including "Christian conference."

---

40. The necessity of faith in such circumstances is a common Protestant emphasis that eliminates the *ex operato* element from such situations. See Wesley's sermons, "The Means of Grace," "The New Birth," "The Marks of the New Birth," and many other places where he stresses that having had the rite of water baptism does not make one a Christian in the present. Even the "almost Christian," in his early parlance, participates in the means of grace in the church. See "The Almost Christian" Sermon 2 (1741), I.7, *Sermons I 1–33*, BEW, 1:134.

41. "Large" *Minutes* (1763), [§ 40.7], *Minutes*, BEW, 10:857–58. See also *Minutes* (1745), [50], ibid., 10:155, where he is talking about entire sanctification:
Q. 11. How should we wait for the fulfilling of this promise?
A. In universal obedience; in keeping all the commandments, in denying ourselves, and taking up our cross daily. These are the general means which God hath ordained for our receiving his sanctifying grace.
Cf. "Doctrinal Minutes" (1749), [50], in 10:791, where this section is included verbatim as Q. 9.

The second are those particular actions that often bear fruit—actions that assist "common Christians," Methodists, and preachers, from the "arts of holy living" to the mundane writing of reports. And the third are those habits and activities that always bear fruit. The third is his list of general means, which includes watching, denying ourselves, and the exercise of the presence of God. The latter he expounds more fully, again in question form, by asking, "Do you endeavour to set God always before you? To see his eye continually fixed upon you?"[42]

This endeavor can and should be the focus of "holy conferencing." The latter cannot be seen as a simple correlation with "Christian conference," the fifth of Wesley's instituted means of grace. But by understanding what is meant by grace, and from there developing a more adequate understanding of the means of grace, one discovers that holy conferencing can be understood either in terms of religious conversation or the meetings that Methodists call Conference. In the 1753 "Large" *Minutes*, before he added his discussion of the means of grace the following decade, Wesley outlined his approach to religious conversation (which he later calls Christian conference):

Q. How may we be more useful in conversation?

1. [A.] Fix the end of each conversation before you begin.
2. Watch and pray during the time.
3. Spend two or three minutes every hour in earnest prayer.
4. Strictly observe the morning and evening hour of retirement.

To these guidelines were added in 1763:

5. Rarely spend above an hour at a time in conversation with anyone.
6. Earnestly recommend the five o'clock hour to all.[43]

While this section deals specifically with conversation, the correlation that Wesley understands between religious conversation and the Annual Conference in his day can be seen in his own use of this type of material in the *Minutes*. In 1747, he had spelled out some guidelines to be used as a

---

42. "Large"*Minutes* (1763), Q. [40.7].4, in *Minutes, BEW*, 10:857–58; cf. *Doctrinal Minutes* (1749), [§ 50], ibid., 10:791.

43. That is, the 5:00 a.m. preaching service, which Wesley felt was a central feature of the movement. For this section, see "Large" *Minutes* (1753), [§ 39], in *Minutes, BEW*, 10:854–55. Cf. his later elucidation of Christian conference in the 1763 "Large"*Minutes* (at n2 above).

proper approach to the meeting of Conference, places toward the front of the Minutes.

> Q. How may the time of this Conference be made more eminently a time of prayer, watching, and self-denial?
>
> 1. [A.] While we are in Conference, let us have an especial care to set God always before us.
> 2. In the intermediate hours let us visit none but the sick, and spend all our time that remain in retirement.
> 3. Let us then give ourselves to prayer for one another, and for a blessing of God upon this our labour.[44]

That entry was then republished six years later in the "Large" *Minutes*, with only a few word changes, as dealing with "conversation."[45]

So whether "holy conferencing" entails religious conversation (as an instituted means of grace), or a session of Conference (as a prudential means of grace), or an opportunity to exercise the presence of God in such individual or communal meetings (as a general means of grace), people who use these activities to open themselves to the power of God in their lives, striving to sense the divine energy transforming them in holiness of heart and mind, are understanding the concept of holy conferencing as a means of grace and are well within the bounds of the Wesleyan heritage.

Methodism itself can thus be seen as a means of grace in the eighteenth century as well as today.[46] The fellowship of believers itself can provide the opportunities for people to experience the presence and power of God in their lives. The church can be catalyst for change by providing occasions for people to exercise the presence and transforming power of God. The multitude of activities that take place under the aegis of the church provide many channels through which members and visitors alike can exercise the presence of God. Even the various levels of conference meetings, from the local Charge Conference to the international General Conference, can become occasions during which participants feel the power and presence of God, and as such are means of grace.

---

44. "The London Conference of June 15–18, 1747," [§ 3], in Minutes, *BEW*, 10:189.

45. "Large" *Minutes* (1753), [§ 1], in Minutes, *BEW*, 10:845. The only major change from the 1747 version, besides the shift from "Conference" to "conversation," is to replace the three-fold goal of "prayer, watching, and self-denial" with simply "watching unto prayer."

46. See Heitzenrater, "Wesleyan Ecclesiology: Methodism as a Means of Grace," in S T Kimbrough Jr., ed., *Orthodox and Wesleyan Ecclesiology* (Crestwood, NY: St. Vladimir's Seminary Press, 2007), 119–28.

Wesley's writings are full of references to "the presence and power of God," his *Journal* frequently recorded that "the power of God was present with us," and his conclusions often state, "God was with us of a truth." He was speaking of the reality of God's grace, the active presence and power of God manifest in human lives. A complex theological idea resolves into a simple rhetorical phrase that evinces a powerful divine reality, recognized by Wesley on his deathbed when he said, "The best of all is, God is with us."

4

Perfecting Plain Truth for Plain People

John Wesley's Sermons

Patrick Streiff

John Wesley's Sermon Corpus

THE CORPUS OF JOHN Wesley's sermons is accessible and well edited since its publication in *The Bicentennial Edition of the Works of John Wesley* in 1984–1987.[1] Albert C. Outler as editor of the sermons added an excellent introduction in general in addition to comments to each individual sermon. The numbering of sermons originated in Wesley's own editing with a mix of topical and chronological order. In total, there are 150 sermons written by John Wesley that are known today.[2] Best known among them are certainly the "*Standard Sermons.*"

In his *Model Deed* (1763), John Wesley made reference to the four volumes of sermons published by him in 1762. These sermons, commonly known as *Standard Sermons*, became the doctrinal reference point for preaching in the meetinghouses of Wesley's *United Societies*. In the British as well as in the American branch of Wesleyan Methodism, the doctrinal standards made reference to the *Standard Sermons*. But the content of these

---

1. *BEW*, 1–4, ed. Albert C. Outler, 1984–1987. Reference to *The Bicentennial Edition* will be given as *BEW* followed by number of the volume, page, and lines. Sermon number will be given in parenthesis.

2. *BEW* 1–4 contains 151 sermons, but sermon three was written by Charles Wesley. It remained in the sermon corpus because it is part of the *Standard Sermons*.

Standard Sermons differed. The British tradition counted forty-four sermons and the American tradition fifty-three. The British tradition relied on Wesley's publication of his sermons in 1762 (*Sermons On Several Occasions,* volumes 1-4) and the American depended on Wesley's publication of his works in 1771 (*The Works of the Rev. John Wesley*). In this chapter, I will concentrate on the development of John Wesley's theology, but without limiting it to the *Standard Sermons*, as it has been done much too often.

"The Path to Perfection: Doctrine, Devotion and Social Concern in Early Methodism" was the well chosen subtitle of one chapter of Henry D. Rack's magnificent biography of John Wesley, aptly titled *Reasonable Enthusiast: John Wesley and the Rise of Methodism*.[3] When Rack published it in 1989, he did not make reference to the sermon volumes in the *Bicentennial Edition*, published shortly before, but he was well aware of a development in Wesley's theology within an overarching theme:

> There are several difficulties in the way of getting a clear picture of Wesley's theology. One is his eclecticism: since he borrowed from a wide range of Christian traditions and then interpreted them through his own selective imagination, it is all too easy for interpreters to seize on one element alone to the exclusion of the others. Furthermore, despite Wesley's repeated claims that he had not changed his views on various doctrines, there is no doubt that he did modify his teaching in significant ways throughout his life, despite some important continuities. Finally, there is a descriptive problem. Wesley composed no systematic theology; . . . Wesley may be said to have focused on the way of sanctification . . . What did matter was doctrine concerned with personal salvation as the achievement of holiness to the point of perfection.[4]

Despite these two important publications in the 1980s, the *Bicentennial Edition* and Henry Rack's *Reasonable Enthusiast*, which grew out of a broad appreciation of John Wesley's theological sources, the analysis of Wesley's theological development has received limited attention. In the following pages I will highlight some of the theological aspects that are linked to the late sermons. Furthermore, an exploration will be offered in particular reference to the ways in which John William Fletcher (1729–1785) has influenced the sermons in the last phase of John Wesley's ministry.

---

3. Henry D. Rack, *Reasonable Enthusiast: John Wesley and the Rise of Methodism.* (London: Epworth, 1989).

4. Ibid., 381–82.

Looking at the published sermons in a chronological sequence, there are some interesting observations for consideration. From the 150 sermons written by John Wesley and published in the *Bicentennial Edition*, nineteen were written prior to the Aldersgate experience of 1738.[5] One of them, the sermon "The Circumcision of the Heart," published in 1733, even found its place among the *Standard Sermons*. A point of historical relevance is the following: Up to 1762, forty-seven other sermons were published and forty-three of them became part of the *Standard Sermons*, thus bringing the number of sermons with particular doctrinal importance to forty-four.[6] From 1762 to 1770 an additional eight were published. They were all included in the edition of the *Works* in 1771 and the number of *Standard Sermons* in the American tradition was then brought to fifty-three.[7] None of the sermons published after 1770 was ever considered as part of the *Standard Sermons*, even if some of them were among the best summaries of John Wesley's theology. Eight sermons were written by Wesley between 1773 and 1778, sixty-two(!) between 1780 and 1789, and seven from 1790 until his death in 1791. Another point of consideration is that the high number of newly written sermons in the last years of his life were readily published due to the regular publication of the *Arminian Magazine* which began in 1778. After 1781, the monthly issues included half of a sermon written by Wesley. Not all of these late sermons are of equal value. Some new topics appear among them; like family life, church history and the development of Methodism, and the cosmic dimension of creation. Interestingly enough, at the end of Wesley's life there were preoccupations which became particularly burdensome for the organizer of the Methodist movement, like the danger of riches among Methodist votaries. And some of these late sermons summarized in condensed form the wisdom of a matured leader of an important religious movement. In his introduction to the *Bicentennial Edition*, Albert C. Outler added a personal note: "the later Wesley who emerges here is the neglected Wesley and that there is a sorely needed redress of this imbalance if the agenda of Wesley studies is ever to regain its due proportion."[8]

---

5. The nineteen sermons with the following numbers 17, 109 and 133–49.

6. Including sermon three, written by Charles Wesley in 1742, and without going into more details about the varying content of sermons in the different editions of volume four of *Sermons on Several Occasions* and its difference to the four volumes in the edition of the *Works* in 1771.

7. Including sermon fifteen (1758) which was not part of the first four volumes of the *Sermons on Several Occasions*.

8. *BEW*, 1:54–55; See also *BEW*, 1:65–66 on "early," "mature" and "late" Wesley.

The Standard Sermons and Their Limitations

Presentations of Wesley's theology heavily relied on the *Standard Sermons*. Outside the English-speaking world, the forty-four or fifty-three *Standard Sermons* are often the only one available in other languages than English. But in the development of Wesley's theology, the sermons of the 1760s already marked a shift, which readers will not find among the edition of the forty-four *Standard Sermons*.[9] The edition of the fifty-three *Standard Sermons* contained the sermons of the 1760s, but no sermon after 1770 was included.[10]

Some recent publications by scholars allude to different stages in the development of his thought. Beginning in the mid 1990s Richard Heitzenrater, in his influential *Wesley and the People Called Methodists* (1995), calls the sermons of the 1760s a maturation of his theology, particularly the sermon "The Scripture Way of Salvation" which was initially published in 1765.[11] What is more, Heitzenrater asserts that the 1760s was a period that can best be understood as a revisionist approach.[12] He mentions a few sermons of the 1780s but only as a theological extension of concerns John Wesley was addressing in the 1760s.[13] Randy Maddox, in his *Responsible Grace: John Wesley's Practical Theology* (1994), introduced a viable grid for current scholarship by making a distinction between the "early Wesley" (1733–1738), the "middle Wesley" (1738–1765) and the "late Wesley" (1765–1791).[14] Among the studies on Methodist theology which have included the sermons of the late Wesley in a prominent way and have contributed to shape a (sometimes diverse) understanding of the mature version of Wesley's theology are to be named beside Maddox: Theodore Runyon[15] and

---

9. The forty-four *Standard Sermons* are not identical with the sermons 1–44, but contain the sermons 1–10, 12, 16–19, 21–42, and 44–50.

10. The fifty-three *Standard Sermons* are the sermons 1–53.

11. "One of the hallmark sermons in the Wesleyan repertoire was published in 1765. 'The Scripture Way of Salvation' signals the maturation of his theology, hammered out during the years of contention and controversy. It stands as perhaps the single best homiletical summary of his soteriology, or doctrine of salvation." Richard P. Heitzenrater, *Wesley and the People Called Methodists* (Nashville: Abingdon, 1995), 220.

12. "The revisionist approach of Wesley's sermons in the 1760s belies his frequent claim that he had been totally consistent in his teachings over the years." Ibid., 229. See also ibid., 261–62.

13. Ibid., 302–03 and 306–07.

14. Randy L. Maddox, *Responsible Grace: John Wesley's Practical Theology.* (Nashville: Kingswood, 1995), 20.

15. Theodore Runyon, *The New Creation: John Wesley's Theology Today* (Nashville: Abingdon, 1998).

Kenneth J. Collins with two major contributions in an interval of ten years:[16] and among non-Methodists, the catholic theologian Thomas Rigl in his dissertation in German language.[17] Additionally, my forthcoming publication in French will present in more depth the unfolding of Wesley's theology based on the sermon corpus.[18] In short, a summary in the development up to 1770 might be framed as follows: the sermons between 1725 and 1738 present the early phase of Wesley's ministry prior to his evangelical conversion. Holiness of heart and life became the aim of his personal life struggle as well as his preaching. The double commandment of love to God and neighbor was at the center of his quest for the "circumcision of the heart" and the renewal of the "image of God." And this aim of his life journey remained the same after 1738 and even into old age.

What changed theologically in 1738 was the means towards attaining the aim. Wesley announced it in a programmatic way in his sermon "Salvation by Faith." From then onwards, justification by faith became the scriptural means for a saving faith and for promoting sanctification. The first three volumes of sermons published by Wesley between 1746 and 1750 fostered this new foundation of salvation. Based on the Sermon on the Mount in the Gospel of Matthew, these volumes included the only sequence of sermons on a continuous biblical text. It was Wesley's exemplification of the "Law established by Faith."

With the fourth volume of sermons in 1760, and more so even with the additional sermons of the 1760s, Wesley's attention shifted from the scriptural foundation of the beginning of salvation (with topics such as repentance, new birth, testimony of the Spirit, the law established by faith, etc.) to the continuing faith journey of the believers with its ups and downs, linked to revivals of perfection as well as to backsliding of believers. "The Scripture Way of Salvation" was an important example of theological method in sermonic form. It not only unfolded in a more prominent way the grace of God as "preventing" (prevenient), "justifying" and "sanctifying," but it also took serious the presence of sin in the lives of believers and pressed them for "that faith whereby we are sanctified, saved from sin and perfected in love."[19] The notion of preventing, justifying, and sanctifying grace had already been

---

16. Kenneth J. Collins, *The Scripture Way of Salvation: The Heart of John Wesley's Theology* (Nashville: Abingdon, 1997) and *The Theology of John Wesley: Holy Love and the Shape of Grace* (Nashville: Abingdon, 2007).

17. Thomas Rigl, *Die Gnade wirken lassen: Methodistische Soteriologie im ökumenischen Dialog* (Paderborn: Bonifatius, 2001).

18. Patrick Ph. Streiff, *John Wesley et ses sermons: Un guide de lecture hisorico-théologique* (Charols: Excelsis, 2015).

19. John Wesley, *Sermons II 34–70*, BEW, 2:167.24–25 (Sermon 43).

present in both earlier periods, before 1738 as well as in sermons of the first years of the Methodist revival.[20] The new attention in the 1760s was more turned towards repentance and faith after justification as part of the journey of sanctification.[21] The sermons "The Scripture Way of Salvation" as well as "The Repentance of Believers" clearly announced the promise of a second instantaneous work of grace whereby believers are delivered from sin and perfected in love.[22] Wesley longed for such a revival of perfect love, despite all the disappointments in reality.[23] As will be demonstrated, the developments of the 1770s again shaped the sermons of Wesley towards a maturation of his theology.

"One Equal to Him I Have Not Known"

"Many exemplary men have I known, holy in heart and life, within fourscore years. But one equal to him I have not known—one so inwardly and outwardly devoted to God. So unblameable a character in every respect I have not found either in Europe or America. Nor do I expect to find another such on this side of eternity,"[24] wrote John Wesley in his sermon on the death of John William Fletcher. Fletcher became known as the theologian and saint of Methodism.[25] As early as 1761, and again in 1773, Wesley had called Fletcher out of his parish in Madeley to become the leader of Methodism, but Fletcher resisted all such calls. Fletcher certainly had close friends on all sides of the wide-spread Methodist movement in the Church of England. But when Wesley was accused of dreadful heresy by Calvinistic

---

20. "He [the Spirit of Christ] alone can quicken those who are dead unto God, can breathe into them the breath of Christian life, and so prevent, accompany, and follow them with his grace as to bring their good desires to good effect." John Wesley, *Sermons I 1–33*, *BEW*, 1:411.8–12 (Sermon 17, 1733) and "By 'means of grace' I understand outward signs, words, or actions ordained of God, and appointed for this end—to be the ordinary channels whereby he might convey to men preventing, justifying, or sanctifying grace." John Wesley, *Sermons I 1–33*, *BEW*, 1:381.3–6 (Sermon 16, 1746).

21. It is a typical example of what Collins calls the conjunctive flavor of Wesley's theology. Collins states as the preferred axial theme or orienting concern the conjunction of both, holiness and grace. See Collins, *Theology of John Wesley*, 6.

22. See John Wesley's sermons 43, parts III.11–18 in *Sermons II 34–70*, *BEW*, 2:166–69, and sermon 14, parts I.20–II.6 in *Sermons I 1–33*, *BEW*, 1:346–50.

23. John Wesley, *Sermons III 71–114*, *BEW*, 3:211–26 (Sermon 86).

24. John Wesley, *Sermons III 71–114*, *BEW*, 3:628.16–21 (Sermon 114).

25. See on Fletcher: Patrick Streiff, *Reluctant Saint? A Theological Biography of Fletcher of Madeley* (Peterborough: Epworth, 2001) and Peter S. Forsaith, *"Unexampled Labours": Letters of the Revd. John Fletcher to leaders in the Evangelical Revival*. (Peterborough: Epworth, 2008).

minded Methodists, Fletcher took up the pen in his defense and, unawares, came into the swirl of a theological controversy over predestination, antinomianism, and Christian perfection. His writings became known as *Checks to Antinomianism*.

In what became Fletcher's *First Check to Antinomianism* (1771), Wesley's thoughts were summed up in such a convincing way that Wesley rushed the manuscript through the press. Wesley had found an able defender who had a profound knowledge and apprehension of his theology combined with a mastery of biblical knowledge. Fletcher rarely quoted from Wesley's sermons or other writings. He could have done so for instance in his *First Check to Antinomianism* in quoting from the sermon, "The Lord Our Righteousness," which in many ways prefigured the controversy of the 1770s. Based on his own reading and studying of the Bible, Fletcher became creative in digging into the controversial debates where Wesley was reluctant and afraid of beginning to "split the hair."

Fletcher who already had tried to build bridges among his close friends in both branches of Methodism in the 1760s listened to arguments of the Calvinistic minded Methodists in the controversy of the 1770s. He developed in detail new approaches to old questions and applied them to the daily life of believers. Space does not allow, however, the place to present the development of this important and volatile controversy,[26] but Fletcher became aware that differing concerns shaped the theological arguments on both sides, for Calvinistic as for Arminian Methodists, and that both had grounding in the biblical message of God's grace and justice. Taken to extremes, each side had its flaws. Reconciliation was only possible in listening to the other side, learning from it, and avoiding extremism in reasoning on each side. Fletcher was convinced that "Bible Arminians" and "Bible Calvinists," as he called them, could perfectly live in harmony, even if they emphasized different parts of the biblical message. His approach to reconciliation probably had more consequences in the revivals in the United States in the 19th century than in Fletcher's own lifetime.[27]

In his theological struggle with a Calvinistic understanding of predestination, Fletcher came to agree that there is an "initial salvation" by an

26. See for more details, Streiff, *Reluctant Saint?*, 149–214.

27. See also Patrick Streiff, "Der ökumenische Geist im frühen Methodismus," in: Alfred Schindler, Rudolf Dellsperger, Martin Brecht, eds., *Hoffnung der Kirche und Erneuerung der Welt: Beiträge zu den ökumenischen, sozialen und politischen Wirkungen des Pietismus* (Göttingen: Vandenhoeck & Ruprecht, 1985), 59–77. At the time I wrote the article, I was not aware of the huge influence of Fletcher's writings in American Methodism and its revivals in the 19th century. With a different purpose in mind, Laurence W. Wood draws attention to it in his book *The Meaning of Pentecost in Early Methodism*. (Lanham: Scarecrow, 2002).

irresistible act of God's grace with all humanity after the initial fall in sin. Thus, no human being is in a "natural state," void of grace and only capable to sin. All have been restored to some freedom to respond to God's ongoing drawings of grace. All can respond to God's grace or refuse it. All are responsible for their way of response. Those who trust in God's grace will be renewed into the image which God initially intended. No one is outside of the realm of grace, but God is free in how much of his grace he bestows on each. Thus, human beings do not live under the horrible alternative that some are predestined and saved and all the others remain under God's wrath. But all live under different dispensations which are different levels how God dispenses his grace to humankind.

What Fletcher developed theologically in writing his *Checks*, was prefigured in earlier sermons and writings of Wesley too. In the sermons "Justification by Faith" and "The Righteousness of Faith," Wesley alluded to the covenant given by Christ, a covenant based on grace and made for the benefit of all humanity.[28] It contained in a nutshell what Fletcher developed theologically as "initial salvation." In the sermon on "Christian Perfection," Wesley referred to biblical passages which distinguished babes, young people, and adults; and then applied it to different stages of faith and Christian perfection. He talked about the Jewish dispensation, about John the Baptist, and the Christian dispensation that was fully manifested on the day of Pentecost.

During the controversy, John Wesley continued to travel the country, to preach, and to organize his evangelistic work. He took oversight for the publication of Fletcher's theological tracts and advertised them in the Methodist societies. He did not see the need to take the pen himself. During all the controversy, Wesley published only one sermon "On Predestination." It was preached in Ireland and written in a calm spirit with a concise style but without fresh thoughts. But Fletcher's approach to unfold the tokens of God's grace in human history would shape John Wesley's own theology in later years.

One of the first hints about Fletcher's influence on Wesley is not in one of Wesley's sermons, but in a re-edition of the *Journal*. Wesley's *Journal* was widely read and went through many editions. In the editions in 1774 (as part of an edition of the *Works*) and 1775 (*Journal* only), Wesley added corrections. He did not change the main text of what he had written, but added rectifying notes to the interpretation of his spiritual condition. These notes were all related to journal entries in the period of his encounter with

---

28. See John Wesley, Sermon 5, parts I.6–9 in *Sermons I 1–33*, *BEW*, 1:185–87 and Sermon 6, Introduction 1–4. Ibid., 1:202–04. See also John Wesley, parts I.4–5 in *Sermons II 34–70*, *BEW*, 2:7–8.

the Moravians and the interpretation of his spiritual condition prior to the Aldersgate experience. In several instances in his *Journal* he had written that he was without faith. In the 1770s, he added the note "I had even then the faith of a servant though not that of a son."[29] The distinction between the faith of a servant and the faith of a son allowed Wesley to overcome the strict alternative of the early years of the revival (no faith at all versus true, Christian faith; the almost Christian versus the altogether Christian) and to move towards a progression of different levels of faith.

Another key topic in the controversy was the role of human accomplishments for salvation. The accusation of "dreadful heresy" against John Wesley arose out of a one-sided summary of doctrine in the minutes of the conference of 1770. The minutes could be interpreted as justification by works if not set into the context of Wesley's other writings. Fletcher, in his *Checks*, provided this context and clarified the origin of human free will and the relationship between God's grace and human activity. The invitation which John Wesley received in 1777 to preach before the Humane Society[30] was an excellent occasion to take up the topic. Wesley preached on "The Reward of Righteousness." In the first part of his sermon, he reflected on good works, drew an overview of the Methodist revival, and the danger of making void the law through faith. Based on the Scripture text of Matt 25:34, Wesley proclaimed:

> And upon his [the Judge of all the earth] authority we must continue to declare that whenever you do good to any for his sake—when you feed the hungry, give drink to the thirsty; when you assist the stranger, or clothe the naked; when you visit them that are sick, or in prison—these are not "splendid sins," as one marvelously calls them, but "sacrifices wherewith God is well pleased."[31] And he went on: "[. . .] good works are so far from being hindrances of our salvation, they are so far from being insignificant, from being of no account in Christianity, that, supposing them to spring from a right principle, they are the perfection of religion. They are the highest part of that spiritual building whereof Jesus Christ is the foundation. To those who attentively consider the thirteenth chapter of the first Epistle to

29. John Wesley, *Journals and Diaries I (1735-1738)*, BEW, 18:215 (Feb. 1, 1738); see also ibid., 235 (April 25, 1738); 242 (in a letter written immediately prior to the Aldersgate experience); 245 and 248 (in a memorandum about his spiritual journey, written after the Aldersgate experience).

30. The Humane Society was established "for the sake of those who seem to be drowned, strangled, or killed by any sudden stroke." See "Introductory Comment," *Sermons III 71114*, BEW, 3:399.

31. John Wesley, *Sermons III 71-114*, BEW, 3:403.29-404.3 (Sermon 99).

the Corinthians it will be undeniably plain that what St. Paul there describes as the highest of all Christian graces is properly and directly the love of our neighbour.[32]

The minutes of the conference in 1770 and the theological controversy which followed debated on key issues in Wesley's theology. Through it all, Fletcher helped to clarify how the manifestation of God's grace in Christ shaped the whole process of salvation. From the seminal theological constructions of Fletcher, Wesley harvested the fruits in his sermons of the 1780s. In two of them, he explicitly mentioned Fletcher's life and contribution, but only after Fletcher's death in 1785.

Fletcher's Influence on Wesley's Late Sermons

John Wesley rarely wrote memorial sermons on the death of a companion. In the entire sermon corpus, there are only two sermons, one on the death of George Whitefield (1770) and one for John Fletcher (1785). There is no memorial sermon on the death of Charles Wesley who died in 1788 and there might be many reasons for it.[33] However, one late sermon is atypical in the number of quotes from Charles's hymns, several of which were from a collection of funeral hymns. The sermon, "Human Life a Dream," might well have been a silent tribute to the life journey that Charles had concluded and John was about to follow.[34]

In 1770, George Whitefield died in the American colonies at age fifty-six. He had expressed his deep desire that his elderly friend and early mentor of student years, John Wesley, would preach the official memorial sermon in England. It was a strong tribute to his friendship with John and Charles, despite the separation which had occurred between the two and developed into Calvinistic and Arminian followers within the Methodist fold. Three months before the funeral eulogy, John Wesley had met with his preachers for the conference in which they had specifically discussed whether they had leaned too much toward Calvinism. When the minutes became known to the Calvinistic minded Methodists, they cried out against what they considered as dreadful heresy. But this outbreak of controversy only happened early in 1771. The memorial service for Whitefield was held

32. Ibid., 3:405.5–14.

33. We may think of several: John Wesley's own old age; how strongly Charles's death moved John emotionally; how distance and disagreements had grown between the two brothers in older age despite their close alliance to each other for many decades of shared ministry.

34. John Wesley, *Sermons IV 115–151*, BEW, 4:109–19 (Sermon 124).

earlier, in mid-November, 1770, when the content of the conference minutes had not yet spread. Nevertheless, the atmosphere was heavy and throughout the year conflicts among followers of the two branches had heightened the tension.

When Wesley preached the memorial sermon[35] he spoke about Whitefield's life and then presented Whitefield's preaching in the following way:

> And, first, let us keep close to the grand scriptural doctrines which he everywhere delivered. There are many doctrines of a less essential nature, with regard to which even the sincere children of God (such is the present weakness of human understanding!) are and have been divided for many ages. In these we may think and let think; we may "agree to disagree." But meantime let us hold fast the essentials of "the faith which was once delivered to the saints," and which this champion of God so strongly insisted on at all times and in all places. His fundamental point was: give God all the glory of whatever is good in man. And in the business of salvation, set Christ as high and man as low as possible. With this point he and his friends at Oxford, the original Methodists (so called), set out.[36]

With his reference to "give God all the glory," Wesley began his exposition with a key term of Calvinistic theology, but then he did not move on to mention predestination with even one single word. As far as fundamental doctrines are concerned, he referred only to the new birth and justification by faith. In the last part of the memorial homily, Wesley spoke about Whitefield's character and spirit: "Is there any other fruit of the grace of God with which he was eminently endowed, and the want of which among the children of God he frequently and passionately lamented? There is one, that is, catholic love: that sincere and tender affection which is due to all those who, we have reason to believe, are children of God by faith."[37] And Wesley's eulogy ended with a prayer that love may prevail among God's children. His plea, however, was not heard. A few weeks later, the schismatic spirit between the two branches of Methodism broke out more violently than ever before. And, what must have grieved Wesley, John Fletcher found himself in the midst of it.

The only other memorial sermon by Wesley was written fifteen years later, on the death of John Fletcher. There was no similar reason due to a particular desire by the deceased as in the case of Whitefield. Fletcher had

---

35. John Wesley, *Sermons II 34–70*, *BEW*, 2:330–47 (Sermon 53).
36. Ibid., 2:341.11–23 (sermon 53).
37. Ibid., 2:344.7–12 (sermon 53).

died after having caught a fever from pastoral visits to some sick individuals. He had been seriously ill, most probably of tuberculosis, towards the end of the controversy and spent a time of convalescence in natal Switzerland. On returning to England, he finally married Mary Bosanquet, one of the early shining lights inspirational herself as one of the women preachers in Methodism. His late marriage gave fresh hope for a more stable health and a longer, ongoing ministry. John Wesley, for his part, continued to invite Fletcher and his wife to travel the country, preach to Methodist Societies, and attend Wesley's conference with the preachers. Charles Wesley also reiterated his hope that a close friendship with Fletcher would be preserved "(after mine and my B[rother]'s departure) to gather up the Wreck."[38] Fletcher, even more so after his intervention at the conference in 1784, was seen as the future leader of the Methodist movement after the death of John and Charles Wesley. But unexpectedly, he died before them in 1785, at age fifty-six.[39]

Wesley wrote in the introduction to his published eulogy that he "hastily put together some memorials of this great man."[40] The text of the sermon gave a short sketch of Fletcher's life and ministry, and of course, mention was made of Fletcher's contribution in the Arminian/Calvinistic controversies of the 1770s. In looking back, Wesley was grateful that his being accused of heresy had led Fletcher to write the *Checks*: "That circular letter was the happy occasion of his writing those excellent Checks to Antinomianism, in which one knows not which to admire most, the purity of the language (such as a foreigner scarce ever wrote before), the strength and clearness of the argument, or the mildness and sweetness of the spirit which breathes throughout the whole."[41]

Wesley did not hide his bewilderment about the reasons why Fletcher remained vicar of Madeley and did not begin to travel and preach throughout the country:

> And I am firmly convinced that had he used this health in travelling all over the kingdom five or six or seven months every year (for which never was man more eminently qualified; no, not Mr. Whitefield himself) he would have done more good than any other man in England. I cannot doubt but this would have been the more excellent way. However, though he did not accept of

---

38. Charles Wesley to John and Mary Fletcher, June 21, 1784, cited in Streiff, *Reluctant Saint*, 273.

39. The same age as George Whitefield. Both had many health issues during their ministry, not the least because of overload of work and inattention to a healthy care for bodily needs.

40. John Wesley, *Sermons III 71–114*, BEW, 3:611.7-8 (sermon 114).

41. Ibid., 3:617.17-22 (sermon 114).

this honour, he did abundance of good in that narrower sphere of action which he chose, and was a pattern well worthy the imitation of all the parochial ministers in the kingdom.[42]

In many instances before, Wesley had praised the sanctified lives of Gregory Lopez and Monsieur de Renty. As he described Fletcher's character, though, Wesley believed that he surpassed their witness to spiritual maturity fundamentally because of his longstanding personal acquaintance with Fletcher. Wesley unabashedly concluded that he had never known a person equal to Fletcher.

Reading the memorial sermon and the short biography published a year later,[43] one can easily understand that Fletcher became known as the "Saint of Methodism." Both texts mention Fletcher's role in the theological controversies of the period, but both also insist on his saintly character. Neither of them is a presentation of his theological writings or contributions. However, Fletcher was more than simply an intelligent and brave scholar who ably defended his theological mentor. And Wesley was aware of it. In one of his late sermons, he paid tribute to his younger and highly esteemed companion. The homily published in 1788, "On Faith," became one of the best expositions of Wesley's mature theology.

Wesley opened the sermon with a definition of faith: "But what is faith? It is a divine 'evidence, and conviction of things not seen;' [. . .] Particularly, it is a divine evidence and conviction of God and of the things of God. This is the most comprehensive definition of faith that ever was or can be given, as including every species of faith, from the lowest to the highest."[44] In this introductory definition, Wesley did not speak of faith only related to a living, saving Christian faith as he had done in early sermons of the revival, but he wanted to include a variety of degrees of faith, from lower to higher. He continued that he did "not remember any eminent writer that has given a full and clear account of the several sorts of it."[45] But then he added in the second paragraph: "Something indeed of a similar kind has been written by that great and good man, Mr. Fletcher, in his treatise on the various dispensations of the grace of God."[46] He then paraphrased Fletcher's presentation of dispensations. He would never have done so if he had not

---

42. Ibid., 3:619.12–21 (sermon 114).

43. John Wesley, *A Short Account of the Life and Death of the Rev. John Fletcher* (London, 1786).

44. John Wesley, *Sermons III 71–114*, BEW, 3:492.1–2, 3–10 (sermon 106).

45. Ibid., 3:492.10–11 (sermon 106).

46. Ibid., 3:492.14–16 (sermon 106).

seen it as a valuable and important theological contribution. Wesley then wrote about Fletcher:

> Herein he [Fletcher] observes that there are four dispensations that are distinguished from each other by the degree of light which God vouchsafes to them that are under each. A small degree of light is given to those that are under the heathen dispensation. These generally believed "that there was a God, and that he was a rewarder of them that diligently sought him." But a far more considerable degree of light was vouchsafed to the Jewish nation; inasmuch as to them were entrusted the grand means of light, the oracles of God. Hence many of these had clear and exalted views of the nature and attributes of God; of their duty to God and man; yea, and of the great promise, made to our first parents and transmitted by them to their posterity, that "the seed of the woman should bruise the serpent's head." But above both the heathen and Jewish dispensation was that of John the Baptist. To him a still clearer light was given: and he was himself "a burning and a shining light." To him it was given to "behold the Lamb of God, that taketh away the sin of the world." Accordingly our Lord himself affirms that, "of all which had been born of women," there had not till that time arisen "a greater than John the Baptist!" But nevertheless, he informs us, "He that is least in the kingdom of God," the Christian dispensation, "is greater than he." By one that is under the Christian dispensation Mr. Fletcher means one that has received the Spirit of adoption, that has the Spirit of God witnessing "with his spirit that he is a child of God."[47]

Based on this paraphrase of Fletcher's writings, Wesley then extended his discussion to point out several sorts of faith and added steps to those outlined by Fletcher. Wesley began with reference to current philosophical thoughts and with what he considered the lowest sort of faith—that of a materialist, then went on to deists, before he came to heathens. "I cannot but prefer this," he wrote, "before the faith of the deists; because, though it embraces nearly the same objects, yet they are rather to be pitied than blamed for the narrowness of their faith. And their not believing the whole truth is not owing to want of sincerity, but merely to want of light."[48] Wesley counted the Muslims among the heathens, and then proceeded to the next level in talking about the Jews. He only briefly mentioned the faith of John the Baptist, a dispensation that had taken more space in Fletcher's

---

47. Ibid., 3:492.16–493.10 (sermon 106).
48. Ibid., 3:494.13–17 (sermon 106).

own writings. Wesley then proceeded on to different Christian beliefs. He began with Roman Catholics and included the following comment on their faith: "If most of these are volunteers in faith, believing more than God has revealed, it cannot be denied that they believe all which God has revealed as necessary to salvation. In this we rejoice on their behalf: we are glad that none of those new articles which were added at the Council of Trent to 'the faith once delivered to the saints,' does so materially contradict any of the ancient articles as to render them of no effect."[49] It echoed and reinforced what Wesley had written earlier in 1750 with his sermon "Catholic Spirit." From Roman Catholics, Wesley moved on to the Protestants and said: "The faith of the Protestants, in general, embraces only those truths as necessary to salvation which are clearly revealed in the oracles of God."[50]

After presenting these different levels of faith, Wesley insisted on an often repeated distinction in many of his published sermons: embracing biblical truth did not necessitate the salvation of the individual; "no more than it could save the devil and his angels—all of whom are convinced that every title of Holy Scripture is true."[51] Right belief is not saving faith! This insight brought Wesley more and more—the older he grew—to limiting the importance of correct belief. Since 1738, Wesley insisted that saving faith goes beyond the mere embracing of true doctrines. But the way he defined saving faith in this late sermon was very different from the early years of the revival: "It is such a divine conviction of God and of the things of God as even in its infant state enables everyone that possesses it to 'fear God and work righteousness.' And whosoever in every nation believes thus far the Apostle declares is 'accepted of him' [. . .] But he is at present only a servant of God, not properly a son. Meantime let it be well observed that 'the wrath of God' no longer 'abideth on him.'"[52] And in order to clarify how far his revision went, he added the following paragraph:

> Indeed nearly fifty years ago, when the preachers commonly called Methodists began to preach that grand scriptural doctrine, salvation by faith, they were not sufficiently apprised of the difference between a servant and a child of God. They did not clearly understand that even one "who feared God, and worketh righteousness, is accepted of him." In consequence of this they were apt to make sad the hearts of those whom God had not made sad. For they frequently asked those who feared God,

---

49. Ibid., 3:496.1–8 (sermon 106).
50. Ibid., 3:496.9–11 (sermon 106).
51. Ibid., 3:497.3–4 (sermon 106).
52. Ibid., 3:497.6–10, 11–13 (sermon 106).

"Do you know that your sins are forgiven?" And upon their answering, "No," immediately replied, "Then you are a child of the devil." No; that does not follow. It might have been said (and it is all that can be said with propriety) 'Hitherto you are only a *servant*; you are not a *child* of God. You have already great reason to praise God that he has called you to his honourable service. Fear not. Continue crying unto him: "and you shall see greater things than these." And, indeed, unless the servants of God halt by the way, they will receive the adoption of sons. They will receive the *faith* of the children of God by his *revealing* his only-begotten Son in their hearts.[53]

As Fletcher did in his writings on the various dispensations, so Wesley also put emphasis on growing beyond lower stages of faith without devaluating them in their own right. Heathens can be saved if they live according to the light which they have received.[54] And the more light someone receives, the deeper they will experience being renewed in God's image and praise God's grace. It is good to press for more light:

> But let us covet the best gifts, and follow the most excellent way. There is no reason why you should be satisfied with the faith of a materialist, a heathen, or a deist; nor indeed with that of a servant: I do not know that God requires it at your hands. Indeed if you have received this you ought not to cast it away; you ought not in any wise to undervalue it, but to be truly thankful for it. Yet, in the meantime, beware how you rest here: press on till you receive the Spirit of adoption. Rest not till that Spirit clearly witnesses with your spirit that you are a child of God.[55]

In the very last paragraph of his sermon, Wesley corrected implicitly such invitations to rest, when he addressed those who had attained a measure of perfect love: "Yea, and when ye have attained a measure of perfect love, when God has 'circumcised your hearts,' and enabled you to love him with all your heart and with all your soul, think not of resting there. That is impossible. You cannot stand still; you must either rise or fall—rise higher or fall lower."[56] Fletcher would have agreed with this last correction, talking of a measure (!) and not simply of the fullness of perfect love. It corresponded

---

53. Ibid., 3:497.14–33 (sermon 106).

54. See Sermon 91, parts I.3 and III.12–13 in *Sermons III 71–114*, BEW, 3: 295–96, 306–07; Sermon 130, part 14 in *Sermons IV 115–151*, BEW, 4:174–75 and implicitly also in Sermon 127, parts 16–19 in *Sermons IV 115–151*, BEW, 4: 146–48.

55. Wesley, *Sermons III 71–114*, BEW, 3:498.16–25 (sermon 106).

56. Ibid., 3:501.2–7 (sermon 106).

to Fletcher's own experience and how he reflected on it when he began to share his testimony. In 1781 Fletcher had written to John Wesley in a letter which is only preserved as a draft among Fletcher's papers. But the draft has all the more interesting deletions (here crossed out) and corrections (here underlined),

> if God ~~blesses~~ smiles upon our [John Fletcher's and Mary Bosanquet's] intimacy by giving us spiritual blessings together, as he did particularly last wednesday when at a Meeting in Miss B. [Bosanquet's] house, I ~~was enabled to see~~ saw my christian privileges so clearly and felt so much of the power of faith and love as to be ~~enabled~~ constrain'd to profess ~~my being entered into the glorious liberty~~ a degree of the glorious liberty of God's children.[57]

Both Fletcher and Wesley, towards the end of their respective lives, interpreted Christian perfection as an ongoing process of growth in love, always grounded and enabled in God's grace. It was different from the expectation of a final second stage, cleansing or blessing, after justification in order to attain Christian perfection, as expressed in earlier sermons, e.g., "The Scripture Way of Salvation." Wesley did not express it as a correction to his earlier views, as he did concerning justification and new birth. But it was in fact quite a congruent shift from an interpretation in opposing alternatives (on a first level: the almost Christian who is not at all a Christian versus the altogether Christian; on a second level: the believer who is still not cleansed from all sin versus the believer who is saved from all sin and perfected in love) to a gradual growth where the lower "levels" of faith and love are not depreciated and growth in faith and love never ends.

The theological struggle about the Holiness movement in Methodism in the 19th century would have greatly benefited from a more explicit reflection on this shift by Wesley himself.[58] Moreover, the staunch believers of that movement would have required a knowledge of John Wesley's late sermons beyond the fifty-three *Standard Sermons*. Of course, Wesley's as well as Fletcher's tracts on Christian perfection included in the end an element that Christian perfection was not a final stage of Christian experience,

---

57. Streiff, *Reluctant Saint?*, 289–90 and n6; for the whole letter, see Forsaith, *Unexampled Labours*, 347–49.

58. Phoebe Palmer's understanding of holiness built on Wesley's sermon: "The Scripture Way of Salvation" which was one among the fifty-three *Standard Sermons*, expecting holiness "*by faith,*" "*as you are,*" and "*now.*" The metaphor of the "altar" which became so prominent in her holiness theology, and the insistence on a "shorter way" radicalized her understanding of Christian perfection on the basis of Wesley's theology of the 1760s. See John Wesley, *Sermons II 34–70, BEW*, 2:155–69.

but allowed for further growth. Both, including Charles Wesley's hymns on perfection, at one point strongly insisted on a second, instantaneous experience which enabled the attainment to the highest level of love. Full salvation was fundamentally being delivered from sin and perfected in love. In the reading of their writings I have offered here, this insistence was strongly linked to a chain of arguments based on the notion of sin and what it meant to experience a compete deliverance from its power. Simply stated, being free from sin reflected a life struggle towards holiness of heart and life. With such reasoning in hand, both Wesley and Fletcher admonished that there was no growth where sin had not been cast out. Furthermore, at least for Fletcher, there was a danger in asserting that God's grace was at work only in the instantaneous bestowing of a (second) blessing. However, the dynamic is different where the chain of arguments is based on the positive content of being filled with love. Then, an ever growing understanding prevails and the divine-human relationship exceeds any alternative of gradual or instantaneous experiences.[59]

Other late sermons rather continued to maintain in similar ways the argument put forward in the 1760s. In his sermon "On Patience," Wesley tried to harvest the controversy on Christian perfection. At first, he seemed to leave open the way Christian perfection was attained, whether "gradual" or "instantaneous"—perhaps because of the difference with his brother Charles in older age:

> But it may be inquired, In what manner does God work this entire, this universal change in the soul of the believer? This strange work, which so many will not believe, though we declare it unto them? Does he work it gradually, by slow degrees? Or instantaneously, in a moment? How many are the disputes upon this head, even among the children of God! . . . And they will be the more resolute herein because the Scriptures are silent upon the subject; because the point is not determined—at least, not in express terms—in any part of the oracles of God . . . Permit me likewise to add one thing more. Be the change instantaneous or gradual, see that you never rest till it is wrought in your own soul, if you desire to dwell with God in glory.[60]

Then Wesley continued to unfold all the testimonies for Christian perfection among Methodists, including the perfectionist revivals of the 1760s. All

---

59. See, also for a contemporary reformulation of Christian perfection, Theodore Runyon, *The New Creation: John Wesley's Theology Today* (Nashville: Abingdon, 1998), 222–33.

60. John Wesley, *Sermons III 71–114*, BEW, 3:176.28–177.2,6–9,12–15 (sermon 83).

testified to an instantaneous deliverance from sin. Therefore, John Wesley concluded that it would commonly be an instantaneous work. And in the last paragraph, he called this work of grace a high degree of holiness: "As if he [the Apostle James] had said, 'ye shall enjoy as high a degree of holiness as is consistent with your present state of pilgrimage.'"[61] Such terminology favored the expectation of a second blessing in the later holiness movement. It again focused on deliverance from sin and therefore envisioned as "high a degree of holiness as is consistent with your present state of pilgrimage" as if it were a final degree of perfection. In "On Patience," a homily written in 1784 and some twenty years on the other side of the perfectionist controversies, Wesley did not reflect on the gradual progression beyond such a "high degree of holiness" as in other late sermons which shifted more towards the positive content of love, growing without end.

Four years later, in 1788, when Wesley came to publish his sermon "On Faith," he alluded to such revisions without critically reflecting on it, as we have seen. Concerning the divine-human relationship that is linked to this topic, Wesley harvested the fruits of the controversy on works as a condition for salvation. Thus another outstanding sermon was written in 1785, "On Working Out Our Own Salvation." In paraphrasing the biblical text of Phil 2:12–13, Wesley developed a sermon in three points: "In these comprehensive words we may observe, First, that grand truth, which ought never to be out of our remembrance, 'It is God that worketh in us, both to will and to do of his own good pleasure'; Secondly, the improvement we ought to make of it: 'Work out your own salvation with fear and trembling'; Thirdly, the connection between them: 'It is God that worketh in you': therefore 'work out your own salvation.'"[62] Wesley inverted the sequence of the biblical text in order to show the preeminence of what God does for and in us human beings. And he again opened the second part of the sermon by insisting on the workings of God's grace, preventing, convincing, justifying, and sanctifying. He expressed a more integrated notion of gradual and instantaneous work:

> All experience, as well as Scripture, shows this salvation to be both instantaneous and gradual. It begins the moment we are justified, in the holy, humble, gentle, patient love of God and man. It gradually increases from that moment, as a "grain of mustard seed, which at first is the least of all seeds, but" gradually "puts forth large branche," and becomes a great tree; till in another instant the heart is cleansed from all sin, and filled with pure love to God and man. But even that love increases more

---

61. Ibid., 3:179.23–24 (sermon 83).
62. John Wesley, *Sermons III 71–114*, BEW, 3:202.8–15 (sermon 85).

and more, till we "grow up in all things into him that is our head," 'till we attain the measure of the stature of the fullness of Christ."[63]

Wesley continued to use the interpretative categories of "gradual" and "instantaneous," but at the same time expressed how intrinsically God and human beings interact: "We know indeed that word of his to be absolutely true, 'Without me ye can do nothing.' But on the other hand we know, every believer can say, 'I can do all things through Christ that strengtheneth me.' Meantime let us remember that God has joined these together in the experience of every believer. And therefore we must take care not to imagine they are ever to be put asunder."[64] We do not know which parts of this late sermon go back to earlier sermons on the same Scripture text prior to 1738:[65] but interestingly, there is the exact same description of God's grace "preventing, accompanying, and following you" as in Wesley's sermon on "The Circumcision of the Heart."[66] In 1785, fifty years later, Wesley concluded his matured exposition of the divine-human synergy with some similar words in the following passage:

> Go on, in virtue of the grace of God, preventing, accompanying, and following you, in "the work of faith, in the patience of hope, and in the labour of love." "Be ye steadfast and immovable; always abounding in the work of the Lord." And "the God of peace, who brought again from the dead the great Shepherd of the sheep,"—Jesus—"make you perfect in every good work to do his will, working in you what is well-pleasing in his sight, through Jesus Christ, to whom be glory for ever and ever!"[67]

Perfecting Plain Truth in Old Age

John Wesley was an ingenious eclectic throughout his life which spanned the eighteenth century. He had been highly gifted in his approach to

---

63. Ibid., 3:204.11–21 (sermon 85).

64. Ibid., 3:208.1–7 (sermon 85).

65. The introductory comment by Albert C. Outler mentioned that Wesley had used the same scripture text Phil 2:12–13 in his preaching four times at Oxford (twice in 1732 and twice in 1734) and then only again in 1781 (*BEW* 3:199). The early preaching does not survive in any written form which would allow a comparison. But it is highly interesting that the matured theology of the late Wesley in many ways brought a more integrated concept of what was dear to Wesley before and after 1738.

66. See quotations in n20.

67. Wesley, *Sermons III 71–114*, *BEW*, 3:209.10–18 (sermon 85).

articulating essential qualities of the Christian life. His theology did not look like a house built with incompatible materials but one that was an integrated and well built edifice. Wesley could indeed take ideas from Christian traditions and theologians of opposite camps, and conjoined into a coherent understanding of the Gospel. His way of editing the most diverse tracts in the fifty volumes of the *Christian Library* (1749–1755) was just one example of this approach. If this essay highlights the influence which Wesley and Fletcher mutually enjoyed with one another, it does in no way exclude or underestimate the influence of external theological resources that figured into their articulation of Christian truth.[68] But for the maturation of Wesley's theology beyond the fifty-three *Standard Sermons* Fletcher was certainly the most influential partner.

When Wesley published his first volume of sermons in 1746, he wrote in his prefatory remarks: "I design plain truth for plain people."[69] And he explained it further: "I have accordingly set down in the following sermons what I find in the Bible concerning the way to heaven, with a view to distinguish this way of God from all those which are the inventions of men. I have endeavoured to describe the true, the scriptural, experimental religion, so as to omit nothing which is a real part thereof, and to add nothing thereto which is not."[70] Already in the Preface, he insisted on the preeminence of love with a rhetorical question: "For how far is love, even with many wrong opinions, to be preferred before truth itself without love?"[71] Thus, when Wesley designed plain truth, he was not interested in doctrinal truth, but in "the way to heaven," in a faith which works by love.

Up to the very last days of his life he continued in perfecting plain truth. A fuller picture of the late sermons would need to mention many other important topics than this brief examination has been able to do. In many ways, the late sermons bring to fruition a divine-human synergy built on the activity of the triune God. Perfecting plain truth, at least in Wesley's way of thinking, served to grow in "the mind of Christ" and follow the Lord's steps. In one of his last sermons, Wesley wrote in opposition to those who insisted on clear views on the capital Christian doctrines:

---

68. E.g., Sermon 77 in Sermons III 71–114, *BEW*, 3: 89–102 and Sermon 67 in *Sermons II 34–70*, *BEW*, 2: 535–50 which make reference to Thomas Crane, *Isagoge ad Dei Providentiam, Or a Prospect of divine Providence* (London, 1672). Wesley published an extract of it in his *Christian Library* which Fletcher also read.

69. John Wesley, *Sermons I 1–33*, *BEW*, 1:104.5 (Preface).

70. Ibid., 1:106.14–19 (Preface).

71. Ibid., 1:107.29–30 (Preface).

> I believe the merciful God regards the lives and tempers of men more than their ideas. I believe he respects the goodness of the heart rather than the clearness of the head; and that if the heart of a man be filled (by the grace of God, and the power of his Spirit) with the humble, gentle, patient love of God and man, God will not cast him into everlasting fire prepared for the devil and his angels because his ideas are not clear, or because his conceptions are confused. Without holiness, I own, no man shall see the Lord; but I dare not add, or clear ideas.[72]

Wesley's focus remained on the renewal of human beings into the image of God through a living and loving faith. In his late sermons, he overcame alternatives of the early revival and perfected "plain truth for plain people" in a more integrated exposition of God's relationship with men and women and with all of creation. God's grace based synergy with humanity enabled and called for being perfected in growing without end in the fruit of faith, particularly in love and praise.

---

72. John Wesley, *Sermons IV 115–51*, *BEW*, 4:175.14–22 (sermon 130).

5

Mission Spirituality in the Early Methodist Preachers

Philip R. Meadows

Introduction

David Lyle Jeffrey claimed that Christian spirituality in the eighteenth century can be divided into two basic kinds.[1] First, the "meditative tradition" has been expressed through poets, hymn writers, mystics, and prayerful intercessors. Second, the "missionary tradition" has been the territory of prophets, preachers, and reformers. The spiritual life and activity of John Wesley and early Methodism has typically been presented as an example of either the meditative or missionary kinds, but the deep logic between them has rarely been noticed and remains largely undeveloped. This chapter argues that early Methodism embodied a form of "mission spirituality," which combined the pursuit of personal holiness with a passion for evangelistic outreach. This reached full expression in the lives and autobiographies of the early Methodist preachers, who were patterns of spirituality for the movement as a whole.

Wesley gathered and published autobiographies of his preachers in the *Arminian Magazine* (1778–1811; latterly renamed the *Methodist Magazine*). Some of these were subsequently collected by Thomas Jackson in *The Lives of Early Methodist Preachers*, which went into a fourth edition (1871), in six

---

1. David Lyle Jeffrey, *English Spirituality in the Age of Wesley* (Vancouver: Regent College, 1987), 24–35.

volumes, and containing forty-one lives.² The present study examines this collection as a provisional "canon" for developing the concept of mission spirituality. There are significant limitations to this approach, such as the omission of female voices,³ and the loss of narratives that didn't make it into the canon. Nevertheless, I aim to make an imperfect beginning at a potentially significant area of research. In general, the importance of these sources has been overshadowed by scholarly interest in the leaders of the movement. Other studies have been focused on ecclesiological and social analyses of the emerging movement;⁴ theological and practical attempts to systematize the principles of early Methodist preaching;⁵ or historical and hagiographical accounts of the preachers as saints and heroes.⁶ The modest aspiration here is to glean insights into the missionary spirit of the Methodist movement, through the autobiographies of its pioneers, and as a contribution to contemporary thinking on the connections between spirituality, discipleship, and mission.⁷

Reading the Early Methodist Preachers

In *The Evangelical Conversion Narrative*, D. Bruce Hindmarsh has provided us with a landmark study of spiritual autobiography in early modern England, including that of the Methodist preachers.⁸ He reminds us that autobiography is both expressive and constructive. On the one hand, it represents an uncomplicated account of facts and experiences; and we can read trustingly. On the other hand, it is a carefully written genre, with specific theological purposes; and we must read critically. He argues that the autobiographies of these preachers have an apologetic function, to

2. *EMP*.

3. Paul Chilcote, *She Offered them Christ* (Eugene, OR: Wipf & Stock, 2001); Paul Chilcote, *Early Methodist Spirituality* (Nashville: Kingswood, 2007).

4. G. Holden Pike, *John Wesley and His Preachers: The Conquest of England* (London: Unwin, 1903); W. L. Dougherty, *John Wesley, His Conference and His Preachers* (London: Wesley Historical Society, 1944); Adrian Burdon, *Authority and Order: John Wesley and His Preachers* (Aldershot: Ashgate, 2005); John Lenton, *John Wesley's Preachers: A Social and Statistical Analysis* (London: Paternoster, 2008).

5. Henry Bett, *The Early Methodist Preachers* (London: Epworth, 1935).

6. Richard Heizenrater, "John Wesley's Principles and Practices of Preaching," in *Lectures on Several Occasions*, no. 1 (Dallas: Perkins School of Theology, 1997).

7. Susan Hope, *Mission-Shaped Spirituality* (London: Church House, 2004); Roger Heland and Leonard Hjalmarson, *Missional Spirituality: Embodying God's Love from the Inside Out* (Leicester: InterVarsity, 2011).

8. D. Bruce Hindmarsh, *The Evangelical Conversion Narrative: Spiritual Autobiography in Early Modern England* (Oxford: Oxford University Press, 2005).

defend an arminian approach to salvation and discipleship; and they have a mimetic function, as a means of defining a "guild" of leaders, whose lives are worthy of imitation by the movement as a whole. For Hindmarsh, the hermeneutical challenge is to "hover" over the sources, on the wings of trust and suspicion.[9]

Hindmarsh operates with what he calls "the evangelical pattern of climactic conversion," found within a long "tradition of crisis conversion" from the apostle Paul to John Wesley.[10] So, he claims "the most distinctive feature" of a preacher's autobiography is "the detailed rehearsal of the subject's conversion."[11] For the women preachers of early Methodism, no less than the men, "conversion was taken up as the theme of one's whole life."[12] This argument is pushed to the limit when he claims that "the whole of their lives have now become explicable in terms of conversion,"[13] as a series of spiritual crises that best describes everything from awakening to perfection and death. "Conversion became not a moment in one's life but the key to interpreting the meaning of one's life from beginning to end."[14] In his review of Hindmarsh's book, Henry Rack notes how "the Arminianism of Wesley's mechanism, unlike the Calvinism of his rivals, meant that conversion was liable to be lifelong," and that "the published *Lives* of early Methodist preachers, written late in life, show the full pattern."[15]

From the perspective of Wesleyan theology, however, this "conversionist" interpretation seems like an over-generalization. The dominant leitmotif in Wesleyan theology is not the navigation of spiritual crises, but the overarching story of God's gracious work in the human heart, and our on-going response of repentance and faith.[16] As we become co-workers with God in working out our own salvation, the story may take dramatic turns in moments of crisis, but it is the journey that defines the moment, not the other way around. When read this way, an autobiography is not just an elaborate account of evangelical conversion, with an agonistic prologue and an extended epilogue of preaching activities. Rather, I argue that these are narratives of a missionary's life, from beginning to end. Conversion does

---

9. Ibid., 12.
10. Ibid., 16.
11. Ibid., 227.
12. Ibid., 238.
13. Ibid., 242.
14. Ibid., 322.
15. Henry D. Rack, *JEH* 65 no. 3 (2006) 620.
16. Kenneth Collins, *The Theology of John Wesley* (Nashville: Abingdon, 2007); Randy Maddox, *Responsible Grace* (Nashville: Kingswood, 1994).

not define the missionary, but being a missionary does define the meaning and importance of conversion. Missionaries are those who have passed through evangelical conversion on the way of holiness, and who are thus empowered to invite others onto that journey.

Since Hindmarsh reduces every kind of spiritual attainment to a crisis moment, he has difficulty accounting for the deeper significance of the whole spiritual journey. So, for instance, the dramatic foretastes of assurance, gained and lost by the awakened seeker, are mistakenly interpreted as examples of justification before the new birth (which Wesley would never admit), or multiple unstable conversions and unresolved oscillations.[17] The deep and formative work of God in the heart and life of the seeker, in the long term making of a missionary, is eclipsed by his conversionist reading. The same kind of reduction can be seen in his approach to the pursuit of Christian perfection; and, indeed, of what it meant to die well.

The argument presented here, is that the dominant leitmotif of the autobiographies is "co-working with God," both in terms of one's own salvation and in the missionary vocation of saving souls. Indeed, this can be seen in James Morgan's own reflections about the importance of spiritual autobiography.[18] In the first place, they provide us with examples of the Christian life worthy of imitation. Unlike some traditions of autobiography, they are not presented as romantic ideals, which can be dismissed as unattainable in everyday life, but as realistic testimonies of how God transforms the lives of ordinary Christians and empowers them for service. Nor are we meant to be enthralled by the narrative of heroic activity as an end in itself, but as a means of grace that inspires the same life of devotion to God and neighbour that they had. They are properly spiritual autobiographies that provide an inner history of the Christian life, connecting the work of God in the heart with the life of discipleship and mission. Rack claims that early Methodist "autobiographies and biographies were to display God's merciful, providential dealings with his people and to act as inspirations and guides to others as well as to show the world what the Methodists were really like."[19]

Morgan laments that "we are too superficially acquainted with ourselves, to get deeply into fellowship with God." These narratives, therefore, provide an example of what it means to strive for an ever deepening and transforming relationship with God. In particular, they serve to reveal the "more internal state" of the preacher "with respect to his daily course of

---

17. Hindmarsh, *Conversion Narrative*, 159, 247, 252.

18. *EMP*, 3:2–10.

19. Henry D. Rack, *Reasonable Enthusiast: John Wesley and the Rise of Methodism* (London: Epworth, 1992), 421.

walking with God; his attainments in the Divine life; together with his last sickness and death." Morgan is convinced, however, that the reader can learn some general "maxims" from these patterns of holiness "which, when adopted into our own conduct, often serve in the room of many rules, and are singular incentives to our diligence and fervour."[20] The method I have adopted is to identify a few of these "maxims" as common patterns of wisdom that emerge from *The Lives of the Early Methodist Preachers*.

The Nature of Mission Spirituality

> *1. Do they know God as a pardoning God? Have they the love of God abiding in them? Do they desire and seek nothing but God? And are they holy in all manner of conversation? 2. Have they gifts (as well as grace) for the work? . . . 3. Have they fruit? Are any truly convinced of sin and converted to God by their preaching?*[21]

Wesley's three marks of a preacher provide a useful foundation for building a formal definition of mission spirituality. The spirit of a missionary has its source in the conscious experience of God's justifying and sanctifying grace, which flows out to others through the gifts of understanding and utterance, and springs up in the fruit of transformed lives. The preacher is not merely thought of as a convert but a seeker, pursuing holiness of heart and life, and inviting others to share this journey into God.

Piety and Proclamation

Although they often preached three or four times a day, the preachers had no shortage of material to draw upon, because their own spiritual discipline and real life experience provided an abundant source. Jackson noted that they followed in the example of Wesley, who learned how to abandon his manuscripts, and "preached out of the fullness of his heart, which was richly charged with gospel truth, and all on fire with holy zeal."[22] Preaching was never about expounding doctrine as a speculative exercise, but exemplifying the truths of scripture through personal testimony. The preachers offered a living exposition of scriptural promises, and an impassioned exhortation that others might prove them true in their own experience.

20. *EMP*, 3:9.
21. Ibid., 1:xiv. Cf. Thomas Jackson, ed. *Minutes of Several Occasions* (London, 1797), 10.
22. *EMP*, 1:xx.

Wesley expected his preachers to grow in both knowledge and vital piety. Alongside the practices of devotion, they were required to adopt the discipline of "spiritual reading" and personal study as a means of grace.[23] To that end, he edited and published the *Christian Library* as a means of feeding the understanding of the preacher, as well as the "whole spirit of Missionaries" itself.[24] So, James Morgan noted that the whole life of Thomas Walsh was "one series of holy living and mental improvement," which had the effect of preserving his heart "like an ever fresh and overflowing fountain, which on every occasion poured forth its fruitful streams of holy doctrine and persuasive exhortation." He continued, "It was easy enough to discern that he felt the things he delivered" and "was himself a pattern of the truths he taught."[25]

Holiness and Usefulness

The nature of mission spirituality can also be traced through the connection between personal "holiness" and spiritual "usefulness." In short, a heart that is deeply rooted in the life of God becomes eminently useful in the hands of God. John Pawson asked, "What can I wish for more, but an increase of the life of God in my own soul, and that His good pleasure may prosper in my hand?"[26]

When the life of God was made visible in the course of their ministry, it was often felt by others as a kind of anointing. Thomas Taylor wondered, "I am at a loss to know what can induce men to preach, who are destitute of the life and power of godliness,"[27] and others observed that there was a "Divine union which generally accompanied his sermons."[28] John Valton advised young preachers not to "seek so much for the art, as for the unction, of preaching. If you have the art, you will please: if you have the unction, you will save men."[29]

James Morgan, one of Wesley's "assistants," wrote that "the most shining abilities, natural or acquired, without 'the wisdom that is from above,' and the anointing of the Holy Ghost, are . . . lighter than vanity."[30] Morgan

23. Jackson, *Minutes*, 21.
24. *EMP*, 5:102.
25. Ibid., 3:149.
26. Ibid., 4:69.
27. Ibid., 5:62.
28. Ibid., 5:102.
29. Ibid., 6:122.
30. Ibid., 3:78.

claimed that all Thomas Walsh's public expressions of prayer and preaching "glowed with the love of God."[31]

Love and Zeal

Mission spirituality also embodies the logic of the Great Commandment. For the preachers, love of God was first about living in the conscious experience of God's own love for them, and the desire it implants to love God fully in return. This wellspring of holy love overflowed in love of neighbour, as the love of God reaching out to others through them. John Gaulter observed that being "converted to God themselves," the preachers "gave efficacy to the savour of their discourses by the active piety of their lives; and their glowing zeal for the salvation of souls."[32]

As a young convert, William Black recounted, "I felt a peculiar love to souls, and seldom passed a man, woman, or child without lifting up my heart to God on their account; or passed a house without praying for all in it . . . so that sometimes I was constrained to speak to them, though I met with rough treatment in return."[33] Beyond conversion, the pursuit of perfect love caused this zeal to take on a highly contagious quality. James Morgan noted that the "whole conversation" of Thomas Walsh "was like fire; warming, refreshing, and comforting all that were about him, and begetting in their souls a measure of the same zealous concern for the glory of God, and the salvation of sinners, which burned in his own breast."[34] In the midst of a powerful love-feast, John Furz recorded how the local leaders became so "filled with zeal for the glory of God, and the good of souls" that "they dispersed themselves on Sundays, went into the country villages, sung and prayed, and exhorted the people to turn to God."[35] By taking up the call to preach, and taking to the road as Wesley's travelling preachers, they spoke of being devoted to "one thing": longing for more of God's love, sharing that love with others, and stirring up the same missionary spirit throughout the movement.

31. Ibid., 3:187.
32. Ibid., 4:208.
33. Ibid., 5:257.
34. Ibid., 3:121.
35. Ibid., 5:127.

The Making of a Missionary

> Q. *What was the rise of Methodism, so called? A. In 1729 the late Mr. Wesley and his brother, saw they could not be saved without holiness; they followed after it, and incited others to do the same. In 1737 they saw holiness comes by faith. They saw likewise that men are justified before they are sanctified: but still holiness was their point. God then thrust them out . . . to raise a holy people.*[36]

The conversion narratives of the early Methodist preachers follow a common pattern. In retrospect, they note how the work of prevenient grace became consciously operative from as early as four years old, implanting a variety of divine "drawings" and desires that could never be shaken off. God both "strives" and "waits" to be gracious in the way of salvation. Growing up, they reported a range of ongoing spiritual experience, from the fear of death to being "athirst for God," along with the desire to forsake sin and improve the "form of godliness" in their lives. These accounts serve to uphold an arminian view of universal and prevenient grace, but only as they narrate a spiritual journey in which the work of God gave birth to a missionary, whose life was preserved and "set apart" for the pioneering task.

Awakening and Longing

In the process of awakening, the Spirit implants a longing for God that can be resisted, but never be satisfied with anything less than holiness of heart and life. Sampson Staniforth remarked, "I that never prayed in my life was continually calling upon God . . . A cry after God was put into my heart, which has never yet ceased, and, I trust, never will."[37] As each narrative progresses, the dance of prevenient grace and human response unfolds through cycles of godly conviction and practical resolution, followed by quenching the Spirit and backsliding. With each cycle, however, the seeker pressed on towards evangelical conversion, by mourning and wrestling for the assurance of forgiveness and the gift of new birth. This journey is reinforced by many "foretastes" of God's love in moments of revelation and spiritual breakthrough. Thomas Walsh observed: "One way, among the diversity of the Holy Ghost's operations, whereby He cleanseth souls, is, to feast them for some moments with so much of the substance of things hoped for, as

---

36. Jackson, *Minutes*, 9–10.
37. *EMP*, 4:118.

shall captivate them for their whole life after; and, in one taste of the sweetness of God, does the work of a thousand arguments."[38]

Thomas Taylor also explained, "I had gracious visits from the Lord, exceedingly sweet to my soul" and in pressing forward, "the Lord continued to visit me with tastes of His love."[39] In this way, a seeker not only learned how to long for God, but also to expect that their longings would be met. Merely believing that God was able to save was eventually superseded by a confidence that God was actually willing to save. The spiritual dynamic was even more subtle, insofar as the Spirit might bring conviction about the need for longing-to-long for God. William Black complained that "I mourned because I could not mourn; and grieved because I could not grieve."[40] He was "greedy of sorrow!" Understanding this process of awakening and longing was more important to the preacher than counting conversions. Once the Spirit began to work these longings in the heart, and given the right guidance, it was only a matter of time before the gospel promises would be fulfilled.

Searching and Guiding

One frequent reason given for slow spiritual progress towards conversion was the lack of a "kind shepherd" or spiritual guide to second the work of prevenient grace in a seeker's life. In the early days of the revival, Christopher Hopper lamented, "I only wanted a spiritual guide to show me the way; but, alas! I could not find him in the country."[41] The need for this kind of guidance, however, is precisely what the emerging Methodist movement promoted and supplied. By some "particular providence," these youthful seekers come across a preacher, or are taken to hear one by a friend, and eventually get mixed up in a Methodist society.

Despite often significant cost to personal reputation and safety, these seekers expressed great and growing affection for the Methodist people and their manner of living. George Story recalled the love and zeal of ordinary members when "the first time I entered a Methodist's house, they went to prayer with me and for me, a considerable time."[42] William Hunter, one of Wesley's longest serving preachers, made mention of the affection he experienced when "the people took notice of me, talked with me, and wished

38. Ibid., 3:51.
39. Ibid., 5:10.
40. Ibid., 5:248.
41. Ibid., 1:185.
42. Ibid., 5:228.

me to cast in my lot amongst them."[43] Once they had been accepted into fellowship, they benefitted from a whole range of transformative practices: from society and class meetings, to participating in love feasts and covenant services. And, in retrospect, Duncan Wright remembered how, "the sight of a Methodist used to set my heart on fire with love."[44]

Seekers did not always attribute the moment of their awakening, or conversion, to evangelistic preaching. Thomas Lee pointed out, "I was not deeply affected under any particular sermon, yet my conscience was gradually enlightened, by hearing, and reading, and conversing, and praying, till I resolved to cast in my lot among them." Subsequently, "in the use of these means, God frequently met me, and comforted my soul." During a moment of private prayer, he rejoiced that "God broke in upon my soul in so wonderful a manner, that I could no longer doubt of His forgiving love."[45]

Converted and Called

These mostly short narratives can belie a very long journey, before the experience of evangelical conversion was attained. Richard Rodda noted that from the time of admission into society, and constantly meeting in class, "I was nearly two years seeking rest for my soul" before "God gave me a clear sense of his forgiving love."[46] Sometimes it is hard to distinguish between foretaste and fulfillment, as these seekers endure multiple cycles of attainment and backsliding, glimpsing assurance, and then sinking back into despair. George Shadford pointed out that "the Lord did not suffer me to take convictions for conversion" and "after those pleasant drawings, I had sorrow and deep distress."[47] This agnostic process is expressed in the language of spiritual warfare. There is a competition for the soul which Satan is intent to win, but doomed to lose. What marks out the moment of conversion is the sense that this cycle of fear, doubt, and despair is finally broken. The experience is not merely a foretaste of forgiveness, but a "clear sense of pardon." It exceeds awakening as an abiding assurance of being embraced by God's love, that endured through the trials and temptations of life to follow.

Henry Rack observes that "early Methodist conversion narratives were punctuated by a variety of supernatural phenomena offering challenges and reassurance on the way to justification and sanctification," often in

---

43. Ibid., 2:242.
44. Ibid., 3:111.
45. Ibid., 4:153–55.
46. Ibid., 2:298–99.
47. Ibid., 6:149.

the form of a supernatural vision and voice.[48] For some seekers, spiritual breakthrough came through a vision of Jesus on the cross through an "eye of faith" and filled them with an assurance of God's forgiving love.[49] For others, it came by hearing the still small voice of God speaking, "Thy sins are forgiven thee."[50] Either way, there is a repeated connection between this overwhelming sense of personal forgiveness and an overflowing love of neighbour. Christopher Hopper confessed, "I found love to my God, to His yoke, to His cross, to His saints, and to His friends and enemies."[51] Here is the thread that connects awakening, conversion and calling in the spirituality of these emerging missionaries. Indeed, the art of preaching meant to "set forth Christ as evidently crucified before their eyes . . . justifying us by his blood, and sanctifying us by his Spirit."[52]

The narrative of being called to preach also has an identifiable narrative pattern; and the experience of Thomas Hanby is somewhat typical.[53] First, there came a "sudden impression" that he "ought to preach the gospel;" an inner compulsion of the Spirit, not an aspiration of the flesh, that leaves him "perplexed." On the one hand, as a relatively untutored and unlettered individual, there was a deep sense of inadequacy for the task: "I cannot preach; for I am a fool, and a child." On the other hand, the tyranny of this anxiety is broken by a desire for obedience: "I was willing to preach, provided I was sure it was the will of God concerning me." This was followed by a period of spiritual wrestling and consulting with friends. Hanby looked for a sign and, while out visiting the sick, God spoke to him through the words of a dying woman: "God has called you to preach the gospel; you have long rejected the call; but He will make you go. Obey the call, obey the call." He was then resolved to "make a trial" by preaching abroad, and noted that "God was pleased to visit us," as some were moved to prayer, and two people received a sense of pardon. Other would-be preachers tested their call by taking on leadership of classes and bands before venturing out. Either way, a degree of liberty in speaking, accompanied by fruitfulness, were looked upon as "seals" of their call to preach.

---

48. Henry D. Rack, "Charles Wesley and the Supernatural," *BJRULM* 88 no. 2 (2006) 67. See also, Rack, "Early Methodist Visions of the Trinity," *PWHS* 46 nos. 2–3 (1988) 38–44 and 57–69.

49. Cf. *EMP*, 4:286; 5:11.

50. Cf. Ibid., 4:122; 5:113.

51. Ibid., 1:189.

52. Jackson, *Minutes*, 27.

53. *EMP*, 2:137–38.

Set Apart and Sent Out

To Wesley's three marks of a preacher, Alexander Mather added a fourth: the "clear conviction that he was called of God to the work; otherwise he could not bear the crosses attending it."[54] A common fear of "running before being sent" was fuelled by the normal expectation that preaching was reserved for ordained clergy of the established Church, or dissenting ministers ordained by congregational appointment. In the face of this, Wesley grounded their authority to preach in the direct call of God, evidenced in sound conversion and fruitful ministry. So, Christian Hopper reasoned, "I have heard and believed the gospel, and found it to be the power of God to the salvation of my own soul" and "I have preached the gospel to sinners dead in sin, and they have been awakened and converted to God." He therefore concluded that his "call to preach the gospel was consistent with Scripture, reason, and experience." He may not be formally ordained by church or congregation, but he can say, "I have now the countenance of my God" and "the hands of His dear Son, the Bishop of my soul, laid upon me."[55]

The long journey of awakening is not merely a prologue to conversion, but training for evangelistic mission. Indeed, it would seem that a preacher's spiritual journey was often longer and more laborious than most. James Morgan observed that "those whom God intends chiefly for the service of other souls, He gives them to feel, as they are able to bear, the uttermost of their nature's death ... before He shows them His salvation." In this way, "they may be the better capable of sympathizing with, and counseling, others in like circumstances, and be quickened in their endeavors of saving souls from death."[56] John Pawson also reflected that, God "took this method with me: He dug deep, and laid the foundation sure, and hath carried on the building to this day!"[57]

The Character of a Missionary

> *Have you a lively faith in Christ? Do you enjoy a clear manifestation of the love of God to your soul? ... Do you expect to be perfected in love in this life? Do you really desire and earnestly*

---

54. Ibid., 2:178.
55. Ibid., 1:193–94.
56. Ibid., 3:51–52.
57. Ibid., 4:19.

seek it? Are you resolved to devote yourself wholly to God, and to his work?[58]

The preachers were committed to the gospel of Christian perfection, variously referred to as entire sanctification, the great salvation or being saved to the uttermost, and especially perfect love. The evolving doctrine, and its experiential proof, was proclaimed as something to be actively pursued, attainable in this life, given in a moment, capable of growing, being lost and regained. It was a promise they proclaimed to all the world, and invited people to seek evangelical conversion as a means to that great end. On his deathbed, John Pawson advised the next generation of preachers to "constantly preach Christ, in all the riches of His grace, and offer in His name a present, free, and full salvation—a salvation from the guilt, the power, and the very being of sin."[59] In an obituary to Pawson, Adam Clarke wrote that "nothing short of this experience he considered as salvation."[60] Christian perfection was not merely a promise for all real Christians, but an experience of God's presence and power that many preachers considered vital for their missionary vocation.

Vocation and Perfection

For around half the autobiographies, the pursuit of perfection is a significant thread in the testimony about being called and empowered as missionary preachers. Among these, there are two basic patterns of experience.

First, there are those who become exhorters and then local preachers relatively soon after conversion. In the course of their ministry, they find themselves subject to trials and temptations, all of which reveal the need for a deeper renewal in grace, and this kindles their pursuit of perfection. The testimony of Alexander Mather is exemplary. The new birth had endowed him with "a continual power over outward and inward sin," yet he explained: "I felt in me what I knew was contrary to the mind which was in Christ, and what hindered me from enjoying and glorifying Him." The context for this revelation was a struggle to fulfill his vocation: "When I saw my call to preach, the difficulties attending that office showed me more and more the need of such a change, that I might bear all things" and "I saw as clearly as I do now, that nothing furthers that end so much as a heart and life wholly devoted to God." For the preacher, attaining perfection was more

---

58. Jackson, *Minutes*, 11.
59. Ibid., 4:89.
60. Ibid., 2:190.

about mission than morality. From that moment, he claimed to have, "an unspeakable pleasure in doing the will of God" and "I had also a power to do it . . . with such a fervent zeal for the glory of God and the good of souls, as swallowed up every other care and consideration."

This conscious state of perfect love was typically given in an instant, but could grow by degrees through "continued watchfulness," or gradually fade away through "wandering thoughts."[61] Either way, the moment left an indelible longing within the soul for the presence and power of God, along with an expectation of ongoing renewal. Mather concludes, "My soul is often on the stretch for the full enjoyment of this without interruption; nor can I discharge my conscience, without urging it upon all believers, now to come unto Him 'who is able to save unto the uttermost!'"[62]

Second, there are those who sensed the need of perfection soon after conversion, and sought it as a proper progression of the holy life.[63] Among these, many testified to the importance of band meetings in wrestling for God's blessing, as well as resisting "Satan's devices" to dampen and derail their spiritual fervour.[64] The call to preach comes either as part of their journey towards perfection in love, or as a consequence of having attained it.

After a remarkable conversion and period of wandering, Thomas Rankin "began to seek this great salvation" and observed "the more I sought it, the more my soul grew in grace."[65] In a time of private prayer, he heard the words, "Whom shall I send?" And, the moment he accepted the call, he said, "I felt such love for the souls of my fellow-creatures" that "I could lay down my life if I might but be anywise instrumental of saving one soul." His initial efforts at preaching, however, were somewhat unsuccessful; and, coupled with an increasing consciousness of his own sinful nature, he was "tempted to preach no more, till God had purified my heart." Nevertheless, he pressed on with the help of his band meeting, until he reported that the power of God "descended upon my soul." As was his practice, Wesley advised Rankin that he would not ultimately find what he was looking for "till you give yourself wholly up to the work of God!" Complete breakthrough came when he "no longer felt reluctance to go out as a poor despised Methodist preacher." Not long after, he was appointed as a travelling preacher, and then sent as a missionary to America.

61. Cf. John Wesley, "Wandering Thoughts," *Sermons II 34–70, BEW*, 2:126–37.

62. *EMP*, 2:194.

63. A cursory survey suggests that this group of preachers undertook their spiritual journey around or after the "holiness revival" of the 1760s, when the intentional pursuit of instantaneous perfection was at its height. See Rack, *Reasonable Enthusiast*, 427.

64. Cf. John Wesley, "Satan's Devices," *Sermons II 34–70, BEW*, 2:139–51.

65. *EMP*, 5:160–72.

For Richard Rodda, the son of a first generation Methodist preacher, it was not moral failure or the call to preach that occasioned his journey into perfection, but the responsibility of praying in public, which he admitted "was a cross to me."[66] After hearing the doctrine of perfection expounded, he "longed to experience it" and "prayed that every thought and desire might centre in God." He recollected, "My soul was now on full stretch after the blessing" and "I not only believed it attainable, but that I should attain it." With the help of his class meeting, he became more earnest in private prayer, until the power of God descended upon him, such that he "could no longer refrain from telling what God had done." Following this, he simultaneously wrestled with the call to preach while becoming captive to wandering thoughts, through which Satan even tempted him to contemplate suicide. Peace only came through accepting the call to preach; first in homes, then abroad, and finally as a travelling preacher.

Although half of the autobiographies do not explicitly speak of pursuing perfection, they are all characterized by a way of holiness that is guided by the vision of perfect love. This vision shaped the missionary character these preachers. What follows is an exploration of their own descriptions of perfection, derived from personal experience, and demonstrating a richness of language not often found in contemporary theological expositions of the doctrine.

Union and Communion

The greatest aspiration was to attain an "uninterrupted communion with God," which meant a "sacred sense" of God's presence and providence that would uphold them throughout the course of their ministry. William Black relished the ability to "see, feel, or taste God in everything."[67] They coveted "having fellowship with the Father and the Son," through an indwelling and abiding witness of the Spirit. Rankin spoke of the desire to walk in a conscious and conversational relationship with God, in the spirit of Abraham and Enoch. The preachers sought a heavenly flame in the heart, that caused them to delight in God and overflow in joyful obedience. They longed for an "inundation of love," and the ability to live in the covenant promise that "Christ is mine, and I am His."[68]

Against accusations of enthusiasm, John Murlin was unashamed to speak of having "a constant communion with Him" and "I pay no regard

66. Ibid., 2:302–9.
67. Ibid., 5:256.
68. Ibid., 6:58.

to those who tell us, 'You must come from the mount.'"[69] John Pawson also "enjoyed the abiding witness of the Spirit" and being "favoured with the continued presence of God."[70] Alexander Mather claimed that perfection is that "communion with God in which is my only happiness" and "that the fullness of the promise is every Christian's privilege." Joseph Benson illustrated further the missionary significance of this communion, by noting that Mather "generally felt himself the truths he delivered to others, and, in consequence thereof, his hearers felt them too." So, "he laboured to diffuse the odor of the knowledge of God, and of the truths of His precious word." His life "was consistent with his teaching."[71]

Intimacy and Power

Mather also claimed that "intimacy with God" is "the life of preaching."[72] In different ways, the journaling of a preacher's ministry narrates the close connection between abidingly deeply with God, and living missionally in the world. George Shadford reflected that, "If we had more of God in our hearts, there would be more of Him on our tongues, and shining in our lives; for out of the abundance of the heart the mouth speaketh."[73] John Valton summed this up: "When I am thus happy in God, my bowels thus yearn after the souls of poor sinners" and "nothing but love glowing in the soul can make us zealous and persevering in every good work." Consequently, "if love decay, we shall soon become unfruitful."[74]

The preachers discovered that a sound conversion was not sufficient to save them from fear, doubt, and despair. The trials they endured, and the temptation to give up their calling, made them vigilant in spiritual warfare and urgent in their pursuit of the perfect love that casts out fear. The ability to spend and be spent in the service of God was not determined by the force of circumstance, but the ability to see his presence, feel his embrace, hear his word of promise, and trust that the future was in his hands. When this connection was threatened or unravelled, the vitality and fruitfulness of the preacher depended upon wrestling for its renewal. James Rogers confessed that "I did not retain the witness of full salvation long;" but, "the Lord has

69. Ibid., 3:300.
70. Ibid., 4:23.
71. Ibid., 2:198–99.
72. Ibid., 2:191.
73. Ibid., 6:176.
74. Ibid., 6:28, 91.

Mission Spirituality in the Early Methodist Preachers 119

graciously restored it to me at different times" enabling him "to feel a measure of the genuine fruits of holiness."[75]

Emptiness and Fullness

The experience of perfection was one of utter moment-by-moment dependence on God's grace, and of patience to receive the gifts of God as the moment required. Far from inducing a sense of pride, the journey into perfection was marked by the humility of knowing oneself to be nothing, to have nothing, and to be capable of nothing, apart from the grace of God alone. George Story "supposed a soul saved from all sin would be a great, wise, and glorious creature" whereas he had "such a discovery of my own nothingness as humbled me to the dust continually."[76] John Valton confessed that "my greatest trials have been timidity" and "standing in that pulpit was like standing to be shot!"[77] The enormous challenges of the missionary vocation, coupled with a sense of inner weakness, left them in little doubt of their own "littleness, helplessness and unworthiness." They understood the necessity of being kept by grace, every moment.

Matthias Joyce felt the call to become a travelling preacher, but knowing that he was insufficient for the task, his prayer for perfection consisted in pleading, "Lord, I am nothing! Lord, I am nothing!" and then "in a moment, found power to obey."[78] Similarly, James Rogers learned from his band meeting that "the blessing of Christian perfection consisted in feeling I am nothing, and Christ is all in all . . . this I found true by experience." He bore witness to being, "so truly humbled with a sense of my own nothingness, that I rejoiced to suffer reproach for the name of Christ."[79]

This experience of nothingness meant being freed from self-centeredness, a deadness or disengagement from the world, and being fully devoted to God. Although many of the preachers were reluctant to speak of perfection as sinlessness, they enthusiastically talked about being "emptied of sin," in order to be "filled with love." Alexander Mather spoke of being "inflamed with great ardor in wrestling with God; determined not to let Him go, till He emptied me of all sin, and filled me with Himself."[80] Jasper Robinson also reflected that "contrary to my former expectation of being

75. Ibid., 4:326.
76. Ibid., 5:236–37.
77. Ibid., 6: 87, 100.
78. Ibid., 4:271.
79. Ibid., 4:290–91.
80. Ibid., 2:191.

something extraordinary when sanctified, I am emptied of self, and sink into an unfeigned nothingness, that Christ may be my all in all."[81] Others also enumerated this sense of emptiness and fullness as two distinct and sequential forms of experience, the latter offering an abiding witness of the Spirit that brings peace and power for missionary service.

Hunger and Thirst

The experience of perfection also filled the early Methodist preachers with a vehement thirst and fervent longing for more of God and a greater conformity to Christ. Being "athirst for God" in personal holiness was inseparable from being "thirsty for souls" in evangelistic mission. Having entered into the experience perfect love, Thomas Walsh recorded in his journal a constant interplay between thirsting for God and neighbor. On one day, he can record, "All the day my soul thirsted for the living God." And a few days later, "I had intercourse with heaven all the day" and "thirsted for the salvation of all men, as for my own soul."[82]

The preachers were not merely thirsty for making converts, but also for a holy people. John Nelson's response to antinomianism was to "create such a hungering and thirsting in them after inward holiness, that they may pant as the hart panteth after the waterbrooks, till all that is in them be made holiness to the Lord!"[83] It was not merely that they proclaimed the gospel of full salvation, but were also witnesses of what it meant to live on full stretch for it. They invited people to long after God in the same way that they did. James Rogers explained: "My soul at present doth hunger and thirst after a more entire conformity to the image of God. I see nothing so desirable as holiness; and I am resolved, through grace, to recommend it to all, both by example and precept."[84] With mission spirituality, the medium is the message.

---

81. Ibid., 6:186.
82. Ibid., 3:215, 223.
83. Ibid., 1:152.
84. Ibid., 4:238.

The Work of a Missionary

> Q. What is the office of a Christian Minister? A. To watch over the souls as he that must give account; to feed and guide the flock. Q. How shall he be qualified for this great work? A. By walking closely with God, and having his work greatly at heart.[85]

The preachers do not talk about "the mission of God," but "the work of God" and being co-workers with God. This way of speaking, however, perfectly captures the essence of the *missio Dei*, as the activity of God in the world, and our participation in it. The calling to be a preacher was understood as being sent out in mission, or having a "commission" from God to be a co-worker in the gospel. The "work of God" was fundamentally what God did to lead people through the whole way of salvation, from awakening to seeking, from seeking to conversion, and from conversion to perfection. These missionary preachers were sent into the world as labourers in God's vineyard, in order to promote salvation to the uttermost. They were co-workers with God's universal and prevenient grace by "preaching broad" in fields, graveyards, and marketplaces. They were co-workers with God's convincing, converting, and perfecting grace through proclaiming the gospel of holiness in society meetings, small groups, and from house to house.

In case anyone was tempted to standardize, predict, or control the work of God, Thomas Walsh commented that one cannot make "the progress of the work of God in one, or a thousand persons, a standard by which to judge of the genuineness of the experience of others."[86] The work of God was continued through many means, and in a diversity of ways, but always with a view to lives perceptibly transformed by grace. One way or another, the preachers were passionate to see the work of God increase, in both the numbers of changed lives, and their progress in the way of salvation. Wesley encouraged them to be observant, and they frequently refer to general trends in the societies, or actual numbers of those awakened, converted and perfected in love. This was not a cult of success, but a conviction that God would "own his work" and prosper it.

Apostolicity and Surrender

As local preachers, they carried out this missionary vocation alongside their ordinary paid employment; but the more it grew, the more they became

---

85. Jackson, *Minutes*, 13.
86. EMP, 3:51.

unsettled and started (or were advised) to consider taking up the apostolic challenge of full-time itinerancy. John Mason explained, "I found a stronger and stronger conviction, that it was my duty to give myself wholly up to the work of God, and to commence an itinerant preacher."[87] Being "given up" to God meant leaving behind the comforts of the settled life and the securities of secular employment, to live by faith and stake their future on the belief that God would prosper both his work and his workers. It also meant being fully surrendered to Wesley's process of stationing, and fully committed to Methodist doctrine and discipline as the particular means through which the work of God was being prospered.

Part of Wesley's appointment process for travelling preachers was to ensure they had the right motivations, and were not proceeding with any romantic illusions about the way of life. He warned Alexander Mather that being "a Methodist preacher is not the way to ease, honor, pleasure, or profit. It is a life of much labour and reproach. They often fare hard, often are in want. They are liable to be stoned, beaten, and abused in various manners. Consider this before you engage in so uncomfortable a way of life."[88] The calling was not merely to do the work of a preacher, but to take up the uncompromising life of a missionary.

They were not all "extraordinary or splendid" as preachers, but their holy love and evangelistic zeal was the foundation of their missionary spirit. They were willing to live and die, spend and be spent, to the glory of God and the salvation of souls. John Pawson repeatedly claimed that "long life never appeared very desirable" compared with the privilege of being a co-worker with God, and being "worn out" in his service.[89] On being invited by Coke to superintend the work in the West Indies, William Black stated, "My great desire is to enjoy God, and to live in His will. Away, ye earthly loves, and leave me to my God! His love, His favour, His will, are dearer to me than life itself."[90]

Being a "good steward" meant recognizing that all they had, and all they were, belonged to God and was to be used in his service. In giving themselves up entirely to the work of God, the preachers were ultimate examples of good stewardship. Christopher Hopper affirmed "I did not want ease, wealth, or honor, but to know, do, and suffer the will of my Lord and Master."[91] At sixty-eight years old, after a lifetime of service, John Pawson

---

87. Ibid., 3:311–12.
88. Ibid., 2:169.
89. Ibid., 4:25.
90. Ibid., 5:288.
91. Ibid., 1:193.

still maintained, "I am in His hand, and at His disposal: let Him do with me as seemeth Him good."[92]

Self-denial and good stewardship were not merely expressed in submission to Wesley's system of circuit appointment, but in surrendering to the providence of God and the impulses of the Spirit, in the daily round of ministry. Hopper noted, "I spent every Sabbath, and all my vacant hours, in preaching, reading, praying, visiting the sick, and conversing with all that Providence put in my way."[93] By setting aside "every other concern and employment," James Morgan commended Thomas Walsh for setting out "with a resolution to give himself up wholly to the dictates of the Holy Ghost, and to be ready to go what way soever the voice of heaven should call him."[94] Having "a heart always at leisure for God, attentive to His teaching, and obedient to His dictates, is the great thing; to which every design and pursuit must give place, if we mean to be truly great in the grace of God."[95]

Fruitfulness and Discipline

Once convinced of their call, the preachers had a spirit of expectancy that God would continue to set his seal to their work, and they would see the fruit of their labours in the salvation of souls. As a young local preacher, Rankin recalled, "I had been led to think, if I really was called of God to preach, the Divine power would attend the word in a very remarkable manner, in the conviction and conversion of sinners."[96] When this did not happen as anticipated, he was tempted to give up. And even as a seasoned travelling preacher, Matthias Joyce confessed, "that which distressed me most was, my not having so many seals of my ministry as I expected." The problem was that "nothing would satisfy me, but hearing the people roar under the sermon, from a sense of their misery" or "shouting for joy, through a sense of pardoning love." When this did not happen, he lamented, "I was almost ready to conclude I was not sent of God."[97]

Joyce found breakthrough by re-examining the nature of fruitfulness itself, and being re-assured of "doing the will of God, from the comfortable testimonies of the people at class-meetings and lovefeasts." Because evangelistic proclamation was inseparably connected to Methodist discipline,

92. Ibid., 4:72.
93. Ibid., 1:195
94. Ibid., 3:85.
95. Ibid., 3:132.
96. Ibid., 5:165.
97. Ibid., 4:265.

those awakened under preaching were more likely to experience and express their life-transforming encounters with God in the class meeting itself. Joyce concluded, "I think it would be well for every young preacher especially, to meet the classes whenever he can" since "nothing has a greater tendency to lift up the hands that hang down, than to hear those who have sat under us relating the good they have received thereby."[98] This connection to Methodist discipline has the effect of chastening any undue dependency on revivalistic enthusiasm to sustain their call to preach, and removing the temptation to confuse being a co-worker with God with the giftedness of the preacher.

Width and Depth

The preachers were equally as concerned for what hindered the work of God as what prospered it. Part of their apostolic task was to confront party spirit and division in the life of the societies, as well as occasions of spiritual and moral declension. Very often, what quenched the spirit of the societies, and broke the hearts of the preachers, was failure to maintain Methodist discipline in the pursuit of perfection.[99] This was not simply a result of spiritual apathy, but also undue enthusiasm. During times of intense revival, some local preachers might be caught up in a spirit of freneticism, and lay aside discipline in the pursuit of more converts. Reflecting on the periodic revivals of the 1770s, Thomas Taylor lamented that "oftentimes God begins a good work, but poor ignorant men will needs take it out of His hand."[100] When not handled well, they complained that revival turned into "wildfire," suggesting that the work of God may spread rapidly but burn out equally fast.[101] When properly connected to Methodist discipline, however, William Hunter celebrated how the revival proceeded with both "swiftness and depth."[102]

There was no doubt that the work of God could proceed with or without the help of human hands, but the preachers were committed to the way God had chosen to bless the ordinary discipline of Methodist society. Later on, in the 1780s, John Pawson noted that there had been "no particular revival" that year, but they did witness "a gradual increase in the societies, as well in number as in grace."[103] James Rogers reflected that the

---

98. Ibid., 4:265.
99. Jackson, *Minutes*, 24–25.
100. *EMP*, 5:86.
101. Ibid., 4:46.
102. Ibid., 2:244–45.
103. Ibid., 4:46.

"congregations continued very large, and the prayer-meetings and classes exceedingly lively" yet "there was scarcely any appearance of what is commonly called wildfire; and the work was not only gradual, but deep in most of them who were the subjects of it."[104] Whether the preachers expected the work of God to result in a rapid or gradual growth of the movement, it was not the speed with which the gospel spread that mattered most, but the depth of its transforming power.

Suffering and Warfare

Where the work of God advanced, they expected spiritual battle.[105] This battle was waged in the flesh through physical injury and illness, the violent persecution of mobs, and the combined powers of church and state to silence the advance of the Methodist movement. In the midst of this, there was also a battle waged in the soul, as the flesh pressed down on the spirit, driving the preachers into times of trial, and sometimes into despair.

Those preachers with private means might well exhaust their personal savings in the course of their calling. Eventually, provision was made to support the domestic needs of their wives and children, but in general it would seem that they received very little income for themselves beyond a small quarterage or an annual allowance. It was anticipated that the circuits would supplement this to cover travelling and living expenses, but often this was not the case, especially were the work was in its infancy.

In addition to being financially stretched, the preachers were often faced with physical endangerment. They constantly travelled from place to place, in all weathers, either on foot or by horse, and from early morning to late at night. At times they might not make it to good lodgings, and have to settle for sleeping rough by roads that were typically nothing more than dirt tracks. James Rogers also recorded an incident in which a travelling preacher was attacked by three highway robbers.[106]

Worse of all, the preachers had to suffer the violence of mobs raised by local clergy and gentry who were determined to rid themselves of the

---

104. Ibid., 4:321.

105. Rack discusses this supernatural interpretation of life in *Reasonable Enthusiast*, 431–32. See also, David Dunn Wilson, *Many Waters Cannot Quench: A Study of Sufferings of Eighteenth Century Methodism and their Significance for John Wesley and the First Methodists* (London: Epworth, 1969). Robert Webster also discusses the "rhetoric of the supernatural" in, *Methodism and the Miraculous: John Wesley's Idea of the Supernatural and the Identification of the Methodists in the Eighteenth Century* (Lexington: Emeth, 2013).

106. *EMP*, 4:323–24.

troublesome Methodist witness. Through all this, the preachers were often taken to within an inch of their lives. Time and again, however, these narratives of persecution conclude with stories of divine providence, as God miraculously protected and delivered them from serious injury and death. They refused to return violence with violence, preferring to stake their lives on the power of God, and then have stories to tell of his ability to save. The work of a Methodist preacher was often at the cost of personal wealth, health, and reputation. Such stewardship and self-denial were undoubtedly at the heart of the missionary spirit, and this was often a difficult price to pay.

Heaviness and Wilderness

Many preachers, like Thomas Lee, described their lives as "continually hung in suspense" between despair and hope.[107] In the midst of seemingly endless trials, this state of suspense was an occasion for both triumph and temptation. They often record a weariness with enduring, and an inner struggle with the temptation to doubt their calling and to quit the rigours of this missionary life for more settled occupations.[108] Christopher Hopper recounted how, sometimes "I was carried above all earthly objects, and had a comfortable view of the heavenly country," but "at other times I was much depressed, and could see nothing but poverty and distress" so that "I staggered through unbelief; and almost yielded to the tempter."[109]

The autobiographies provide an inner history of spiritual struggle through times of heaviness and even wilderness.[110] On the one hand, heaviness is a kind of spiritual depression that drags down the soul, but never finally extinguishes the assurance of God's presence and love. The journal of Thomas Walsh can read like a spiritual roller coaster, oscillating between moments of profound communion with God and times of severe heaviness through manifold temptations. On the other hand, wilderness is the experience of losing the sense God's presence and the assurance of forgiveness. John Haime confessed to enduring an inner wilderness for some twenty years as the result of personal sin, arising from a failure to watch and pray.[111]

Under a variety of circumstances, some preachers chose to settle down and resume regular employment, or take up paid leadership in dissenting

---

107. Ibid., 4:161.
108. Cf. Ibid., 2:273–74.
109. Ibid., 1:191.
110. John Wesley, "On Satan's Devices," and "Heaviness through Manifold Temptations," *Sermons II 34–70, BEW*, 2:222–35.
111. *EMP*, 1:308.

congregations. For those who persevered to the end, however, God continued to prosper his work despite their various inner and outer conflicts, and brought redemption in the midst of them.

Intrepidity and Prosperity

After Thomas Taylor's death, the minutes of Conference recorded how, "when Methodism was but in its infancy," the preachers had to "endure much from hunger, cold, weariness, and persecution;" but they "met and surmounted those difficulties with a truly apostolical intrepidity."[112]

If there is one overarching missionary motivation that emerges from these autobiographies, it is a passion and longing for the work of God to prosper in the lives of individuals and whole societies. "My soul thirsts for the prosperity of Sion."[113] This was not merely reflected in their tireless ministry, but also in their fervent devotion. John Pawson reflected about Alexander Mather: "For as no one had the prosperity of the work of God more deeply at heart, so, I believe, no man more constantly and fervently wrestled with the Lord in prayer for the enlargement, as well as the establishment, of the Redeemer's kingdom in the world, than he did."[114] Indeed, Pawson himself wrote: "The deep concern I felt for the prosperity of the work of God led me to earnest prayer; so that my own soul was kept alive, and I got clearer views of the gracious designs of God."[115]

Wesley was convinced that the spiritual and physical health of the preacher was connected to the fulfillment of his duties. Personal renewal did not come from retirement, but being caught up in the work of God. As John Milner wrote to Jonathan Maskew, "I doubt not but the work of God prospers in your hand, and rejoice to hear that as your day so your strength is; that the more you labor the more you prosper both in soul and body. Verily, we may say we serve a good Master."[116] Whether in the vigour of life or the rigours of death, it was their mission spirituality that shone through; a deep communion with God, a longing for holiness, and a zeal for the salvation of souls. Their deathbed testimonies and detailed obituaries affirmed the blessedness of living well, through the witness of dying well.[117] Henry D. Rack argues that deathbed biography in early Methodism had a deeply

112. Ibid., 5:104.
113. Ibid., 1:224.
114. Ibid., 2:217–18.
115. Ibid., 4:55.
116. Ibid., 4:212.
117. Joseph McPherson, *Our People Die Well* (Bloomington: Author House, 2008).

apologetic purpose, insofar as "holy dying seemed to prove the truth of the message preached by the dying saint."[118]

Conclusion

John Pawson summarized the importance of mission spirituality in his appeal to the next generation of preachers:

> Forgive me, brethren, if on this occasion I drop a tear, and in the fullness of my heart pray, that a double portion of that Spirit which influenced the first Methodist preachers may rest upon you who are likely to be their successors . . . labor with all your might in maintaining the life and power of godliness, both in your own souls and those who hear you. Promote old genuine Methodism, which stands in the renewal of the soul in righteousness and true holiness. Remember, brethren, that the whole weight of the cause of God will very soon rest upon your shoulders and seriously consider, how much will then depend upon your walking closely with God . . . and labour in his vineyard.[119]

I have read the spiritual autobiographies of the early Methodist preachers as narratives of mission spirituality. From a missiological perspective, they can be seen as pioneers of a movement, whose goal was to make disciples and not just converts. Their overarching concern was for "spreading scriptural holiness across the land."[120] Methodist discipline embodied a spiritual journey that passed through the two defining moments of evangelical conversion and perfection in love. It was not the moments that mattered most, however, but the resulting consciousness relationship of union and communion with God that empowered growth in grace. The way of holiness was about becoming a co-worker with God in working out one's own salvation. Mission spirituality, however, is about becoming a co-worker with God in the salvation of others. This can be seen as a mark of the whole Methodist movement, insofar as they were a people committed to helping each other work out their salvation with fear and trembling.

An overly strong conversionist reading of these autobiographies can tend to reduce the preacher's mission to making converts, and reduce discipleship to the endless pursuit of conversion-type crisis experiences.

---

118. Henry Rack, "Evangelical Endings: Death-Beds in Evangelical Biography," *BJRULM* 74 no. 1 (1992) 48.

119. *EMP*, 2:152.

120. Jackson, *Minutes*, 9.

Historically, this way of thinking has caused evangelicals to truncate the journey of awakening, and fail at making disciples by making conversion an end in itself. Focusing on the moments themselves can eclipse the ordinary moment-by-moment way of growth in holiness they are meant to promote.

From this Wesleyan perspective, therefore, evangelism is a complex task that involves proclaiming the gospel of perfect love, awakening people to seek after it, and initiating them into form of discipline that helps them pursue it. Salvation is not fundamentally about guilt management or moral development, but a life-transforming journey of entering, deepening and perfecting one's communion with the triune God. It is a way marked by an insatiable longing to be emptied of self, to be filled with the Spirit of love, and to grow in Christlikeness. It is a way marked by spiritual discipline and spiritual warfare, as one seeks God's blessings and resists Satan's devices in the means of grace. It is a way marked by Christian fellowship, in which mutual accountability and spiritual direction become the rhythm of one's walk with God and growth in holy love.

Mission spirituality is about being filled, transformed and overflowing with the holy love of God and neighbour. This is why Pawson pleaded with the next generation of preachers, to "labour with all your might in maintaining the life and power of godliness, both in your own souls and those who hear you." Mission promotes a movement when ordinary people become recipients of God's love, and are moved themselves to become participants in God's mission.

6

Medicine on Demand

John Wesley's Enlightened Treatment of the Sick

Deborah Madden

These seeds of heavenly fire
With strength innate would to their source aspire,
But that their earthly limbs obstruct their flight,
And check their soaring to the plains of light.

—Virgil, *Aeneid*[1]

1: Fons et Origo Mali

THE FLESHLY LIMITATION OF human existence is marked out here by earthly limbs, which place a natural check on Man "soaring to the plains of light." This fragment from Virgil's *Aeneid* was cited by John Wesley in its original Latin, but translated into English for Methodist readers. It appeared in a sermon written on June 17, 1790, during one of his extensive preaching tours around the British Isles, though it was published posthumously in the *Arminian Magazine* as "Heavenly Treasure in Earthen Vessels" (1792).[2]

---

1. Virgil, *Aeneid* 6.730–32, in John Wesley, "Potta [Potto], June 17, 1790," published posthumously as "Heavenly Treasure in Earthen Vessels," *AM* 15 (1792) 117–20, 173–76. Also see, John Wesley, "Heavenly Treasure in Earthen Vessels," *Sermons IV 115–151*, ed. Albert C. Outler, *BEW*, 4:161–67.

2. Wesley, "Heavenly Treasure in Earthen Vessels," *Sermons IV 115–151, BEW*, 4:164.

Here, exegesis also turns on a metaphor used by St Paul in 2 Corinthians; that of the "earthen vessels" (4:7), which Wesley described as being "exquisitely proper."[3] Like "earthen ware," our mortal bodies are weak, corruptible and easily broken: wrought from dust, to dust they will return.[4] The metaphor, which denotes "the brittleness of the vessels, and the meanness of the matter they are made of," probably resonated further because Wesley was feeling the limitation of his own mortal body. Just eleven days after writing the sermon, a journal entry for Monday, June 28, 1790, made the following candid observation:

> This day I enter into my eighty-eighth year. For above eighty-six years, I found none of the infirmities of old age: my eyes did not wax dim, neither was my natural strength abated. But last August, I found almost a sudden change. My eyes were so dim that no glasses could help me. My strength likewise now quite forsook me and probably will not return in this world. But I feel no pain from head to foot, only it seems nature is exhausted and, humanly speaking, will sink more and more, till "the weary springs of life stand still at last."[5]

Perhaps it was his birthday that prompted these reflections about declining bodily strength, though the biblical and theological themes elucidated in Wesley's sermon on earthen vessels epitomize deeply held beliefs. These beliefs were forged in the fires of his evangelical ministry, which was extraordinary for its impact, longevity, and enduring legacy.

All of the sermons written during the last year of Wesley's life crystallize a repeated insistence about the limitation of fleshly existence and the folly of trying to soar towards "plains of light."[6] Yet Wesley also reminded faithful believers that, unlike Classical poets and philosophers, Christians could attain an apperception of the "treasure" contained within their corruptible bodies. This apperception was mediated through the gospel of salvation; St Paul taught that humility and following Christ's pattern would reveal a foretaste of the world to come.[7] This was God's gift to humanity and it promised the light of true knowledge—as opposed to the superficial learn-

---

3. Ibid., 164.

4. John Wesley, *Journal and Diaries VII (1787–1791)*, eds. W. Reginald Ward and Richard P. Heitzenrater, *BEW*, 24:182.

5. Details about Wesley's last sermons, as well as the "four manuscript sermons" found in his study at Bristol, and the chronology of their posthumous publication in the *Arminian Magazine*, can be found in Outler's "Introductory Comment" to "The Deceitfulness of the Human Heart," in Wesley, *Sermons IV 115–151*, *BEW*, 4:149–50.

6. Wesley, "Heavenly Treasure in Earthen Vessels," *BEW*, 4:164.

7. Outler, "Introductory Comment," *BEW*, 4:161.

ing of philosophical wisdom. Revealed knowledge, through faith, involved a complete renewal, or new birth, in God's image.[8] The gospel of salvation offered an authentic transformation of mind, body, and soul: *saluus*, the hope of immortality. Wesley's conception of mind, body and soul, which is captured so vividly in the "Heavenly Treasure in Earthen Vessels," was another riposte to Enlightenment assumptions about human perfectibility and the certainties of reason insisted upon by rationalists.[9] Wesley's writings about the fallen condition of humanity in his last sermons condense earlier ideas about the holistic relationship between fleshly existence and a life of faith in Christ's body.[10] Fleshly existence—flawed, imperfect, and corruptible—placed inevitable limits on Man's understanding. Moreover, deceit in the human heart led to an outright denial of this limitation.[11] Deceit was inextricably linked with intellectual pride; this was the source and origin of evil—the *fons et origo mali*. Pride and deceit produced an over-inflated confidence in human autonomy and infallibility. Wesley's critical admiration for enlightened thought thus worked within these parameters. His distrust of Enlightenment rationalism was informed by an acknowledgement of intellectual pride and an insistence on the Scriptural way to salvation. This can be seen in a sermon he wrote on April 21, 1790, about the "deceitfulness" of the human heart. Enlightenment sentiments about humanity's innate wisdom, virtue, and happiness are rebutted here in fairly blunt terms. Such sentiments, he argued, are far worse than any hubris peddled by "ancient heathens." This modern delusion denied the importance of faith and revelation, both of which connected humanity to God. Without this, Man would only remain "a mystery to himself":

> O show thou me what spirit I am of, and let me not deceive my own soul. Let me not "think myself more highly than I ought to think." But let me always "think soberly, according as thou hast given me the measure of faith!"[12]

Pride and deceit, which led to Adam's rebellion, accounted for all of the inconsistencies in human nature. Wesley summarized this in the sermon on "Heavenly Treasure in Earthen Vessels":

---

8. Outler, "Introductory Comment," *BEW*, 4:149

9. John Wesley, "On the Wedding Garment," *Sermons IV 115–151*, *BEW*, 4:139–48, 147; John Wesley, "On Worldly Folly," *Sermons IV 115–151*, *BEW*, 4:131–38, 137.

10. Wesley, "The Deceitfulness of the Human Heart," *BEW*, 4:149–60, 151.

11. Wesley, "The Deceitfulness of the Human Heart," *BEW*, 4:160. The sermon was given this title posthumously and published in the *Arminian Magazine* in 1792.

12. Wesley, "Heavenly Treasure in Earthen Vessels," *BEW*, 4:163.

> The greatest and littleness, the dignity and baseness, the happiness and misery of [Man's] present state, are no longer a mystery, but clear consequences of his original state, and his rebellion against God. This is the key that opens the whole mystery, that removes all the difficulty, by showing what God made Man at first, and what Man has made himself.[13]

He deployed medical language in this sermon to suggest that a new throng of fevers fell upon humanity in the immediate aftermath of Adam's sin. An "unknown army of consumptions, fevers, sickness [and] pain of every kind, fixed their camp upon earth"—all of which paved the way for Man's last enemy: death.[14]

The theological detail of "Heavenly Treasure in Earthen Vessels" bears more than a striking resemblance to the Preface of *Primitive Physic*, (1747), a medical manual designed by Wesley to assist the poor with their health and well-being:

> Since Man rebelled against the Sovereign of heaven and earth, how entirely is the scene changed! The incorruptible frame hath put on corruption, the immortal has put on mortality. The seeds of weakness and pain, of sickness and death, are now lodged in our inmost substance; whence a thousand disorders continually spring, even without the aid of external violence.[15]

A proper understanding of humanity, both before and after the Fall, was the only way that Man could find his way back to pristine purity (wholeness), before the corruption of Original Sin. Revelation, through faith, brought clarity on how Adam contributed to his own downfall. Understanding how and why the human condition had become so corrupted would also reveal where Man's "everlasting" strength lay. This was the antidote to Original Sin. Apart from guarding against the sin of pride, Man needed to ask God exactly "what spirit" he was made.[16] Knowing that humanity was comprised of more than "mere machines, stocks, and stones," or that Man was governed by an internal monitor—natural or superadded by the grace of God—was not sufficient. Wesley insisted that true believers should enjoy "that peace of God which passeth all understanding;" that their soul might "rejoice" from

---

13. Ibid., 163. For the medical allusions in Wesley's sermons, see Phillip W. Ott, "Medicine as Metaphor: John Wesley on Therapy of the Soul," *MH* 33 (1995) 178–91 and Deborah Madden, "*A Cheap, Safe and Natural Medicine*": *Religion, Medicine and Culture in John Wesley's Primitive Physic* (Amsterdam: Rodopi, 2007).

14. Ibid., 165.

15. John Wesley, *Primitive Physic*, 1st ed. (London, 1747), iii.

16. Wesley, "The Deceitfulness of the Human Heart," *BEW*, 4:160.

the everlasting strength of justifying faith and "redemption in the blood of Jesus."[17] The "heavenly treasure" of which St Paul spoke was not just the residual image of God in Man—an immaterial principle or spiritual nature left intact after the Fall. Nor was it what the philosophers called natural conscience. Rather, the "heavenly treasure" referred to by St Paul entailed an absolute faith in Christ, which would see a complete "renewal in the whole image of God." This repaired the violence of Adam's sin and set Christian believers free from "the fear of death." That is to say: Christ the physician restored eternal life.[18]

Faith was the mechanism that would open Man's soul to produce a "new set of senses." By asking God what spirit he was made of, Man opened the door to faith. The spiritual "senses" allowed humans to glimpse, albeit imperfectly, "evidence of things unseen."[19] "Spiritual "senses," felt in Man's heart, but discerned in his soul, cannot be worked out intellectually; they flow only through faith, as indicated in Charles Wesley's hymn, "The Life of Faith":

> The things unknown to feeble sense,
> Unseen by reason's glimmering ray,
> With strong, commanding evidence
> Their heav'nly origin display.
> Faith lends its realising light:
> The clouds disperse, the shadows fly;
> Th' Invisible appears in sight,
> And God is seen by mortal eye.[20]

Only faith could produce a true "realising light." By the time Wesley experienced his Aldersgate conversion in 1738, he had become dissatisfied with a purely Lockean definition of the human faculties and the relationship between faith and reason that this implied. Locke's philosophy could not sufficiently account for what Wesley recognized as a spiritual "sense" of an immaterial "reality."[21] Close attention to the spiritual senses, produced by faith, and working through love, led to humility and charity. Humility, *imatatio Christi*, was essential because it ameliorated the sin of pride

---

17. Wesley, "Heavenly Treasure in Earthen Vessels," in *BEW*, 4:164–65.

18. Ibid., 164–65.

19. John Wesley, "On Faith," *Sermons IV 115–151*, *BEW*, 4:187–200, 200. This sermon is thought to be Wesley's last-written, dated "London, January 17, 1791." It was published posthumously as "Sermon LXIV. On Hebrews xi.1" in the *Arminian Magazine* in 1792.

20. Charles Wesley, "The Life of Faith," sts. 5–6, *Hymns and Sacred Poems* (1740), in John Wesley, "On Faith," *BEW*, 4:200.

21. Laura Bartels Felleman, "John Wesley and Dr George Cheyne on the Spiritual Senses," *WTJ* 39 no. 1 (2004) 163–72.

(Adam's Original Sin): "all who have received this treasure might continually cry, 'Not unto us, but unto thee, O Lord.'"[22] Humility enabled Christians to recognize their human weakness, whilst also getting a glimpse of "the world to come."[23] Wesley suggested that this Pauline vision of salvation, through faith, hope, and love (1 Cor 13:13), encompassed the whole of God's created order: "the love of God shed abroad in their [Christians'] hearts, with love to every child of Man, and a renewal in the whole image of God, in all righteousness and true holiness. This is properly and directly the treasure concerning which the Apostle is here speaking."[24]

The legacy of Adam's sin meant that this heavenly "treasure" was contained within "earthen vessels"—a "vile house of clay": our "earthly, mortal corruptible bodies."[25] The "corruptible" human body, which had once been "incorruptible and immortal," now pressed down upon the soul. As a result, the soul was unable to exert as much influence as it should: "Consequently, if these instruments by which the soul works are disordered, the soul itself must be hindered in its operations. Let a musician be ever so skilful, he will make but poor music if his instrument be out of tune."[26] Man's post-lapsed condition was one of disequilibrium—like a musical instrument played out of tune. His "house of clay" implied sickness, suffering and pain, until, bearing the afflictions no more, the body relinquished itself into the "dust of death." But despite this gloomy prognosis, it was only through bodily affliction that Man would find health (salvation) though Christ. This was the central message of Christ's Incarnation:

> Come on then, disease, weakness, pain, afflictions (in the language of men). Shall we not be infinite gainers by them? Gainers for ever and ever! Seeing "these light afflictions, which are but for a moment, work out for us a far more exceeding and eternal weight of glory!"[27]

Christ's suffering thus serves as the archetypal Christian struggle for eternal life: "trust in the Lord Jehovah, for in him is everlasting strength."[28]

---

22. Wesley, "Heavenly Treasure in Earthen Vessels," *BEW*, 4:167.

23. Ibid., 164.

24. Ibid., 164.

25. Ibid., 164. "Vile house of clay" is a line from a verse quoted by Wesley in his sermon. The verse has been extracted from John and Charles Wesley's *Hymns for Those That Seek and Those That Have Redemption* (London, 1747).

26. Wesley, "Heavenly Treasure in Earthen Vessels," in *BEW*, 4:165–66.

27. Ibid., 167. Wesley quotes from 2 Cor 4:17 here.

28. Ibid., 167.

Wesley believed that nourishment of faith equated to spiritual equilibrium of the soul, which, in turn, had a bearing on the physical health of mind and body—our house of clay.[29] There was no contradiction in keeping a balance between the spiritual senses and an empirical approach to rationalism or the medical sciences.[30] The balance between spiritual and physical realms is most apparent in Wesley's medical manual, *Primitive Physic*, where diseases of the flesh are treated by recourse to a medical model that is thoroughly empirical and disease is not catalogued in a spiritual manner. Indeed, emphasis upon looking after the body and preventing illness via a moderate regimen amply testifies to this. Furthermore, Wesley insisted that the sick should consult the best medical advice available.

The remedies listed in *Primitive Physic* can be traced to contemporary "orthodox" medical sources and Wesley was not peddling "kitchen-physic" recipes from a by-gone era. In this respect, the manual best represents Wesley's role as what Henry D. Rack terms "cultural mediator."[31] Complex medical knowledge was mediated by Wesley and made accessible to the poor. The physicians Wesley admired, he described in *Primitive Physic* as "lovers of Mankind who have endeavoured, even contrary to their own interest, to reduce physick to its ancient standard."[32] Those he held in esteem were "the great and good Dr Sydenham" and his pupil Thomas Dover—the latter wrote a manual on self-medication entitled *The Ancient Physician's Legacy to his Country* (1732). Wesley displayed his admiration for "the learned and ingenious" George Cheyne by citing many of the remedies he had set out in his *Essay of Health and Long Life* (1724), but use was also made of Cheyne's *Natural Method of Curing Most Diseases* (1742).[33]

Wesley quoted too from other well-known physicians, such as Richard Mead and John Huxham, but also the Dutch physician and botanist, Hermann Boerhaave and Swiss professor of medicine Samuel Tissot—Wesley's

---

29. Deborah Madden, "Introduction. Saving Souls and Saving Lives: John Wesley's 'Inward and Outward' Health," in ed. Deborah Madden, *"Inward and Outward Health": John Wesley's Holistic Concept of Medical Science, the Environment and Holy Living* (London: Epworth, 2008), 1–13.

30. Madden, *"A Cheap, Safe and Natural Medicine"*; Madden, "Introduction. Saving Souls and Saving Lives: John Wesley's 'Inward and Outward' Health."

31. Henry D. Rack, *Reasonable Enthusiast. John Wesley and the Rise of Methodism*, 2nd ed. (London: Epworth, 1992).

32. Wesley, *Primitive Physic*, 1st ed., viii; Madden, "*A Cheap, Safe and Natural Medicine.*"

33. Wesley, *Primitive Physic*, 1st ed., viii; George Cheyne, *The Natural Method of Curing Most Diseases of the Body, and the Disorders of the Mind Depending on the Body*, 1st ed. (London, 1742).

medical writing was greatly affected by *L'Avis au Peuple sur sa Sante* (1765).[34] Tissot lived in Lausanne but his text went to nine editions throughout Europe. *L'Avis* sprang from a concern about depopulation in Switzerland, but, again, it would be a mistake to simply regard this text as merely "popular"; Tissot, in fact, wrote it so that country clergymen could mediate important medical advice to a wider audience.[35] Wesley did not obtain any of the remedies for the first edition of *Primitive Physic* from Tissot, though he subsequently integrated the doctor's findings into later editions. He also anonymously produced an abridged version of *L'Avis* in 1769, which was entitled *Advice with Respect to Health*. In the introduction, Wesley praised Tissot for his plain language, use of regimen, and empirical approach to medicine. He commended Tissot for his humanity—the qualities identified by Wesley were those he sought to represent in *Primitive Physic*. He was not, however, completely uncritical and castigated Tissot for recommending the use of clysters (enemas), and his "violent fondness for bleeding," which Wesley thought was recommended "on the most trifling occasions." He also severely criticized Tissot for recommending internal medicine for the external skin complaint, scabies.[36] Wesley did not simply cull from leading authoritative medical texts to source his remedies, but critically engaged with other physicians, using his experience to make cautious changes to subsequent editions of *Primitive Physic*. The manual went to twenty-three editions during his lifetime—the last edited by Wesley was in 1791, though it continued to be published well into the nineteenth century. With each revision he incorporated the latest scientific advances available. An example of this can be seen in his advocacy of electrical therapy from 1760 onwards.

Wesley's interest in the spiritual health (salvation) of the poor included a concern for their physical welfare. His interest was underpinned by the vocation of Anglican practical piety, from which he also developed a holistic view of nature and healing inspired by Primitive Christianity. Ministering to the poor beyond the confines of church buildings and parish boundaries increased his awareness of the need for urgent medical attention. In a letter to his friend Vincent Perronet, the Vicar of Shoreham, he explained how he

---

34. Samuel August Andre Tissot, *L'Avis au Peuple sur sa Sante*, trans. J. Kirkpatrick, 2nd ed. (London, 1765). This was the version Wesley used and abridged. Wesley was also familiar with Tissot's other works, *Onanism* (1760), *Treatise On Epilepsy* (1770), *Nervous Diseases* (1782), and *Diseases of the Men of the World* (1770).

35. A. Wesley Hill, *John Wesley Amongst the Physicians* (London: Epworth, 1958) 55–56.

36. The original title of Tissot's work was altered for the 6th edition of 1797 to *The Family Physician: or Advice with Respect to Health*; John Wesley ed. "Introduction," *Advice with Respect to Health* (London, 1769) 3–5.

had decided to "prepare and give physic" out of sheer necessity—this was in 1746 and that same year he opened dispensaries in London and Bristol.[37] One year later *Primitive Physic* was produced from a list of "receipts," arranged in alphabetical order, which were drawn from Wesley's own experience, though always grounded in reliable medical practice. These "receipts" were used to guide other Methodists when visiting the sick.[38]

The correlation between physical and spiritual health, albeit in the context of Man's fallen state, was revealed to those who adopted a life of simplicity or regimen *imatatio Christi*—a life that would not only alleviate diseases of the flesh, but which could also mitigate the misery of Original Sin.[39] In this he was heavily influenced by the pietist physician, George Cheyne, who believed that the mind, body, and soul were separate, but inextricably linked categories.[40] These relationships were made explicit in the Preface to *Primitive Physic*, but recur throughout all of his sermons. Illness and death, the result of Original Sin and Man's fall, are unavoidable, but Christ, the ultimate physician, healed the sick and bore the sins of man *bodily* on the cross. Christ the physician, healer of body and soul, served to link the material and spiritual worlds, but Wesley did not suggest that health of the body and soul were one and the same. He evoked the divine physician, but did not simply believe in providential medicine. The spiritual world could not affect man's physical organs. The Incarnation gave tremendous significance to the body as something holding intrinsic value in its own right. Man's body belonged to God and, as the locus of ordered limits, transgression was sacrilegious. The body was a gift and as such, one had to take care of that "exquisitely wrought machine."[41]

---

37. John Wesley to Vincent Perronet, 1748, *LJWT*, 2:292–307. This was also noted by Wesley in his *Journal* for December 4, 1746. See John Wesley, *Journal and Diaries III (1743–1754)*, *BEW*, 20:150–51. See also, Madden, "A Cheap, Safe and Natural Medicine."

38. Eunice Bonow Bardell, "Primitive Physick: John Wesley's Receipts," *Pharmacy in History* 21 (1979) 111–21, 116. The 1745 pamphlet, *Collection of Receipts for the Use of the Poor*, was enlarged and corrected to a 119-page book, *Primitive Physic*, including a twenty-four page preface. The diseases increased from 93 to 243, whilst the remedies increased from 227 to 725—by the 23rd edition this had increased to 288 diseases and 824 remedies. Wesley's name did not appear on the volume until the 9th edition. See Bardell, "Primitive Physick," 111–21.

39. Madden, "*A Cheap, Safe and Natural Medicine*"; Madden, "John Wesley as Medical Advisor on Health and Healing," in *Cambridge Companion to John Wesley*, eds. Randy L. Maddox and Jason E. Vickers (Cambridge: Cambridge University Press, 2009), 176–89.

40. Madden, "*A Cheap, Safe and Natural Medicine*"; Madden, "Pastor and Physician: John Wesley's Cures for Consumption," in "*Inward and Outward Health*," 94–139.

41. Madden, "*A Cheap, Safe and Natural Medicine.*"

The sermons written in 1790 and 1791 demonstrate with poignancy the extent to which Wesley remained committed to this holistic concept of spiritual and physical health. They also show how he exemplified some of the contradictions that lay at the heart of English enlightened thinking. As a learned, classical scholar, who was deeply engaged with practical piety, Wesley confounds simplistic polarities about the Enlightenment and some of its more complex and controversial figures. This original insight was provided, of course, by Henry D. Rack, whose seminal work, *Reasonable Enthusiast* (1989) fully contextualized a subtle thinker hitherto only regarded as anti or "counter" Enlightenment.[42] Rack's definitive biography illuminated the intricacies involved with Wesley's theology, whilst simultaneously undercutting interpretations that pitted "orthodox" against "unorthodox" Christianity, or "reason" against "enthusiasm." Rack's work has been enormously influential, not only amongst Methodist scholars, but within eighteenth-century intellectual, religious, and cultural histories; which, in turn, have helped to alter perceptions about Wesley's medical and scientific activities.[43] In addition to this, eighteenth-century historiography has, over the last twenty years or so, reconfigured the Enlightenment so that its project of "modernity" is greeted with suspicion and the era is now regarded as being more akin to a variegated geography with some common themes. Refiguring the Enlightenment in this way has meant that Wesley is now much less a "counter" Enlightenment figure and more typical of someone writing within the context of Christian enlightened thought.[44]

Using a selection of sermons, letters and journal entries for 1790 and 1791, this chapter shows that, even as his own bodily strength waned, Wesley ministered to the physical and spiritual welfare of the poor, applying remedies for the body, or prayer for the soul, as and when appropriate.[45] Despite an ingrained skepticism about the capacity of worldly knowledge, he utilized an enlightened empiricism to relieve the most severe physical conditions and intractable diseases.[46] His practical treatment and Christian compassion when treating bodily disease, provides an extremely useful

---

42. Rack, *Reasonable Enthusiast*.

43. My own work on Wesley's medical activity is deeply indebted to Rack's biography, but original inspiration grew from reading his earlier article, "Doctors, Demons and Early Methodist Healing," ed. William. J. Shiels, *The Church and Healing*, (Oxford: Basil Blackwell, 1982).

44. Madden, "A Cheap, Safe and Natural Medicine."

45. Madden, "Introduction. Saving Souls and Saving Lives."

46. Madden, "A Cheap, Safe and Natural Medicine."

heuristic device for a fuller understanding of his enlightened medical holism, which was a consistent theme throughout his life.[47]

2: These Houses of Clay

On April 11, 1790, just a month or so before he wrote his sermon on "Heavenly Treasure," Wesley penned the following letter to his niece, Sarah:

> My Dear Sally,
>
> Persons may judge I am not so well as I was once because I seldom preach early in the morning. But I have been no otherwise indisposed than by the heat and dryness of my mouth, which usually begins between one and two and ends between seven and eight. In other respects I am no worse but rather better than I was six months ago. How much care must we take of these houses of clay that they sink not into the dust before time! All the advice which the art of man can give, my sister will hear from Dr Whitehead. But, indeed, in most chronical cases vain is the help of man![48]

This letter is the first in a series to his niece for 1790 where a combination of spiritual and medical advice is offered. Dr John Whitehead—a Quaker who converted to Methodism in 1784—was Wesley's trusted physician, not least because of his God-fearing credentials. Wesley's mention of not being able to preach early in the morning recurs in several letters for this period and is obviously a source of anxiety. The allusion to "houses of clay" captures the immediate concerns confronting Wesley, whilst revealing his consistently holistic approach to health of the body and soul.

Wesley's passion for the "noble medicine" of early-morning preaching was conveyed in a letter to Henry Moore for June 1, 1790, where he again expressed apprehension about not being able to carry out what had become a distinctive feature of Methodist worship. Convinced that early-morning preaching was good for both body and soul, he tells Moore that his health and strength are unlikely to fully recover without it.[49] The importance of early-morning preaching was something dear to Wesley's heart. On discovering that the practice of early-morning preaching had been dropped in several circuits around the country in 1784, he warned followers that Methodism would simply degenerate into a dry sect unless it was taken up

---

47. Madden, "Introduction. Saving Souls and Saving Lives."
48. John Wesley to Sarah Wesley, April 11, 1790, *LJWT*, 8:213.
49. John Wesley to Henry Moore, June 1, 1790, *LJWT*, 8:220.

again.[50] Methodists were reminded that Wesley himself had been dedicated to early-morning preaching during his missionary days in Georgia and he believed this had helped sustain the evangelical revival on British soil. In 1787 Wesley instructed ministers at the Foundry in London to go to bed at 9:00 pm so that they could rise early to preach at 5:00 am.[51]

Georgia had been the key to Wesley developing his theological understanding of Primitive Christianity and its practical application in the form of preaching, giving alms, and following a simple regimen *imitatio Christi*.[52] As Rack remarks, this "primitive" and "natural" habitat, which, by turns, was also a difficult and inhospitable environment, served as a "theatre" for individual piety—a life of piety that frequently threw man back upon his "naked self," forcing him to confront "inward problems," thus offering a "disturbing challenge" and reminding him of what he lacked.[53] Although his primitivist ideals would change, especially in the immediate aftermath of his Aldersgate experience, Wesley retained particular tenets of practical piety that had been bedded down in Georgia. These tenets included early-morning preaching, giving alms to the sick, and fasting. Indeed, in a letter addressed to James MacDonald for October 23, 1790, Wesley tells the preacher to exhort his brethren in Newry to pray and fast for God. The latter, so Wesley lamented, had been "almost universally neglected" by Methodists in England and Ireland. His letter to MacDonald ended with a quotation from Thomas à Kempis: "the more thou deniest thyself, the more thy wilt grow in grace."[54]

Wesley taught that self-denial and tribulation should be cherished like treasure; the challenge involved with suffering and self-sacrifice would bring Methodists closer to God. On December 15, 1790, Wesley wrote to one of his closest friends, Ann Bolton, to explain that her "inward holiness," works of charity and personal suffering would be justly rewarded in the eternal realm.[55] Christian struggle and self-denial would, by steady degrees, lead to a truly holy (whole) and happy (sinless) state of perfection—as it was in the beginning, before the slow, languid poison of Original Sin had worked its pernicious influence. This noxious influence had created sickness in the

---

50. Richard P. Heitzenrater, "John Wesley's Principles and Practice of Preaching," *MH* 37 (1999) 89–106.

51. Heitzenrater, "John Wesley's Principles and Practices of Preaching," 95.

52. Rack, *Reasonable Enthusiast*; L. L. Keefer, "John Wesley: Disciple of Early Christianity," *WTJ* 19 (1984) 23–32; Ted Campbell, *John Wesley and Christian Antiquity: Religious Vision and Cultural Change* (Nashville: Kingswood, 1991).

53. Rack, *Reasonable Enthusiast*, 97, 133–36, 146–47.

54. John Wesley to James MacDonald, October 23, 1790, *LJWT*, 8:242–43.

55. John Wesley to Ann Bolton, December 15, 1790, *LJWT*, 8:250–51.

body and soul. In the "Preface" to *Primitive Physic* Wesley stated that Man first came out of the Creator's hands, "clothed in body as well as in soul, with immortality and incorruption." In this state of sinless perfection, there was no place for physic or the art of healing.[56]

Wesley's advocacy of early-morning preaching was, of course, inextricably linked to an insistence on the efficacy of early rising. The merits of early rising formed an important part of following a simple regimen *imatatio Christi*. Influenced by the medical works of Cheyne, regimen had been the cornerstone of *Primitive Physic* and a useful strategy for preventing disease and poor health. The "Preface" to *Primitive Physic* spelt out the importance of regimen for "preserving health" and long life:

> Observe all the time the greatest exactness in your regimen or manner of living. Abstain from all mixed, all high-seasoned food. Use plain diet, easy of digestion; and this as sparingly as you can, consistent with ease and strength. Drink only water, if it agrees with your stomach; if not, good clear, small beer. Use as much exercise daily in the open air, as you can without weariness. Sup at six or seven, on the lightest food: go to bed early, and rise betimes. To preserve with steadiness in this course, is often more than half the cure. Above all, add to the rest, (for it is not labour lost) that old fashionable medicine, Prayer. And have faith in God who *killeth and maketh alive, who bringeth down to the grave, and bringeth up.*[57]

Commitment to a constant regimen achieved harmony, and harmony was the resolution of contradictory forces. Avoidance of excess in the nonnaturals increased longevity and Wesley insisted upon the importance of avoiding all extremes in food, drink, and the passions. He did not advocate a complete ban on alcohol but suggested drinking "clear beer" and wine in moderation. Indeed, clear beer was preferable to drinking tea or coffee. In 1746 he identified the effect of caffeine and understood that it could produce unwanted symptoms, such as trembling or shaking. He recommended temperance and regarded spirits, especially gin, as thoroughly poisonous and the cause of many nervous disorders.[58]

Religion and medicine may have converged for Wesley on a theological level, but *Primitive Physic* was empirically grounded in its suggested

---

56. Wesley, *Primitive Physic*, 24th ed. (London, 1792), iii; Madden, "Introduction. Saving Souls and Saving Lives."

57. Wesley, *Primitive Physic*, 24th ed., i. For a detailed analysis of Wesley's regimen, see Madden, "*A Cheap, Safe and Natural Medicine*."

58. Madden, "*A Cheap, Safe and Natural Medicine*."

regimen and remedies. Characterized by Wesley's "plain style" of writing, its theoretical structure was informed by the commonly used regimen of the six "non-naturals" (diet, exercise, sleep, air, evacuations, passions), whilst the remedies contained within were underpinned by contemporary medical practice. Emphasis on preventive strategies was how Wesley sought to increase awareness about health and hygiene in a way that was cost-effective. This consisted of a sparing diet, copious amounts of water, and as much exercise as possible, preferably in the open air.

Methodist itinerants devoted to a life of practical piety were well placed to enjoy a virtuous circle that ensured physical health whilst keeping their eyes fixed on the eternal realm. Wesley was convinced that his own hardy constitution and long life was directly linked to travelling on horseback, which took him preaching and open-air preaching around the country. Concerned about the health of Robert Carr Brackenbury in September 1790, Wesley explained that horseback riding and open-air preaching had restored his own "worn out" body: "Moderate riding on horseback, chiefly in the South of England, would improve your health. If you choose to accompany me in any of my little journeys on this side of Christmas, whenever you [were] tired you might go into my carriage."[59] This letter is immediately striking for the kindness and sympathy Wesley showed for someone afflicted with poor health. His letters are full of medical advice and instructions on how to keep the mind, body and soul in a healthy state. In June 1790, for example, he wrote several letters to the friends and family of preacher Adam Clarke. Fearing that Clarke would "preach himself to death," Wesley was keen to find a circuit that made less exerting demands. Writing to Clarke's wife, Wesley suggested a reduction in preaching duties. He also advised Clarke to ride horseback to Hot Wells every day—the spa's healing waters, combined with riding, would restore the ailing minister's physical health.[60]

Old age and infirmity did little to diminish Wesley's horse-riding and open-air preaching. This can be seen in his observations about what would turn out to be his last open-air preaching in Winchelsea on October 7, 1790:

> I went over to that poor skeleton of ancient Winchelsea. It is beautifully situated on the top of a steep hill, and was regularly built in broad streets, crossing each other, and encompassing a very large square, in the midst of which was a large church, now in ruins. I stood under a large tree, on the side of it, and called to most of the inhabitants of the town, "the kingdom of heaven

---

59. John Wesley to Robert Carr Brackenbury, September 15, 1790, *LJWT*, 8:237–38.
60. John Wesley to Mrs Adam Clarke, June 1, 1790, *LJWT*, 8:220.

is at hand: repent, and believe the Gospel." It seemed as if all that heard were, for the present, almost persuaded to be Christians.[61]

It is true to say that Wesley often felt ambivalent about open-air preaching.[62] However, when undertaken properly, the nexus of early rising, fasting, open-air preaching, and horseback itinerancy could create a virtuous circle of physical and spiritual health. The positive pursuit of health, hygiene, regimen, and temperance went beyond medicine and into the spiritual realm of morality, virtue, healing, purity, and thus wholeness. By contrast, Wesley was quick to point out when an ascetic regimen was taken to extremes. Whilst preaching in Hartlepool, in June 1790, he received an account of a female follower with a "lively imagination" and an over-zealous penchant for fasting:

> She is given up to a strong delusion (whether natural or diabolical I know not) to believe a lie. One proof may suffice: some time since, she told the community, as from God, that the Day of Judgment would begin that evening. But how could she come off when the event did not answer? Easily enough. "Moses," said she, "could not see the face of God, till he had fasted forty days and forty nights. We must all do the same." So for three weeks they took no sustenance, but three gills of water per day: and three weeks more they took each three gills of water gruel per day. What a mercy that half of them did not die in making the experiment.[63]

Wesley made a direct and simple connection between regimen, health, and the medical sciences, but never conflated medicine and religion. In his journals, diaries, and *Arminian Magazine*, which were meant to aid spiritual inspiration and enlightenment, Wesley retained a place for faith-healing and the supernatural or "miraculous" instances of recovery and cure. Thus after his open-air preaching in Winchelsea, Wesley's *Journal* reported on a "strange account" given by an "eminently pious woman, Mrs Jones":

> Many years since she was much hurt in lying in. She had various physicians, but still grew worse and worse, till perceiving herself to be no better, she left them off. She had continual pain in her groin, with such *prolepsis uteri*, as soon confined to her bed; there she lay two months, helpless and hopeless, till a thought came one day into her mind, "Lord, if thou wilt, thou canst make

---

61. Wesley, *Journal and Diaries VII (1787–1791)*, BEW, 24:191.
62. Heitzenrater, "John Wesley's Principles and Practices of Preaching," 95.
63. Wesley, *Journal and Diaries VII (1787–1791)*, BEW, 24:180.

me whole: be it according to thy will!" Immediately the pain and disorder ceased. Feeling herself well, she rose and dressed herself: her husband coming in, and seeing her in tears, asked, "are those tears of serious joy?" She said, "of joy!" On which they wept together. From that hour she has felt no pain, but enjoyed perfect health. I think our Lord never wrought a plainer miracle, even in the days of his flesh.[64]

Such spiritual episodes and testimonies about the power of prayer recur frequently throughout his journals and diaries but were not included in the main body of *Primitive Physic*, which offered purely practical advice to those needing urgent medical attention for physical symptoms.[65] Wesley certainly believed in the power of spiritual healing and prayer—it is advocated in the "Preface" to *Primitive Physic*. But this was only through God's grace; Wesley denounced any attempt to assert faith as a curative power for physical diseases. All too often this was countered by the reality of natural suffering.[66]

Wesley argued that preventing disease involved adopting a sensible regimen; a simple life was a healthy life. Natural diseases were not spiritualized in a Puritan fashion, though for Wesley health was not merely physical. The motivating force behind Wesley's broader religious aim was a desire to achieve the common life in the "body of Christ." The good and holy life was an active discipline and he sought to show that the goal of all self-aware Christians involved a struggle to find the golden mean. Understanding this, however, did not preclude the medical sciences from improving the human condition in a fallen world. When writing *Primitive Physic*, Wesley committed to paper his belief that ordinary people could themselves relieve every day common diseases. In his letters he therefore encouraged friends, family, and followers to use the manual for this very purpose: To Sarah Wesley, for instance, he wrote: "If your hurt is not yet healed, apply thereupon the poultice of powdered coal prescribed in the *Primitive Physic*. In a few days it will cure any sore on a human body. I scarce knew it fail."[67] His niece Sarah was suffering from "scorbutic sores" (ulcers). The above letter was written in June 1790 and several more were sent with medical advice on how to treat this condition. The remedy in *Primitive Physic* can be traced back to Dr John Huxham. In September that year Wesley also encouraged her to spend some time sea-bathing in Margate to ease the ulcers, but told her to fast and

---

64. Ibid., 191.
65. In the "Preface" Wesley suggested that the love of God is the "sovereign remedy" for all miseries—because it keeps the "passions" within "due bounds."
66. Madden, "*A Cheap, Safe and Natural Medicine.*"
67. John Wesley to Sarah Wesley, July 31, 1790, *LJWT*, 8:229.

take the "diet drink," specifically prescribed in *Primitive Physic* for scorbutic sores.[68] Sea-bathing, of course, was generally regarded as a panacea for most ills in the Georgian period. But *Primitive Physic* provided a choice of remedies for individuals to select and encouraged them to be pro-active in their own physical well-being.

Primitive Physic was Wesley's way of making sure that the poor had a physician in their home—one who could be called upon at any time, and one who was cost-effective. It was crucial to take care of our "houses of clay" to ensure that they did not sink into the dust before their time. For this reason the manual was included as part of the essential corpus of works to be disseminated by preachers amongst their Methodist circuits.[69] Whilst he had faith in God's ability to restore body and soul, this did not prevent physicians and patients from ameliorating the worst effects of fleshly disease. For Wesley, God's preternatural element was the framework into which the natural world fitted. He therefore informs his niece Sarah that God was the best physician for a "sin-sick soul," cheerfully adding: "and we may safely say 'I'll trust my great physician's skill; what He prescribes can ne'er be ill.'"[70] Wesley's medical holism was linked to a profound faith in God's grace, which he believed could produce "true holiness," wholeness (*saluus*) and happiness: "choose holiness by my grace, which is the way, the only way, to everlasting life. He cries aloud, be holy, and be happy; happy in this world, and happy in the world to come."[71]

---

68. John Wesley to Sarah Wesley, September 17, 1790, *LJWT*, 8:238.
69. Madden, "*A Cheap, Safe and Natural Medicine*."
70. John Wesley to Sarah Wesley," July 31, 1790, *LJWT*, 8:229.
71. Wesley, "On the Wedding Garment," *BEW*, 4:139–148, 148.

7

Wesley's Invisible World

Witchcraft and the Temperature of Preternatural Belief

 *Owen Davies*

> With my latest breath will I bear my testimony against giving up to Infidels, one great proof of the invisible world. I mean, that of Witchcraft and Apparitions, confirmed by the testimony of all ages.[1]

BORN IN 1703, JOHN Wesley was nine years old when Jane Wenham was convicted and condemned to death at Hertford assizes for conversing with the Devil in the form of a cat, and thirteen when the family home at Epworth was the scene of a noisy haunting that we would now describe as poltergeist phenomena. Wesley was thirty-three when the Witchcraft Act was passed by the British parliament. This statute repealed the Witchcraft and Conjuration Act of 1604, and redefined witchcraft and magic as fraudulent crimes and not diabolic realities. That a young Anglican clergyman such as Wesley might believe in an invisible world of witches, ghosts, devils, and angels does not seem odd when viewed in this context. The most ardent and vocal persecutor of Jane Wenham was, after all, an ambitious young high church clergyman, Francis Bragge Jr., not some foaming ranter or aged clergyman mentally and theologically stuck in the seventeenth century.[2]

1. John Wesley, ed., *AM* 5 (1782) 366.
2. Owen Davies, "Decriminalising the Witch: The Origin of and Response to the 1736 Witchcraft Act," in John Newton and Jo Bath, eds. *Witchcraft and the Act of 1604* (Leiden: Brill, 2008), 207–32. On Bragge, see Mark Knights, *The Devil in Disguise: Deception, Delusion, and Fanaticism in the Early English Enlightenment* (Oxford: Oxford University Press, 2011), 215–16, 220–33, 237–38.

Wesley wrote no more than a few paragraphs in all expressing his belief in witchcraft and ghosts, but during his lifetime, and after, the founder of Methodism was portrayed as the last of the demonologists, and his followers the sowers of counter-Enlightenment superstition.[3] In this context, he has been, and continues to be, a magnet for those seeking to exemplify counter currents in eighteenth-century educated society. It has been all too easy for historians to fill in the gaps of Wesley's demonology, to attribute to him all the characteristics of the devout intellectual witch believer of the witch-trial era. Historians who are usually sensitive to nuance can fall into this "Wesley trap." Others and I have stated, for example, that Wesley staunchly opposed the Witchcraft Act of 1736. Yet nowhere did he explicitly state this opposition.[4] It is based on inference. So what exactly did Wesley write about witchcraft, where did he write it, why, and when? Context is the key to providing a more nuanced understanding of Wesley's demonology.

The link between Nonconformity and credulity regarding the preternatural was already well established by the late seventeenth century, with the Society of Friends, Presbyterians, and Baptists being the focus of attacks.[5] In the 1650s the Quaker movement, like the Baptists, faced accusations of witchcraft and diabolism, but the subtle intellectual shift from a Neoplatonic to a Cartesian world over the ensuing decades led to a realignment of both groups with "superstition." Accusations of witchcraft were increasingly used as a political and religious metaphor, rather than a reference to the criminal offence.[6] Come the early years of the eighteenth century and witchcraft and apparitions became ammunition in the debate that raged between Angli-

---

3. Owen Davies, "Methodism, the Clergy, and the Popular Belief in Witchcraft and Magic," *History* 82 (1997) 252–65.

4. Owen Davies, *Witchcraft, Magic, and Culture, 1736-1951* (Manchester: University of Manchester Press, 1999), 12; Phyllis Mack, *Heart Religion in the British Enlightenment: Gender and Emotion in Early Methodism* (Cambridge: Cambridge University Press, 2008), 225.

5. See Clarke Garrett, *Spirit Possession and Popular Religion from the Camisards to the Shakers* (Baltimore: John Hopkins University Press, 1987); Nathan Johnstone, *The Devil and Demonism in Early Modern England* (Cambridge: Cambridge University Press, 2006), 265–86; Jane Shaw, *Miracles in Enlightenment England* (New Haven: Yale University Press, 2006), esp. 51–73.

6. Peter Elmer, "'Saints or Sorcerers': Quakerism, Demonology and the Decline of Witchcraft in Seventeenth-Century England," in Jonathan Barry, Marianne Hester, and Gareth Roberts, eds. *Witchcraft in Early Modern Europe* (Cambridge: Cambridge University Press, 1996), esp. 167–69; Sue Friday, "Witchcraft and Quaker Convincements: Lynn, Massachusetts, 1692," *Quaker History* 84 no. 2 (1995) 89–115; Ian Bostridge, *Witchcraft and its Transformations, c.1650–c.1750* (Oxford: Clarendon Press, 1997); Malcolm Gaskill, *Crime and Mentalities in Early Modern England* (Cambridge: Cambridge University Press, 2000), 96–105.

cans, Dissenters, Deists, and Theists about whether God continued to allow miracles. To deny the continued existence of the invisible world was tantamount to atheism said one side. To believing in it was a mark of irrationality, credulity, or enthusiasm said the other.

We can see how these discourses played out in the case of the possession of the young Lancastrian Richard Dugdale, better known as the Surrey Demoniac, who in 1689–1690 vomited nails and stones in his fits.[7] Two notable Dissenters, Thomas Jollie and John Carrington, were involved in the dispossession and published an account of their success in 1697. Anglican clergyman Zachary Taylor, a splenetic critic of Catholics and Dissenters, responded with *Popery, Superstition, Ignorance and Knavery* (1698–1699), accusing Dissenters of "whoring," "forgeries," and "superstition." The influential Anglican clergyman, Francis Hutchinson, in his *Historical Essay Concerning Witchcraft* (1720), referred to the "folly" and "vanity" of the Dissenters involved in the case. Dugdale's father had sought out Anglican clergy but found them unresponsive to the issue, so he went to the Dissenters. "Five or six of their Ministers were there at a Time," Hutchinson noted, continuing with smug satisfaction that, "all the Country flock'd in to see and hear them. At first they admired them; but after some Time, they began to make themselves merry with them."[8]

By the 1720s, the Quakers had distanced themselves from the miraculous spiritual milieu their founder had promoted—and on which his popular reputation was built, and retired from the public if not the private debate about ghosts.[9] Other well established dissenting groups had also, by and large, become publicly silent on the matter of the invisible world. Then Methodism emerged, breathing new life into the cinders of spiritual and providential discourse. The old accusations thrown at dissenting religion were dusted off, namely that enthusiasm was a front for sexual licentiousness

---

7. Henry D. Rack, "Doctors, Demons and Early Methodist Healing," in William J. Sheils, ed. *The Church and Healing* (Oxford: Basil Blackwell, 1982), 137–52; Dewey D. Wallace, *Shapers of English Calvinism, 1660–1714: Variety, Persistence, and Transformation* (Oxford: Oxford University Press, 2011), 40.

8. Francis Hutchinson, *An Historical Essay Concerning Witchcraft*, 2nd ed. (London, 1720), 159. On Hutchinson's skeptical views with regard to the invisible world see Andrew Sneddon, *Witchcraft and Whigs: The Life of Bishop Francis Hutchinson, 1660–1739* (Manchester: Manchester University Press, 2008), 77–129.

9. Rosemary Moore, "Late Seventeenth-Century Quakerism and the Miraculous: A New Look at George Fox's 'Book of Miracles,'" in Kate Cooper and Jeremy Gregory, eds. *Signs, Wonders, Miracles: Representations of Divine Power in the Life of the Church* (Woodbridge: Boydell, 2005), 342–43; Sasha Handley, *Visions of an Unseen World: Ghost Beliefs and Ghost Stories in Eighteenth-Century England* (London: Pickering & Chatto, 2007), 172–74.

and wild superstition. This is illustrated by Charles Macklin's 1746 comedy, *A Will and No Will, Or a Bone for the Lawyers*, in which the sexually incontinent Widow Bumper, with fifteenth children and another on the way, stated:

> You must know, Uncle, I am greatly addicted to be afraid of Spirits, Ghosts, Witches, and Fairies, and so to prevent terrifying Dreams and Apparitions, *I took a Religious Gentleman, a very good Man to bed with me—an Itinerant Methodist, one Doctor Preach Field.*
>
> *Skin.*[uncle] Doctor Preach Field. I have heard of him.
>
> Widow Bumper: O he's a very good man, Uncle, I assure you, and very full of the Spirit.[10]

When not being denounced as crypto-Catholics, critics likened this new outburst of enthusiasm to the sexual, political, and religious chaos that inspired various radical sects during the Civil War. Methodists were rabble rousers threatening social order as well as Protestant orthodoxy, preying on the poor, weak, and mentally ill for their own political ends.[11] Methodism, with its appeal to the emotions and the invisible world was quickly pathologized as a mania by the nascent psychiatric profession. Claims that the mad houses were full of Methodists were wide of the truth but effective propaganda. The pioneering insanity doctor James Monro Sr., did battle with Wesley and Whitefield over the incarceration of Methodists in Bethlem hospital. What Monro and others diagnosed and treated as forms of insanity, Wesley and Whitefield believed were instances of divine or diabolic intercession, arguing that the treatment required was spiritual succour not vomits and purges.[12]

All the ingredients of these attacks on Methodism were represented in Hogarth's famous work *Credulity, Superstition, and Fanaticism* (1762). This popular engraving was a version of an unpublished double satire of Methodism and art connoisseurship entitled *Enthusiasm Delineated* that Hogarth had produced two years earlier.[13] The latter, inspired by George

---

10. Charles Macklin, *A Will and No Will, Or a Bone for the Lawyers* (London, 1746).

11. See, for example, David Hempton, *Methodism: Empire of the Spirit* (New Haven: Yale University Press, 2005), 32–54.

12. Jonathan Andrews and Andrew Scull, *Undertaker of the Mind: John Munro and Mad-Doctoring in Eighteenth-Century England* (Berkeley: University of California Press, 2001), 81–93.

13. See Bernd Krysmanski, "We see a Ghost: Hogarth's Satire on Methodists and Connoisseurs," *The Art Bulletin* 80 no. 2 (1998) 292–310; Jane Shaw, "Mary Toft, Religion and National Memory in Eighteenth-Century England," *Journal of Eighteenth-Century Studies* 32 no. 3 (2009) 321–38; Misty G. Anderson, *Imagining Methodism in*

Whitefield's chapel in Tottenham Court Road, which opened in 1756, depicted a Methodist preacher in full flow with his wig flying off to reveal the tonsure of a Jesuit. A puppet of God (mimicking a depiction of God in a Raphael painting) hangs from one hand and the Devil from the other. A large thermometer with a Methodist's brain for a base gauges the religious and sexual fervour in the chapel. In *Credulity, Superstition, and Fanaticism*, Hogarth reworked the engraving by putting in a heap of references to notorious cases of gullibility and supernatural sensations, most within living memory, some stretching back to the early seventeenth century. So the puppet of God was changed to one of a witch on a broomstick, a woman on the floor is turned into Mary Toft the rabbit woman. The figures of Christ held be three women in the congregation in *Enthusiasm Delineated* are now transformed into figures of the Cock Lane ghost, and the top section of the thermometer now has images representing the same. Perched on top is a figure of the Tedworth Drummer, who was the central actor in the noisy haunting of the house of John Mompesson in the early 1660s. Denounced as a fraud by some at the time, Wesley reported in his *Journal* for 1768 that his eldest brother had discussed the affair with Mompesson's son at Oxford, and that from the evidence he, Wesley, concluded the case was no trick but a diabolic manifestation.[14]

A youth sitting under the lectern now spews pins to represent the notorious Bilson boy possession case of 1620, while a copy of "Whitfield's Journal" lies in a basket at his side along with the accoutrements of a shoeblack. The brain and thermometer now rest on two books entitled "Westley's Sermons" and "Glanvil on witches." John Trusler (1735–1820), the Church of England clergyman and publisher who wrote the first compendious analysis of Hogarth's work in 1768, commented that the inclusion of these two titles was intended "to shew us, that superstition and credulity is the groundwork of fanaticism." A footnote explained that "Westley" is "a leader of a sect, called Methodist."[15] Three large puppets dangle from the pulpit each representing a well-known apparition—"expressive of the people's weakness" explained Trusler. There is the ghost of Julius Caesar, as described in Shakespeare's *Julius Caesar*; the ghost of Mrs Veal, a "true" story, which was made popular by Daniel Defoe in his pamphlet, *A True Relation of the Apparition of One Mrs. Veal* (1706); and another famous ghost story in popular

---

Eighteenth-Century Britain: Enthusiasm, Belief and the Borders of the Self (Baltimore: John Hopkins University Press, 2012), 150–69.

14. Michael Hunter, "New Light on the 'Drummer of Tedworth': Conflicting Narratives of Witchcraft in Restoration England," *Historical Research* 78 (2005) 311–53.

15. John Trusler, *Hogarth Moralized. Being a Complete Edition of Hogarth's Work* (London, 1768), 113.

literature, that of the ghost of George Villiers, whose apparition appeared to prophesy the murder of his son, the notorious Duke of Buckingham.

The Cock Lane haunting was widely held as a beacon of superstitious credulity that reflected badly on all concerned. This included such notable figures as Samuel Johnson.[16] Most of those exhibiting an active interest were firm Anglicans yet most of the criticisms were directed at clergy who had Methodist alignments, though no leading Methodists were directly involved in the case.[17] Still, two of the key clergymen who investigated the affair had sympathies with the movement. One, John Moore, Rector of St Bartholomew the Great, remained an Anglican minister all his life, and the other Thomas Broughton (1712–1777), while being an early supporter of Methodism, likewise remained firmly in the fold of the established church. Horace Walpole was one of the loudest critics in public and private, painting Cock Lane as a Methodist plot, insinuating that its adherents had whipped up three such ghost sensations in Warwickshire to further their popularity.[18] In a 1766 publication he wrote of the Cock Lane ghost that "the Methodists expected such a rich Harvest, (for what might not a rising Church promise itself from such well imagined Nonsense as the Apparition of a Noise?)."[19] He expressed the same sentiments in earlier private correspondence, remarking that the Methodists "were glad to have such a key to the credulity of the mob. Our bishops, who do not discount an imposture, even in the subdivision of their religion, looked mighty wise, and only took care not to say anything silly."[20]

Although it did not attract the same national notoriety as Cock Lane, in the same year a possession case at the Lamb Inn, Bristol, became a touchstone for similar private and public debates about the invisible world,

---

16. See Owen Davies, *The Haunted: A Social History of Ghosts* (Basingstoke: Palgrave, 2007), 125.

17. On the Methodist involvement in the Cock Lane affair see, Handley, *Visions of an Unseen World*, 142–48; Davies, *The Haunted*, 82–83; Travis Glasson, "Missionaries, Methodists, and a Ghost: Philip Quaque in London and Cape Coast, 1756–1816," *Journal of British Studies* 48 no. 1 (2009) 36–40.

18. This may refer in part to the case recorded in Richard Jago, *A Sermon Preach'd at Harbury in Warwickshire, May 4. 1744. On Occasion of a Conversation said to have Pass'd Between one of the Inhabitants, and an Apparition* (Oxford, 1755). See Handley, *Visions of an Unseen World*, 162–64.

19. Horace Walpole, *An Account of the Giants Lately Discovered; In a Letter to a Friend in the Country* (London, 1766), 2.

20. Horace Walpole to Sir Horace Mann, February 25, 1762, in *Letters of Horace Walpole* (London: Richard Bentley, 1843), 1:70; Letter from Horace Walpole to George Montague, February 2, 1762, in *Letters from the Hon. Horace Walpole to George Montagu, Esq.* (London: Rodwell and Martin, 1818), 277–78.

anti-Newtonian philosophy, religious infidelity, Methodism, and credulity. On this occasion much of our knowledge of the case derives from private not printed sources, particularly the diary of the Bristol accountant William Dyer and the narrative account written by his friend the chemist Henry Durbin, which Durbin instructed be published after his death to avoid reinvigorating the abuse he received in the newspapers for his "credulity." Both men were Wesleyan Methodists, and Jonathan Barry's meticulous analysis of the case shows how they wrestled with the veracity and import of the antics of the supposedly bewitched Lamb Inn girls. Their belief in the case ebbed and flowed depending on their empirical assessment of the girls' behaviour, the observable influence of prayer and fasting, and the rough and tumble of the public debate.[21] They struggled in private with the sentiments expressed by Wesley in his *Journal* for 1764 regarding apparition accounts: "How hard it is to keep the middle way! not to believe too little, or too much."[22]

So the portrayal of early Methodism as a dustbin of debunked supernaturalism and old-fashioned providentialism was sketched in part from received and well-worn criticisms of religious enthusiasm, but there is no doubt that early Methodism drew from and appealed to the widespread popular belief in magic, providence, spirits, dream interpretation, and faith healing. Methodism made theology relevant once again to the lives of the poor for whom the preternatural was fundamental to understanding and dealing with the harsh, chaotic world in which they lived.[23] Wesley was well aware of this, but he was also acutely conscious that the movement should reform and not foster various aspects of popular religion as well as culture. So magic was an iniquity however practiced, and the popular resort to cunning-folk and fortune-tellers for cure and comfort had to be strongly condemned, and indeed such people were the target of the Witchcraft Act of 1736. Wesley may have shared the popular belief in witches, furthermore, but Wesley's witches were a different breed to those feared by the common people. Wesley defined witchcraft largely in terms of diabolic possession, a satanic affliction. There is little reference to the figure of the witch in Wesley's comments. He was not interested, it would seem, in the popular concerns and accounts of neighbourhood witches and *maleficium*,

---

21. Jonathan Barry, *Witchcraft and Demonology in South-West England, 1640–1789* (Basingstoke: Palgrave, 2012), 165–206.

22. John Wesley, *An Extract of the Rev. Mr. John Wesley's Journal, from October 29, 1762, to May 25, 1765* (Bristol, 1768), 103.

23. Rack, *Reasonable Enthusiast*, 431–36; John Rule, "Methodism, Popular Beliefs and Village Culture in Cornwall, 1800–1850," in Robert Storch, ed. *Popular Culture and Custom in Nineteenth-Century England* (London: Croom Helm, 1982), 48–70; Davies, "Methodism, the Clergy"; Davies, *Witchcraft, Magic, and Culture*.

of witches inflicting debilitating illnesses, bewitching chickens, overlooking pigs, drying up milk cows, and causing misfortune in the dairy. Yet, such accusations were the substance of the vast majority of witchcraft accusations during and after the witch-trial era.

As Henry D. Rack has explored, Wesley was careful in positioning himself as a "reasonable enthusiast," well exemplified by his damage limitation exercise in the early 1760s with regard to the publicity generated by the prophetic enthusiasm of George Bell.[24] The nuanced but fundamental differences regarding certain aspects of Methodism and popular religion were easily misunderstood or deliberately warped by critical audiences eager for the Methodists to provide rope with which to hang them in the court of public opinion. No wonder, then, that Wesley was cautious about the media in which he chose to promote the preternatural, witchcraft in particular. The astute American Methodist clergyman Abel Stevens (1815–1897) explained in an apologia for Wesley's "credulity" that as "a noteworthy proof of his good sense, they [accounts of the invisible world] seldom or never appear in his standard theological writings, hardly tinge the works which he left for the practical guidance of his people, but are almost invariably given as matters of curiosity and inquiry in his miscellaneous and fugitive writings."[25] So in Wesley's published sermons we find one on "Evil Angels" in which he explored how they ranged abroad—"we know that Satan and all his angels are continually warring against us, and watching over every child of man," a theme he continued in another sermon on "Wandering Thoughts," but there is nothing in the sermons on witchcraft and ghosts.[26] The invisible world was almost exclusively restricted to Wesley's *Journal* and the *Arminian Magazine*, and it is from these sources that the persona of Wesley as demonologist has been drawn.

Wesley's *Journal* may be a frustrating source in terms of understanding Wesley's inner spiritual life and theology, but it is a fascinating cultural document. More than any other Methodist work it helped shape the public perception, critical and sympathetic, of early Methodism, and provides the basis of any social history of the movement. Its publication history is

---

24. Kenneth G. C. Newport and Gareth Lloyd, "George Bell and Early Methodist Enthusiasm: A New Manuscript Source from the Manchester Archives," *BJRULM* (1998) 89–101; Kenneth Newport, "George Bell: Prophet and Enthusiast," *MH* 35 no. 2 (1997) 95–105. On Methodist prophetic culture more generally, see Kenneth G. C. Newport, *Apocalypse and Millennium: Studies in Biblical Eisegesis* (Cambridge: Cambridge University Press, 2008), 91–118.

25. Abel Stevens, *The History of the Religious Movement of the Eighteenth Century called Methodism* (New York: Carleton & Porter, 1859), 2:397–98.

26. John Emory, ed., *The Works of the Reverend John Wesley* (New York: Waugh & Mason, 1835), 2:142.

revealing in itself, its cultural significance exemplified by the use of the passages regarding witchcraft and apparitions. While over the last two centuries it has often been read as a single volume collection, sometimes abridged, the *Journal* was not a diary of private reflection published as a single defining account after the author's death. It was, in fact, published in twenty-one cheap pamphlet instalments produced every four years on average between 1740 and 1791, each bearing the title *An Extract of the Rev. Mr. John Wesley's Journal*.[27] It was inspired by a familiar literary religious genre of published letters and godly lives, and was intended as a vehicle for cementing and promoting the identity of a growing *national* community, and as a means of communicating with it in a familiar as well as a didactic way. Wesley expended much time and effort editing the journal extracts for publication, so his references to witchcraft, apparitions, and other manifestations of the invisible world were undoubtedly included to serve a purpose. Attention to the chronology is important. Wesley had referred very briefly to witchcraft in entries for 1751 and 1764, but the first explicit defence of its reality and iniquity appeared in his *Journal* dated 1768, which was first published in 1774; so, over thirty years after the first volume was published, and at a time when the criticism of Methodist credulity had long been articulated.

In *Credulity, Superstition, and Fanaticism* the pin-spewing shoeblack's basket stands upon a book entitled "Demonology by K. James 1st," which, Trusler explained, was "a proof that these idle notions existed as well among the great and learned, as among the poor and illiterate."[28] This gets to the core of a fundamental intellectual chasm between Wesley and his critics. For Wesley, apart from the Bible, there was no greater evidence for the supernatural than the weight of credible testimony and venerable authority. History could not be re-written, and the opinions of the great minds of the past were not to be dismissed, excused, or reinterpreted lightly. As he wrote in his *Journal*, with regard to witchcraft, "I have sometimes been inclined to wonder, at the pert, saucy, indecent manner, wherein some of those trample, upon men far wiser than themselves: At their speaking so dogmatically against what not only the whole world, Heathen and Christian, believed in all past ages, but thousands, learned as well as unlearned, firmly believe at this day." That said, his empiricism required him to weigh the quality of the

---

27. See Frank Baker, "The Birth of John Wesley's Journal," *MH* 8 (1970) 25–32; Michael Mascuch, "John Wesley, Superstar: Periodicity, Celebrity, and the Sensibility of Methodist Society in Wesley's Journal (1740–1791)," in Rudolf Dekker, ed. *Egodocuments and History: Autobiographical Writing in its Social Context since the Middle Ages* (Rotterdam: Verloren, 2002), 137–61.

28. Trusler, *Hogarth Moralized*, 115.

evidence before him, and to question the presentation and analysis of it.[29] Each instance or relation had to be judged individually on its worthiness as testimony. This is evident in Wesley's comments on one of his much-thumbed late-seventeenth century defenses of the invisible world, Richard Baxter's *The Certainty of the Worlds of Spirits* (1691). Wesley admired much of Baxter's theology and works, but was not going to relax his empirical approach to Baxter's evidence. In the *Journal* for 1764 he wrote: "Mon. 10, and the three following days, I visited Canterbury, Dover, and Sandwich, and returned to London on Friday, the 14th. In the machine I read Mr. Baxter's book upon apparitions: it contains several well-attested accounts; but there are some which I cannot subscribe to."[30]

Wesley has often been written about as the heir or defender of Joseph Glanvill (1636–1680), and even described as an "admirer" by one historian.[31] He was certainly very familiar with Glanvill's work, particularly the posthumously published *Sadducismus Triumphatus, or Full and Plain Evidence Concerning Witches and Apparitions* (1681), which grew from an earlier work entitled *Philosophical Considerations Touching the Being of Witches and Witchcraft* (1666). But in his printed comments, he was not exactly fulsome in his praise. In his first published opinion on witchcraft, in the *Journal* for 1751, he wrote: "We rode to Camelford. In the way I read Mr. Glanvill's Relations of Witchcraft. I wish the facts had had a more judicious relater; one who would not have given a fair pretence for denying the whole, by his awkward manner of accounting for some of the circumstances."[32] In 1769 he was immersed in Glanvill again, and had not changed his opinion:

> At my leisure minutes yesterday and to-day, I read Mr. Glanvill's Sadducismus Triumphatus. But some of his relations I cannot receive; and much less his way of accounting for them. All his talk of Aerial and Astral Spirits, I take to be stark nonsense. Indeed, supposing the facts true, I wonder a man of sense should

---

29. On Wesley's empiricism see Frederick Dreyer, "Faith and Experience in the Thoughts of John Wesley," *American Historical Review* 88 no. 1 (1983) 12–30, esp. 23–24; Rack, *Reasonable Enthusiast*, 384–88.

30. John Wesley, *An Extract from the Rev. Mr. John Wesley's Journal, From October 29, 1762, to May 25, 1765* (Bristol, 1768), 103.

31. Walter Stephens, "Strategies of Interspecies Communication, 1100–2000," in Joad Raymond and Lauren Kassell, eds. *Conversations with Angels: Essays Towards a History of Spiritual Communication, 1100–1700* (Basingstoke: Palgrave, 2011), 40.

32. John Wesley, *An Extract from the Rev. Mr. John Wesley's Journal, from July 20, 1749, to October 30, 1751* (London, 1756), 104–5.

attempt to account for them at all. For who can explain the things of the invisible world, but the inhabitants of it?[33]

Wesley bridled at the presumptuousness that humans could or should seek to explain everything in nature. "I endeavour throughout not to account for things," he wrote in *A Survey of the Wisdom of God* (1763), "but only to describe them. I undertake barely to set down what appears in nature; not the cause of those appearances."[34] Glanvill, by contrast, while sharing the hatred of atheism born of materialism, and also the bottom line that denying witchcraft was giving up God, criticized the "superficial" enquiries of religious dogmatists (which could be fairly applied to Wesley in this respect). As a founding member of the Royal Society, Glanvill promoted the scientific principle of confirming or proving the existence of the invisible world through not only the quality of testimony, but the application of the scientific method. He wrote of "resolving natural Phanenomena," while cautioning, "we can only assign the probable *causes*, shewing how things *may be* not presuming how they *are*."[35] In short, Glanvill speculated about the invisible world and Wesley did not.

As already mentioned, Wesley's first published defense of the reality of witchcraft appeared in his *Journal* for 1768 (published in 1774). It evidently provoked complaints from his brother Charles. In a letter dated May 6, 1774, John Wesley replied to him: "I have no doubt of the substance, both of Glanvil's and Cotton Mather's narratives. Therefore, in this point, you that are otherwise minded, bear with me. *Veniam petimusque damusque vicissim.* Remember, I am, upon full consideration, and seventy years' experience, just as obstinate in my opinion as you are in yours."[36] The extent and nature of Wesley's everyday discourse on witchcraft is unknown, though one assumes he was frequently broached regarding the subject on his many travels. We get a glimpse of the tenor of such conversations from an account of a Dublin dinner party attended in 1787 by the learned Methodist critic William Hales the Rector of Killesandra, Ireland, Thomas Coke (then President of the Irish Methodist Church), several assistant Methodist preachers, and member of the Dublin Society. According to Hale's recollection:

33. John Wesley, *An Extract from the Rev. Mr. John Wesley's Journal, from May 14, 1768, to Sept 1, 1770* (London, 1790), 48.

34. John Wesley, *A Survey of the Wisdom of God in the Creation: or a Compendium of Natural Philosophy*, 3 vols. (Bristol, 1763), 1: v.

35. Joseph Glanvil, *A Blow at Modern Sadducism* (London, 1688), 15.

36. John Wesley to Charles Wesley, May 6, 1774, *LJWT*, 6:82. Printed also in the *Wesleyan-Methodist Magazine* 1 2 4th Series (1845) 991; Luke Tyerman, *Life and Times of the Rev. John Wesley, M.A., Founder of the Methodists* (London: Hodder & Stoughton, 1871), 3:171.

> The conversation during dinner, happening to turn on the subject of Witchcraft, I asked Mr. Wesley whether he had read, and if so, what he thought of Bishop Hutchinson's book upon Witches?—After some pause, finding that he made no answer, I repeated the question; on which he declared, that Bishop Hutchinson and the whole bench of Bishops together, could not invalidate the reality of witchcraft.[37]

To prove his point he typically referred not to an instance of *maleficium* but to a case of possible possession in Northern England concerning a man who confessed that he and two of his brothers had committed murder. The three were executed but the supposed victim reappeared, it transpiring that he had fled to France for non-payment of debts. Wesley asked Hales, "was that not plain evidence of witchcraft or demoniacal possession?" "I rather ascribed it to phrenzy or madness," wrote Hales. One of the preachers chipped in with a case of a violent haunting in Dungannon involving a malicious potato-throwing spirit. The conversation then took a familiar turn as to the falsity of Catholic miracles before Wesley looked at his watch and said he had to attend the Liffey-Street Chapel where ministers were gathered to pray over a woman possessed with an evil spirit. Responding to Hale's doubts about their success, Wesley "declared, in a solemn tone of voice, that much might be done in this way by prayer and fasting"—though he clearly had not been fasting himself that day. Still, when he rejoined the party again that evening for tea, he reported that their efforts had not been in vain.

Despite all the brickbats that came his way due to his published and conversational thoughts on the invisible world, Wesley had no intention of keeping quiet for the better reception of his broader theology. The creation of the *Arminian Magazine*, a monthly publication that ran between 1778 and 1797, and which Wesley devised and edited until his death in 1791, provided another vehicle for amplifying the defense of the invisible world. The *Magazine* had a circulation of around 7000 copies a month by 1791, which was more than that contemporary literary institution the *Gentleman's Magazine*. Wesley kept a close control over what his followers published and read, obliging his preachers to promote and sell his publications at every opportunity. As one critic noted in 1795: "There are thousands in this society who will never read anything besides the Bible, and books published by Mr Wesley."[38]

---

37. William Hales, *Methodism Inspected, Part II* (1805). Extract reprinted in *The Orthodox Churchman's Magazine and Review* 10 (1806) 143–44.

38. Cited in David W Bebbington, *Evangelicalism in Modern Britain: A History from the 1730s to 1980s* (London: Routledge, 1989), 68.

John Hampson Jr., a one-time Methodist preacher who disassociated himself from the movement in 1784, and became a Church of England clergyman, commented in his *Memoirs of the Late Rev. John Wesley*, that to give the *Arminian Magazine* "a just character, were no easy task. It is a strange medley of heterogeneous matter . . . a snug corner is reserved for witches and apparitions."[39] Hales pointedly asked Wesley, "whether such imposing relations of witchcraft and ghosts, might not tend to support the spurious *popish miracles*?"[40]

After Wesley's death, the criticisms were less diplomatically expressed. "Mr. John Wesley was remarkably superstitious this way"; observed an essayist in 1822, "the early volumes of the *Arminian Magazine*, done especially under his own eye, are full of the most appalling, but incredibly-fanciful stories." In his biography of Wesley, Robert Southey referred to these accounts as "so silly, as well as monstrous, that they might have nauseated the coarsest appetite for wonder." [41]Charlotte Brontë almost certainly had the *Arminian Magazine* in mind when one of the two lead female characters in the novel *Shirley*, Caroline Helstone, described a pile of "mad Methodists Magazines" as "full of miracles and apparitions, of preternatural warnings, ominous dreams, and frenzied fanaticism."[42]

The *Magazine* had a much wider cultural reach than the few thousand Wesleyan households that purchased it. Copies were lent to friends and fellow members, read aloud at gatherings, distributed via circulating and chapel libraries. Children were encouraged to read it as part of their education. It was also perused out of casual curiosity by those who had no Methodist sympathies. So the readership must have been in the tens of thousands, and extended across the social strata. During the early nineteenth century, furthermore, some of the stories in Wesley's *Journal* and *Arminian Magazine* were reprinted in a popular compilation of preternatural phenomena, *News from the Invisible World*, produced by the former Cornish itinerant Wesleyan preacher John Tregortha. He settled down in the Midlands town of Burslem in 1790 where he kept a circulating library and churned out cheap

---

39. John Sampson, *Memoirs of the Late Rev. John Wesley, A.M. With a Review of his Life and Writings*, 3 vols. (Sunderland, 1791), 3:154. On Sampson see Henry D. Rack, "Wesley Portrayed: Character and Criticism in Some Early Biographies," *MH* 43 no. 2 (2005) 90–114.

40. See Davies, "Methodism, the Clergy."

41. "Ghosts," *The Recreative Review* 3 (1822) 439; Robert Southey, *The Life of Wesley: And the Rise and Progress of Methodism* (London: n.p.: 1820), 2:413. See also William Howells, "Cambrian Superstitions," *Westminster Review* 17 (1832) 402.

42. See Lee A. Talley, "Jane Eyre's Little-Known Debt to the Methodist Magazine," *Brontë Studies* 33 (2008) 109–19.

tracts. Tregortha's stated aim in gathering numerous accounts of prophetic dreams and apparitions from "respectable" but deceased authors, was for the "support of our faith, and practice."[43] The Wesleyan content and purpose of the publication led the Quaker writer and chronicler William Howitt to mistakenly attribute authorship of *News from the Invisible World* to Wesley.[44]

A recent analysis of the preternatural content of the *Arminian Magazine* concluded that the vast majority of relations concerned dreams (mostly of Christ, Hell, and Judgement Day), divine communications, and the seeing and hearing of spiritual beings. There were a few cases of miraculous healing and confrontations with the demonic.[45] Not surprisingly extracts from Baxter's *The Certainty of the Worlds of Spirits* were given an airing, as was Glanvill's account of the Tedworth Drummer, and the first substantive account of the now well-known account of the noisy haunting of the Wesleys' Epworth home in 1716–17. Let us focus, though, on the several accounts of witchcraft found in the "snug corner" of the *Arminian Magazine*. Considering his penchant for seventeenth century proofs, there was a huge amount of material from which to draw upon. What exactly did Wesley chose to include? What did he choose to ignore?

In 1782 Wesley included an account of the "Devil of Mascon," which had first been published in French in 1656, with an English edition appearing two years later with a preface by the philosopher Robert Boyle.[46] The *Arminian Magazine*'s reprint of this was prefaced with the quote that began this chapter—and the sentence that followed, to wit, that the truth of witchcraft "was in the last Century acknowledge by all Europe." To further support this statement, in 1785 the *Magazine* reprinted an account taken from *Saducismus Triumphatus* of the 1669 Mora witch trials in Lutheran Sweden, relating how numerous children accused adults of riding them to witches sabbats. Then in 1787 there was an account of the confession of Alice Huson at the York Assizes (1664), from Matthew Hale's *A Collection of Modern Relations of Matter of Fact Concerning Witches & Witchcraft* (1693).[47] The

43. Owen Davies, *Ghosts: A Social History* (London: Pickering & Chatto, 2010), 2: xiii–xiv.

44. William Howitt, *The Rural Life of England* (London: n.p., 1838), 2:220.

45. See Liam Iwig-O'Byrne, "How Methodists were Made: The *Arminian Magazine* and Spiritual Transformation in the Transatlantic World, 1778–1803" (PhD dissertation, University of Texas at Arlington, 2008), 76–92. See also, Richard Bell, "'Our people die well': Deathbed Scenes in John Wesley's Arminian magazine," *Mortality* 10 no. 3 (2005) 210–23.

46. François Perrault, *The Devill of Mascon, Or, A True Relation of the Chiefe Things which an Unclean Spirit did* (Oxford, 1658).

47. Matthew Hale's *A Collection of Modern Relations of Matter of Fact Concerning Witches & Witchcraft* (London, 1693), 58–59.

young daughter of the Corbet family, of Burton Agnes, fell inexplicably ill. The girl claimed she was bewitched, but her parents were not persuaded. She was treated for natural ailments by physicians but to no avail. Only after four years did the parents come round to the conviction that witchcraft was responsible. Alice Huson and Doll Bilby stood trial for the crime. Bilby was found not guilty, while Huson was condemned but later reprieved. The Corbet's journey from skepticism to belief after exhausting all other avenues appealed to Wesley's empiricism, and Huson's voluntary confession that she had made a pact with the Devil was worthy evidence of Satanic interference. Apart from the Mascon account these cases were printed without any editorial commentary. Abel Stevens approved: "he seldom gives a direct opinion of the supposed preternatural cases which he so often records ... they are presented with circumstantial particularity as the data for an opinion on the part of others."[48]

One of the most telling relations in the *Arminian Magazine* appeared in 1786 and concerned an account of the possession of Mary Glover, a notorious case that spiralled into a sensational religious and medical conflict. In the spring of 1602 Mary Glover, a fourteen-year-old London servant girl began to exhibit the symptoms of possession. Friends and neighbours suspected she had been bewitched by an elderly neighbour named Elizabeth Jackson. Multitudes flocked to see Glover's fits. The Bishop of London, Richard Bancroft, saw trouble in the oxygen given to the case, and so when Jackson was tried for witchcraft he appointed two respected physicians Edward Jorden and John Argent to assess Glover's condition. They duly testified that Glover suffered from natural causes. Although still found guilty, Jackson was soon released, perhaps due to Bancroft's influence. Glover's torments continued.

In December 1602, Six puritan ministers, including Lewes Hughes, curate of the significant London parish of Great St Helen's, Bishopsgate, in which Glover lived, "performed that good work of prayer, fasting, and supplication" to expel the devil. Hughes was holding Glover when the Devil apparently fled her body. This result he reported to Bancroft, who was outraged not only that no permission had been given to the ministers, who were, therefore, guilty of illegal conventicle, but that the Church had been dragged further into this popular London sensation. Only the month before, Bancroft had sanctioned the Oxford Professor Thomas Holland to preach at Paul's Cross, with a message denouncing those who sought "to show the truth of religion by casting out devils." Indeed, decades later Hughes recalled that, at the time, Bancroft had called him a "Rascall and varlot," and

---

48. Stevens, *The History of the Religious Movement*, 397.

he and his fellow minsters "Devill finders, Devill puffers, and Devill prayers, and such as could start a devil in a lane, as soone as an hare in Waltham Forrest."[49] Hughes was imprisoned and on gaining his freedom he left for Bermuda to set up a dissenting church.[50]

The *Arminian Magazine*'s account was based solely on Hughes's version of events published in the early 1640s when he was back in England pursuing his attacks against the Bishops of the Church of England—or Antichrists as he called them. Wesley would have seen Hughes in a sympathetic light, and the *Arminian Magazine* commentary on the case, no doubt written by Wesley, concluded:

> Seeing he [Hughes] has attested it as an affair in which five other Ministers, together with Dr. *Bencroft*, Lord Chief Justice *Anderson* and Sir *George Crook*, Recorder of *London*, were concerned; and seeing it was publicly tried at the Old Bailey, and the account published while the parties concerned were still living; is it not far more absurd to *doubt* the truth of it, than to *believe* it?[51]

As the details of the case given above show, though, Wesley's critical faculties were little in operation in writing this statement, which seemed to suggest that Bancroft was a fellow believer in the case. Wesley made no reference to the malign powers or otherwise of Elizabeth Jackson. He was clearly convinced of the possession but was he convinced of the witch's guilt and the appropriateness of her prosecution?

The only contemporary account of witchcraft included in the *Arminian Magazine* concerned the bewitchment and possession of a young woman of Cannoby (Canonbie) in Dumfries, a few miles from the English border. It was a parish described in 1855 by working-class autobiographer James Dawson Burn as one of "the most noted places for witches and fairies that I remember, and where they lingered longest in the face of civilization."[52] On November 3, 1781, a young woman of Canonbie dreamed that a local

---

49. Lewes Hughes, *Certaine Grievances, or the Errours of the Service-Booke Plainely Layd Open* (London, 1641), 15.

50. Details of the case are discussed in Michael MacDonald, ed. *Witchcraft and Hysteria in Elizabethan London: Edward Jorden and the Mary Glover Case* (London: Routledge, 1991); Thomas Freeman, "Demons, Deviance and Defiance: John Darrell and the Politics of Exorcism in Late Elizabethan England," in Peter Lake and Michael C. Questier, eds. *Conformity and Orthodoxy in the English Church, c. 1560–1660* (Woodbridge: Boydell, 2000), 56–61; Kathleen R. Sands, *Demon Possession in Elizabethan England* (Westport: Praeger, 2004), 175–91.

51. "Some Account of M. Jackson's Witchcraft," *AM* 9 (1786) 265.

52. James Dawson Burn, *The Autobiography of a Beggar Boy* (London: William Tweedie, 1855), 33.

woman commonly thought to be a witch was to obtain power over her for a period of twenty weeks, after which she would either die or be freed from her possession. The next day the woman began to experience fits and the usual symptoms of the possessed. At the expiration of the twenty weeks the symptoms ceased and "she then desired thanks to be returned to Almighty God for her deliverance." A letter describing the case, written by one who had been an eye and ear witness, was sent to the *Dumfries Weekly Journal* and passed on to Wesley. The facts of the matter were apparently investigated before being included in the *Arminian Magazine*. There was no need for further editorial commentary as the views of the letter writer, although nowhere stated to be a Methodist, accorded perfectly with Wesley's. "What is very remarkable," said the author, is that "some who formerly denied the existence of Witches, were that night fully convinced of their mistake, and I believe still continue so."[53]

The *Arminian Magazine* studiously avoided well-reported contemporary cases of witchcraft. Wesley had no wish to be tainted by association with popular prejudice or popular justice against suspected witches, so several instances of witch swimming reported in the press, such as that at Tring in 1751, which resulted in one of the ring-leaders being hanged, another at Burton Overy, Leicestershire, in 1760, and a further case of swimming at Aston, Leicestershire, in 1776, went unremarked.[54] Unattributed newspaper reports, furthermore, did not pass Wesley's empirical standards. Better to stick to venerable accounts verified by learned individuals.

In 1788 the temperature raised by the *Arminian Magazine* was heightened by a sensational possession case in Somerset. George Lukins of the village of Yatton, Somerset, had exhibited the signs of possession on and off for nearly twenty years, but in May 1788 a former neighbour requested the evangelical Joseph Easterbrook, vicar of Temple Church, Bristol, to say prayers over the afflicted man. Easterbrook obliged, requesting that Lukins be brought to Bristol. Here he was visited by various Anglican and Dissenting clergymen. When it came to participating in collective prayer over Lukins, though, the case became a decidedly Wesleyan Methodist affair. "I applied to such of the clergy of the established church . . . as I conceived to be the most cordial in the belief in supernatural influences," Easterbrook wrote, "but though they acknowledged it as their opinion, that his was a supernatural affliction, I could not prevail upon them to join with me, in this attempt to relieve him."[55] The six men who eventually joined Easterbrook

53. John Wesley, ed., *AM* 6 (1783) 100–102, 153–56.

54. See Davies, *Witchcraft, Magic, and Culture*, 96–97.

55. Joseph Easterbrook, *An Appeal to the Public Respecting George Lukins* (Bristol, 1788), 7. The case has been meticulously studied in Barry, *Witchcraft and Demonology*, 206–56.

were Thomas McGeary, headmaster of the Wesleyan Kingswood School and five Wesleyan ministers on the Bristol circuit. The critics had a field day in the press, and the Lukins affair became another Cock Lane remembered for decades as an example of Methodist credulity and opportunism.[56]

Both the Lukins affair and the *Arminian Magazine* caused a boom in public debates about the invisible world. Methodist doctrine was also a frequent topic for London's debating societies, and Methodists were keen participants.[57] While before 1788 there are only two recorded debates about apparitions, between 1789 and 1799 there were thirty-three.[58] In 1788, the Capel-Court Debating Society, Bartholomew Lane, for instance, held three successive Monday meetings on the question, "Is the Rev. Mr. Wesley censurable for publicly maintaining the Existence of Witches, the Doctrine of Apparitions, and Demoniac Possessions?" The Society's debates apparently attracted those of a Radical bent. The advertisement for the second meeting noted that a false report had been spread that Wesley was the author of the question under debate and he was to attend to rebut the proposition. The proprietors of Capel-Court distanced themselves from the rumours, and opined "Whether Mr. Wesley will speak to this question time alone can determine." The follow week they reported that the second debate had inspired "a wonderful assemblage of Wit, Ingenuity, and Metaphysical Disquisition," with a clergyman concluding at the end that "it would be unfair to condemn Mr. Wesley unheard." An adjournment was then agreed upon and apparently warmly supported by several of Wesley's friends in attendance who agreed to try and coax Wesley to honour the final debate. Wesley did not oblige, but the Society's organizers reported that those who attended were "numerous, brilliant, and respectable: Several characters of the first eminence among the Clergy and Laity honoured and assisted a Debate with their abilities, which after three evening's investigation, terminated in Mr. Wesley's favour."[59] A fascinating outcome suggesting that Wesley's defence of the invisible world was by no means the isolated conviction of a cranky aging enthusiast.

Wesley was no public advocate of the witch trials—of the campaign to exterminate those pitiful folk who supposedly succumbed to the Devil's blandishments and intimidation; his was a battle cry against the Devil

---

56. See, for example, *The London Magazine* 2 (1820) 193; *The Church Magazine* 1 (1839) 178.

57. Mary Thale, "Deists, Papists and Methodists at London Debating Societies, 1749–1799," *History* 86 (2001) 328–47; Donna T. Andrew, ed. *London Debating Societies, 1776–1799* (London: London Record Society, 1994).

58. Thale, "Deists, Papists and Methodists," 334; Davies, *The Haunted*, 128.

59. *World*, July 14, July 21, and July 28, 1788.

himself. He extracted and abstracted witches from the received concept of witchcraft better to defend and simplify his war against the continued satanic threat. But in clinging to the language of witchcraft he only served to isolate himself publicly from the broader and well-engrained institutional acceptance of Satanic influence, which pervaded the rhetoric, rubric, and testimony of criminality and British jurisprudence in the Enlightenment period.[60]

With the death of Wesley the temperature of the Methodist brain began to drop. In 1798 the *Arminian Magazine* was re-titled the *Methodist Magazine*. Once out of Wesley's hands the "snug corner" dedicated to the invisible world was closed down, and under the editorship of Joseph Benson between 1803 and 1821 the *Magazine* distanced itself more generally from Wesley's preoccupations, including the promotion of female preachers and reports of exciting revival meetings: in short it became a more sober, conservative, rationalist, Nonconformist publication reflecting the general shift of Methodism away from the providential and evangelical to the institutional.[61] References to witchcraft were concerned strictly with Biblical reflection and with the "heathenish" beliefs encountered overseas by Methodist missionaries. The invisible world was a matter for the pagan "other": witchcraft *belief* and not *witchcraft* was now the problem.[62] So, when the young Wesleyan missionary William Binnington Boyce reported back from South Africa in 1831, he described having to deal not only with the murder of a suspected witch, justified by the locals "on the plea of ancient usage," but also native suspicions that the missionaries had the power to bewitch. "Superstition results as naturally from Atheism, as from the most corrupted systems of Paganism," he concluded.[63]

60. See Owen Davies, "Talk of the Devil: Crime and Satanic Inspiration in Eighteenth-Century England," (2007), http://www.academia.edu/224811/Talk_of_the_Devil_Crime_and_Satanic_Inspiration_in_Eighteenth-Century_England. Erik Midelfort has observed the development of a similar discourse on "witchcraft without witches" in eighteenth-century Germany. See, Erik Midelfort, *Exorcism and Enlightenment: Johann Joseph Gassner and the Demons of Eighteenth-Century Germany* (New Haven: Yale University Press, 2005).

61. See Josef L. Altholz, *The Religious Press in Britain, 1760–1900* (New York: Greenwood, 1989); Jonathan R. Topham, "The *Wesleyan-Methodist Magazine* and Religious Monthlies in Early Nineteenth-Century Britain," in Geoffrey Cantor et al., *Science in the Nineteenth-Century Periodical: Reading the Magazine of Nature* (Cambridge: Cambridge University Press, 2004), 67–91; Louis Billington, "The Religious Periodical and Newspaper Press, 1760–1870," in Michael Harris and Alan Lee, eds. *The Press in English Society from the Seventeenth to Nineteenth Centuries* (Rutherford: Fairleigh Dickinson University Press,1986), esp. 115–19.

62. See Owen Davies, *Paganism: A Very Short Introduction* (Oxford: Oxford University Press, 2011), 65–83.

63. *Wesleyan-Methodist Magazine* 10 3rd Series (1831) 860–62.

In 1845 the *Arminian Magazine*, renamed the *Wesleyan-Methodist Magazine*, included a brief note by Thomas Marriott, once dubbed the "Methodist antiquary" for his accumulation of works and manuscripts on the history of Methodism, compiling everything Wesley said on witchcraft in his published works. The article only stretched to two pages in all. There was no commentary other than that Samuel Wesley opposed his views on the subject. Two further articles appeared over the next few years, though, that attacked such beliefs without mentioning Wesley's name. In 1847 it printed an article on the "Sources of Superstition" by the Independent minister, Rev. James Godkin, who was a missionary in Ulster. Godkin held that "credulity has always fostered superstition" and that while both Protestants and Catholics were prone to it and the marvellous stories that fed it, the "former generally condemn and resist them, while by the latter they are generally sanctioned and fostered." Four years later, another piece "On the history of witchcraft" described how the witch trials of the seventeenth century were "a sort of infectious disease of the intelligence—a plague-spot of the age," and once the absurdity of the accusations became clear to judges and juries witchcraft ceased to exist.[64] The message was clear: mainstream Methodism had purged itself of Wesley's preternatural views. But stray from the orthodox organs of the churches and theologians, and Wesley's invisible world reveals itself here and there in the grassroots during the early nineteenth century.

Between 1819 and 1820 two cases of witch-induced possession excited the people of south Devon. The first concerned the four daughters of a grocer and lay preacher named John Kennard. The girls, like most of the supposedly possessed, were aged between seven and sixteen, and exhibited such characteristic symptoms as fits, running up walls, superhuman strength, moving objects, and vomiting pins. Blame was placed upon an old woman who had an altercation with one of the girls. The case was reported in the local press, but does not seem to have been broadcast more widely by national newspapers. This was done by the Wesleyan Methodist preacher John Heaton.[65]

64. Thomas Marriott, "The Rev. John Wesley on Apparitions and Witchcraft," *Wesleyan-Methodist Magazine* 1, 2 4th Series (1845) 989–91; *Wesleyan-Methodist Magazine* 3 4th Series (1847) 397–400; *Wesleyan-Methodist Magazine* 7 4th Series (1851) 37.

65. James Heaton, *The Demon Expelled: Or, The Influence of Satan, and the Power of Christ, displayed in the Extraordinary Affliction, and Gracious Relief of a Boy* (Plymouth Dock: n.p., 1820); Idem., *The Extraordinary Affliction and Gracious Relief of a Little Boy* (Plymouth: n.p., 1822); Idem., *Farther Observations on Demoniac Possession, and Animadversions on Some of the Curious Arts of Superstition, &c.* (Frome: n.p., 1822). The case has been skilfully analysed in Jason Semmens, "'I will not go to the Devil for a Cure': Witchcraft, Demonic Possession, and Spiritual Healing in Nineteenth-Century

In his late thirties, Heaton (1782–1862), the son of Methodists, had, from around 1810, been a minister on the Truro circuit in Cornwall, becoming a preacher at the Ker Street chapel in Plymouth Dock in 1818, a community that supported a range of Nonconformist congregations. He was Wesleyan to the bone, admiring the founder's public defence of the reality of witchcraft and the invisible world. "Those who have said he was *credulous*," Heaton wrote, "have never yet shown a reason why he should not give proportionate credence to what he knew to be sterling evidence." There were no better collective proofs than the word of God, one's own eyes, and the "faithful testimony of men of sound judgment and unimpeachable veracity."[66]

After service at Windmill-Hill Chapel on the February 29, 1820, Heaton was approached by a neighbour named John Lose, who told him that his stepson John Evens exhibited all the signs of demonic possession—convulsions, barking like a dog, swearing, suicide attempts, and "a furious antipathy to anything sacred." It is likely that Evens was influenced by hearing of the Kennard case. The contagious effect of possession is well documented. John Kennard, who was on the District Committee of the Plymouth Dock Methodist Auxiliary Missionary Society, came to see Evens, telling his family and assembled witnesses that the boy was clearly troubled with the same satanic malady as his daughters. Heaton thought Evens suffered from occasional epilepsy, but this was merely an effect of his possession and not the cause. Medical men could not cure him, and so Heaton began to attend the boy on a daily basis. On March 22nd, a concerted attempt to dispel the demon by prayer was apparently successful. But the symptoms commenced again soon afterwards. A second demon expelling was attempted on April 19th. Those who aided Heaton in his prayers over the boy included Thomas Robinson a Wesleyan Methodist minister attached to the Ebenezer Chapel, Eastlake Street, Plymouth; William Coath, a rope manufacturer associated with the Wesleyan Methodist Chapel, Gloucester Street, Plymouth; John Rendle of Polperro, a cordwainer and notably active Wesleyan lay preacher living in Bideford at the time; Thomas Sibly, who was possibly one and the same as the Thomas Sibly who was a geometry teacher at Kingswood Methodist School in 1833 and later Headmaster of the Wesleyan College, Taunton; Thomas May, who was on the District Committee of the Plymouth

---

Devon," *Journal for the Academic Study of Magic* 2 (2004) 132–55; Jason Semmens, "The Dock Dæmoniac: Or, A Study of Possession, Dissent, and Healing in Early Nineteenth Century Plymouth" (Master's thesis, Exeter University, 2001).

66. Heaton, *The Extraordinary Affliction*, 126–27.

Dock Methodist Auxiliary Missionary Society; and William Almond, a baker who paid subscription to the Plymouth Dock circuit.[67]

Evens said he was "overlooked" and described the witch responsible; "in several things, he imitated her exactly," Heaton observed. But Heaton's interpretation of this attempt to confirm the guilt of a suspected witch before a community of believers is highly significant, for he articulates what I think is Wesley's position with regard to witches. Evens "asserting that he was bewitched, is not a sufficient proof of the fact: and it would be cruel to criminate a poor old woman without substantial evidence of guilt," wrote Heaton. "If it were true, that a wicked human being had employed evil arts to afflict him, that injury could not have been inflicted but by the agency of an evil spirit; therefore, to this great cause of the mischief our attention should be chiefly directed."[68] Heaton, like Wesley it would seem, had no interest in punishing or ostracizing witches.

Heaton was also acutely conscious of the pitfalls of debate on the subject of witchcraft and possession: "Though frequently requested," he reflected, "he did not think it prudent to narrate the case in public congregations; his words might have been misunderstood and misrepresented."[69] To write long letters to friends and acquaintances would have been too much of a burden on his time, so publication seemed "the safest, the least objectionable, the most useful and satisfactory, and, all things considered—the best" means of proving the case and defending his involvement. Heaton had read Durbin's posthumously published account of the Lamb Inn possession, and drew upon the stylistic narrative and empirical approach of that account. As Jason Semmens has observed, where it departed was in Heaton's interjection of his own interpretations and the ascription of motive with regard to events.[70] The result was three pamphlets, beginning with *The Demon Expelled: Or, The Influence of Satan, and the Power of Christ*. Heaton produced a second enlarged edition with the more subtle title *The Extraordinary Affliction and Gracious Relief of a Little Boy: Supposed to be the Effects of Spiritual Agency*. Heaton explained that the first edition "was received with more satisfaction and approbation than the writer anticipated," but there

---

67. *The Annual Report of the Methodist Auxiliary Missionary Society, for the Plymouth Dock District* (Plymouth Dock: n.p., 1820), 16; Plymouth and North Devon Record Office, PH/146; John Gould Hayman, *A History of the Methodist Revival of the Last Century, in its Relations to North Devon* (London: Woolmer, 1885), 101, 118; *The History of Kingswood by Three Old Boys* (London: , 1898), 137; Semmens, "The Dock Dæmoniac," 22.

68. Heaton, *The Extraordinary Affliction*, 30–31.

69. Heaton, *The Extraordinary Affliction*, iii.

70. Semmens, "'I will not go to the Devil for a Cure,'" 135–36.

had been criticisms, not least that the original title was "so bold as to startle some readers, and prevent deliberate examination of their propriety."[71] A third pamphlet entitled *Farther Observations on Demoniac Possession* developed the themes of the wickedness of resorting to charms and cunning-folk, and the falsity of Catholic exorcism.

The three pamphlets were studiously ignored by the *Methodist Magazine*, though *The Extraordinary Affliction* received a critical review in the *Imperial Magazine*, which was edited by the Cornish Methodist theologian Samuel Drew (1765–1833). The reviewer opined that the account might have served a useful purpose if Heaton had acted the "disinterested historian" and left it the readers to draw their own conclusions rather than be subjected to special pleading.[72] It circulated widely enough though. In 1848 George Sandby, Vicar of Flixton, Suffolk, commented that the *Demon Expelled* had sold well, and used it as a good contemporary example of how possession cases could be explained away as mesmeric illness.[73] William Howitt sent a copy of one of one of Heaton's "curious" pamphlets on the case to Sir Walter Scott, who said he intended to make use of it in his work. Howitt referred to it as an example of how Methodists in general were "firmly persuaded of demoniacal possession," which was far from the truth at the time.[74] A correspondent to *Notes and Queries* in 1870 remarked that he knew Heaton and had discussed the matter of demoniacs with him, describing Heaton's published accounts as "very curious books."[75] Its curiosity value clearly piqued Lewis Carroll's interest, for we find a copy of *Demon Expelled* in his library.

In 1853 the *Local Preachers' Magazine*, the authorized organ of the Wesleyan Methodist Local Preachers, included an anonymous account of possible demoniacal possession observed the previous year. The author recalled reading Heaton's *Extraordinary Affliction* a quarter of a century before, and used the account to compare with the details of the one he had recently witnessed. It concerned a thirty-seven-year-old man, who had been inspired to attend class after hearing the revivalist Methodist minister

---

71. Heaton, *The Extraordinary Affliction*, iii, vi.

72. *Imperial Magazine* 5 (1823) 270–72; cited in Semmens, "'I will not go the Devil for a Cure,'" 136. On Drew and Cornish Methodist critique see Clive D. Field, "The Mania of Methodism Reconsidered: Richard Polwhele's Polemics against the Methodists, 1799–1836," *Journal of the Royal Institution of Cornwall*, New Series 2 4 (1997) 75–89.

73. George Sandby, *Mesmerism and its Opponents*, 2nd ed. (London: Longman, 1848), 288.

74. Howitt, *Rural Life*, 2:220.

75. William Bates, "Demoniacs," *Notes and Queries* 4th Series, 6 (1870) 79.

James Caughey, whose sermons were full of the Devil and hell fire.[76] After three months he began to have fits, swearing terribly, and uncontrollably. In short he was convinced he was possessed. His family had him removed to a lunatic asylum, where he was visited by a dissenting minister, a Primitive Methodist minister, and the author (presumably a Wesleyan). On one occasion the man was released for a day to visit his sister—which became a pretext to have him "exorcised." Those gathered for the task were the aforementioned ministers, a preacher of the Wesleyan Association, and another of the New Connexion Methodists, plus a couple of other men of prayer. After several hours, they failed to expel the devil, but were heartened that they had weakened its power over the man. The author of the account was perplexed: "are the facts of this case sufficient to sustain the belief that it is a case of demoniacal possession? I cannot determine that question." "Mr. Wesley laid great stress upon such cases, as evidence of satanic influence and of the reality of the spiritual world. I wait for more light, and shall be glad to receive it from any of my brethren," he concluded.[77] Such a letter would never have been included in the *Wesleyan-Methodist Magazine*, but the fact that it was in the organ of the "Wesleyan Local Preachers" suggests a greater grassroots adherence to Wesleyan spiritualism, and the facts of the case show how such instances of demonianism brought together interested parties from a variety of Methodist and Independent groups.

The sensational trial of William Dove in 1856 provided a belated opportunity for the critics of Methodism to wheel out the old accusations of credulity and superstition. From one of the most respected and influential Wesleyan families in Leeds, and brought up in the best Wesleyan schools, Dove fell in thrall to the supposed powers of a local wizard named Henry Harrison who inadvertently inspired Dove to poisoning his own wife. While in gaol, Dove wrote a pact with the Devil in his own blood, requesting his satanic majesty get him "clear at the assizes." It was a sign of how mainstream the Methodist movement had become that no mud was flung in public with regard to Dove's beliefs. Wesleyan Methodist newspapers were keen to portray him as a sad lunatic, other sections of the press denounced him as a cool, cold killer.

As Methodism became part of the establishment, new evangelical revivalist groups emerged who kept Wesley's invisible world alive, thereby maintaining that earthy link with popular spiritual concerns and folk

---

76. See, for example, James Caughey and Daniel Wise, *Earnest Christianity Illustrated* (Boston: n.p., 1855).

77. "Demoniacal Possession," *The Local Preachers' Magazine and Christian Family Record* New Series, 1(1853) 10–13.

beliefs, and attracting familiar criticisms.[78] Hugh Bourne, leader of the Camp Meeting Methodists, wrote of reading about visions and trances in Wesley's *Journals*, and at least for a short while he believed in the power of witches thanks to the influence of James Crawfoot, leader of the Forest or Magic Methodists. The two men first met in 1807 and over the next few years they worked closely together. Crawfoot was more heavily engaged in the battle against Satan and his minions, expelling demons and combating the powers of suspected witches. In one journal entry Bourne wrote that "it appears that they [witches] have been engaged against James Crawfoot ever since he had a terrible time praying with and for a woman who was in witchcraft."[79] The extent of Crawfoot's influence upon Bourne is a matter of debate, but it would seem that Bourne distanced himself from such views, or was at least silent regarding them, from 1813 onwards.[80]

Some of these various groups fed into what became the Primitive Methodist movement, with Hugh Bourne taking a lead role in its establishment and growth. But by the 1840s the Primitive Methodist establishment had already distanced itself from Wesleyan preternaturalism and Bourne's early adherence to Wesley's invisible world. The "Family Department" section of the *Primitive Methodist Magazine* for 1849, for instance, advised that telling children stories of witches, ghosts and goblins was "Abominable! Such impressions are often ruinous, lasting as eternity. Some children have been actually frightened to death!"[81] By the 1870s a Primitive Methodist chronicler of Skelmanthorpe, Yorkshire, could recall that the Wesleyans had done much to improve the moral character of the inhabitants but were unable to cope with a growing population who believed in witches and omens, and who were addicted to cock-fighting and foolishness—until the Primitive Methodist preachers arrived and "took a bold stand against the

78. James Obelkevich, *Religion and Rural Society: South Lindsey 1825–1875* (Oxford: Clarendon Press, 1976), 231–32; Deborah M. Valenze, *Prophetic Sons and Daughters* (Princeton: Princeton University Press, 1985), 247–48; Robert Colls, *The Pitmen of the Northern Coalfield: Work, Culture, and Protest, 1790–1850* (Manchester: Manchester University Press, 1987), 173.

79. Quoted in W. R. Ward, "The Religion of the People and the Problem of Control, 1760–1830," in Geoffrey J. Cuming and Derek Baker, eds. *Popular Belief and Practice* (Cambridge: Cambridge University Press, 1972), 242.

80. See John N. Brittain, "Hugh Bourne and the Magic Methodists," *MH* 46 no. 3 (2008) 132–40; John W. B. Tomlinson, "The Magic Methodists and their Influence on the Early Primitive Methodist Movement," in Kate Cooper and Jeremy Gregory, eds. *Signs, Wonders, Miracles: Representations of Divine Power in the Life of the Church* (Woodbridge: Boydell, 2005), 389–400; Henry D. Rack, *James Crawfoot and the Magic Methodists* (Englesea Brook: Englesea Brook Primitive Methodist Museum, 2003). My thanks to Jill Barber for providing a copy of the latter.

81. *Primitive Methodist Magazine* 3rd Series 7 (1849) 103.

follies and vices of the people."[82] Once again the erstwhile witch believers had become the foes of "superstition." Yet as we have seen, on the ground Wesleyans and Primitive Methodists continued to share interest and belief in the possibility of diabolic possession, if not witches.

The mid-nineteenth century saw various Methodist apologias for Wesley's belief in the invisible world, usually along the lines of that expressed by Abel Stevens: "When it is remembered that Wesley's age was one of general scepticism among thinkers, we cannot be surprised if he revolted, in his great work, to the opposite extreme, and the error was certainly on the best side. Credulity might injure his work, but scepticism would have ruined it, or rather would have rendered it impossible."[83] But then the growing enthusiasm for spiritualism in the 1850s held out the possibility that Wesley was right after all: the spirit realm could and did interact with the living. The age of miracles and providence was not dead. The first volume of *The Spiritual Magazine* in 1860 included an essay on "Spiritualism and John Wesley" in which the author claimed Wesley "was a Spiritualist, and dared to avow his spiritualism in the midst of the faithless, we had almost said, godless eighteenth century in which he lived. Yes, we repeat it, Wesley was an avowed spiritualist." The account of the Epworth haunting from the *Arminian Magazine* was held up by spiritualists as important evidence that the spirit rapping at séances had precedence from a source of the highest worth. So the front cover of the first edition of the *Spiritualist* newspaper in 1869 concerned the Epworth haunting.[84] Just as Wesley had based his convictions on the evidence of divines and philosophers born two or three generations before himself, so Wesley was now cited as venerable proof by subsequent generations of spiritual seekers. His views on witchcraft, which were inextricably tied to his belief in the spirit realm, were conveniently ignored in the process.

---

82. *Primitive Methodist Magazine*, New Series 12 (1874) 680–81. See also Obelkevich, *Religion and Rural Society*, 254.

83. Stevens, *The History of the Religious Movement*, 397.

84. *The Spiritual Magazine* 1 (1860) 178; Georgina Byrne, *Modern Spiritualism and the Church of England, 1850–1939* (Woodbridge: Boydell, 2010), 104–105.

8

John Wesley and Francis Asbury

John Wigger

PICTURE FRANCIS ASBURY AND John Wesley sitting in a pub somewhere in England, perhaps like the one across the road from Asbury's childhood home. The room is bustling but not crowded and they have a quiet table in the corner. It is sometime in the late 1780s, after Wesley ordained Thomas Coke and sent him to America to ordain Asbury, and after the Americans formed themselves into the Methodist Episcopal Church. Wesley is in his eighties and Asbury is in his mid-forties. For some reason the two men have been left alone for a few hours with only each other for company. Each has a pint in front of him, enjoying it with the leisure of someone who has nothing better to do.

Of course, no such meeting ever occurred, either in England or America. Wesley never crossed the Atlantic after his mostly unsuccessful mission to Georgia in 1736–1737 and Asbury never returned home after he left for the colonies in 1771. But if he had, and if the two men had found themselves alone without any pressing business, what would they have talked about? What was there that would have bound them together, and what would have pulled them apart?

There was much that divided Wesley and Asbury, beginning with their upbringings and family backgrounds. Wesley's parents, Samuel and Susanna, were part of England's educated elite, though their means always remained modest by gentry standards. While his father and grandfather were Dissenting ministers, Samuel Wesley became a High Church Tory. Susanna Wesley, the daughter of a prominent Dissenting minister, joined the Church of England in her teens. Educated at Oxford, albeit as a servitor, Samuel received his living at Epworth in 1695 and remained there until his death in 1735. He was, by any broad measure, a solid and respectable gentleman.

The Wesleys admittedly had their share of family turmoil. Samuel and Susanna had between seventeen and nineteen children, of which John was the thirteenth or fourteenth and only the second of three sons to survive childhood. It was, to say the least, a large and boisterous family. Samuel and Susanna were a study in contrasts. "Temperamentally, it seems painfully clear, they were poles apart," writes Henry D. Rack. Where Susanna was "competent, businesslike and possessed of a cool, rational mentality," Samuel was "learned, zealous, pious, affectionate" but also "prone to self-dramatization." The effect was "almost uniformly disastrous" for the Wesley girls, as Rack notes, but not for John. His upbringing provided him with a confident sense of his place in the world and a firm conviction that he had an important place in English society.[1]

Asbury's upbringing was far humbler. As a child he had no expectations of a life beyond his village and a trade. His parents, Joseph and Elizabeth, were married on May 30, 1742, when he was about twenty-nine and she about twenty-seven. They had two children, Sarah, born on May 3, 1743, and Francis, born on August 20 or 21, 1745. He was never exactly sure of the date since his parents, who were not particularly religious during much of his childhood, may never have had him baptized.[2]

Francis, or Frank as the family called him, grew up in the West Midlands of England, near Birmingham, in Great Barr, near Wednesbury and West Bromwich. His father was an agricultural laborer and gardener employed, according to most accounts, by two local, wealthy families. Their cottage was attached to a brewery indicating that Joseph likely worked at the nearby brewery farm, with the cottage as part of his compensation. Soundly built, the cottage was lived in until the 1950s. It consists of two bedrooms upstairs, two rooms downstairs, and a cellar, a comfortable home for the family of a gardener but nothing to compare to the Epworth rectory. Reflecting on this period, Asbury recalled that his parents "were people in common life; were remarkable for honesty and industry, and had all things needful to enjoy."[3]

---

1. Henry Rack, *Reasonable Enthusiast: John Wesley and the Rise of Methodism* (London: Epworth, 1989), 5–51; Richard P. Heitzenrater, *Wesley and the People Called Methodists* (Nashville: Abingdon, 1995), 25–32.

2. John Wigger, *American Saint: Francis Asbury and the Methodists* (New York: Oxford University Press, 2009), 15–16; *JLFA*, 1:720; David J. A. Hallam, *Eliza Asbury: Her Cottage and Her Son* (Studley, England: Berwin, 2003), 1–7, 12–15; Henry Herbert Prince, *The Romance of Early Methodism in and around West Bromwich and Wednesbury* (West Bromwich: Published by the author, 1925), 39–40; Parish Register and Bishops Transcript for St. Mary Parish, Handsworth, 1743–1745, City Archives and Local History Department, Birmingham Public Library, Birmingham, England.

3. Wigger, *American Saint*, 16; *JLFA*, 1:720; W. C. Sheldon, "The Landmarks of

But he also added, "had my father been as saving as laborious, he might have been wealthy." Did Joseph gamble or drink their money away, as proximity to the brewery might suggest? Whatever his failing, it cast a cloud over the family. About 1796, two years before Joseph's death, the American preacher Jeremiah Minter asked Asbury, "I have often heard you mention your Mother, but never heard you mention your Father, is he living or is he dead?" When Asbury didn't reply another preacher answered for him: "It may be that he has no Father." At least not that he cared to discuss. Samuel Wesley had his faults (chronic debt among them), but they did not leave John Wesley too embarrassed to even acknowledge him.[4]

Education also separated Wesley and Asbury. John Wesley went up to Oxford, to Christ Church, in June 1720. Oxford was formative for Wesley and would remain a central axis of his life ever after. It conferred on him the respectability and dignity of England's educated elite. Wesley was ordained a deacon in the Church of England in September 1725 and a priest in September 1728. He was elected a fellow of Lincoln College in March 1726, a fellowship he continued to hold until his marriage in 1751. The fellowship paid him a stipend of £18 to £80 per year, though it was usually about £30. "This was comfortable enough for a young bachelor," writes Rack, and provided the kind of security that Asbury could never have dreamt of.[5]

Wesley's education and upbringing allowed him to become a prolific author and the dominant theological voice of Methodism in Britain and America. If we count the later holiness and Pentecostal movements as part of the Wesleyan family, then Wesley's theology, particularly his doctrine of Christian perfection, is key to understanding the development of Protestant evangelicalism from the mid-eighteenth century to the present. Francis Asbury produced no similar body of literature. Though he diligently kept a journal for forty-five years and wrote thousands of letters, Asbury never published a book or treatise of any note. He was a voracious reader, particularly of Wesley's works, but he simply did not have the intellectual tools to do more with pen and paper.

Bishop Asbury's Childhood and Youth," *PWHS* 12 (1920) 97–103; Frederick W. Briggs, *Bishop Asbury: A Biographical Study for Christian Workers*, 3rd ed. (1874; repr., London: Wesleyan Conference Office, 1880s), 9–10; J. M. Day, *Asbury Cottage, Newton Road, Great Barr, Restored, re-opened and dedicated on Friday, 27th November, 1959* (Printed and published by the Metropolitan Borough of Sandwell, n.d.), 6–7.

4. Wigger, *American Saint*, 16–18; *JLFA*, 1:720; Jeremiah Minter, *A Brief Account of the Religious Experience, Travels, Preaching, Persecutions From Evil Men, and God's Special Helps in the Faith and Life, &c. of Jerem. Minter, Minister of the Gospel of Christ* (Washington City: Printed for the Author, 1817), 26.

5. Rack, *Reasonable Enthusiast*, 68–76; Heitzenrater, *Wesley and the People Called Methodists*, 33–58.

Asbury's parents had done the best they could, beginning with the best education they could imagine or afford. By age five his mother had taught him to read the Bible, and he remained "remarkably fond of reading" during his childhood. He later recalled that "my father having but one son, greatly desired to keep me at school he cared not how long." They sent Frank to the only school in the area at Sneal's Green, a free school about a quarter mile from their cottage. Unfortunately the school's master was "a great churl, and used to beat me cruelly," Asbury later remembered. His severity "filled me with such horrible dread, that with me anything was preferable to going to school."[6]

At about age thirteen Asbury entered an apprenticeship to a local metalworker. The six and a half years he spent as a metalworker left an indelible mark on him. West Midlands manufacturers had a keen eye for what would sell. Asbury later applied this same market sense to the American religious landscape. Having seen a consumer revolution in material goods he was better prepared to appreciate a consumer revolution in spiritual ideas, exactly what he would encounter in America.[7]

Nevertheless, a metalworker's shop was not Oxford. Wesley's family may have been only moderately wealthy by gentry standards, but he could still command the attention of the well-heeled. There was much about his Oxford experience that Wesley later rejected, but he usually included the title "Fellow of Lincoln College" on the title pages of his books. He had great sympathy and even admiration for the working people of England, but it was the sympathy of an outsider. When he traveled, Wesley routinely lodged with wealthy supporters, who were nevertheless not Methodists, rather than stay in the homes of more humble members. Asbury never adopted a similar practice. His early life was more commonplace than Wesley's and he never expected to be treated like a gentleman.[8]

The event that would drive a wedge between Wesley and Asbury was the American Revolution. At the outset it was not obvious that Wesley would oppose the American cause. Writing in June 1775 to the Earl of Dartmouth, secretary of state for the colonies, Wesley confessed that he could not help but think of Americans as "an oppressed people" who "ask for nothing more than their legal rights, and that in the most modest and inoffensive manner that the nature of the thing would allow."[9]

6. Wigger, *American Saint*, 19; *JLFA*, 1:720–21.
7. Wigger, *American Saint*, 20–24.
8. Rack, *Reasonable Enthusiast*, 45–49, 105; Wigger, *American Saint*, 91.
9. John Wesley to William Legge, June 14, 1775, *JWLT*, 6:142, 156; Wigger, *American Saint*, 87–88.

All of this changed for Wesley once the disruptive social and economic impact of the revolution became clear, particularly its hostility to the king. Wesley was not so much concerned with what the revolution would do to America as with what it might do to England. "If a blow is struck, I give *America* for lost, and perhaps *England* too," he wrote to his brother Charles in June 1775.[10] Wesley wrote to the Earl of Dartmouth to counter reports "that trade was as plentiful & flourishing as ever, & the people as well employed & as well satisfied." From Wesley's observations, just the opposite was true. "In every part of England where I have been (& I have been East, West, North & South within these two years) trade in general is exceedingly decayed, & thousands of people are quite unemployed." Food was so scarce that many were reduced to "walking shadows." Wesley found that people mostly blamed the king. "They heartily despise his Majesty, & hate him with a perfect Hatred. They wish to embrue their hands in his blood; they are full of ye Spirit of Murder and Rebellion." This was a dangerous situation and Wesley saw it as his duty to speak out.[11]

At about the same time that he wrote to Dartmouth, Wesley came across Samuel Johnson's pamphlet *Taxation No Tyranny*. Borrowing liberally from Johnson (his critics would say plagiarizing), Wesley reduced Johnson's argument in length and complexity, making it more suitable for a broad audience. Published as *A Calm Address to Our American Colonies*, the pamphlet sold for two pence, but did little to calm anyone's feelings. Wesley reminded his readers that England enjoyed more civil and religious liberty than any nation on earth. Why would anyone rebel against such a benevolent government? The answer, Wesley wrote, was that "designing men" in England had duped the Americans into believing that they were oppressed. "Determined enemies to monarchy," these men were willing to risk all to bring down the king and replace him with a republican form of government. "Would a republican government give you more liberty, either religious or civil?" Wesley asked. Far from it. "No governments under heaven are so despotic as the republican; no subjects are governed in so arbitrary a manner as those of a commonwealth. . . . Republics show no mercy." The only sensible course was to "fear God and honour the King!" Following up a theme from his earlier pamphlet, *Thoughts Upon Slavery* (1772), Wesley reminded readers that the only real slave in America was "that Negro, fainting under the load, bleeding under the lash!"[12]

10. John Wesley to Charles Wesley, June 2, 1775, *LJWT*, 6:152.

11. John Wesley to William Legge, Aug. 23, 1775, Staffordshire Record Office, Stafford, England; Wigger, *American Saint*, 88.

12. *JWJW*, 11:80–90; Frank Baker, "The Shaping of Wesley's *Calm Address*," *MH* 14 no. 1 (1975) 3–12; Heitzenrater, *Wesley and the People Called Methodists*, 262–64; Wigger, *American Saint*, 88.

Wesley's pamphlet sold a hundred thousand copies in a few months, creating a storm of protest in the process. Though few copies reached America, his views became generally known, and he continued to publish on the topic for several years. In subsequent pamphlets, particularly *A Calm Address to the Inhabitants of England* (1777), Wesley shifted much of the blame for the war from anti-monarchists in England to the Americans themselves, and he continued to call for loyalty to the king. "Do any of you *blaspheme God*, or *the King*?" Wesley asked his fellow Methodists. "None of you, I trust, who are in connexion with *me*. I would no more continue in fellowship with those, who continue in such a practice, than with whore-mongers, or sabbath-breakers, or thieves, or drunkards, or common swearers."[13]

Other British Methodists, including John Fletcher, joined John Wesley in criticizing the Americans. Charles Wesley wrote hundreds of pages of poetry condemning American patriots, those "fiends from hell," and the conduct of British leaders who had bungled the war effort. Like John, Charles drew a connection between the American Revolution and the English Civil War. The American patriots, according to Charles, were guilty of conducting the war,

> By burnings, ravages, and rapes,
> And villainy in a thousand shapes

By comparison, John Wesley seemed a moderate.[14]

British preachers in America could easily perceive the direction of the Wesleys' opinions and increasingly spoke out against the American cause. Except for Asbury. After receiving an "affectionate letter" from John Wesley in early 1776, Asbury declared that he was "truly sorry that the venerable man ever dipped into the politics of America." Had Wesley "been a subject of America, no doubt he would have been as zealous an advocate of the American cause" as he now was of the British. The gulf between Wesley and Asbury in this regard ran deep. Wesley was an Oxford-educated clergyman and gentleman who saw it as his duty to uphold church and king. For Wesley, republicanism undercut the essential social hierarchy that supported the moral order of the universe. Asbury had come to the more American view

---

13. John Wesley, *A Calm Address to the Inhabitants of England*, 2nd ed. (London, 1777); *JWJW*, 12:9–40; *JWLT*, 6:182; Donald H. Kirkham, "John Wesley's *Calm Address*: The Response of the Critics," *MH* 14 no. 1 (1975) 13–23; David Hempton, *The Religion of the People: Methodism and Popular Religion c. 1750–1900* (London: Routledge, 1996), 77–90; Rack, *Reasonable Enthusiast*, 376–77; Wigger, *American Saint*, 89.

14. Charles Wesley, *The Unpublished Poetry of Charles Wesley*, eds. S. T. Kimbrough Jr. and Oliver A. Beckerlegge, 3 vols. (Nashville: Kingswood, 1988), 1:72, 96, 104, 109; Wigger, *American Saint*, 89.

that the old order was inherently flawed, a human invention, and not a very good one at that. None of this is surprising given that Wesley was a priest of the established church and Asbury was not. Asbury had grown up within sight of political power (Dartmouth's estate was within two miles of the Asburys' cottage), but without any expectation that it would ever concern him directly. Of Wesley's licensed missionaries to America, only Asbury divided Wesley's theology from his political and social views. Asbury's position on the war was much closer to that of the majority of the American preachers, who eventually supported the American cause.[15]

So it would seem that Wesley and Asbury had little in common. But there are other ways of looking at the two that make them appear much more alike, and that shed light on what Methodism was really all about.

First, Wesley and Asbury shared a core sense of piety and spiritual devotion. At Oxford Wesley began to fashion a life of spiritual discipline that he would hold to, in its broad outline, for the remainder of his life. He determined to rise at 5:00 a.m. for prayer, though it was a practice "only gradually achieved," as Professor Rack writes. While still in his twenties he developed a "passion for an organized life of piety" that, for Wesley at least, laid the foundation for the so-called "Holy Club." There is much about Wesley's conversion, whether at Aldersgate or at some other point, and his quest for assurance that remains difficult to pin down. In a remarkable letter to his brother Charles on June 27, 1766, John wrote, "[I] do not feel the wrath of God abiding on [me]; nor can I believe it does. And yet (this is the mystery) [I do not love God. I never did.] Therefore [I never] *believed* in the Christian sense of the word."[16] This was more than an isolated moment of doubt, but it does not mean that Wesley's piety was feigned or insincere. Wesley was a mediator of religious experience for his followers, even when he had not had the kind of direct, emotional experience he preached. For all the vicissitudes of his faith, Wesley's life was defined by his practice, his method, of piety.[17]

Asbury's life was also defined by his piety, though with fewer doubts, so far as we know. He ate sparingly and usually rose at 4 or 5 a.m. to pray for an hour in the stillness before dawn. He never married or owned a home and could carry nearly all of his possessions on horseback. During his forty-five years in America he essentially lived as a houseguest in thousands of other people's homes across the nation. This manner of life "exposed him, continually, to public and private observation and inspection, and subjected

---

15. *JLFA*, 1:181; Wigger, *American Saint*, 89–90.
16. John Wesley to Charles Wesley, June 27, 1766, *JWLT*, 5:16.
17. Rack, *Reasonable Enthusiast*, 83, 544–49.

him to a constant and critical review, and that from day to day, and from year to year," wrote Ezekiel Cooper, who knew Asbury for more than thirty years. Asbury lived one of the most transparent lives imaginable. People saw him at unguarded moments, when he was tired and sick, when he went to bed at night and got up in the morning. If his piety had been less than sincere it would have been obvious. It is therefore all the more revealing that the closer people got to him, the more they respected the integrity of his faith.[18]

Wesley and Asbury agreed on the danger that wealth posed to true spiritual devotion. Wesley was always suspicious of the consumer revolution taking shape in the eighteenth century, and his economic teaching was hardly a model for acquisitive capitalism. He never ceased to warn Methodists against the evil of stockpiling wealth. They were to work diligently within the bounds of the law, regarding their labor as a divine calling. The object of their financial ambitions ought to be charity, not luxury. They should provide for their families "plain, cheap, wholesome food, which most promotes health both of body and mind" and whatever else was "needful for life and godliness," and then "fix [their] purpose to 'gain no more.'" Laying up treasures on earth "our Lord as flatly forbids as murder and adultery."[19]

Wesley mostly practiced what he preached, but a growing number of his followers did not. Methodist discipline gave them the tools they needed to gain a measure of financial success, but they proved reluctant to give it away. As early as 1765, Wesley was complaining that "many Methodists" had grown "*rich*, and thereby *lovers* of the present *world*." In a 1784 sermon, he lamented that "of all temptations none so struck at the whole work of God as 'the deceitfulness of riches.'" Too many were "indulging 'the pride of life,'" and "seeking the honour that cometh of men." "They *gain all they can*, honestly and conscientiously. They *save all they can*, by cutting off all needless expense, by adding frugality to diligence. And so far all is right.

---

18. Ezekiel Cooper, *The Substance of a Funeral Discourse, Delivered at the Request of the Annual Conference, on Tuesday, the 23d of April, 1816, in St. George's Church, Philadelphia: on the Death of the Rev. Francis Asbury, Superintendent, or Senior Bishop, of the Methodist Episcopal Church* (Philadelphia: Jonathan Pounder, 1819), 21; Wigger, *American Saint*, 3, 5.

19. John Wesley, "The More Excellent Way," *Sermons III 71–114*, ed. Albert C. Outler, BEW, 3:270, 276; John Walsh, "John Wesley and the Community of Goods," in *Protestant Evangelicalism: Britain, Ireland, Germany, and America c.1750–c.1950: Essays in Honour of W. R. Ward*, ed. Keith Robbins (Oxford: Basil Blackwell, 1990), 25–50; Wigger, *American Saint*, 36. The quotations from Wesley are from the sermon "The More Excellent Way." Also see Wesley's sermon "The Danger of Increasing Riches," *Sermons IV 115–151*, ed, Albert C. Outler, BEW, 4:178–86. The works by William Law that most impressed Wesley in this regard were *A Practical Treatise Upon Christian Perfection* and *A Serious Call to a Holy Life*.

This is the duty of everyone that fears God. But they do not *give all they can*; without which they must needs grow more and more earthly-minded." In short, because of their unwillingness to detach themselves from the world around them, many lost their spiritual edge.[20]

Not Asbury. Perhaps more so than any of Wesley's followers Asbury lived out the patterns of Wesleyan piety and discipline. Though he spent his life on the road he insisted on riding inexpensive horses and using cheap saddles and riding gear. He relentlessly pushed himself to the breaking point of his health, seldom asking more of other Methodists then he was willing to do. Asbury rode more than 130,000 miles during his career in America, on mostly bad backcountry roads and through all kinds of weather. In 1810, at age sixty-five and in precarious health, he sold a two-wheeled sulky he had used for a couple of years and returned to riding horseback. Without the carriage he could "better turn aside to visit the poor; I can get along more difficult and intricate roads; I shall save money to give away to the needy; and, lastly, I can be more tender to my poor, faithful beast."[21]

Even more so than Wesley, Asbury gave away nearly all the money that came his way. While riding through Virginia in March 1800 a "friend" asked to borrow £50. "He might as well have asked for Peru," Asbury joked. "I showed him all the money I had in the world—about twelve dollars, and gave him five ... I will live and die a poor man." "He would divide his last dollar with a Methodist preacher," recalled Henry Boehm, who traveled some 25,000 miles with Asbury from 1808 to 1813. "He was restless till it was gone, so anxious was he to do good with it." Once, in Ohio, Asbury and Boehm came across a widow whose only cow was about to be sold to pay her debts. Determining that "It must not be," Asbury gave what he had and solicited enough from bystanders to pay the woman's bills. "His charity knew no bounds but the limits of its resources, nor did I ever know him let an object of charity pass without contributing something for their relief," wrote John Wesley Bond, who traveled with Asbury during the last years

---

20. John Wesley, "The Wisdom of God's Counsel," *Sermons II 34–70*, ed. Albert C. Outler, *BEW*, 2:560–61; *Minutes of the Methodist Conferences, From the First, Held in London, By the Rev. John Wesley, A. M. In the year 1744*, vols. 1–2 (London: Conference Office, 1812, 1813), 1:50. Also see John Wesley's "The Use of Money," *Sermons II 34–70*, *BEW*, 2:268–80.

21. *JLFA*, 2:610, 612, 614, 652, 656, 3:406–8; Wigger, *American Saint*, 3, 5, 368. "Since I am on horseback my fetters are gone," Asbury wrote on Nov. 19, 1810, after selling the sulky. Asbury, *JLFA*, 2:653. Asbury's austerity sometimes led to misunderstandings. In rural Maryland in March 1810 he apparently offended locals by refusing a ride in a coach. "Will my character never be understood? But gossips will talk. If we want plenty of good eating and new suits of clothes, let us come to Baltimore; but we want souls." *JLFA*, 2:632.

of his life and who, like Boehm, kept track of Asbury's money. "To begin at the right end of the work is to go first to the *poor*; these *will*, the rich *may possibly*, hear the truth," Asbury observed in 1789.[22]

Like Wesley, Asbury believed that wealth was a snare. Toward the end of his career the growing prosperity of American Methodists increasingly alarmed Asbury. After the end of Thomas Jefferson's unpopular trade embargo with Europe in 1809, he could not help but "fear much that these expected *good times* will injure us:—the prosperity of fools will destroy; therefore affliction may be best, and God may send it, for this is a favored land: Lord save us from ruin as a people!" He feared that creeping affluence would lead to complacency and pride. "Our *ease in Zion* makes me feel awful," he wrote in July 1810. "Ah, poor dead Methodists! I have seen preachers' children wearing gold—brought up in pride. Ah, mercy, mercy!" One can hardly doubt that Wesley would have agreed.[23]

Asbury and Wesley were alike in a second crucial way, their ability to negotiate between competing religious and cultural worlds. In his magisterial biography of John Wesley, Rack argues persuasively that Wesley acted as a "cultural middleman" between Methodists on the one hand and clergymen and educated gentlemen on the other. Asbury used this same mediating impulse to shape Wesley's system for America. What Wesley and Asbury both understood was that the church was failing to reach large numbers of people with the gospel. In England the greatest areas of need were the newly industrializing towns and cities. In 1700 only about nineteen percent of the English population lived in a town of more than 2500 people. By 1801 it was nearly thirty-one percent. These were the people that the Church of England was largely failing to minister to in Wesley's day. In America urbanization was never much of a factor during Asbury's lifetime but rapid geographic expansion was. England's expansion was more intensive and America's more diffuse, but the effect was the same. Both were societies in rapid transition where the old ways of connecting with people would not suffice.[24]

Wesley blended the theology of the Church of England and the eighteenth century's emphasis on reason with the more "supernaturalist mentality and religious tastes" of common people, making him indeed a "reasonable enthusiast." To provide preaching to places that did not have it

22. *JLFA*, 1:440, 445, 601, 607, 2:223–31; Henry Boehm, *Reminiscences, Historical and Biographical, of Sixty-Four Years in the Ministry* (New York: Carlton & Porter, 1866), 445, 454–55; John Wesley Bond, "Anecdotes of Bishop Asbury, No. 4," Methodist Archives and History Center, Drew University, Madison, N. J.; Wigger, *American Saint*, 12, 175, 288.

23. *JLFA*, 2:600, 602, 603, 643, 666; Wigger, *American Saint*, 367.

24. Rack, *Reasonable Enthusiast*, 2, 352; Wigger, *American Saint*, 7.

he licensed lay preachers and appointed them to circuits. To provide pastoral care he created class meetings. In the process this gentleman priest gave voice to a much wider range of people than had ever been the case before in England.[25]

Asbury maintained this system, this method, in America throughout his career. Yet Asbury's own cultural sensitivity led him to do things in America that he would not have done in England, some of which Wesley disapproved. Asbury accepted the emotionalism of southern worship in the 1770s, promoted camp meetings in the early 1800s, and reluctantly acquiesced to southern Methodists holding slaves. This mediating impulse, transmitted from Wesley through Asbury, became a trademark of American Methodism. An episode involving Thomas Rankin, one of the preachers Wesley trusted most, illustrates Asbury's close understanding of American culture.[26]

Wesley sent Rankin to America to enforce the discipline of the class meetings and love feasts, which Wesley's first appointed preachers to America, Joseph Pilmore and Richard Boardman, had neglected. "There has been good, much good done in America, and would have been abundantly more had Brother Boardman and Pilmoor continued genuine Methodists both in doctrine and discipline. It is your part to supply what was wanting in them," Wesley wrote to Rankin shortly after his arrival. Asbury initially welcomed Rankin's mission, hoping that he would have the weight to deal with lax members, particularly in New York and Philadelphia. But Rankin had little of Asbury's understanding of, or sympathy for, how American culture differed from English ways.[27]

Beginning in 1775 Methodism was growing by leaps and bounds in southern Virginia and North Carolina. Asbury first visited there in late 1775 and early 1776, writing that January, "Virginia pleases me in preference to all other places where I have been." It did not please Thomas Rankin. Rankin toured southern Virginia for the first time in the summer of 1776, where he saw the revival in full swing. When he preached at Boisseau's (often written Bushill's) chapel in Dinwiddie County and White's chapel in Amelia County he could hardly be heard over the shouting, crying, and extemporaneous prayers of his listeners.[28]

When Rankin returned to Boisseau's Chapel a few weeks later he was determined to quiet things down. That morning, according to the American

---

25. Rack, *Reasonable Enthusiast*, 352.
26. Wigger, *American Saint*, 7.
27. *EMP*, 6: 23, 57; Wigger, *American Saint*, 62.
28. *JLFA*, 1:166, 167, 168, 178; Wigger, *American Saint*, 80, 82.

preacher Jesse Lee, Rankin "gave us a good discourse ... and tried to keep the people from making any noise while he was speaking." But as soon as Rankin left to "get his dinner," "the people felt at liberty, and began to sing, pray, and talk to friends, till the heavenly flame kindled in their souls, and sinners were conquered, and twelve to fifteen souls were converted to God." Rankin returned to preach again in the afternoon, though most of the people seem to have wished he hadn't. When he could not stop them from crying aloud and shouting out prayers while he spoke, he finally gave up and turned the meeting over to George Shadford, who had come to America with Rankin and was one of Wesley's most dynamic preachers. Shadford strode to the front and "cried out in his usual manner, 'Who wants a Saviour? The first that believes shall be justified.'" That did it; the place erupted. Shadford embraced the assembly's emotional energy such that "in a few minutes the house was ringing with the cries of broken hearted sinners, and the shouts of happy believers." Rankin could only look on in dismay.[29]

As Rankin's opposition to southern Methodist worship grew, Asbury was determined to defend the revival. He and Rankin had both come to Virginia with high hopes. While Rankin left disturbed that American Methodists were moving beyond English patterns, Asbury, who had always been on better terms with the mostly young southern preachers, embraced the new style. At a subsequent conference of the preachers, Rankin launched into a tirade against "the spirit of the Americans," criticizing southern Methodists for putting up with "noise" and "wild enthusiasm" in their meetings. He urged that "a stop must absolutely be put to the prevailing wild-fire, or it would prove ruinous." Though he "had done all he could to suppress it," Rankin was "ashamed to say that some of his brethren, the preachers, were infected with it." As Rankin railed on, Asbury "became alarmed, and deemed it absolutely necessary that a stop should be put to the debate, and this he thought could be most easily and safely done by a stroke of humour," according to Thomas Ware, who witnessed the event. Jumping up, Asbury pointed across the room and said, "I thought,-I thought,-I thought," to which Rankin asked, "pray ... what did you thought?" "I thought I saw a mouse!" Asbury replied. This joke, which must have been perfectly timed because otherwise it isn't that funny, "electrified" the preachers, and in the

---

29. Jesse Lee, *A Short History of the Methodists, in the United States of America; Beginning in 1766, and Continued till 1809. To Which is Prefixed a Brief Account of Their Rise in England, in the year 1729, &c.* (Baltimore: Magill and Clime, 1810), 51–52; Wigger, *American Saint*, 82–83. Rankin said little about this meeting in his diary, except that "It fell far short of what we enjoyed the first Sunday I preached there." Thomas Rankin, untitled manuscript journal, Garrett Evangelical Theological Seminary, Evanston, Ill. (July 14, 1776), 104.

ensuing laughter Rankin realized that he had lost. From the American perspective his concerns amounted to little more than a mouse in the corner of the room. The result was "alike gratifying to the preachers generally, and mortifying to the person concerned," according to Ware.[30]

This episode reveals the degree to which Asbury had quickly come to understand Americans. While he was no enthusiast—he seems never to have been among the shouters, jumpers, and fainters at these noisy meetings—he did not share Rankin's fears about southern worship. If this was the way that southerners took to the gospel, then Asbury was willing to make room for it, as all the preachers could now see. "Mr. Asbury always sided with those who deemed it dangerous to" oppose "those gusts of feeling that always did accompany deep and lasting revivals of religion," Ware wrote. "The friends of order, he used to say, may well allow a guilty mortal to tremble at God's word, for to such the Lord will look; and the saints to cry out and shout when the Holy One is in the midst of them."[31]

This exchange also helps explain Asbury's quirky (from an eighteenth-century perspective) ability to control small group discussions, something that many contemporaries alluded to, but few attempted to explain. Laughing in public wasn't something early Methodists encouraged, and Asbury often chided himself for excessive "mirth." Salvation was serious business, and the eternal fate of souls was never to be taken lightly. And yet it was Asbury's ability to use humor to redirect potentially explosive discussions that in part made him so effective in these situations. The danger of looking foolish would have been great, but Asbury knew his audience. Whether Wesley would have had more sympathy for Rankin or Asbury in this instance is difficult to say. But the point is that in the same way that Wesley understood England, Asbury understood America.[32]

Finally, Wesley and Asbury were alike in their organizational ability. Both were central to the creation of religious organizations that have endured to the present. Wesley created a system of class meetings, societies, circuits, and conferences that Asbury adjusted for the American setting. Though there are important theological issues tied to Wesley's ordination of

---

30. Thomas Ware, *Sketches of the Life and Travels of Rev. Thomas Ware, Who Has Been an Itinerant Methodist Preacher for More Than Fifty Years* (New York: T. Mason and G. Lane, 1840), 252–53; Thomas Ware, "The Christmas Conference of 1784," *Methodist Magazine and Quarterly Review* 14 no. 1 (January 1832) 96–104; Wigger, *American Saint*, 83. This exchange between Rankin and Asbury probably took place at the May 1777 conference at Deer Creek, in Harford County, Md. See *JLFA*, 1:238–39; Rankin, mss. journal (May 18, 1777), 136–37.

31. Ware, "Christmas Conference," 103.

32. Wigger, *American Saint*, 84.

Thomas Coke and Asbury as superintendents of American Methodism (the Americans later adopted the title of bishop, much to Wesley's dismay) it was also a brilliant administrative decision. Wesley and Asbury understood that religion meant little apart from community. Dramatic public meetings were well and good, but they amounted to little without sustained nurturing.[33]

American Methodists trusted Asbury because he knew the church better than anyone else. He traveled relentlessly for forty-five years and crossed the Allegheny Mountains some sixty times. For many years he visited nearly every state once a year, and traveled more extensively across the American landscape than probably anyone else of his time. He was more widely recognized face to face than any person of his generation, including such national figures as Thomas Jefferson and George Washington. Landlords and tavern keepers knew him on sight in every region, and parents named more than a thousand children after him. People called out his name as he passed by on the road.[34]

Asbury did not just travel; he listened and talked. People loved to have him in their homes. Asbury often chided himself for talking too much and too freely, especially late at night. He considered this love of close, often lighthearted conversation a drain on his piety. In reality it was one of his greatest strengths, allowing him to build deep and lasting relationships and to feel closely the pulse of the church and the nation. Asbury was not born in America, but he came to understand ordinary Americans as well as anyone of his generation. Nathan Bangs, who knew Asbury and wrote one of the first comprehensive histories of American Methodism, believed that the key to Asbury's leadership was his ability to connect with people "in whatever company he appeared, whether religious or irreligious, whether high or low, learned or unlearned."[35]

In the same manner Wesley traveled at least 200,000 miles over the course of his career. Wesley had few close friends and notoriously confusing relationships with women, but he nevertheless understood the needs of his followers. Though he was an Oxford educated priest of the Church of England, he had a remarkable feel for the sensibilities of ordinary people. As a leader he was more authoritarian than Asbury, but then English society was more hierarchical than American. What worked in one setting would

---

33. On Wesley's ordination of Coke and Asbury see Rack, *Reasonable Enthusiast*, 506–34; Wigger, *American Saint*, 140–47, 161–65.

34. Wigger, *American Saint*, 5.

35. Nathan Bangs, *A History of the Methodist Episcopal Church*, 3rd ed., 4 vols. (New York: T. Mason and G. Lane, 1839–1840), 2:411; Wigger, *American Saint*, 6, 406–7.

not necessarily work in the other, something that Wesley and Asbury both broadly understood even if they did not always agree on specifics.[36]

One of Asbury's strengths was his willingness to tolerate strong personalities in leadership positions, even when they cut across his views. He was "unwilling to cut off any member, whether in, or out of conference, until every prudential and Christian means, to reclaim, recover, and save them, had been used," wrote Ezekiel Cooper, who knew Asbury for more than thirty years. Once Asbury was gone the church reaped the benefits of this pattern. Perhaps even more so than was the case with Wesley in England, Asbury left behind a movement culture that could thrive without him. Much as Wesley had no single successor in England, Asbury had none in America, but the church did not decline as a result.[37]

The movement that John Wesley founded is often called Wesleyanism; there is no Asburyianism. Yet without Asbury there probably would have been little Wesleyanism in America after the Revolution. The preachers in the South, where most Methodists lived and where the movement was growing the fastest, would have broken completely with John Wesley and gone their own way. Asbury barely persuaded them to suspend their decision to ordain one another and instead appeal to Wesley for a solution to the so-called sacramental crisis of 1779–1780. The eventual result was Wesley's ordinations of 1784. If not for Asbury it is anybody's guess where the southern preachers would have ended up, but it would not have been Methodism as we know it.[38]

Francis Asbury did more than maintain the Wesleyan line in America. He adapted Wesley's practice to fit a new social and cultural setting. And yet he did so using decidedly Wesleyan principles. The combined influence of these two remarkable leaders is responsible for much of the Wesleyan, holiness, and Pentecostal movements that have so significantly shaped religion in America, Britain, and around the world to the present day.

So why is Wesley so much better known than Asbury? In part because of the skill of Professor Rack and others who have analyzed Wesley's thought and actions with such perception. Rack's ability to place Wesley in the broader context of eighteenth-century English life is stunning. Wesley was an innovative theologian and prolific author who understood how the world was changing, exactly the kind of leader we might expect to find at the heart of a movement like Methodism. Asbury is a more surprising leader, and therefore easier to overlook. His legacy was not in books published or

---

36. Rack, *Reasonable Enthusiast*, 535; Wigger, *American Saint*, 350.
37. Wigger, *American Saint*, 417.
38. Ibid., 112–22.

memorable sermons, but in the convictions about what it meant to be pious, connected, and organized that he instilled in his people one conversation at a time. The sensitivity that Henry Rack applies to his study of John Wesley not only tells us much about Wesley and his times, it is also a model for how we might more broadly understand Methodism and religious movements like it.

9

Echoes of Wesley on the US Southwestern Frontier

The *Autobiography* of William Stevenson

Ted A. Campbell

AT THE CONCLUSION OF his biography of John Wesley, *Reasonable Enthusiast*, Henry D. Rack observes, "Wesley's most obvious and measurable achievement and legacy must necessarily be the Methodist churches worldwide," noting, in particular, the strength of Methodist churches in the United States.[1] What follows is an account of how the biography of John Wesley came to be echoed in the autobiography of a pioneering Methodist itinerant on the southwestern frontier of the United States in the early 1800s, William Stevenson. In the year after John Wesley died, Stevenson set out from his home in South Carolina to follow the lure of the American frontier. He was one of the first preachers in the Louisiana Territory and his name is known in my native region as the first Methodist, indeed the first Protestant of any denomination, to preach within the bounds of what is now Texas.[2]

Although he was baptized as a Presbyterian and his mother became a Baptist early in his life, Stevenson was attracted to Methodism after leaving home, and the *Autobiography of the Rev. William Stevenson*, written in 1841 and serialized in the *New Orleans Christian Advocate* in 1858, reveals multiple points at which the legacy of John Wesley's writings influenced him.

---

1. Henry D. Rack, *Reasonable Enthusiast: John Wesley and the Rise of Methodism* (Philadelphia: Trinity Press International, 1989), 550.

2. Walter N. Vernon published a brief but well documented biography entitled *William Stevenson: Riding Preacher* (Dallas: SMU Press, 1964). This essay will have reference to Vernon's work, but focuses on Stevenson's *Autobiography* as published in the *New Orleans Christian Advocate*.

But the *Autobiography* also shows some of the particular ways in which the inheritance of Wesleyanism was transmitted in Methodist folk culture. It reveals a Methodist culture based on a very restricted body of Wesley literature, namely, the *Standard Sermons* and material about Wesley's biography that reflect portions of Wesley's *Journal* and Thomas Coke's and Henry Moore's *Life of the Reverend John Wesley* which was itself substantially based on the *Journal*.[3]

Introduction: The Life of William Stevenson

William Stevenson was born on October 4, 1768, the son of James Stevenson (1735–1778) and Elizabeth Pankney (1735–1773), in a frontier settlement that was and still is called Ninety Six, South Carolina, about 170 miles inland from Charleston. Early settlers reckoned that the community was only ninety-six miles east of the nearest Cherokee village, hence the name. Stevenson himself alludes to this when he says that he was raised on "a frontier not far from the Cherokee line."[4] This means that almost his entire life, up to his last decades, was spent in frontier areas. He became one of the earliest British-American travelers to many of these areas, including Missouri, Arkansas, and Texas.

In the fall of 1792, at the age of twenty-four, Stevenson left his home in South Carolina in the company of a cousin whose name was Stevenson Fowler. William Stevenson recalled his motivations for leaving home: his family "had suffered greatly in the revolutionary war," "the pressure of the times was great, money very scarce, lands poor, and little encouragement for a young man to begin the world or make a living." By contrast, "we had

---

3. [Thomas] Coke and [Henry] Moore, *The Life of the Rev. John Wesley, A. M.: Including an Account of the Great Revival of Religion, in Europe and America, of which He was the First and Chief Instrument* (London, 1793). Coke, Moore, and John Whitehead had been authorized by John Wesley to produce a biography, but Whitehead had taken many of John Wesley's papers into his own private possession and proceeded to write his own biography, leaving Coke and Moore to work largely from the printed (*Journal*) sources. Whitehead's two-volume *Life of the Rev. John Wesley, A. M.* was published in 1793 and 1796.

4. I will refer to William Stevenson's *Autobiography* by the date when specific sections were published in the *New Orleans Christian Advocate*. In each case, the excerpt from Stevenson's *Autobiography* appears on the first page of the issue of the *New Orleans Christian Advocate* that is identified. In this case, the citation is from the first sentences of the initial section published on March 13, 1858. The *Autobiography* has now been published in a single volume that I edited: Ted A. Campbell, ed., *The Autobiography of William Stevenson* (Dallas, TX: Bridwell Library, 2015; ISBN 0–941881–41–5).

fine news from the West. Kentucky and Tennessee were fine countries, land plenty and good: so I set out to explore, settle and get rich."[5]

Stevenson and Fowler traveled north and west. They crossed the Watauga and Nolichucky Rivers in western North Carolina. "All was new," he wrote of this journey, "mountains, beautiful springs, and small rivers, rich valleys bearing fine crops of corn."[6] He settled in Green County, then a western county of North Carolina but which four years later (1796) became a county of the newly-formed state of Tennessee. The area was still contested by Native American groups, and Stevenson recorded frequent conflicts with them. During his six years in Green County, he heard a moderate Presbyterian minister, Hezekiah Balch. He also met and married Virginia native Jane Campbell (1773–1846), and they eventually had eleven children.

On March 1, 1798, Stevenson set out for Kentucky, apparently leaving his wife and children in the care of her parents in Virginia. He stayed in Lexington, Kentucky, for a year, then moved to Shelby County, Kentucky, where Jane and the children joined him. Here he came under the influence of Methodist preachers, including Rev. Gabriel Woodfield, and had an experience of religious awakening or conviction. This was followed in May, 1800, by a vivid experience of conversion, including a sense of assurance of the forgiveness of his sins.[7] He joined a Methodist class and society, and his wife joined the society soon after.[8]

In the fall of 1800, the Stevenson family moved again, this time two hundred miles south to Smith County, in Middle Tennessee, east of Nashville. They joined a Methodist society there, participated in camp meetings, and heard Bishops Whatcoat, Asbury, and McKendree preach. It was here that Stevenson was appointed a class leader and was licensed to preach.[9] It was also during their nine years in Smith County, Tennessee, that Jane Stevenson had a conversion experience parallel to William's.

In 1803 the United States acquired from France a vast territory west of the Mississippi River, the Louisiana Territory. Six years later, William Stevenson and his family yet again followed the lure of the frontier, crossing

---

5. Stevenson, *Autobiography*, the section published on March 13, 1858; cf. Vernon, *William Stevenson*, 3–7.

6. Stevenson, *Autobiography*, the section published on March 20, 1858.

7. Ibid.

8. Stevenson, *Autobiography*, the section published on March 27, 1858.

9. Stevenson, *Autobiography*, the sections published on April 3 and 10, 1858. Stevenson stated only that they moved to the "Cumberland" region of Tennessee, that is, the region along the Cumberland River, but Vernon identified the specific area as Smith County, Tennessee; Vernon, *William Stevenson*, 17–18.

the Mississippi and settling in Bellview, Missouri.[10] He found Methodist elders Samuel Parker and David Young already at work there, and joined their efforts. He was in Missouri at the time of the New Madrid earthquakes that began on December 16, 1811, and described vividly the destruction wrought by them. In his early years in Missouri, Stevenson was ordained deacon by Bishops Asbury and McKendree.[11]

In 1813, responding to a request from his brother James Stevenson, William Stevenson traveled south of Missouri to the Arkansas Territory. He was instrumental in some religious awakenings among the population there, organized a few societies, and promised he would return. Back at home in Bellview in 1814, he indicated his intention to preach again in Arkansas. He also ran, unsuccessfully, for the office of representative to the General Assembly of the Missouri Territory. His opponent in this election was Stephen F. Austin, who would later lead the settlement of English-speaking peoples in Texas.[12] Stevenson was ordained as an elder and joined the Missouri Annual Conference of the Methodist Episcopal Church in that year, and in 1815 returned to Arkansas, preaching and organizing societies. It was during this itineration that Stevenson crossed the Red River a few miles west of the present site of Texarkana, Texas, and entered the Viceroyalty of New Spain to preach to a small settlement of British-American people at a place called Pecan Point.[13] He also organized a society there that lasted for several decades. Walter N. Vernon points out that the Pecan Point settlement was comprised of settlers from Smith County, Tennessee, with whom Stevenson would have been familiar.[14]

Stevenson's *Autobiography*, with which this essay is concerned, stopped in 1815. After that year, Stevenson and his family and a colony of settlers from Bellview, Missouri, moved together to Mound Prairie, Arkansas, where he lived for many decades and served as a presiding elder, organizing congregations there. In 1820 he was elected to the first General Assembly of the Arkansas territory and served as a chaplain to the territorial Assembly. He was eventually named as a missionary supported by the Missionary

---

10. This is Bellview in Washington County, Missouri, just one county west of the Mississippi River; cf. Vernon, *William Stevenson*, 32. Stevenson himself wrote "Belview"; Vernon consistently used the spelling "Bellevue." Although there is no longer a community by this name, there remains a township in Washington County that is today identified as "Bellview."

11. Stevenson, *Autobiography*, the section published on April 17, 1858.

12. Vernon, *William Stevenson*, 30.

13. Stevenson, *Autobiography*, the section published on April 24, 1858.

14. Vernon, *William Stevenson*, 38–39.

Society of the Methodist Episcopal Church, and continued to foster missions to Texas in that role.[15] Around 1825 he moved to Louisiana, probably to live with his children who had settled there, and continued to preach and to organize new Methodist societies. He died in 1857 in Claiborne Parish, Louisiana, at the age of 89.[16]

Stevenson's *Autobiography*, serialized in the *New Orleans Christian Advocate*, concluded with his 1815 preaching tour of Arkansas and Texas. He wrote it in 1841 while living in Louisiana. The *Autobiography* was published in the spring of the year after his death (1858) in seven sequential sections that appeared in weekly issues of the *Advocate* between March 13 and April 24 of that year. The first section included a note by the editor, Dr. Holland N. McTyeire, indicating that it was to be the first in a series of articles "on experimental and practical religion, readable and edifying."[17]

A Catholic Spirit among Presbyterians and Baptists

It comes as no surprise that Stevenson's early life was dominated by Baptist and Presbyterian cultures. These, along with Methodist culture, would be the principal forms of Christian faith that prevailed in the southern and southwestern US in the early 1800s, at least away from the East Coast where Anglican (later Episcopalian) congregations had existed since the colonial period. But Stevenson never lived near the coast. His *Autobiography* shows consistent evidence of engagement with Baptists and Presbyterians, and his arguments against both groups reflected his Wesleyan grounding.

Stevenson consistently represented Methodists as holding openminded attitudes towards church doctrines. "I was a little acquainted with the Methodists, and as far as I could judge I liked their liberal doctrines, their general spirit, and above all the life of religion I saw many of them had attained unto."[18] In one case he utilized language echoing John Wesley's sermon on a "Catholic Spirit": "O when will Christians all rally around the standard of love and cease to judge and condemn one another on those non-essential points on which God has given every man liberty to think for himself."[19] The reference to "non-essential points" echoes Wesley's concern in "Catholic Spirit" to find unanimity in "the main branches of

---

15. Ibid., 40–52.
16. Ibid., 53–63.
17. Stevenson, *Autobiography*, a preface to the section published on March 13, 1858.
18. Stevenson, *Autobiography*, the section published on March 27, 1858.
19. Stevenson, *Autobiography*, the section published on April 17, 1858.

Christian doctrine," but to allow for differences over "opinions" and "modes of worship."[20]

Presbyterians

Presbyterianism had come to the southern colonies by a wave of immigration between 1715 and 1775 that brought colonists from Scotland, Northern Ireland (Scots-Irish or Ulster Scots), and the northernmost English counties that border on Scotland. Presbyterianism was by far the dominant religious culture of these immigrants, who tended to arrive in the American colonies by the port of Philadelphia but moved inland rapidly, turned south at Gettysburg, and populated the Shenandoah Valley of Virginia with its numerous trails leading westward across the Appalachians into Kentucky and Tennessee.[21]

The Presbyterian culture that came to this region was not at all the staid, traditional Presbyterianism of the East Coast. It had been deeply influenced by a series of religious revivals in Ulster and then in the southern counties of Scotland from the 1620s. Part of this culture, in the British Isles and then in America, involved emotional preaching about the "order of salvation," often dramatized in large, outdoor communion gatherings in which preachers would lead hearers through the stages of effectual calling, justification, assurance, sanctification, and glorification, culminating in the celebration of the Supper for those who had been issued appropriate tickets. It was demonstrated in the 1980s that these Scots-Irish Presbyterian communion gatherings were the immediate predecessors of American frontier camp meetings.[22] Although the traditional Reformed teachings about election and limited atonement were maintained by most Presbyterian leaders, the doctrine of election was openly questioned within Presbyterian ranks, and a separate denomination, the Cumberland Presbyterian Church, emerged in this frontier area, rejecting the doctrine of limited atonement but maintaining the teaching about the eternal security of believers.

---

20. John Wesley, "Catholic Spirit," *Sermons II 34–70*, ed. Albert C. Outler, *BEW*, 2:81–95.

21. David Hackett Fischer, *Albion's Seed: Four British Folkways in America* (New York: Oxford University Press, 1989), 605–39.

22. Marilyn J. Westerkamp, *The Triumph of the Laity: Scots-Irish Piety and the Great Awakening, 1625–1760* (New York: Oxford University Press, 1988); Leigh Eric Schmidt, *Holy Fairs: Scottish Communions and American Revivals in the Early Modern Period* (Princeton: Princeton University Press, 1989).

From the first page of his *Autobiography*, Stevenson indicated his qualms with and arguments against the ideas of election and limited atonement. Even as a child, he worried about these teachings:

> I frequently heard, in my raising, much said in favor of the doctrine of decrees, unconditional election, and reprobation; but I never could believe that a God, just and merciful, would ever *will* much less *decree* great abominations, and even in my boyhood, before I was ten years of age, I seriously doubted any man who said he believed that doctrine.[23]

Upon his departure from South Carolina in 1792, Stevenson Fowler's father gave William some books on Reformed theology, "hoping that I would be saved from those great errors, propagated by Arminians."[24] Stevenson was willing to listen to Presbyterians, such as Hezekiah Balch ("he was a predestinarian; but moderate."), but objected strongly to those who were "quibblers about foreknowledge, unconditional election and final perseverance."[25] His principal objection to the doctrines of election and limited atonement was essentially the objection that John Wesley expressed in his sermon on "Free Grace," namely, that these doctrines made God into a monster that delighted in the damnation of his creatures.[26]

Baptists

Baptists had proliferated in the southern states from the time of the First Great Awakening in the American colonies, that is, from about the 1740s. Stevenson's mother had been converted under the influence of Baptists. "Some of them," Stevenson wrote, "were warm hearted, shouting Christians, and my mother obtained like precious faith."[27] Stevenson concurred with the Baptists on the need for an affective experience of conversion, and he indicated that early on that, like the Baptists, he had preferred immersion as the appropriate mode of baptism.

Stevenson's most consistent objection to Baptists had to do with their limitation of baptism and church membership to believers. His opposition was consistent with other Methodists who appealed to Jesus's words about receiving the kingdom like little children, "and why, I thought, reject

---

23. Stevenson, *Autobiography*, the section published on March 13, 1858.
24. Stevenson, *Autobiography*, the section published on March 20, 1858.
25. Ibid., further down in the section.
26. John Wesley, "Free Grace," par. 23 in *Sermons III 71–114*, BEW, 3:554.
27. Stevenson, *Autobiography*, the section published on March 13, 1858.

infants, when Christ received them and declared them to be subjects of the kingdom." He also appealed to the parallel between circumcision on the eighth day after birth and Christian baptism. Baptism represented the church's act in setting a person apart for Christ, "I become perfectly satisfied that baptism was the setting of the subject apart from God, and the sooner the better."[28]

Stevenson's logic about infant baptism seemed to be that infants were simply incorporated into the church and thus were appropriate subjects of baptism. What he did not say was that infants were regenerated or born again in baptism. Although John Wesley made this claim,[29] Stevenson seemed to be unacquainted with the idea. Wesley's view would be rediscovered by Methodists in the twentieth century, but it was submerged in an American Methodist culture that argued simply for the inclusion of infants in the Christian community but did not claim the grace of regeneration as a concomitant of infant baptism.

Stevenson's logic in defending infant baptism is related to a larger argument about the great advantage of Methodism in incorporating persons who were not yet believers into Methodist classes and societies. The "General Rules" had specified that the only requirement for membership in a Methodist class was "a sincere desire to flee from the wrath that is to come," that is, participants were not required to profess Christian faith or a conversion experience. Stevenson stated that his wife was admitted to a Methodist society as a "seeker," that is, one who had not yet professed a conversion experience.[30] He claimed, moreover, that he himself would have become a Christian much earlier than he did if he had been a Methodist, "for had I an opportunity of knowing the people called Methodists and been admitted on trial as a seeker and attended prayer and class meeting, I should have had religion many years before I obtained it."[31]

Against Baptists as well as Presbyterians, Stevenson argued that believers could truly fall away from faith in Christ and forfeit their justification. This was the subject of one of the first Methodist sermons that Stevenson ever heard when he was still living in South Carolina. The sermon was on John 15:6, "If a man abide not in me, he is cast forth as a branch, and is withered." Stevenson and a companion who heard the sermon understood it to mean that they could not rely on a guarantee of election or of "eternal security" (the expression preferred by Baptists) for their salvation. When

---

28. Stevenson, *Autobiography*, the section published on March 27, 1858.
29. John Wesley, "The New Birth," IV:1–2, *Sermons II 34–71*, *BEW*, 2:196–98.
30. Stevenson, *Autobiography*, the section published on March 27, 1858.
31. Stevenson, *Autobiography*, the section published on March 13, 1858.

Stevenson recounted the sermon to Rev. James Fowler, a Baptist minister and the father of his companion Stevenson Fowler, Rev. Fowler expressed his objections and argued for the teaching of the eternal security of a believer. Stevenson's comment on this was that if doctrines "act as opiates to keep us easy in our sins they are of the devil."[32] John Wesley had referred to the same biblical text, John 15:6, in his fourth sermon "Upon Our Lord's Sermon on the Mount" as a way of reinforcing the possibility of falling away from the grace of justification.[33] Doubtless this passage was emerging as a standard piece of Methodist ammunition in defending "the amissibility of grace" against Presbyterian arguments for predestination and Baptist arguments for "eternal security." But Stevenson's logic was also Wesleyan, pointing to the practical problems involved in a theological claim that could act as an "opiate" to reassure Christians that they did not need to be concerned about their fidelity once assured of their election.

Stevenson's *Autobiography* and the "Way of Salvation"

William Stevenson's *Autobiography* followed the recognizable pattern of the "way of salvation" that Methodists since Wesley's time had consistently taught in sermons, hymns, and catechetical materials. Wesley himself had summarized the "way of salvation" as involving repentance, faith, and holiness, or preventing grace (divine grace coming before justification), justifying grace (the divine grace by which believers are justified), and sanctifying grace (the divine grace that leads believers to greater and greater holiness).[34] In popular Methodist culture in the United States, these stages were often summarized utilizing the terms "conviction," "conversion," and "sanctification," and in popular Methodist culture those who gave testimonies to their experiences following these patterns often included detailed descriptions of the trials of the soul before and after their conversion experiences.[35]

---

32. Ibid.

33. John Wesley, "Upon our Lord's Sermon on the Mount, Discourse the Fourth," I: 8–9, *Sermons I 1–33, BEW*, 1:537–38.

34. The references are to John Wesley, "The Principles of a Methodist Farther Explained" (1746), VI:4–6, *The Methodist Societies: History, Nature and Design*, ed. Rupert E. Davies, BEW, 9:195, and John Wesley, "The Means of Grace," I:1 and II:1, *Sermons I 1–33, BEW*, 1:378 and 381. On Wesley's various expressions of the "way of salvation," see Ted A. Campbell, *Wesleyan Beliefs: Formal and Popular Expressions of the Core Beliefs of Wesleyan Communities* (Nashville: Kingswood, 2010), 73–82.

35. Cf. Campbell, *Wesleyan Beliefs*, 147–66.

Stevenson's *Autobiography* displays all of these elements of the "way of salvation" in describing his own spiritual journey and those of other Christians.

Experiential Religion and Miraculous Interventions

Stevenson's *Autobiography* is infused with a consistent confidence that God was regularly at work in the events of his life, revealed in a variety of religious experiences and in occasional miraculous occurrences. John Wesley had claimed that "perceptible inspiration" was "the main doctrine of the Methodists," and Methodists from his time regarded their religious experiences as indications of God's direct work in their souls.[36] Many interpreters have understood the emphasis on religious experience to be one of the most distinctive marks of the Wesleyan movement.[37]

Stevenson's *Autobiography* was replete with accounts of religious experiences, his own and those of others, and he especially associated vivid emotional experiences as indications of divine work. Noting that many of the Baptists with whom his mother had identified were "warm-hearted, shouting Christians," he also noted that they "were looked upon by the old, calm, still-born regulars, as a kind of weak, enthusiastic brethren, but good Christians, and should be born with in the Church."[38] Prior to his own conversion, he wrote, "I had daily the witness of condemnation in my own heart."[39] Describing gatherings for revivals and preaching, he would comment, "it appeared to me that the power of God filled the whole house."[40] Stevenson described even more vivid experiences, "I saw a young man in this place, who had been very wicked; he was struck with a power which jerked him with great force. He commenced a kind of dance, looking and talking hopelessly."[41] As we will see in what follows, Stevenson associated specific moments in the "way of salvation" with particular religious experiences.

In addition to his belief in religious experiences, John Wesley also believed that God intervenes directly in the material world and that Christians

---

36. The quotation is from John Wesley's letter to the anonymous correspondent who signed his letters, "John Smith," 1745-12-30, ¶ 13; in Letters II 1740–1755, ed. Frank Baker, *BEW*, 26:181–82; cf. John Wesley to John Smith, March 22, 1748, ¶ 7, ibid., 289.

37. Campbell, *Wesleyan Beliefs*, 72–73, 215–19.

38. Stevenson, *Autobiography*, the section published on March 13, 1858.

39. Ibid.

40. Ibid.

41. Stevenson, *Autobiography*, the section published on April 10, 1858.

can identify such miraculous interventions.⁴² This too became a part of Methodist culture, and William Stevenson recounted a number of events that he took to be miraculous signs of divine intervention. In his early life he recalled having been struck by a branch of a tree that removed his eyeball from its socket. He replaced it, and came to believe that his healing was an act of divine intervention. He also recalled in his early life falling from a high floor of a house that was under construction and being miraculously delivered from injury. "Love thou the Lord," he commented, "for thou hast been plucked as a brand from the burning."⁴³ Here he echoes a frequently repeated saying associated with John Wesley's deliverance from the Epworth fire in Wesley's youth, a saying that Wesley took as a slogan and occasionally used in his own branding.⁴⁴ Stevenson recalled stories of miraculous healing. A man who was "brought to the door of death to all appearances" and "medical aid failed." He was healed by using "the scriptural means pointed out by St. James," i.e., anointing with oil with prayers for healing, "and from that hour his pain and fever left him."⁴⁵

Perhaps most importantly, as an echo of John Wesley's writings, Stevenson understood the New Madrid earthquakes of 1811–1812 as a divine intervention, "seeming to warn the unbelievers that hell was moving from beneath them to meet them at their coming." "About this time," he wrote further, "it was easy to preach to the people; all seemed to be humbled and came together in crowds to hear what they must do to be saved."⁴⁶ Stevenson's sentiments echoed John Wesley's beliefs about the great Lisbon earthquake of 1755, in response to which Wesley had written his *Serious Thoughts occasioned by the late Earthquake at Lisbon* within a month of the earthquake that occurred there on November 1 of that year. In his *Serious Thoughts*, John Wesley attributed the Lisbon earthquake to the direct intervention of God to judge the sins of the Portuguese nation.⁴⁷ Although Stevenson may

---

42. Ted A. Campbell, "John Wesley and Conyers Middleton on Divine Intervention in History," *Church History* 55 no. 1 (1986) 39–49; William J. Abraham, *Aldersgate and Athens: John Wesley and the Foundations of Christian Belief* (Waco: Baylor University Press, 2010), 41–60.

43. All of these instances, and the quotation, are from Stevenson, *Autobiography*, the section published on March 13, 1858.

44. Cf. Richard P. Heitzenrater, *The Elusive Mr. Wesley*, 2nd rev. ed. (Nashville: Abingdon, 2003), 42–46.

45. Stevenson, *Autobiography*, the section published on April 10, 1858.

46. Stevenson, *Autobiography*, the section published on April 17, 1858.

47. John Wesley, *Serious Thoughts occasioned by the late Earthquake at Lisbon*, JWJW, 11:1–13.

not have had direct access to the *Serious Thoughts*, John Wesley had written about the *Serious Thoughts* in his *Journal*.[48]

Awakening and Conviction

Stevenson's *Autobiography* recounted his own experience of awakening, a typical experience that was often referred to in popular Methodist circles as an experience of "conviction" prior to conversion. Describing his earlier life, Stevenson wrote that, "I had daily the witness of condemnation in my own heart."[49] On May 11, 1800, he went to hear a Methodist itinerant, Gabriel Woodfield, preach. "When we kneeled in prayer," he wrote, "my heart was broke for sorrow to think that I had been so ungrateful, to so good a father and preserver as God had always been to me. I wept all the time the preacher was preaching."[50]

As Stevenson described it, consistent with accounts in John Wesley's *Journal*, awakening was a terrifying experience, typically involving a sense of damnation hanging over a person and an accompanying awareness of one's inability to do anything about it apart from the assistance of divine grace. The result of such an experience was to cry out to God for mercy and help.[51] Stevenson had a number of accounts of such experiences. One woman had come to a Methodist meeting in Kentucky determined to shout "glory to the devil," but Stevenson continued,

> she arose and stood on one of the seats to do what she had promised; but her mouth was stopped and she fell on the floor, lay some time like a dead person, after which she cried out, "I am damned, I am damned; hell is my portion: there is no mercy for me. I am gone, eternally gone, hell is my portion.[52]

After a day or so in a state of despair, Stevenson explained, "she began to pray for mercy, and God in great mercy spoke peace to her soul."[53]

---

48. John Wesley's journal entry for November 26, 1755, in *Journal and Diaries IV (1755–1765)*, eds. W. Reginald Ward and Richard P. Heitzenrater, *BEW*, 21:35. At several subsequent points in the *Journal*, Wesley gave accounts of people who had been in Lisbon at the time of the earthquake.

49. Stevenson, *Autobiography*, the section published on March 13, 1858.
50. Stevenson, *Autobiography*, the section published on March 20, 1858.
51. Cf. Campbell, *Wesleyan Beliefs*, 158–59, 220–21.
52. Stevenson, *Autobiography*, the section published on April 10, 1858.
53. Ibid.

Conversion, Justification and Assurance

The previous instance of the woman in Kentucky includes both an account of her sense of conviction (awakening) and her receiving the assurance of pardon that was associated with conversion. John Wesley had not typically spoken of "conversion," but wrote of justification as pardon for sin that occurred on the basis if living faith in Christ. He also described the sense of assurance that he took to be the normal accompaniment of justification. In the popular experience of American Methodists, justification and assurance were typically spoken of together as "conversion."[54]

William Stevenson's own conversion experience came just three weeks after his experience of awakening (described above). He had continued to seek "the witness of God's spirit in me that I am born again." Then on Sunday morning, June 1, 1800,

> I fell on my knees to pray; but the Holy Spirit was beforehand with me, and on me, and in me. Before I made one petition, my intended prayer was turned into praises to Him who had loved me and washed me in his own blood. I had the witness, God's spirit bearing witness with my spirit that I was a child of God.[55]

Stevenson also described his experience as "the witness of my acceptance with God," and "the witness of the conversion of the soul."[56] His wife and his daughter Elizabeth had similar experiences a few years later when they were living in Tennessee.[57] Such accounts of conversion experiences, accompanied by assurance, are common in Stevenson's *Autobiography*, as the concluding lines of the previous subsection indicate. Walter Vernon points out that William Stevenson's own conversion experienced occurred during a well-known period of frontier revivalism in Kentucky and Tennessee, the great revival of 1800.[58]

Those familiar with John Wesley's writings on justification and assurance may be aware of the fact that, although John Wesley thought of the experience of assurance of pardon as the normal accompaniment of the experience of justifying faith, he did allow for what he called "exempt cases" in which persons believed in Christ without the experience of assurance.[59] There was no such nuance in Stevenson's thought. He followed his account

---

54. Cf. Campbell, *Wesleyan Beliefs*, 73–82, 113–14, 159–61.
55. Stevenson, *Autobiography*, the section published on March 20, 1858.
56. Ibid., in the text following the account of his conversion experience.
57. Stevenson, *Autobiography*, the section published on April 10, 1858.
58. Vernon, *William Stevenson*, 20–24.
59. Campbell, *Wesleyan Beliefs*, 226–29.

of his own experience of conversion accompanied by assurance with an exhortation for seekers not to rest until they have experienced the full assurance of pardon:

> And now, reader, I *hope* you will never rest if you have not got the witness in your heart that God, for Christ's sake, has pardoned your sins. Until you get it, take no man's word; no, not even the decisions of a whole Church in your favor. Let nothing stop you until Jesus speaks, "Go in peace, thy sins are forgiven thee." Do not say, I *hope* I have religion; but press and pray on until God speaks to thy heart and thou canst say, I *know* that my Redeemer liveth.[60]

The strong impression one has from this account is that if one does not have the inward witness of assurance, one is really not pardoned, not justified. This point of view would become the norm in popular American Methodist experience through the nineteenth century. In the twentieth century, American Methodists were surprised to learn of Wesley's nuances on the matter.

Trials of the Soul

John Wesley developed a taxonomy of spiritual problems that can follow after justification and along the way to entire sanctification. These include spiritual pride, "wandering thoughts," "heaviness" (a kind of spiritual depression), and "the wilderness state" (loss of faith and of justification).[61] Methodist hymnals typically included a section of hymns on the trials of believers, and Methodist spiritual autobiographies often devoted long sections on the trials, temptations, and tribulations faced by believers on the way to the goal of perfect love for God and neighbor.[62]

Stevenson gave some indications of trials of the soul, though this is not as prominent in his account as it was in other Methodist accounts of the nineteenth century. He states on another occasion:

> I was often troubled and tempted, especially after being very happy, that I had deceived myself and was not what I felt. I was

---

60. Stevenson, *Autobiography*, the conclusion of the section published on March 20, 1858.

61. Spiritual pride is described in John Wesley's "The Scripture Way of Salvation," I:5–7, *Sermons 2 34–70, BEW*, 2:158–59. Wesley wrote complete sermons on the other spiritual problems identified here: "Wandering Thoughts," *Sermons II 34–70, BEW*, 2:125–37, "Heaviness Through Manifold Temptations," *Sermons II 34–70, BEW*, 2:222–35, and "The Wilderness State," *Sermons II 34–70, BEW*, 2:202–223.

62. Campbell, *Wesleyan Beliefs*, 148–56, 161–62.

troubled with evil thoughts, which I hated; but thought they must proceed from the heart; therefore my heart was not right with God. This gave me much pain until I could again receive the witness that the Lord was mine.[63]

He was also troubled about doctrinal disputes in this period, so he indicated that when he first attended a Methodist class meeting, "the power of God was present to heal the wounds I had received from some who contend more about unprofitable doctrine than against sin."[64] He also suffered deprivations through his life as an itinerant and found grace to bear with them.[65]

Entire Sanctification

One of John Wesley's most distinctive teachings, at least compared to other Protestants, was his claim that Christians should not only aspire to perfect love for God and for their neighbors, but that God would empower them to attain this great goal by divine grace. This became a consistent mark of the Methodist movement, and nineteenth-century spiritual autobiographies are replete with accounts of "entire sanctification" or "Christian perfection," though by the nineteenth century the term "sanctification" was beginning to be used in popular Methodist circles as a shorthand way of saying "entire sanctification."[66]

William Stevenson understood from very early after his conversion experience that he was to seek the gift of entire sanctification. Though troubled by doctrinal disputes between Christians, "on reading God's holy word I saw that it was my duty to leave these things [doctrinal disputes] behind and to go on unto perfection, not laying again the foundation from dead works."[67] Reflecting on Christians who had an initial conversion experience but then fell away, Stevenson commented, "I therefore felt determined, by the assistance of divine grace, to seek a clean heart which I desired above all things." The expression "clean heart" was a popular Methodist term for a heart that has been entirely sanctified. He also seems to have associated

---

63. Stevenson, *Autobiography*, the section published on April 3, 1858.

64. Stevenson, *Autobiography*, the section published on March 27, 1858.

65. Stevenson, *Autobiography*, the section published on April 24, 1858, recounted diseases and suffering that Stevenson had endured, leading him to include the hymn, "O what are all my sufferings here," etc.

66. Campbell, *Wesleyan Beliefs*, 82–84, 114–15, 155–56, 162–63, 165, 231–33.

67. Stevenson, *Autobiography*, the very end of the section published on March 27, 1858.

entire sanctification with "the abiding witness," that is, the continual experience of assurance.[68]

Stevenson recounted his experience of entire of sanctification matter-of-factly. It occurred about a year after his conversion at a class meeting where the leader had called on him to pray. He knelt with the group, and as he knelt he thought of a dying woman and he "entreated God on her behalf, that he would sanctify her soul before it left the body." At this point, he recounted:

> I felt assured that God would save her from all sin, and take her soul to heaven, and at the same time I had the witness that God, for Christ [sic] sake, had given me a clean heart and that I should doubt no more. At the same moment, I felt such a blessing as I had never felt before. It was indeed unspeakably glorious. At the same time the whole room seemed to be filled with the glory of God, and it was an uncommon time of rejoicing.[69]

Stevenson used in this account the terminology of a "clean heart," and in the next paragraph he referred to the experience as "my sanctification from all sin." The experience was, he said, an "unspeakable blessing." His statement that "the whole room seemed to be filled with the glory of God" parallels other Methodist accounts of entire sanctification that describe manifestations of divine glory in entire sanctification. A member of the African Methodist Episcopal Zion Church, Julia A. J. Foote, described her experience of entire sanctification, saying that, "The glory of God seemed almost to prostrate me to the floor. There was indeed, a weight of glory resting upon me."[70]

Immediately after this experience, Stevenson hesitated to give a testimony to the experience: "a thought struck me that they would not believe me, and that it would appear like boasting; and if my life after should not accord with my profession, I would be a reproach to the good cause."[71] He went on, though, to profess the experience. As indicated above, Stevenson came to associate the experience of entire sanctification with the "abiding witness" that he was accepted by Christ that is, after his conversion and up to the time of this experience, he had continuing doubted about the validity of his conversion experience. From the time of his experience of entire sanctification, he no longer doubted the validity of his conversion.

68. Stevenson, *Autobiography*, the section published on April 3, 1858.
69. Ibid.
70. Julia A. J. Foote, an account of her experience given in Campbell, *Wesleyan Beliefs*, 163.
71. Stevenson, *Autobiography*, the section published on April 3, 1858.

The latter point about "the abiding witness" seems to be an element of American folk Methodism, not something that had been transmitted from John Wesley. Also, Stevenson completely identified entire sanctification with this particular, vivid, spiritual experience. John Wesley himself maintained that, although entire sanctification itself must be momentary because there must be a moment when a believer passes from loving God less than completely to completely, believers nevertheless might not "advert to the moment" when entire sanctification occurred. That is to say, Wesley allowed that a believer might not be cognizant of the moment when entire sanctification occurred.[72] There seems, again, to be no such nuance in Stevenson's *Autobiography*. Entire sanctification seems to have been identified wholly with the conscious experience of entire sanctification. Stevenson's account of entire sanctification indicates the way in which this experience was to be understood consistently in folk Methodism in the nineteenth century, and eventually in the Holiness Movement.

Social Reformation

The Minutes of the early Methodist conferences in Britain indicated that the primary goal or mission of the Methodist movement was "To reform the nation, and in particular the Church, to spread scriptural holiness over the land."[73] This had been revised in the earliest *Disciplines* of the Methodist Episcopal Church in the United States to state that the goal of Methodism in America was "to reform the Continent, and to spread scripture Holiness over these Lands."[74] "Reform" was a central objective in these statements, and it denoted "the reformation of manners," that is, reform of a people's ways of life to be transformed not only among Methodist societies, but in British or American society more broadly.

William Stevenson's *Autobiography* offers examples of social reformation that came about as a result of Methodist work. Speaking of the revival of 1800 during which he was awakened and converted, Stevenson wrote that "men of sound thinking and morale always acknowledged that the people were greatly reformed and made better under these extraordinary

---

72. John Wesley, "The Scripture Way of Salvation," III:18, *Sermons II 34–70, BEW*, 2:168–69.

73. The "Large Minutes," in Henry D. Rack, ed. *The Methodist Societies: The Minutes of the Conference, BEW*, 10: 303.

74. *A Form of Discipline for the Ministers, Preachers, and Members of the Methodist Episcopal Church in America, Considered and Approved at a Conference held at Baltimore, in the State of Maryland, On Monday the 27th of December, 1784* (New York, 1787), 4.

visitations."[75] The principle need in the wilderness settlements, as Stevenson saw it, was for regular preaching, "Prayer in families and the gospel preached was a new thing; but all, with few exceptions, received us, joined in family prayer, or at least had nothing against it."[76] At the conclusion of his *Autobiography*, Stevenson commented that "even those who did not unite with us in the Church had sound reason and good sense and courage to know and say that the gospel of Christ was the only means which God generally made use of to civilize, moralize, and Christianize a country."[77] By the 1860s, Methodists were making the case that Methodism was God's intended instrument to civilize and Christianize the North American continent.[78] Stevenson's *Autobiography* indicates that Methodists had already begun to sound this theme in the 1840s or earlier.

Conclusion

William Stevenson's *Autobiography* demonstrates how the legacy of John Wesley was employed on the US frontier in the early decades of the nineteenth century. His *Autobiography* not only echoed the general outlines of the "way of salvation" that John Wesley and subsequent Methodists had expressed, but at points it specifically echoed language derived from John Wesley's sermons and Wesley's *Journal*, for example, his claim that after a miraculous deliverance he had been "plucked as a brand from the burning."[79] But Stevenson's *Autobiography* also shows some of the ways in which the Wesleyan inheritance was being transformed in its re-telling on the American frontier.

As suggested above, it was a small selection of Wesley's writings that seem to have been familiar to Stevenson. Walter Vernon's biography of Stevenson indicated that one of Stevenson's mentors in Tennessee, Rev. John Page, served as a book agent for the denomination and carried a stock of books by and about John Wesley.[80] It was undoubtedly through such litera-

---

75. Stevenson, *Autobiography*, the section published on April 10, 1858.

76. Stevenson, *Autobiography*, the section published on April 24, 1858.

77. Ibid.

78. Abel Stevens, *A Compendious History of American Methodism: Abridged from the Author's "History of the Methodist Episcopal Church"* (New York: Phillips and Hunt, and Cincinnati: Walden and Stowe, 1867, although a preface printed in the book carries the date 1868). The providential role of Methodism in civilizing and Christianizing the North American continent is a consistent theme in Stevens's work, but cf. page 78 for a specific claim to this effect.

79. Stevenson, *Autobiography*, the section published on March 13, 1858.

80. Vernon, *William Stevenson*, 25.

ture and the common telling and re-telling of the narrative of John Wesley that Stevenson encountered the Wesleyan tradition. But there would have been only a small selection of Wesleyan and Methodist literature available in the frontier areas where Stevenson spent his career, and almost all of his references or allusions to Wesleyan materials can be accounted for by familiarity with John Wesley's Standard Sermons, Wesley's *Journal*, and the biography of John Wesley that Thomas Coke and Henry Moore had prepared rapidly after John Wesley's death, *The Life of the Reverend John Wesley* (1793), which was itself substantially based on the *Journal*.

Stevenson's *Autobiography* is not exceptional in this respect but probably representative of frontier Methodism at large. The form of Wesleyanism that emerges from the pages of his *Autobiography* lacks nuance on many points of theology and practice, for example, in regarding a particular kind of conversion experience accompanied by the assurance of pardon as an absolutely necessary sign of true Christian faith and the concomitant belief that those who had not experienced such a conversion could not be accounted as true Christians. Similarly, whatever nuances Wesley may have expressed about the doctrine and experience of entire sanctification, it appears in Stevenson's *Autobiography* as a type of vivid religious experience akin to the experience of conversion, accompanied by its own version of assurance. One can see in this a foreshadowing of the understandings of entire sanctification that would divide advocates of the Holiness Movement from other Wesleyans in the later decades of the nineteenth century. Similarly, Stevenson's attitude toward divine intervention and miracles was one of simple trust and thanksgiving for the direct work of God that he saw going on around him. He did not harbor the suspicions of popular accounts of religious experiences and miraculous claims that John Wesley sometimes expressed and that Charles Wesley seems to have espoused consistently from the decade of the 1750s, often in opposition to his brother John.

William Stevenson's *Autobiography*, then, shows how Wesleyanism was being transmitted on the American southwestern frontier in the early decades of the nineteenth century. It illustrates the vitality of frontier Methodism as well as the folk theology that was growing from its Wesleyan roots in this period. It offers a little cameo of Methodist culture in a crucial period when Methodism was becoming a dominant force in popular religious life in the United States.

---- 10 ----

"Did God Do That?"

Common and Separating Factors of Eighteenth-Century Methodism and Contemporary Pentecostal and Charismatic Renewal

 *Robert Webster* ────────

I am not afraid that the people called Methodists should ever cease to exist in Europe or America. But I am afraid lest they should only exist as a dead sect, having the form of religion without the power. And this undoubtedly will be the case unless they hold fast both the doctrine, spirit, and discipline with which they first set out.[1]

At one meeting when I was through the slain of the Lord lay all over the floor. I looked for the preachers behind me and they lay stretched out on the floor too . . . It was a cyclonic manifestation of the power of God.[2]

Today as we celebrate the 250th anniversary of John Wesley's conversion, let us pause to reflect soberly . . . . Methodism has lost its savour and we do not see the power there[i]n. Our pulpits are filled with preachers who preach "Fairy tales." Class meetings are led by leaders who are not spirit-filled. The causes of such a divergence are to be found in the neglect of old-time religion . . . . We say John Wesley was an evangelical and Pentecostal, but what do we see here, a cold and lack-lustre Church

---

1. John Wesley, *Thoughts upon Methodism,* in *The Methodist Societies: History, Nature, and Design,* eds. Rupert E. Davis , *BEW,* 9:527. This document was also published in John Wesley, ed. *AM* 10 (1787) 100–2, 155–56.

2. Frank Bartleman, *Azusa Street* (South Plainfield, NJ: Bridge, 1980), 125–26.

> ... sustained by the faithful few who are filled by the Holy Spirit. To bring the religion of the old times, then, there is need to allow the fullest Holy Spirit operation in our Church.[3]

IN WRITING HIS HISTORY of the Methodist movement, David Hempton makes a very interesting observation about the historical connection of Methodism and Pentecostalism. Like bookends to a fascinating exploration of historical Methodism, the Dean of the Harvard Divinity School declares: "Above all, Pentecostalism is an enormously successful continuation of Methodism's energy and mobility, which transformed the religious landscape of the North Atlantic region and beyond in the eighteenth and nineteenth centuries. The next Christendom, already under construction in the global south, would not look the same if Methodism had never existed."[4] Philip Jenkins, in his study of global Christianity has also noted a fascinating statistic that by the year 2050 Pentecostals will boast of one billion members which will be as many Hindus and twice the number of Buddhists in the world. What Jenkins's study reveals, however, is that Pentecostals are less concerned about statistical information than transformative principles. He writes:

> Their exact numbers are none too clear, since they are too busy baptizing newcomers to be counting them very precisely. By most accounts, membership in Pentecostal and independent churches already runs into the hundreds of millions, and congregations are located in precisely the regions of fastest population growth. Within a few decades, such denominations will represent a far larger segment of global Christianity, and just conceivably a majority. These newer churches preach deep personal faith and communal orthodoxy, mysticism, and puritanism, all founded on clear scriptural authority. They preach messages that, to a Westerner, appear simplistically charismatic, visionary, and apocalyptic. In this thought world, prophecy is an everyday reality, while faith-healing, exorcism, and dream-visions are all fundamental parts of religious sensibility. For better or worse, the dominant churches of the future could have much in common with those of medieval or early modern times.[5]

---

3. Cephas N. Omenyo, "New Wine in an Old Wine Bottle? Charismatic Healing in the Mainline Churches in Ghana," in Candy Gunther Brown, ed. *Global Pentecostal and Charismatic Healing* (Oxford: Oxford University Press, 2011), 240–41.

4. David Hempton, *Methodism: Empire of the Spirit* (New Haven: Yale University Press, 2005), 209.

5. Philip Jenkins, *The Next Christendom: The Coming of Global Christianity*, rev. ed. (Oxford: Oxford University Press, 2007), 8.

All this brings an interesting thesis for the scope of this essay: In what aspects has the Pentecostal-Charismatic movement become the successor of eighteenth-century Methodism? Scholars have noted the sequential developments between the two movements in the eighteenth and twentieth centuries.[6] Issues such as mobility, empowerment of women, organizational acumen, the interfacing of religious expression against political realities, and the embracement of popular piety as normative for living out Christian faithfulness have been vital in understanding the existence and relationship between the two.[7] Nobody disputes that these issues were important for both movements. What is more critical and one that has not been taken into account by historians, sociologists, and theologians in previous treatments, is what were the dynamics that both fuelled the Pentecostal and Charismatic movements while simultaneously being in decline or modified in the Methodist church. David Hempton, who concludes his study with a treatment of Methodist expansion in the north Atlantic world of the nineteenth century, makes an interesting observation: "Wherever in the world Methodism took root, its disciplined and respectable piety inexorably eroded the primitive supernatural excitement that accompanied its own growth."[8]

In the following essay I will take up Hempton's thesis about eighteenth-century Methodism and twentieth-century Pentecostalism with the intent of examining these important questions of decline and growth. Obviously the terrain of both eighteenth-century Methodism and twentieth-century Pentecostalism is vast. Both Methodism with its influence in the nineteenth century holiness movement and Pentecostal and Charismatic renewal are complex and multifaceted. For the purposes here we will confine our conversations to some basic themes that were important to both movements and the metanarratives they constructed. To do this there will be an examination of three important aspects of these religious and spiritual movements. First, a treatment of the social environment of both Methodism and Pentecostalism will be offered. What was it about the environs of both the eighteenth-century English and the twentieth-century American movements that allowed for the birthing of these powerful and transformative

---

6. Note the essays in Henry H. Knight, III, ed. *From Aldersgate to Azusa Street: Wesleyan, Holiness, and Pentecostal Visions of the New Creation* (Eugene, OR: Pickwick, 2010) and more recently Knight's *Anticipating Heaven Below: Optimism of Grace from Wesley to the Pentecostals* (Eugene, OR: Cascade, 2014).

7. See my book, *Methodism and the Miraculous: John Wesley's Idea of the Supernatural and the Identification of Methodists in the Eighteenth Century* (Lexington, KY: Emeth, 2013), for a treatment of this on the Methodist side of things.

8. David Hempton, *The Religion of the People: Methodism and Popular Religion c. 1750–1900* (London: Routledge, 1996), 27.

constructs of human spirituality? Second, in what ways has the doctrine of sanctification become a linchpin for understanding the vitality of Methodists and Pentecostals throughout the last three hundred years? Certainly John Wesley's understanding of sanctification became the chief identifying mark of the Methodists during the Enlightenment. Henry D. Rack has put it succinctly: "It should be clear . . . that for Wesley the true goal of the Christian life is sanctification, holiness, even to the point of perfection."[9] There is more than ample evidence that supports the claim that sanctification for the Methodists in the eighteenth century and the Baptism of the Holy Spirit for Pentecostals in the modern world have been defining benchmarks in their self-identifications. Both Methodists and Pentecostals faced tremendous opposition over their theological understanding and pastoral application of these Christian teachings. On the one hand, Methodists with their idea of the place of perfection went through various and sundry theological disputes in the eighteenth century; not the least were the perfectionist controversies of the early 1760s. John Wesley recorded in his *Journal* over a decade later, for example, his despondency over the society in Launceston and their neglect in maintaining its importance. For August 14, 1776, he cited:

> Here I found the plain reason why the work of God had gained no ground in this circuit all the year. The preachers had given up the Methodist testimony. Either they did not speak of perfection at all (the peculiar doctrine committed to our trust), or they spoke of it only in general terms, without urging the believers to "go on to perfection," and to expect it every moment. And wherever this is not earnestly done the work of God does not prosper.[10]

Wesley's language was revealing. The idea that the teaching of perfection had been deposited to the Methodists as its guardian ("committed to our trust") not only referenced the importance which Wesley placed on the doctrine but the necessity of its inculcation within the Methodist societies.

Pentecostals, on the other hand, with their emphasis on the gifts of the Holy Spirit and particularly Speaking in Tongues (*Glossalia*) have faced a variety of misunderstandings, disputes, and cynical ridicule. Like Methodists and their views of spiritual perfection, Pentecostals and their ideas of Holy Spirit baptism are an identifying mark for those inside and outside the family of faith. American historian, Grant Wacker, correctly maintains that the

---

9. Henry D. Rack, *Reasonable Enthusiast: John Wesley and the Rise of Methodism*, 3rd ed. (London: Epworth, 2002), 395.

10. John Wesley, *Journal and Diaries VI (1776–1786)*, eds. W. Reginald Ward and Richard P. Heitzenrater, *BEW*, 23:28.

teaching plays a formidable role in properly defining who the Pentecostal is in the modern world: "When early pentecostals, wanted to explain themselves to the outside world—indeed when they wanted to explain themselves to each other—they usually started with the experience of Holy Spirit baptism signified by speaking in tongues."[11] A cursory look at the opening pages of the *The Apostolic Faith*, a widely read publication chronicling the religious and supernatural experiences of those involved in the Azusa Street revival at the beginning of the twentieth century, indicates that *glossalia* was experienced predominately with the occurrence of Spirit baptism.[12] Though, for some modern interpreters of the movement, the doctrine of Holy Spirit baptism misplaces the identity of the Pentecostal which is better represented by the idea of spiritual healing.[13] Regardless of these competing categories it seems overwhelmingly fair to say that the baptism of the Holy Spirit has been a primal category for understanding the self-identification of Pentecostals and Charismatics.[14] Finally, a consideration will be given to the role of a supernatural rhetoric in both movements. The belief in an invisible world at various junctures has been fundamental to understanding the religious topography of both Methodists and Pentecostals. A discussion of this aspect of their faith and work will be instrumental in comprehending not only their ministry but their mission as well.

---

11. "Speaking in tongues, in a fundamental sense, became the oral manifestation of the Pentecostal imagination." Grant Wacker, *Heaven Below: Early Pentecostals and American Culture* (Cambridge, MA: Harvard University Press, 2001), 35. Wolfgang Vondey, *Beyond Pentecostalism: The Crisis of Global Christianity and the Renewal of the Theological Agenda* (Grand Rapids, MI: William B. Eerdmans, 2010), 30.

12. See William J. Seymour, ed., *The Azusa Street Papers: A Reprint of The Apostolic Faith Mission Publications Los Angeles, California (1906–1908)* (Foley, AL: Together in the Harvest, 1997).

13. "Divine healing practices are an essential marker of Pentecostal and Charismatic Christianity." Candy Gunther Brown, "Introduction: Pentecostalism and the Globalization of Illness and Healing," in Candy Gunther Brown, ed. *Global Pentecostal and Charismatic Healing* (Oxford: Oxford University Press, 2011), 3. Brown further cites Luis Lugo, et. al., *Spirit and Power: A 10-Country Survey of Pentecostals* (Washington, D. C.: Pew Forum on Religion and Public Life, Oct. 2006) and notes: "The Pew survey singles out divine healing—more so than any other factor, including speaking in tongues and financial prosperity—as distinguishing Pentecostals and Charismatics from other Christians."

14. See Frank D. Macchia's *Baptized in the Spirit: A Global Pentecostal Theology* (Grand Rapids, MI: Zondervan, 2006) for a detailed theological treatment of this category.

Making Room for the Spirit

Historians and theologians alike have been in agreement on at least one point in evaluating Methodists and Pentecostals. Despite being separated by a century both religious movements were radical and transformative in their theological orientation and social influence on society. The Methodists, on the one hand, generated an impact that was phenomenal by any standard. To properly understand Methodism is a complex matter however. In the eighteenth and nineteenth centuries one must take into account the organizational strategies of the societies and class meetings but also the dynamics of such issues as agency, a psychology of the unconscious, self-identification, and spiritual inculcation techniques. Phyllis Mack writes in the beginning of her study on gender and emotion in the period that the genius of the Methodists during the modern world amounted to maintaining a healthy tension between self-abnegation and self-transformation.[15] How that was often played out was contradictory to an Enlightenment ideology that increasingly referred to "faith" pejoratively and attempted to posit reason as the adjudicating category in all of its pursuits. However, for the Methodists, the success of connecting with the primal qualities of human nature proved to be critical to reaching individuals at various levels of social existence.[16]

For John Wesley and his Methodist followers, the attraction of a supernatural dimension of existence not only served to solidify their self-identification but provided an appeal to the masses. The belief in the existence of the miraculous gave them a certain sense of validity that they were being claimed for a special purpose. Despite this rationale for life within the Methodist fold, John and Charles Wesley often defended their followers against attacks of enthusiasm and quackery. In an exchange with Thomas Church, Vicar of Battersea and Prebendary of St. Paul's, for example, John Wesley was quick to argue for the validity of supernatural experiences.[17]

---

15. Phyllis Mack, *Heart Religion in the British Enlightenment: Gender and Emotion in Early Methodism* (Cambridge: Cambridge University Press, 2008), 14.

16. "I now write (as I generally speak) *ad populum*—to the bulk of mankind—to those who neither relish nor understand the art of speaking, but who notwithstanding are competent judges of those truths which are necessary to present and future happiness. I mention this that curious readers may spare themselves the labour of seeking for what they will not find. I design plain truth for plain people." John Wesley, *Sermons I 1–33*, ed. Albert C. Outler, *BEW*, 1:103–4.

17. "I believe there was a *supernatural* power on the minds of the persons there mentioned [in his earlier response to Church in correspondence], which occasioned their bodies to be so affected by the *natural* laws of the vital union." Wesley, *The Principles of a Methodist Farther Explained: Occasioned by the Reverend Mr. Church's Second Letter to Mr. Wesley: In a Second Letter to that Gentleman*, *BEW*, 9:208.

After several pages of argumentation in his letter to Church where Wesley cited what he considered empirical evidence for the healed states of others and himself, an invitation was extended to Church about the mission of the Methodists: "O that it were possible for you to consider calmly whether the *success* of the gospel of Jesus Christ, even as it is preached by us, the least of his servants, be not itself a *miracle*, never to be forgotten!"[18] It is certain, despite some reservations lodged by those inside and outside the Methodists, that this belief not only confirmed God's favor in their understandings of supernatural occurrences but also fueled their evangelistic intensity as they promoted a gospel that was designed to convert sinners, heal the sick, and perform exorcism of demonic spirits. In North America too during the nineteenth century there was an attraction to the Methodist cause as they became the fastest growing church at the beginning of the century. Richard Carwardine writes concerning their social impact: "Numbering only 73,000 members in 1800, the Methodist Episcopal Church [MEC] grew at a rate that terrified other religious bodies, reached a membership of a quarter of million by 1820, doubled its members in the following decade, penetrated into every quarter of the country, including traditionally hostile New England, and became the largest denomination in America."[19] This supernatural rhetoric that contributed to a powerful narrative for understanding their social existence, in both England and North America, also hit a chord in the culture in which they found themselves and they readily took advantage of it in ways that bolstered their cause.[20]

For Pentecostals too, a supernatural consciousness has not only marked its identity but functioned as a key element of its rhetoric which has appealed on a variety of social, economic, and global fronts. Furthermore, it is not uncommon to discover among the leaders of the Pentecostal movement a self-avowed connection to Methodism—historically and theologically. Vinson Synan's opening sentence in his treatment of the Pentecostal movement, for instance, clearly marks this distinction: "John Wesley, the indomitable founder of Methodism, was also the spiritual and intellectual father of the modern holiness and Pentecostal movements, which arose

---

18. Ibid., 222.

19. Richard Carwardine, "Methodist Ministers and the Second Party System," in Russell E. Richey, Kenneth E. Rowe, and Jean Miller Schmidt, eds. *Perspectives on American Methodism: Interpretative Essays* (Nashville, TN: Kingswood, 1993), 159.

20. For treatment of this supernatural rhetoric among Methodists in England see my *Methodism and the Miraculous*, for its influence in American Methodism consult John H. Wigger, *Taking Heaven by Storm: Methodism and the Rise of Popular Christianity in America* (New York: Oxford University Press, 1998) and Lester Ruth's *Early Methodist Life and Spirituality: A Reader* (Nashville, TN: Kingswood, 2005).

from Methodism in the last century."[21] It has almost become folklore to begin a study of Pentecostalism by noting that the now famous meetinghouse of the Azusa revival, once located on 312 Azusa Street in Los Angeles, was an abandoned Methodist church building. However, as I noted in the introduction to this essay, there was a massive "come-outism" from Methodism that fueled the initial drive of Pentecostalism in various ways.[22] The Methodists, who had become convinced that there was something more than what they were experiencing in the spiritual life of their own respective churches, found in Pentecostal circles an emphasis on holiness that they could identify with and embrace. Frank Bartleman who himself came from Methodist circles and wrote an eye-witness account of the Azusa Street revival often quoted or explained passages from John Wesley's own writings. An unidentified source that cited Wesley, for instance, fueled Bartleman's reflection when he delineated the spiritual vitality that was realized in the midst of great opposition. Bartleman recounted with approval:

> When John Wesley ignored all church restrictions and religious propriety and preached in the fields and by-ways, men declared his reputation was ruined. So it has been in all ages. When the religious condition of the times called for men who were willing to sacrifice all for Christ, the demand created the supply, and there have always been found a few who were willing to be regarded reckless for the Lord.[23]

Both the Methodists and those enamored by the spiritual fires that were ignited by those gathered on Azusa Street were excited and perplexed by the presence of earthquakes and saw in their occurrence a reason for considering spiritual truth. Much like the Wesleys' and their consideration of the Lisbon earthquake, Frank Barleman asserted that people were convinced that God was at work in the terrible earthquake in San Francisco on April 18, 1906. Bartleman wrote on it and declared what many people were thinking: "The

---

21. Vinson Synan, *The Holiness—Pentecostal Tradition: Charismatic Movements in the Twentieth Century*, 3rd ed. (Grand Rapids, MI: William B. Eerdmans, 1997), 1.

22. The following list of individuals contain just a few who were either raised in, converted from, or had significant identities with the Methodists: Charles Parham, William J. Seymour, Agnes Ozman, Frank Bartleman, Francisio Olazábal, Rachel Sizelove, Wade Harris, Willis Hoover, Minnie Abrams, Phoebe Palmer, Benjamin Hardin Irwin, Smith Wigglesworth, Maria B. Woodworth-Etter, G. B. Cashwell, William Taylor, Mary Stone, Oral Roberts, Melvin Hodges, Bishop Randolph S. Foster, John G. Lake, and Julia Foote. Thus: "The most disturbing development to loyal churchmen was the appearance of a "come-outism" movement during the 1880's among the more radical holiness spokesmen." Synan, *The Holiness—Pentecostal Tradition*, 35.

23. Bartleman, *Azusa Street*, 46.

question in almost every heart was, 'Did God do that?' But instinct taught men on the spot that He had. Even the wicked were conscious of the fact."[24]

The Pentecostal and Charismatic movements that has penetrated contemporary religious consciousness with phenomenal growth has lodged itself not merely as a marker in contemporary religious movements but one that has embedded itself as epochal in the history of Christianity. Harvey Cox has compared Pentecostalism with the Reformation in its scope and importance! In his forward to a volume on Pentecostal and Charismatic healing practices he links the European Reformation of the sixteenth century to the one that has been spearheaded by the Pentecostal faith. He maintains that "the main bearers of this new reformation do not, by and large, represent the historic denominations that emerged from that sixteenth-century turmoil. Rather, they are the children of a powerful spiritual movement that appeared in its present form only at the beginning of the twentieth century, namely, the Pentecostal-Charismatic movement."[25]

A brief look at the demographics of this movement supports Cox's statement. Amos Yong, one of the leading Pentecostal scholars and Professor of Theology and Mission at Fuller Theological Seminary, writes of an impressive level of penetration by Pentecostals on the global market.[26] Yong writes that at the turn of the second millennium Pentecostals made up twenty-eight percent of the total Christian population. Of these Pentecostals, Charismatics, and neo-Charismatics, seventy-six percent were located in Latin America, Africa, and Asia. An examination of the statistics for Pentecostal and Charismatic growth, shows like the Methodists in the eighteenth century, a steady increase of votaries has been among the poor and disenfranchised. In 2008 at the Society for Pentecostal Studies held on the campus of the Methodist affiliated Duke University, Jürgen Moltmann

---

24. Bartleman, *Azusa Street*, 50. For an examination of John and Charles Wesley's treatments of natural catastrophes see my chapter "The Lisbon Earthquake: John and Charles Wesley Reconsidered," in *The Lisbon Earthquake of 1755: Representations and Reactions*, Theodore E. D. Braun and John B. Radner, eds. (Oxford: The Voltaire Foundation, 2005), 116–26.

25. Harvey Cox, "Forward," in Brown, *Global Pentecostal and Charismatic Healing*, xvii. Furthermore, Cox maintains that any adequate reflection on contemporary religion must seriously look through Pentecostalism to get an accurate vantage point. "The more I read abut [sic] the Pentecostal-Charismatic tsunami, and the more I participate in and observe its many manifestations, the more convinced I become that, in addition to being a beguiling phenomenon on its own, it also provides an invaluable lens through which to watch the whole religious resurgence." Ibid., xx.

26. Amos Yong, *The Spirit Poured Out on All Flesh: Pentecostalism and the Possibility of Global Theology* (Grand Rapids, MI: Baker Academic, 2005), 19. For extensive analysis of Pentecostalism's global impact and influence see Walter J. Hollenweger, *Pentecostalism: Origins and Developments Worldwide* (Peabody, MA: Hendrickson, 1997).

recalled a conversation he had in Lima, Peru, with the noted Liberation theologian, Gustavo Gutiérrez. Pointing to the barrios, Gutiérrez exclaimed to Moltmann: "Out there, it is the Pentecostals who are going into the barrios [to reach the poor]."[27]

But, what has led to this rapid global expansion for the Pentecostals. Harvey Cox is surely correct when he sized up the movement: "However small the sparks at Azusa Street were, within a few decades, Pentecostalism had become a full-fledged forest fire."[28] In the remainder of this essay, I will examine the dynamics of that forest fire and how it surpassed what was found in its Methodist origins.

A Second Blessing or A Forest of Fallen Trees

When John Wesley came to describe the destiny and purpose of Methodists in the eighteenth century he often noted that they had been raised up by God to "spread Scriptural holiness over the land."[29] What Wesley meant followed in the next answer to the conference question:

> Q4. What was the rise of Methodism so called?
>
> A. In 1729, two young men, reading the Bible, saw they could not be saved without holiness, followed after it, and incited others so to do. In 1737 they saw holiness comes by faith. They saw likewise, that men are justified before they are sanctified; but still holiness was their point. God then thrust them out, utterly against their will, to raise a holy people. When Satan could no otherwise hinder this, he threw Calvinism in the way; and then Antinomianism, which strikes directly at the root of all holiness.[30]

Despite the contradiction of Wesley's own language of "being thrust out, utterly against their own will" while denouncing Calvinism, his assertion was that the call to holiness was a defining characteristic of the rise of Methodism in the eighteenth century. How the call to holiness was played out in the Enlightenment by the Wesleys' was not only in preaching and inculcating

27. Joseph Davis, "The Movement Toward Mysticism in Gustavo Gutiérrez's Thought: Is This an Open Door to Pentecostal Dialogue?" *Pneuma* 33 no. 1 (2011) 5.

28. Harvey Cox, *Fire from Heaven: The Rise of Pentecostal Spirituality and the Reshaping of Religion in the Twenty-first Century* (Reading, MA: Addison-Wesley, 1995), 71.

29. John Wesley, *Large Minutes*, Thomas Jackson, ed. *JWJW*, 3rd ed. (1872; repr., Grand Rapids, MI: Baker, 2007), 8:299.

30. Ibid., 300.

the doctrines of justification and sanctification but in writing religious verse and establishing societies wherever they travelled.[31]

At the center of Wesley's understanding of sanctifying grace and Christian perfection was an experience that was accessed by the faith of the believer and subsequent to justification.[32] The goal of the experience was to realize the controlling influence of God's love in such a way that sin would be overcome. The experience of spiritual perfection must be seen within the terrain of sanctifying grace but there is little doubt that it was also an experience within itself which both Methodists and members of the Pentecostal family considered vital for their spiritual identification. In his treatment of the subject, Timothy L. Smith wrote: "But in the fall of 1739 he [John Wesley] came to the clear conviction that a second and instantaneous experience was essential to that process. In that moment, believers were filled with the Holy Spirit, their hearts were cleansed from the remains of inbred sin, and they were perfected in love."[33] Certainly Wesley encouraged his Methodist followers to seek after the experience, even to the point of enlisting children in the pursuit of a second blessing! In a letter to Jane Salkeld, who was schoolmistress at Weardale, Wesley wrote with approval: "I want you to hold fast all that you have already received, and to receive more and more . . . Exhort all the little ones that believe to make haste and not delay the time of receiving the second blessing; and be not backward to declare what God has done for your soul to any that truly fear him."[34] So impressed was Wesley with the revival that he included a comparative analysis of the revivals of Weardale and Everton. Everton had individuals who testified to dreams and visions but Weardale not only exhibited more people who had experienced justification but experienced conversion at a swifter rate than those at Everton; especially the children. In his *Journal* for June 5, 1772, Wesley recorded his evaluation of Everton and Weardale:

---

31. "If any theme defined Charles Wesley's approach to religion it was the struggle for Christian perfection." Andrew Pratt, "The Influence of Charles Wesley in Contemporary Hymnody," in *Charles Wesley: Life, Literature & Legacy*, eds. Kenneth G. C. Newport and Ted A. Campbell (Peterborough: Epworth, 2007), 407. For issues relating to Christian perfection in Methodist societies see David Lowes Watson, *The Early Methodist Class Meeting: Its Origin and Significance* (1985; repr., Nashville, TN: Discipleship Resources, 1995), 62–65 and more recently, Kevin M. Watson, *Pursuing Social Holiness: The Band Meeting in Wesley's Thought and Popular Methodist Practice* (Oxford: Oxford University Press, 2014).

32. John Wesley, *A Plain Account of Christian Perfection*, in *Doctrinal and Controversial Treatises II*, eds. Paul Wesley Chilcote and Kenneth J. Collins, BEW, 13:167.

33. Timothy L. Smith, "John Wesley and The Second Blessing," *WTJ* 21 no. 1 (1986) 138.

34. John Wesley, *LJWT*, 5:333.

And hence, we may easily account for the grand difference between the former and the latter work; namely, that the one was so shallow, there scarce being any subjects rising above an infant state of grace; the other so deep, many, both men, women, and children, being what St John terms "young men" in Christ. Yea, many children here have had far deeper experience, and more constant fellowship with God, than the oldest man or woman at Everton which I have seen or heard of. So that upon the whole, we may affirm such a work of God as this has not been seen before in the three kingdoms.[35]

For Wesley the Second Blessing was a sign that one had experienced authentic sanctification. To a Mrs. Barton who had inquired whether Wesley believed she had the gift of grace, he responded: "It is exceeding certain that God did give you the second blessing, properly so called. He delivered you from the root of bitterness, from inbred as well as actual sin."[36] However, it was possible to lose the strength of this blessing. Later in the same letter Wesley indicated that this was indeed the case with both Mrs. Barton and her husband.

The fundamental starting point of the Second Blessing was not merely a feeling or experience, however. This was the mistake that some Methodists who sought out Christian Perfection in its extreme forms. Thomas Maxfield and to a greater extent George Bell had misapplied John Wesley's teaching about sanctification and ended up elevating themselves as models of perfection among a Methodist society in London.[37] There were several claims not the least of which was the performance of exorcism, resurrection of the dead, and the prediction by George Bell that the world would come to a cataclysmic end on February 28, 1763.[38] John Wesley had several disputes with Maxfield and Bell and the two renegades removed themselves from the Methodist connexion on February 5, 1763.

Particularly informative of John Wesley's view of the Second Blessing experience is a correspondence of letters that Wesley exchanged with Dorothy Furley, a Methodist who also corresponded with leading female

35. John Wesley, *Journal and Diaries V (1765–1775)*, BEW, 5:337.
36. Wesley, *LJWT*, 6:116.
37. See my treatment of this in Webster, *Methodism and the Miraculous*, 138–44.
38. I have transcribed a letter that John Walsh, the Deist turned Methodist, wrote to Charles Wesley about the extravagant claims of Maxfield and Bell. See Ibid., 209–25. See my chapter, "The Holy Spirit and the Miraculous: John Wesley's Egalitarian View of the Supernatural and its Problems," in Wolfgang Vondey, ed. *The Holy Spirit and the Christian Life: Historical, Interdisciplinary, and Renewal Perspectives* (New York: Macmillan and Palgrave, 2014). Also John Wesley, *A Plain Account of Christian Perfection*, in *Doctrinal and Controversial Treatises II*, BEW, 13: 179–87.

Methodists of her day, like Sarah Crosby, Sarah Ryan, Elizabet Edgecomb, and Mary Bosanquet. Furley wrote to Wesley several times from June 14, 1757 through December 15, 1763, where she engaged the respected Wesley about issues relating to the doctrines of Justification and Sanctification and wanted to know how they functioned in the *ordo salutis*. In response, Wesley addressed several issues, including Furley's prolonged illness, which factored into her questions about God's favor in her life. It is obvious that she felt a sense of urgency because of Wesley's own understanding that nobody would enter heaven who had not experienced sanctification. For Wesley's part, he continually encouraged Furley to seek after the experience and indicated that he did not subscribe to the idea that its normal reception was at death or that it was confined to a process of gradual progression—in other words one could receive the blessing instantaneously.[39]

But what was it that one was experiencing instantaneously? Briefly stated: divine love was the foundation, rationale, and legitimacy for both justification and sanctification. What happened in the Second Blessing, however, was a deeper awareness of love and the elimination of actual and inbred sin. The followers of Maxfield and Bell had misapplied perfection to mean a spiritual superiority and located supernatural manifestations as a verification of their superior Christian character. According to Walsh, he had heard George Bell declare that he "could not fall from your perfect State, unless GOD himself could fall from his Throne."[40] To Wesley, the Christian doctrine of perfection had never been about perfectionism but a sense of Godly love where sin did not play a defining role in the believer's life and witness. To Dorothy Furly he wrote on September 15, 1762—just seven months after the expulsion of Maxfield and Bell: "I want you to be all love. This is the perfection I believe and teach. And this perfection is consistent with a thousand nervous disorders, which that high-strained perfection is not."[41] Still one must seek for this deeper experience of love. Wesley to Furley on December 15, 1763:

> You experienced a taste of it when you were justified; you since experienced the thing itself, only in a low degree; and God gave you His Spirit that you might know the things which He had freely given you. Hold fast the beginning of your confidence steadfast unto the end. You are continually apt to throw away

---

39. Wesley, *LJWT*, 3:221 and 4:188–89. In another letter, Ibid., 3:214–15, one could lose the blessing by: 1) committing sin, 2) omitting duty, 3) giving place to pride, anger, or in other inward sin or 4) not watching in prayer to spiritual sloth.

40. John Walsh, "Letter to Charles Wesley, 1762," in Webster, *Methodism and the Miraculous*, 218.

41. Wesley, *LJWT*, 4:188.

what you have for what you want. However, you are right in looking for a farther instantaneous change as well as a constant gradual one.[42]

Others too in the eighteenth century sought after the Second Blessing. The Irish Methodist, Thomas Walsh, for example.[43] However, by the nineteenth century the teaching had waned along with preaching on sanctification among American Methodists. John Littlejohn, for one, summarized the condition of religion in America as "superficial" and observed that this demise was largely due to the fact that Methodist preachers no longer preached on sanctification.[44]

Despite American Methodists continual boredom and lack of interest with this issue there is an overwhelming amount of documentation that demonstrates that the Pentecostals at the beginning of the twentieth century looked at Wesley's instruction about sanctification with favor. However, nowhere in the history of Methodism did sanctification or the idea of a Second Blessing carry the lasting force that the baptism of the Holy Spirit has been for modern day Pentecostalism. Amos Yong in his treatment of the topic maintains that this understanding of the Holy Spirit is vitally important to Pentecostals for properly understanding the *ordo salutis*.[45] The issue for Pentecostals is part of a broader theological agenda that summons internal and external reformations, which in turn, fosters renewal. Frank D. Macchia stipulates:

---

42. John Wesley, *LJWT*, 4: 25.

43. Thomas Walsh, *The Life and Death of Mr. Thomas Walsh Composed in Great Part for the Accounts Left By Himself.* Compiled by James Morgan. (1763; repr., London, 1866).

44. John Littlejohn, "Journal of John Littlejohn," in Wigger, *Taking Heaven by Storm*, 184. However, see the testimonies of sanctification in American Methodism collected in Lester Ruth, *Early Methodist Life and Spirituality* (Nashville: Kingswood, 2005), 119–33. For Phoebe Palmer's view of sanctification and its role in American holiness circles, see Jonathan Dodrill, "From Second Blessing to Second Coming: The Evolution of Dispensationalism within the Holiness Hermeneutic," *WTJ* 47 no. 1 (2012) 150–61.

45. Yong, *The Spirit Poured Out on All Flesh*, 102. Yong insists on a sextuple configuration of the experience of Holy Spirit Baptism: 1) Anticipated and Precipitated by Jesus's offering the spirit to all humanity; 2) The culmination of Christian initiation; 3) A metaphor that connects the biblical understanding that Jesus was raised for the justification of the sinner by the power of the Spirit and the forgiveness of sins; 4) A connecting link between God *declaring* sinners righteous in justification and *making* sinners righteous in sanctification; 5) Unites believers to Christ through the power of the Holy Spirit for ministry to the world through the church; and 6) Baptism of the Holy Spirit is the down payment for the eschatological redemption of God.

> Spirit baptism is a liberating force that reorders our lives according to the loving reign of God in the world. It is fulfilled in the renewal of creation with apocalyptic signs in the heavens and the earth. Until then, sons and daughters, rich and poor, young and old are all caught up in the liberating service of God's loving reign in the world to the glory of God (Acts 2:17–21). Spirit baptism constitutes the church and causes the church to missionize for the sake of the kingdom. But Spirit baptism also transcends the church because it inaugurates the kingdom.[46]

There is little disputing that the idea of Spirit baptism has played a central place in Charismatic and Pentecostal renewal.[47] But how did that come about? To get some historical bearings on the importance of this experience and how it has developed within Pentecostal circles one must go back to Charles Parham and William Seymour. Parham had started his religious career as a supply pastor in the Methodist Episcopal Church in Kansas. He had received the gift of "entire Sanctification," as it was sometimes called and preached by Methodists. During the 1880s Parham had come into contact with holiness preachers and when "come-outism" became prevalent after 1895 he decided to leave the Methodist church. Later he opened a healing home in Topeka but soon decided to start teaching in his own Bible college because he was convinced a new demonstration of the Holy Spirit's power would be needed to meet the evangelistic and missional challenges of the new century. On New Year's Eve in 1900, Parham and his students were praying and searching the Scriptures. One of Parham's students, another Methodist—Agnes Ozman, requested Parham lay hands on her and pray that she would receive the Holy Spirit and the gift of speaking in Tongues. As the New Year was brought in, Ozman "gave evidence" by speaking in the Chinese language. Subsequently, for three days, she could not speak and when she attempted to write her thoughts on paper she uncontrollably wrote in Chinese.[48] The news became electric and soon was featured in the local newspapers. At another school which Parham began in 1905, "The Bible Training School" located in Houston, William Seymour was not allowed to officially enroll and attend because of the racial divide that existed

---

46. Macchia, *Baptized in the Spirit*, 106.

47. "This motif of a universal outpouring of the Spirit is integral to Pentecostalism's understanding of its purpose." William K. Kay, *Pentecostalism: A Very Short Introduction* (Oxford: Oxford University Press, 2011), 6.

48. Synan, *The Holiness—Pentecostal Tradition*, 90–92. A remarkable claim was that there were among the students twenty-one known languages spoken including French, German, Swedish, Bohemian, Chinese, Japanese, Hungarian, Bulgarian, Russian, Italian, Spanish, and Norwegian.

in the United States at the time.[49] However, Parham allowed Seymour to attend classes and sit in the hallways where he could overhear Parham lecturing in his classroom. Seymour, who had been raised in a Baptist home and then later attended an African Methodist Episcopal church in Indianapolis, found under Parham's instruction a renewed excitement for the doctrine of the Holy Spirit and the power of Spirit baptism for living out his biblical faith. Seymour accepted Parham's understanding of *glossalia* as the only true evidence of the Spirit baptism, even though he had not experienced it himself while a student at the bible college.[50]

Later Seymour came to Los Angeles to accept the invitation to be pastor of a small mission under the direction of the Southern California Holiness Association. Arriving there in February of 1906 he began to preach his understanding of the Baptism of the Holy Spirit and the gift of Tongues. The leadership of the Association, however, felt that Seymour's preaching was contrary to Scripture and so he was padlocked out the next night. Seymour had received a mixed review of his message but when Richard Asbery (one who did not accept his teaching but nevertheless invited him to his home on Bonnie Brae Street) allowed him to preach from his living room, a spiritual confirmation was the result. The success was almost immediate and within a few weeks it was obvious, after people were filling the neighborhood streets to hear Seymour that a new place would be needed. The abandoned African Methodist Episcopal Church was found in the downtown business section of the city.[51] When Seymour started preaching, "a monumental revival began."[52] People responded to his preaching with religious fervor, and experiences of being "slain in the spirit," and speaking in Tongues. Of course they prayed for it, much like the Methodists had prayed for sanctification in the eighteenth century. Frank Bartleman, an eyewitness to the revival, commented,

> Some one might be speaking. Suddenly the Spirit would fall upon the congregation. God himself would give the altar call. Men would fall all over the house, like the slain in battle, or rush for the altar enmasse, to seek God. The scene often resembled a forest of fallen trees. Such a scene cannot be imitated. I never saw an altar call given in those early days. God himself would

---

49. Hollenweger, *Pentecostalism*, 20, notes during Seymour's adulthood 3,436 were lynched—nearly two a week!

50. Vinson Synan and Charles R. Fox, Jr., *William J. Seymour: Pioneer of the Azusa Street Revival* (Alachua, FL: Bridge Logos Foundation, 2012).

51. The church once it was abandoned also served as combined tenement house and livery stable before Seymour found it.

52. Synan, *The Holiness-Pentecostal Tradition*, 97

call them. And the preacher knew when to quit. When He spoke all obeyed. It seemed a fearful thing to hinder or grieve the Spirit. The whole place was steeped in prayer. God was in His holy temple. It was for man to keep silent. The shekinah glory rested there. In fact some claim to have seen the glory by night over the building ... The presence of the Lord was so real.[53]

The newspaper of the movement, *The Apostolic Faith*, was filled with reports of powerful displays of divine presence. In many of these cases the Baptism of the Holy Spirit was accompanied by the gift of a language that individuals had no training or knowledge previously to speak, in addition to miraculous healings, exorcisms, and an assortment of dreams and visions.[54] The tragjectory of miraculous manifestations in the Pentecostal and Charismatic movements simply cannot be ignored by the intellectual historian. What the experience of Spirit baptism and Tongues has come to mean for those within the fold of Pentecostalism is quite another question.

At its most fundamental level the theological and practical affirmation of Spirit baptism among Pentecostals has become a metanarrative for those who have asserted the theological legitimacy of the experience. Much like the affirmation of sanctification among eighteenth-century Methodists, the Baptism of the Holy Spirit has been a defining mark of Pentecostal existence. Harvey Cox, the noted cultural theologian, for one, has written about his own discovery of Pentecostalism: "As I pored over these archaic accounts, it became clear to me that for those early converts, the baptism of the Spirit did not just change their religious affiliation or their way of worship. It changed everything. They literally saw the whole world in a new light. Spirit baptism was not just an initiation rite, it was a mystical encounter."[55] Indeed, it is hard to configure a history of Pentecostalism without taking into consideration the teaching of Spirit baptism and the corollary experience of speaking in a spiritual language. In a powerful way, this teaching has served to be an identifying mark of Pentecostals and their place in the religious marketplace. This meant not only a misunderstanding

---

53. Bartleman, *Azusa Street*, 59–60.

54. "We cannot tell how many people have been saved, and sanctified, and baptized with the Holy Ghost, and healed of all manner of sickness. Many are speaking in new tongues, and some are on their way to the foreign fields, with the gift of the language. We are going on to get more of the power of God." Seymour, ed. *The Azusa Street Papers*, 10.

55. Cox, *Fire From Heaven*, 70. Also, "Jesus considered the baptism of the Holy Spirit so important that He expressly forbade His disciples to begin their ministry until they had received it." Don Basham, *A Handbook on Holy Spirit Baptism* (Pittsburgh, PA: Whitaker House, 1969), 24.

of the teaching by those outside of the fold but these misconceptions of the teaching served to bolster the cause rather than detract from it. For the Pentecostal and Charismatic the teaching of Spirit baptism demonstrates a certain sense of ownership—that is, by experiencing Spirit baptism, the Pentecostal understands his religious self-identification to be divine in origin. F. E. Hill, wrote about the Pentecostal experiences in San Diego in 1907 in a way that could hardly be contained in human speech but nevertheless affirmed the connection with the Azusa Street revival:

> Praise God! The fire still burns, sinners coming home to God, believers being sanctified and baptized with the Holy Ghost, speaking with other tongues as the Spirit gives them utterance. We joined with you all of like precious faith on April 9th, and commemorated the anniversary of the Pentecostal outpouring in California. We had a most blessed and victorious day. Hallelujah! The streams of living water and salvation flowed, and glorious deliverance came to some precious souls. The tide is rising higher and higher, the conviction going deeper and deeper, and the way growing brighter day by day. Oh, Glory! Hallelujah! This little army is marching on to sure and glorious victory through the precious blood of the Lamb.[56]

The theme of the Pentecostal movement has been one of a continual flame that has burned from generation to generation without losing the essence of Spirit baptism in its root form. Frank Macchia, in his book on the theology of Spirit Baptism, has centered the teaching on an eschatological understanding of the work of the Spirit where the work of God is seen in a liberating paradigm. Macchia contends that a proper understanding of the experience as the work of the Spirit and not merely as a human configuration of religious experience must take this into account. Thus, a spiritual immersion into the Holy Spirit is defined in ways that places the believer in the midst of true freedom to be an authentic and powerful witness in and to the world about the power of the Spirit's transformational mission. Yet, the sanctifying work of the Spirit needs to be revealed in life through powerful experiences of renewal and charismatic enrichment that propel the believer towards vibrant praise, healing reconciliations, enriched *koinonia*, and enhanced gifting for empowered service.[57] It is the Pentecostal's understanding of the Baptism of the Holy Spirit that truly defines its understanding of Christian existence.

---

56. Seymour, *The Apostolic Faith*, 38.
57. Macchia, *Baptized in the Spirit*, 145.

Rhetorical Supernaturalism

Both the Methodists during the Enlightenment and modern day Pentecostals have had a profound respect for the affirmation of an invisible world. In the history of the Methodists in the eighteenth century, many noted and asserted that John Wesley had a firm belief in the supernatural. Only recently has a serious examination been given to Wesley's understanding of the supernatural in a way that would place it against the background of Enlightenment history and what it meant for Methodists to develop a self-identification that gave significant place to a belief in supernatural occurrences.[58] What I suggest in this section is that for both Methodists (eighteenth century) and Pentecostals and Charismatics (twentieth and twenty-first centuries), the belief in the supernatural was not just a naïve form of biblicalism but a theological articulation of its faith that has proved to be integral to its evangelical success.

For John Wesley, and to a lesser extent Charles Wesley, the belief in the supernatural was a confirmation that God was at work in the life and ministry of the church. Henry H. Knight, III, correctly notes at the beginning of his collection of essays on Wesleyan and Pentecostal mentalities:

> One way to put this is that, especially in their [both Methodists and Pentecostals] early decades, participants in these movements experienced themselves living in a world permeated by God's activity. For many this included divine guidance or calling through dreams, visions, prayer, devotional reading of scripture, and even through seemingly ordinary circumstances or coincidences. They expected to meet God in the everyday activities of life as well as in times of corporate worship and personal or small group devotions.[59]

John Wesley faced sundry and serious issues about the topic of the supernatural and its place in the life of the Methodist movement which he supervised in the eighteenth century.[60] Throughout his life Wesley answered the

---

58. My book, *Methodism and the Miraculous*, deals with John Wesley's idea of the supernatural and how Wesley developed a "rhetoric of the supernatural" for Methodists living in the eighteenth century. Contrary to previous historiographical treatments of the period, the belief in supernatural occurrences was not eclipsed from the mindset of people living in the era and Wesley served in the words of Henry D Rack as a "cultural middleman." See Rack, *Reasonable Enthusiast*, 433. Therefore, it is inaccurate to view Wesley as out of touch with the era in which he lived with his belief in various aspects of an invisible or supernatural world.

59. Knight, *From Aldersgate to Azusa Street*, 4.

60. I have given extensive treatment to the epistemological, political, and theological issues that Wesley faced in *Methodism and the Miraculous*.

call to defend the Methodists against charges of Enthusiasm by both secular and ecclesiastical opponents. To some, like Bishop Joseph Butler (1692–1752), he was able to create a common ground of understanding.[61] On other occasions, Wesley found himself asserting the priority of supernatural occurrences against agnostic and religious skeptics. Space will not allow a detailed recounting of Wesley's view of dreams, visions, religious convulsions, demonic possession, exorcism, and spiritual healings.[62] However, an examination of a letter that Wesley wrote to the agnostic classicist, Conyers Middleton (1683–1750), should give us insight into how Wesley viewed a rhetoric of the supernatural and how he conceived a belief in miraculous events should function for those who called themselves Methodists.

Conyers Middleton, a noted classicist at Cambridge University wrote and published a series of books in which he questioned the belief in miraculous occurrences.[63] As indicated by the lengthy subtitle of his treatises, Middleton had developed a cessationist position. That is to say: when the apostolic period ended so did the continued presence of miracles along with the gifts of the Holy Spirit in the life of the church. Middleton, however, did not stop there but went on to argue that the supernatural gifts of the early church were based on deception and therefore all Christian testimony which was based upon the witness of the primitive position was unreliable. Indeed in the preface to his work, Middleton claimed that the whole question which affirmed the credibility of a continual presence of supernatural occurrences throughout Christian history depended "on the joint credibility of the facts, pretended to have been produced by those powers, and of the witnesses,

---

61. For the interview between Joseph Butler and John Wesley, Frank Baker, "John Wesley and Bishop Joseph Butler: A Fragment of John Wesley's Manuscript Journal 16th to 24th August 1739," *PWHS* 42 (1980) 93–100. The essence of the interview between Bishop Butler and John Wesley is also found in Wesley's *Journal*. See Nehemiah Curnock, ed. *The Journal of John Wesley* (London: Epworth, 1938), 2:256–57 and W. R. Ward, ed. "Appendix B: Wesley's Interview with Bishop Butler, August 16 and 18, 1739," *BEW*, 19:471–74.

62. For treatment of these categories in Wesley and the early Methodists see Webster, *Methodism and the Miraculous*, 63–194.

63. Conyers Middleton, *An Introductory Discourse to a Larger Work, Designed Hereafter to be Published, Concerning the Miraculous Powers which are Supposed to have subsisted in the CHRISTIAN CHURCH, from the Earliest Ages, through Several Successive Centuries; Tending to Shew, that we have no Sufficient Reason to Believe, upon the Authority of the PRIMITIVE FATHERS, that any such Power were Continued to CHURCH, after the Days of the Apostles . . .* (London, 1747) and *A Free Inquiry into the Miraculous Powers, which are Supposed to have Subsisted in the Christian Church, from the Earliest Ages through Several Successive Centuries. By Which is Shewn, that we have no Sufficient Reason to Believe, upon the Authority of the Primitive Fathers, that any such Powers were Continued to the Church, after the Days of the Apostles* (London, 1749).

who attest them."[64] In addition, to take up Middleton's point, why was the gift of Tongues absent in the church's affirmation of the supernatural at the end of the apostolic period? The skeptic suggested that the church found belief in Tongues embarrassing and untenable. If the church would become more honest about supernatural speculations, Middleton suggested, then it would assert that all supernatural and miraculous gifts should be eclipsed from Christian discourse. The Cambridge scholar asserted:

> If this then appears to have been the case of this particular gift [γλωσσαις]; that false claim to it was made by the early Fathers, and held up for a while, till it could no longer be supported; it is sufficient, one would think, of itself, to blasé the general credit of all the rest, tho' no particular mark of fraud could have been fixed on each of them separately: but when there is not a single one among them all, which either from it's nature, or end, or manner of exertion, or the character of it's witness, does not furnish just ground to suspect it as fictitious, it must needs persuade every rational inquirer, that they were all derived from the same source of craft and imposture.[65]

Middleton's arguments infuriated John Wesley and he took the time to break from his preaching tour to respond in a letter that consisted of over two hundred pages![66] The letter will be considered as a theological document in and of itself in a forthcoming volume of the critical *BEW*.[67] For Wesley's part, Middleton had revealed a fundamental flaw in approaching the Bible. The Scriptures were not to be read primarily through the lenses of skepticism but faith. Surely after the third century, Wesley conceded with Middleton, superstition had arisen in various hagiographic stories of miracles in the life of the saints. However, to begin an analysis of Holy Scripture with an eye of doubt certainly invited a spirit of inaccuracy into the hermeneutical project. "Surely," wrote Wesley to Middleton, "there is something very peculiar in this—something extraordinary, though not miraculous—that a man who is too wise to believe the Bible should believe everything but the Bible! should [sic] swallow any take, so God be out of the question, though ever

---

64. Middleton, *Free Enquiry*, ix.

65. Ibid., 121–22.

66. "Wesley's swift reading and response to Middleton's work indicate the seriousness with which Wesley regarded Middleton's argument." Ted Campbell, "John Wesley and Conyers Middleton on Divine Intervention in History," *Church History* 55 no. 1 (1986) 43.

67. According to Richard P. Heitzenrater, editor-in-chief of the project, the letter will be published in Volume 16 and due out in 2018. For now, see *LJWT*, 2:312–88.

so improbable, ever so impossible!"⁶⁸ In relation to Middleton's assertion that all miracles are fabricated, Wesley wanted proof: "I should desire you to prove that the miracles of the fourth century were all forged."⁶⁹

To construct blanket generalizations against the existence of miracles was fallacious and could not be sustained in Wesley's estimation. Always the empiricist, John Wesley considered each miraculous claim on its own merit. Some, like those he received from the French Prophets were not to be believed. However, that did not exclude all claims as erroneous and not worthy of consideration. At a deeper level of historical inquiry was Middleton's disparagement of Christian testimony and the validity of a continuum of witnesses to supernatural occurrences. With a catalogue of Christian witnesses from the ancient church, Wesley documented those who attested to the personal experiences of miraculous events: Justin Martyr (who Wesley translated from the Greek for Middleton), Irenaeus, Theophilus, Tertullain, Minutius Felix, Origin, Cyprian, Arnobius, and Lactantius. These spoke loudly about the presence of miracles in the early church.⁷⁰ However, what is most disturbing to Wesley about Middleton's analysis is his refusal to allow for the contemporary revival of primitive spiritual realities. For Wesley's part, to discard all witnesses concerning miraculous occurrences, was to disregard all history. Indeed all of science and history had been built on the knowledge communicated through human testimony.⁷¹ Instead, Wesley argued, by faith a Christian may see past "the veil into the world of spirits, into things invisible and eternal; a power to discern those things which with eyes of flesh and blood no man hath seen or can see, either by reason or their nature, which (though they surround us on every side) is not perceivable by these gross senses, or by reason of their distance, as being yet afar off in the bosom of eternity."⁷² It is in faith as a spiritual sense that one could properly perceive the miraculous and invisible world.⁷³ When this is done, Welsey reasoned, a whole world opens to the believer. A world where the

---

68. Wesley, *LJWT*, 2:368.

69. Wesley, Ibid., 2:321.

70. "Surely, sir, you talk in your sleep: you could never talk thus, if you had your eyes open and your understanding about you." Wesley, *LJWT*, 2:337.

71. In his brilliant study of testimony, C. A. J. Coady makes a similar argument against David Hume. See, C. A. J. Coady, *Testimony: A Philosophical Study* (Oxford: Oxford University Press, 1992), 79–100.

72. Wesley, *LJWT*, 2:382.

73. For more on this see my "Sensing the Supernatural: John Wesley's Empirical Epistemology and the Pursuit of Divine Knowledge," *Sewanee Theological Review* 54 no. 3 (2011) 254–81.

supernatural is not a part of a cloudy historical past but vividly seen harmonious with real Christianity.[74]

Not since the eighteenth century and its disparagement among intellectuals in the nineteenth century has the world see such a dramatic onslaught of a group demonstrating a rhetoric of the supernatural, as it did with twentieth century Pentecostalism. In the development of a rhetoric of the supernatural, Pentecostals and Charismatics have had two important differences from the Methodists of the Enlightenment. First, with regard to the supernatural manifestations, Methodists tended to downplay the issue of the gifts of the Holy Spirit (*charismata*) and especially the gift of Tongues. For Pentecostals and to a lesser extent Charismatics, Tongues has been affirmed in a bold and unapologetic way and been developed into an *apologia* for understanding their place in the history of the church. There are obvious points of disagreement among scholars of the Pentecostal movement on this marking of identification.[75] However, my point here is that it would be a hard-pressed exercise to locate the historical significance of Pentecostalism without considering the gifts and especially *glossalia*. Even among Charismatics who give Tongues an important place in its spirituality, the spiritual operation of this gift in the community of faith has a primordial role. Mark J. Cartledge explains: "In charismatic spirituality inspired speech is a constant thread that runs right through its process and is seen at various points in the framework."[76] There is little disputing the idea that classical and modern Pentecostals have expended quite a bit of energy in grappling with the function of inspired speech and its role in defining Pentecostalism.

Still there are other issues that play a fundamental role in defining this movement that has grown exponentially in the contemporary world. The idea of exorcism and supernatural healing have been powerful displays of how much the Pentecostal faith has placed on the human body in developing

---

74. "I reverence them, because they were Christians . . . And I reverence their writings, because they describe true, genuine Christianity, and direct us to the strongest evidence of Christian doctrine." John Wesley, *LJWT*, 2:387.

75. There is some contention in contemporary thought as to whether *glossalia* is the central category for understanding the Pentecostal movement. See Vondey, *Beyond Pentecostalism*, 182–85 and Brown, *Global Pentecostal and Charismatic Healing*, 3–13. See also Yong, *The Spirit Poured Out on All Flesh*, 89–91, who more broadly defines Pentecostal essentials as Forgiveness of Sins, Deliverance from the devil, the demonic, healing of the sick, taking care of the poor, and an eschatological dimension that is inclusive of realized and future moments.

76. Mark J. Cartledge, *Encountering The Spirit: The Charismatic Tradition* (Maryknoll, NY: Orbis, 2007), 69. For a fuller treatment of *glossalia* see Cartledge, *The Gift of Speaking in Tongues: The Holy Spirit, the Human Spirit and the Gift of Holy Speech* (Cambridge: Grove, 2005).

its understanding of God's love and compassion. From Dorothy Trudel's healing house in Switzerland to the evangelical and healing services of Carlos Annacondia, the experience of healing in Pentecostal services has truly become an egalitarian experience.[77] For many, especially among the marginalized communities, healing has become a point of hope that is extended to various and sundry issues that are present in their lives. It has not become uncommon for Pentecostals to apply the category of healing to physical and metaphysical issues.[78] Benno Schoeneich, missionary in Nicaragua wrote of his experiences in Africa: "nearly everyday someone gets healed. Healing is part of the Gospel. It not only includes the healing of the soul, but of the body as well."[79] Certainly the Pentecostal community has made a place for healing in modern religious discourse and the existence of healing services throughout mainstream Christianity is due in large measure to the degree that healing has become a major theological category in the defense of the supernatural in the daily life of the believer.

A final dimension of the supernatural rhetoric that Pentecostals are quick to defend is the continual presence of the supernatural in modern religious discourse. Though those who claim, like Conyers Middleton in the eighteenth century, that miracles died out in the Apostolic period are hard to find though they do climb out of the theological woodwork from time to time.[80] This contribution to the history of miracles has found no greater defense in the history of Christianity than the one provided by scholars of Pentecostalism. While it is certainly true that it is not the sole issue that concerns those who write and work within the Pentecostal family it is certainly one that has become *articulus stantis et cadentis ecclesiae* (the

---

77. "One of great appeals of the pentecostal faith is that anyone can walk into a church service and request divine healing or participate in the rituals happening during the service." Rebecca Pierce Bomann, "The Salve of Divine Healing: Essential Rituals for Survival among Working-Class Pentecostals in Bogotá, Columbia," in Brown, *Global Pentecostal and Charismatic Healing*, 196. See also Heather D. Curtis, *Faith in the Great Physician: Suffering and Divine Healing in American Culture, 1860–1900* (Baltimore, MD: John Hopkins University Press, 2007); James Robinson's *Divine Healing: The Formative Years, 1830–1890: Theological Roots in the Transatlantic World* (Eugene, OR: Pickwick, 2011) and *Divine Healing: The Holiness-Pentecostal Transition Years, 1890–1906: Theological Transposition in the Transatlantic World* (Eugene, OR: Pickwick, 2013), for an analysis of healing in the Holiness movement of the nineteenth century.

78. Joseph W. Williams, *Spirit Cure: A History of Pentecostal Healing* (Oxford: Oxford University Press, 2013).

79. Benno Schoeneich, "Telling the Gospel Story in Nicaragua," Quoted in Gary B. McGee, *Miracles, Missions, & American Pentecostalism* (Maryknoll, NY: Orbis, 2010), 146.

80. The most recent example is John MacArthur's *Strange Fire: The Danger of Offending The Holy Spirit with Counterfeit Worship* (Nashville, TN: Nelson, 2013).

article on which the church stands or falls). In a provocative and highly interesting book, Gary McGee argued for the the existence of a supernatural world-view as an essential part of the mission and ministry of radical Evangelicals and Pentecostals. McGee wrote:

> At the core of radical evangelical thinking stood not only the Lord's soon return, but the concept of expectant faith, a rock-solid confidence that God would empower believers and answer their prayers, whether for money, provisions, physical healing, or sundry other needs. In regard to the financial operation of missions, while virtually all agency leaders and missionaries agreed on the importance of faith in raising funds, many radical evangelicals pressed the issue farther by advocating faith for God's direct provision as the intended norm.[81]

The supernatural was neither for eighteenth century Methodists nor twentieth century Pentecostals merely a narrative whereby one could be encouraged by the experiences of others but a metanarrative whereby those stories, individually and collectively, should be understood as the story of redemption itself. There are many more chapters in this story that time will not allow that would be valuable for consideration and conversations. The style of worship, music, and economics just name a few. However, maybe a good place to end this study is with the words of Frank Bartleman, who had an experience of consulting a Methodist commentary through the means of *biblicae sorte*, a practice that John Wesley and the early Methodists utilized in the previous century:

> I wanted a quotation of two lines from a volume of Clarke's Commentaries. There were four volumes. Each contained 1000 pages. I only had a few minutes to find it. Prayerfully I chose one of the volumes, closed my eyes and let the book drop open itself. It was not marked or pressed at that particular page, but wonderful to relate, the book opened exactly at the right place and my eyes fell directly on the quotation that I wanted. This would have been impossible in the natural. I had not at all known where in the book to find it. I only remembered having read it. This strengthened my faith greatly for the message. But I certainly would not, of course, advise this as a practice.[82]

---

81. McGee, *Miracles, Missions, & American Pentecostalism*, 45. For an evaluation of the radical financial and healing dimensions of the Pentecostal movement, see Kate Bowler's *Blessed: A History of the American Prosperity Gospel* (Oxford: Oxford University Press, 2013). Bowler sees the Penteocostal informed Prosperity movement as unique to American self-reliance culture and defined primarily as a comprehensive hermeneutical tool of the self.

82. Bartleman, *Azusa Street*, 23.

11

The Oxford Movement and Evangelicalism

Parallels and Contrasts in Two Nineteenth-Century Movements of Religious Revival

Peter B. Nockles

A WELCOME TREND IN the recent historiography of modern British religious history has been a focus on revival, revivals, and revivalism. The literature on "evangelical revival" (and notably the specifically "Evangelical Revival" of the "long" eighteenth century), especially in regard to its origins and genesis, is vast and has been crowned by David Bebbington's magisterial *Victorian Religious Revivals* (2011).[1] This essay will reconsider the Oxford Movement as a manifestation of religious revival, almost a century after the so-called "Evangelical Revival" associated with John and Charles Wesley, George Whitefield, Howell Harris, Daniel Rowland and others, and that in North America known as the "Great Awakening" and spearheaded by Jonathan Edwards.[2] It will place the Oxford Movement in relation to the Evangelical Revival's nineteenth-century Anglican Evangelical successors.

The Oxford Movement has rarely been studied from the perspective of a religious "revival" in the classic "evangelical" sense of individual

---

1. David W. Bebbington, *Victorian Religious Revivals: Culture and Piety in Local and Global Contexts* (Oxford: Oxford University Press, 2012). See also Andrew Walker & Kristin Aune, eds. *On Revival: A Critical Examination* (London: Paternoster, 2003).

2. There have been attempts by American scholars to distinguish "revivals" from "awakenings." See William Gerald McLoughlin, *Revivals, Awakenings, and Reform* (Chicago: University of Chicago Press, 1978). I owe this reference to Dr John Walsh, Emeritus Fellow, Jesus College, Oxford. I also wish to thank Dr Walsh for his helpful reading of and comments on earlier versions of this essay.

spiritual conversions for which there were certain prerequisites or criteria laid down and which conformed in some way to the four main characteristics of Evangelicalism—the Quadrilateral—as defined by David Bebbington: conversionism, activism, Biblicism, and crucicentrism.[3] Of course, the Methodist movements inspired by John Wesley and George Whitefield respectively have been recognized as national revivals and Henry D. Rack, who stands out as the foremost biographer in his generation of John Wesley, has done much to enrich our understanding of Wesley as a great revivalist leader.[4] Nonetheless, the evangelical understanding of a "revival movement" has tended to be applied to local communities and to short-term "revivals" and "revivalism" within a wider tradition. Rack himself has focused on an unusual local Methodist revival in rural Cheshire.[5] In short, the emphasis has often been on the "-ism." Revival in this sense may not always have been a mark of success. However, an "evangelical" revival could also encompass wider and broader institutional aspects. One important dimension of an "evangelical" revival, that of marking a season of renewal ordained by God awakening the Church as a whole to its mission after a period of neglect or decline, as traditionally applied to Wesleyan Methodism, can be also applied to the Oxford Movement.

One of the key criteria for "a genuine revival of religion" laid down in 1851 by Daniel Wilson the younger, the influential Evangelical Vicar of Islington and successor to his father, was that of "a return to vigour and energy after a state of torpor and inactivity"; a "religious revival," he explained, was "accordingly a return of spiritual life to a languid church."[6] Another criterion as laid down by Daniel Wilson was that of the raising up of individuals as agents of revival endowed with special gifts.[7] Many Victorian British Evangelicals of course emphasized that the Evangelical Revival had been a revival of the doctrines of the English Reformers as well as of the interior spiritual life of individuals and churches. The doctrines themselves may have been in conflict, but the early Tractarian leaders likewise regarded the Oxford Movement as a doctrinal recovery as well as spiritual renewal. They were also conscious of a need—not always found in the evangelical

---

3. David W. Bebbington, *Evangelicalism in Modern Britain: A History from the 1730s to the 1980s* (London: Unwin Hyman Ltd., 1989), 2–17.

4. Henry D. Rack, *Reasonable Enthusiast: John Wesley and the Rise of Methodism* (London: Epworth Press, 1989).

5. Henry D. Rack, "Early Methodist Visions of the Trinity," *PWHS* 46 nos. 2–3 (1987) 38–44, 57–69.

6. Daniel Wilson, *A Revival of Spiritual Religion the only effectual remedy for the dangers which now threaten the Church of England* (London: Hatchard, 1851), 4.

7. Ibid., 5.

understanding of revival—for a renewal of the church's corporate practical life as well as its doctrine and theological resources.

Although it is not appropriate to use the terminology of "revivalism" or "revivals" in the plural in this context, the idea of a "Church" or "Catholic" institutional revival was to become commonplace in the literature on Tractarianism from supporters and opponents alike from at least the 1860s onwards, as is attested by such titles as *The Anglican Revival, The Catholic Revival, The Church Revival,* even *The Orthodox Revival.* In fact, the term "revival" was used as early as 1840 by Samuel Francis Wood, one of Newman's Oriel pupils and disciples, in his manuscript account of the Oxford Movement up to that early date, significantly entitled *The Revival of Primitive Doctrine:* a document which James Pereiro has uncovered in the Halifax papers in the Borthwick Institute, York.[8]

The Swedish Lutheran author, Yngve Brilioth's masterly *Anglican Revival: Studies in the Oxford Movement,* published in 1925 has been one of the few studies on the Oxford Movement to understand it in terms of a theological and religious revival (in both individual and corporate terms). For the Tractarian reinvigoration of the Church of England as a whole after 1833 to a large extent was nourished on a preceding renewal of the individual interior life of its leading participants, a renewal sometimes fostered, as we shall see, as much by the influence of Evangelicalism as by traditional high churchmanship. In short, the "Church Revival" depended on the ground prepared by an earlier more individualistic revival of personal religion.

A full understanding of the religious core of the Oxford Movement has been obscured by a focus on the political context and contingent origins of its birth, and by the ecclesiastical controversies and polemics which it inspired both within and without the Church of England, in which "Tractarians" and "Evangelicals" were in conflict. Evidence for opposition to Evangelicalism abounds. From an early date in the Movement, Hurrell Froude's, albeit playful and facetious, nickname for Evangelicals—"the *Peculiars*" was widely adopted in the private correspondence of the Tractarian leaders (though it should be noted that the term then denoted distinctiveness rather than oddity).[9] More significantly, it has become an axiom that nineteenth-century Wesleyan Methodism was pushed further

---

8. York, Borthwick Institute, Halifax Papers, Box A2 42.3; Samuel Francis Wood, "The Revival of Primitive Doctrine" [1840]. See James Pereiro, *"Ethos" and the Oxford Movement: At the Heart of Tractarianism* (Oxford: Oxford University Press, 2007), 252–65.

9. Hurrell Froude used the epithet frequently, e.g., *The Autobiography of Isaac Williams, B. D. . . . Edited by his brother-in-law the Ven. Sir George Prevost* (London: Longmans, Green, & Co., 1892), 63.

away from the established Church and towards the Nonconformist or "Free Church" camp than might otherwise have been the case, in reaction against the "sacerdotalism" of the Oxford Movement—a direct consequence of Tractarianism's supposed undermining of the Protestant credentials of the Church of England.[10] Anglican Evangelicals would certainly raise an outcry against Tractarian teaching. Daniel Wilson was adamant that his definition of a religious revival excluded the Oxford Movement, though he conceded that it was widely so regarded, and did not scruple to refer to what he called "the Tractarian heresy."[11]

In his controversial biography of Newman, the late Frank Turner framed his exhaustive study of the Anglican Newman and his leadership of the Oxford Movement in terms of a direct and deliberate reaction against Evangelical religion.[12] There is nothing new in this charge—it had been made by many others, including Newman's own brother Francis writing shortly after John Henry's death in a work which has been condemned as an act almost of "fratricide," and by Edwin Abbot.[13] Like them, Turner overstated his case and while rich in documentation his interpretation lacked nuance and overlooked much contrary evidence. In truth, Newman's belief that the Movement was primarily directed against liberalism should be taken at face value rather than as a later "smokescreen" for what Turner suggested was Newman's real *bête noir* at the time, Evangelicalism.

In the post-Tractarian epoch, attitudes hardened. If on the Anglican Evangelical side, figures such as Dean Francis Close, Bishop J. C. Ryle, and Walter Walsh (in his notorious *Secret History of the Oxford Movement* published in 1898) represented a high water-mark of antipathy to all that the Oxford Movement stood for, their antipathy was matched, if not exceeded by Anglo-Catholic polemics against Evangelicalism, a genre represented by H. L. Proby's *Annals of the Low Church Party* (1888) and Sabine Baring-Gould's *The Church Revival* (1914), on the other side. For Close and Walsh, the Oxford Movement and (arguably) its apparent offspring Ritualism, represented a gigantic conspiracy to subvert the Protestantism of the Church of

---

10. Mats Selen, *The Oxford Movement and Wesleyan Methodism in England 1833–1882: A Study in Religious Conflict* (Lund: Lund University Press, 1992), 1–2. 35–6; John .Munsey Turner, *Conflict and Reconciliation. Studies in Ecumenism in England, 1740–1932* (London: Epworth, 1985).

11. Wilson, *Revival of Spiritual Religion*, 15.

12. Frank M. Turner, *John Henry Newman and the Challenge to Evangelical Religion* (New Haven: Yale University Press, 2002).

13. Francis Newman, *Contributions Chiefly to the Early History of the Late Cardinal Newman. With Comments*, 2nd ed. (London: Kegan Paul, Trench, Truebner & Co., 1891); Edwin A. Abbott, *The Anglican Career of Cardinal Newman*, 2 vols. (London: Macmillan & Co., 1892).

England from within and to advance what Walsh called "the Papal Apostasy."[14] On the other hand, if for hard-line Anglican Evangelicals of Ryle's stamp, Tractarians and Anglo-Catholics were merely traitors bent on doing Rome's work, for Anglo-Catholics such as Baring-Gould, the Evangelical party was an alien element introduced into a native English Church by Huguenot and continental Protestant immigration. For Baring-Gould, Evangelicalism "did not spring out of the Church herself."[15] Herein is a reminder that an emphasis on nationalism and the "Englishness" of Anglicanism, features which the Tractarian deplored and which the early Oxford Movement repudiated, was reintroduced within later Anglo-Catholicism and was not intrinsic to Protestant understandings of the Church of England. Thus, Baring-Gould was quite unable to share the admiration for Evangelicalism which had marked the first-generation Tractarians and he dismissed Evangelical religion as being "of a miserably partial quality, not partaking of the fullness of the spirituality that is found among Catholics, English or Roman."[16] Of the Evangelicals of his own generation, Baring-Gould was scathing:

> Most of the Evangelicals whom I met and knew were formal; and smugness was the badge of their tribe. They were all, without exception, men of very narrow views. Religion with them was subjective, emotional, concentrated on self ... They conceived of God in no other capacity than that of being engaged over individuals, like a scientist examining, feeding and providing for animalcules, and unconcerned about creation at large. Of worship they had no conception at all.[17]

It is possible, however, to get behind the well-rehearsed polemics which initially came to divide Tractarians and Evangelicals and which solidified in succeeding generations into the often harsh and bitter rhetoric cited above, and to view the real spiritual affinities which both movements originally had in common; a fact perhaps the less surprising when it is realized just how many adherents and followers of the Oxford Movement had come from Evangelical households or had had an early Evangelical career. Moreover, certain individuals such as the Irish high churchman, Alexander Knox (1757–1831) and his friend and life-long correspondent, John Jebb (1775–1833), bishop of Limerick, acted as bridge figures who managed to

---

14. Walter Walsh, *The Secret History of the Oxford Movement* (London: Swan Sonnenschein & Co., 1898), esp. chaps 9–11.

15. Sabine Baring-Gould, *The Church Revival. Thoughts thereon and Reminiscences* (London: Methuen & Co., 1914), 86.

16. Ibid., 81.

17. Ibid., 88.

span the Evangelical/High Church divide and ensured that what became known as Tractarianism retained components of Evangelicalism and even elements characteristic of Wesleyan Methodism. Alexander Knox as a boy and young man had had contact with John Wesley and was the recipient of twenty letters of religious and practical advice from the founder of Methodism. It was one of Knox's contentions that the Church of England since the Reformation had neglected an emphasis on the interior life partly out of an excessive fear of "popery."[18] He regarded Evangelicalism and Methodism as supplying that deficiency but his real hope for was a reinvigoration of a dormant high church Anglicanism which might harness the best in both competing spiritual traditions. For this reason, he and Bishop Jebb have been regarded as precursors of the Oxford Movement,[19] though it has recently been rightly argued that Jebb should be regarded as a creative and original theologian in his own right who rose above party labels.[20]

It was with neglected but crucial figures such as Alexander Knox and John Jebb in mind that Brilioth maintained that the nineteenth-century revival in the Church of England commonly known as the Oxford Movement might be better and more broadly described as the "Anglican Renaissance" or revival of "Neo-Anglicanism."[21] There was no wholesale repudiation of Evangelicalism. In Newman's case, there seems to have been a link between his conversion to Rome in 1845 and his first "evangelical" conversion in 1816 at the age of fifteen. In short, Newman's second conversion can be presented as an affirmation and completion, not repudiation, of his Evangelical past. Others have argued that the "Calvinist influences of his youth" and a belief in a form of personal election by grace always remained with Newman, casting what has been called "a dark shadow" over his preaching. It has also been plausibly suggested that Newman's acknowledged difficulty in finding in the everyday material world any "reflection of its Creator," gave him a gloomier and more severe outlook than that of even a typical Evangelical.[22] It is significant that Newman could be scathing about "cold Arminian doctrine" as representing "the first stage of liberalism" and of the malign

---

18. *Remains of Alexander Knox*, [ed. James J. Hornby], 4 vols. (London: James Duncan, 1834–1837), 3:208.

19. See Peter B. Nockles, "Church or Protestant sect? The Church of Ireland, High Churchmanship, and the Oxford Movement, 1822–1869," *Historical Journal* 41 no. 2 (1998) 457–93, at 464–65; Alan Acheson, *Bishop Jebb and the Nineteenth-Century Anglican Renaissance* (Toronto: Clements, 2013) esp. chaps 3 & 4.

20. Acheson, *Bishop Jebb*.

21. Ynvge Brilioth, *The Anglican Revival. Studies in the Oxford Movement* (London: Longmans, Green, and Co, 1925).

22. Turner, *John Henry Newman*, 64.

influence of Dutch Arminian divines such as Hugo Grotius (1583–1645) and Philipp van Limborch (1633–1712) in laying the foundations of eighteenth-century Anglican latitudinarianism,[23] while remaining respectful of the Calvinist system. His antipathy to John Wesley and qualified admiration for the Calvinist George Whitefield and Selina, Countess of Huntingdon, also fits this pattern. As he informed his sister Harriett in 1837: "I have nearly finished Southey's 'Wesley' . . . I do not like Wesley—putting aside his exceeding self-confidence, he seems to me to have a very black self-will, a bitterness of religious passion, which is very unamiable. Whitefield seems far better."[24] Newman especially disapproved of what he perceived as a sectarian tendency in John Wesley's religious activity. As Mozley recalled:

> For as long as I can remember him he would have shuddered at the very thought of founding a sect or creating a schism. He desired to modify the Church of England as others have modified it. . . . It would not have suited his nature or his habits to go about from town to town, telling the people everywhere they were in bad hands and take care of themselves, forming them into communities and putting ministers over them.[25]

Frank Turner's suggestion that the "deathbed Anglican" Newman might have contemplated creating such a schism on his own terms seems particularly wide of the mark.[26] Yet for all his dislike of John Wesley, Newman retained a high estimate of the Methodist movement as a whole, as is clear from his review of a new biography of Selina Countess of Huntingdon, in the *British Critic* in October 1840, in which his powers of satire were given full expression. Methodism, in Newman's view, had recovered hidden spiritual treasures out of the Church's store-house, and the Anglican bishops of the day had blundered badly in their inconsistent and ineffectual response to it.[27] Newman was probably drawing a parallel here with the blundering episcopal response to the Oxford Movement—in both cases an Anglican

---

23. [John.Henry Newman], "Le Bas's Life of Archbishop Laud," *British Critic* 19 (1836) 368.

24. John Henry Newman to Mrs J. Mozley, January 19, 1837, in *Letters and Diaries of John Henry Newman*, ed. Gerard Tracey (Oxford: Clarendon Press, 1984), 6:16.

25. Thomas Mozley, *Reminiscences of Oriel College and the Oxford Movement*, 2 vols. (London: Longmans, Green, and Co., 1882,), 2:440–41.

26. See Turner, *John Henry Newman*, chap. 9: "In Schism with all Christendom."

27. [John Henry. Newman], "Life of Selina Countess of Huntington," *British Critic* 28 (1840) 405.

hierarchy could be shown up to be incapable of responding coherently to something new and vital.[28]

One often unrecognized link between the Oxford Movement and the Evangelical Revival was the former's adoption of the same medium of communication perfected by the latter—the publication of (initially) short and pithy printed tracts. Hurrell Froude made this point to Isaac Williams as a justification for commencing the *Tracts for the Times*: "Isaac, we must make a row in the world. Why should we not? Only consider what the Peculiars, i.e. the Evangelicals have done with a few half truths to work upon! And with our principles, if we set resolutely to work, we can do the same."[29] Moreover, there were things which the early Tractarians and Evangelicals could agree upon. The extent of the Church of England's apparent decay in the later eighteenth and nineteenth centuries has been contested in recent "revisionist" scholarship, with studies of the Hanoverian church revising some of the Oxford Movement's criticism of the state of the pre-Tractarian Church of England. Nonetheless, contemporary perceptions of the Church of England's condition in that era were often no less negative. In fact, the Tractarians built upon earlier criticisms of the late-eighteenth and early-nineteenth century Church of England made by Evangelicals, though each emphasized different aspects and causes of spiritual decay or decline.

Some of the early numbers of the *Tracts for the Times*, notably Number Nine, "The Gospel a Law of Liberty" appealed to Evangelicals and were intended to do so. However, an early stumbling block for Evangelicals soon appeared in the Tractarian approach to the doctrine of the Atonement and the preaching thereof. What can be called a Tractarian *ethos* found expression in the theological principle as well as moral temper of "Reserve." This notion had been touched upon by Newman in his *Arians of the Fourth Century*: it was a method of communicating religious knowledge in a gradual and progressive way whereby some truths might be withheld for a time from those being initiated in them. Newman found evidence that the early church had practised this principle in the instruction of those who wanted to become Christians or in disputation with pagans.[30]

The doctrine was developed more fully by Isaac Williams in two of the *Tracts for the Times* (Numbers Eighty and Eighty-Seven), in reaction against what the Tractarians regarded as the emotional excesses of popular

---

28. This analogy was suggested to me by Andrew Nash, editor of a new edition for Gracewing/Notre Dame University Press of Newman's *Essays Critical and Historical*, in which Newman's original review article was republished.

29. Isaac Williams, *Autobiography of Isaac Williams*, 63.

30. See Robin C. Selby, *The Principle of Reserve in the Writings of John Henry Cardinal Newman* (Oxford: Oxford University Press, 1975).

Evangelical religiosity, manifested itself in an unwillingness to speak of religious experience and sacred matters in familiar discourse; it was a principle which dictated strict reticence when communicating religious knowledge, especially in relation to the doctrine of the Atonement which Evangelicals tended to place at the forefront of their teaching and evangelization. Moreover, there appears to have been an element of conscious repudiation of Evangelical practice in Isaac Williams's enunciation of the principle. In his *Autobiography* (published in 1892, after his death), Williams maintained that the Evangelical outcry over his Tracts on Reserve was, "to be expected—it was against their hollow mode of proceeding; it was understood as it was meant, and of this I do not complain."[31] It was certainly thus understood by that vitriolic anti-Tractarian author, Walter Walsh, in his conviction that secrecy underlay the whole movement, as evidenced by his polemic being entitled *The Secret History* and by its first chapter being called "Secret Teachings." Walsh regarded Newman's *Arians of the Fourth Century* (1833) in which the concept of the *disciplina arcanae* or "secret teaching" was promulgated and justified from the precedent that in the Church of Alexandria the catechumens were not taught all the doctrines of the Christian Faith, as the "seed from which many a noxious weed has grown."[32]

The Tractarian theological *ethos* also encompassed an eventual rejection of the evidential approach to Christian apologetic associated with William Paley (1743–1804), author of *A View of the Evidences of Christianity* (1794) and derived earlier from the writings of John Locke. The younger Newman, however, in line with many Evangelical contemporaries, had retained an adherence to a Lockean and Enlightenment apologetic tradition that manifested itself in over a century of religious controversy between English Protestants and their Deist and Freethinking opponents. The young Newman utilized this apologetic method in his correspondence with his sceptical younger brother Charles in the 1820s. However, Newman's abandonment of his earlier Evangelicalism was accompanied by a reappraisal of this apologetic approach in favour of one more rooted in the sacramental principle and mysticism.[33] For the Tractarian Newman, the prerequisites for

---

31. Williams, *Autobiography of Isaac Williams*, 91.

32. Walsh, *Secret History of the Oxford Movement*, 1. See also Martin Wellings, "The Oxford Movement in late nineteenth-century retrospect. R. W. Church, J. H. Rigg and Walter Walsh," in *The Church Retrospective*, ed. Roger Swanson, (Woodbridge, Boydell, 1997), 511–15.

33. I owe this insight to Geerjtan Zuijdegt who is currently developing this connection in a University of Leuven doctoral dissertation. For a recognition that Newman's apologetic changed after the mid-1820s, see Francis McGrath, *John Henry Newman: Universal Revelation* (Macon, GA.: Mercer University Press, 1997), 99–100.

the reception of the truths of the Gospel were to become the humility and receptivity of a child, not mere intellectual attainment or a rational enquiring mind. For Newman, the Paleyite emphasis on a study of the evidences was now deemed to encourage an "evil frame of mind" whereby "the learner is supposed external to the system."[34] For the Tractarians, Paley's argument from design was superficial because it failed to engage with those deeper moral truths that lay above and beyond nature, in the unseen world. Evangelicals, with their belief in biblical typology which sought to harmonize the teaching of the Old and New Testaments, were not per se opposed to this Tractarian methodology. The Tractarians, however, drew out more explicit sacramental implications, arguing that material phenomena were both the types and instruments of things unseen. As Pusey maintained in his unpublished *Lectures on Types and Prophecies* (1836), God had created, "a sort of sacramental union between the type and the archetype, such that the type is meaningful only to the extent that it expresses the archetype, and the archetype can be grasped only by means of embodiment within the type."[35]

The Tractarian and Evangelical movements also paralleled each other in their utilization of literary forms of expression. Tractarian ideas reached a far wider popular social constituency than the *Tracts for the Times* could have reached due to the literary medium of historical novels and tales, notably those from the pens of William Gresley (1801–1876), Francis Paget (1806–1882), and William Edward Heygate (1816–1902).[36] However, this had its counterpart in the much better studied Evangelical literary popularizers. Recent scholarship has highlighted the extent to which Evangelicals were active in Victorian print culture, publishing novels, poems and ballads, as well as works of biography, theology and periodical literature.[37] Newman himself, of course, was the author of a semi-autobiographical novel of conversion, *Loss and Gain* (1848), and that masterpiece of the autobiographical form, his *Apologia pro vita sua* (1864), but here again one can find parallels with a long established Evangelical genre of introspective journal-keeping

---

34. John Henry Newman to A. P. Perceval, January 11, 1835, in Henry Parry Liddon, *Life of Edward Bouverie Pusey*, 4th ed. 4 vols. (London: Longmans, Green, & Co., 1894), 1:301.

35. Edward Bouverie Pusey, MS "Lectures on Types and Prophecies," Pusey House Library, Oxford. An edition of this manuscript by the Rev. George Westhaver is in progress at the time of writing.

36. See Simon Skinner, *Tractarians and the Condition of England: the Social and Political Thought of the Oxford Movement* (Oxford: Oxford University Press, 2004); George Herring, "W. E. Heygate: Tractarian Clerical Novelist," in *The Church and Literature*, eds. Peter Clarke & Charlotte Methuen (Woodbridge: Boydell, 2012), 259–70.

37. For example, see Elizabeth Jay, *The Religion of the Heart. Anglican Evangelicalism and the Nineteenth-Century Novel* (Oxford: Oxford University Press, 1979).

and autobiography. Newman's *Apologia* lay squarely within the tradition of classic religious conversion narratives such as St Augustine's *Confessions* and John Bunyan's *Grace Abounding*. It is impossible to underestimate the influential force of this medium of writing. As one Tractarian Anglican reviewer of the *Apologia*, William Irons, put it, appealing to the authority of an observation made by Hurrell Froude for his view that

> there is no vehicle, comparable to biography, for the propagation of opinion and for the creation of those sympathies which influence life and action so much more than argument.... That interest in a hero which so soon becomes interest in his cause, that plot which belongs to a true life which men are eagerly unravelling will tend to give them, as they read, a sort of complicity in the result.[38]

Such a comment could just as well as fit the Evangelical variant of the spiritual autobiography. It was for this reason that Newman and Keble had risked publishing Froude's own often-controversial theological views and ascetical practices in their edition of his *Remains* (1838–1839). In the event, that move backfired, and several contemporary critics compared the *Remains* unfavourably with the Evangelical genre of spiritual diary as exemplified in a new edition of the diaries of the Evangelical Henry Martyn (the very fact of such comparisons being drawn is significant).[39]

One of the key aspects of the Christian tradition which Evangelicals had always emphasized, and which the leaders of the Oxford Movement sought to revive and put at the heart of their message, was a high view of the ministerial office and calling. The excited theological atmosphere generated by the Oxford Movement was certainly in part a response to a political crisis in church and state, but it was one which necessarily forced Anglican churchmen to re-examine the very roots and basis of their spiritual authority. The inadequacies of resting on the security of establishment and the state were revealed by the challenge of Whig governmental reforms which seemed set to undermine the independence of the church's ministry. The early numbers of the *Tracts for the Times*, were a call to the clergy to magnify their office and recognize their sacred calling and responsibilities. The rights of the "Visible" Church had been violated and laymen were interfering in matters of the clergy. The British legislature had superseded the ecclesiastical power. As Tract Two argued, the Church was a divine foundation not

---

38. William.Josiah Irons, *"Apologia pro vitae Eccleiae Anglicanae": In reply to John Henry Newman D. D.* (Oxford: J. H. & J. Parker, 1864), 5.

39. [James Stephen], "The Lives of Whitefield and Froude—Oxford Catholicism," *Edinburgh Review* 67 (1838) 500–35.

created by the State. The Church had an existence independent of the State, and the State had no right religiously to interfere with its internal concerns.[40] This essentially anti-Erastian argument had a wide resonance for churchmen of all shades, not merely high churchmen but Evangelical churchmen.

There was another aspect of the message of protest in the early Tracts that might appeal to Evangelicals. In the face of the Whig government's interference in church affairs, the very basis of pastoral responsibility and a spiritual cure of souls seemed to be at stake. The Tractarian *ethos* already ensured a rejection of the *mores* and values of the so-called "fox hunting parson" of an earlier generation and often associated with the so-called "high and dry" or "two bottle orthodox" tradition of churchmanship. The air of crisis in 1833 reinforced this outlook. It was an attitude that struck a wide cord and resonance, bringing many anxious and conscientious churchmen within the Movement's orbit. One such was Henry Edward Manning, the future Roman Catholic convert, Archbishop, and Cardinal. As Manning later noted in his private *Journal*, when looking back to his early time as curate at Lavington, Sussex, in the 1830s:

> The first question that rose in my mind was, What right have you to be teaching, admonishing, rebuking others? By what authority do you lift the latch of a poor man's door and enter and sit down and begin to instruct or correct him? This train of thought forced me to see that no culture or knowledge of Greek or Latin would suffice for this. That if I was not a messenger sent from God, I was an intruder and impertinent.[41]

Here was a concern which followers of the Oxford Movement certainly shared with disciples of the Evangelical Revival—the importance of not only the ministerial calling but also of the ministerial commission as the basis of ministerial authority.

Frank Turner's argument that the Oxford Movement was almost inspired by a wholesale repudiation of Evangelical religion of course merely mirrored the line purveyed by the Movement's contemporary Evangelical critics. It rests on a selective and retrospective re-reading of the background and early phase of the Movement's history. Looking back from the vantage point of 1869, Bishop Samuel Wilberforce was closer to the mark with his observation that in the early-1830s it was the Anglican Evangelicals

---

40. *Tracts for the Times, By Members of the University of Oxford*, vol. 1 for 1833–34 (London: Rivington, 1840), Tract 2: "The Catholic Church" [1833], 1–2.

41. Cited in James Pereiro, *Cardinal Manning. An Intellectual Biography* (Oxford: Oxford University Press, 1998), 14.

rather than "high and dry" churchmen who were its most natural potential supporters:

> To both parties the claims of their Church as a leading member of the great Catholic body were substantially unknown. Amongst the orthodox the existence of such claims was still held as a respectable tradition, dormant under the spell of worldly-mindedness, and without any living power; amongst the Evangelicals they were generally unknown and regarded as hindrances to that inner individual spiritual life which it had been the glory of their party to revive ... In many instances the earliest Tracts met with a warmer reception from the latter class than from the former, because whilst the remaining receptiveness of life was most awake amongst the younger Evangelicals, the older and more lethargic party feared even a threatening external change less than internal wakening. Accordingly, many of those who most eagerly received the new enthusiasm, had been bred up in the Evangelical camp.[42]

Certainly, the "high and dry" churchman Godfrey Faussett, Margaret Professor of Divinity at Oxford, in 1838 first turned against the Tractarians on the ground that they were not only revivers of "popery" but also, citing the evidence of Froude's *Remains*, that they were religious "enthusiasts" intent on destabilizing the established church. Faussett's castigation of the recently published *Remains* of Hurrell Froude, as containing "the wild and visionary sentiments of an enthusiastic mind,"[43] echoed the anti-Methodist polemic of a century earlier. The similarities in tone and content of Faussett's critique with Bishop George Lavington's *The Enthusiasm of Methodists and Papists Compared* (1749-1751) directed against the movement of Wesley and Whitefield, and the 1730s and 1740s sermons of Joseph Trapp against the "monstrous enthusiastical absurdities" of the Wesleys, Whitefield, and William Law,[44] are striking.

In the generations prior to the dawn of the Movement, Anglican Evangelicals had asserted an increasingly conservative emphasis on church order and discipline and the binding ties of church and state. The stigma of

---

42. Samuel Wilberforce, "Keble's Biography," in *Essays Contributed to the Quarterly Review*, 2 vols. (London: John Murray, 1874), 2:222-76, at 260.

43. Godfrey Faussett, *The Revival of Popery. A Sermon preached before the University of Oxford at St Mary's ... 20 May 1838* (Oxford: At the University Press, for the Author, 1838), 13.

44. Joseph Trapp, *The Nature, Usefulness, and Regulation of Religious Zeal. A Sermon preached at St Mary's, Oxford, August 2, 1739* (Oxford, 1739), 7; Joseph Trapp, *A Reply to Mr Law's Earnest and Serious Answer* (London, 1741), esp. 41, 117.

itinerancy and irregularity had been repudiated. Moreover, as Alexander Knox's friend, Bishop Jebb noted (about twenty years before the dawn of the Oxford Movement), an interest in the Fathers was being kindled even then among Anglican Evangelicals. As a writer in the Evangelical *Christian Observer* put it in 1816: "the communion of the Church of England with the primitive church may have been too little insisted upon in late times."[45] Newman's own abiding imaginative interest in the Fathers and church of antiquity had been first fired not by any high church source but by the Anglican Evangelical Joseph Milner's evocative *History of the Church of Christ*. As Newman later related in his *Apologia*: he, "was nothing short of enamoured of the long extracts from St Augustine and the other Fathers which I read there. I read them as being the religion of the primitive Christians."[46]

Pusey's biographer, Henry Parry Liddon, later observed that Milner's *Church History* "gave evidence of a sense of the spiritual beauty of the ancient church."[47] Milner's *History* avoided doctrinal controversies and revealed no trace of the party spirit that was to afflict Evangelicalism in the Tractarian era. On the contrary, Milner celebrated examples of genuine piety and "vital" Christianity, even among medieval as well as patristic era saints, St Bernard of Clairvaux being one of his particular favourites.[48] John Wesley had adopted a somewhat similar methodology in his *Concise Ecclesiastical History* (1781).[49] In the words of Henry Rack, like Joseph Milner, John Wesley "picked out scattered sparks of light in the dark ages of popery which preserved the truth until the Reformation dawned."[50] The wider reception of Wesley's views of church history will become clearer in the light of wider current research on John Wesley's *History of England*.[51] However, unlike the "irregular" Evangelical Thomas Haweis's *Church History* (1801), Milner's *History of the Church of Christ* was admired by not only moderate Anglican

---

45. *Christian Observer* 15 no. 175 (1816) 420.

46. Newman, *Apologia*, 121.

47. Liddon, *Life of Edward Bouverie Pusey*, 1:414.

48. John D. Walsh, "Joseph Milner's Evangelical Church History," *JEH* 10 no. 2 (October 1959) 174–87.

49. See Darren Schmidt, "The Pattern of Revival. John Wesley's Vision of 'Iniquity' and 'Godliness' in Church history," in *Revival and Resurgence in Christian History*, eds. Kate Cooper & Jeremy Gregory, (Woodbridge, Boydell, 2008), 142–53 at 150–51. For a fuller exploration of the exploration of the Christian past by Milner and other Evangelicals, see Darren Schmidt, "Reviving the Past: Eighteenth-Century Evangelical Interpretations of Church History," (Ph.D. thesis, St Andrews University, 2009).

50. Rack, *Reasonable Enthusiast*, 349.

51. Professor William Gibson is publishing on John Wesley as an historian.

Evangelicals but, with notable exceptions, by many high churchmen.[52] Thus the Tractarian appeal to the Fathers of the early church was initially by no means per se unacceptable to Anglican Evangelicals.

It is clear that what drew some young Anglican churchmen who had been either reared in Evangelical households or who had come under some form of Evangelical influence to the nascent Oxford Movement was an apparent harnessing of the "objective" with the "subjective" aspects of the Christian religion. Henry Edward Manning was one of several churchmen who fell into this category. Manning himself had been reared in a stiffly "high and dry" church household but seems in his later undergraduate years to have come under the Evangelical influence of the Bevan family. As James Pereiro has demonstrated, Manning found much contemporary high churchmanship in the 1820s to be too spiritually "arid" and "rational" in its emphasis on an evidential apologetic. He felt the want of a richer devotional religion of the heart and found it in Evangelicalism. However, while embracing Evangelical devotional and practical views and emphases, he refrained from accepting Evangelical dogma and retained his inherited high church doctrinal outlook. The result was something of a fusion between high church principles and Evangelical piety.[53]

This combination of Evangelical spiritual fervour and personal religion with formal high-church dogma and ecclesial order was widely replicated. It was particularly pronounced among those who had been through an unqualified Evangelical phase after a formalistic high-church upbringing, such as Walter Kerr Hamilton, later made bishop of Salisbury in 1854 and regarded as the first Tractarian bishop. Moreover, many reared in the Evangelical tradition made this transition. The later skeptic Mark Pattison, as well as the Wilberforce brothers (Henry and Robert), were actually drawn into Tractarianism by what Pattison felt to be the inner force of an inherited *pietisme* of an evangelical type.[54] Such one-time Evangelicals were attracted by the Tractarian emphasis on the pursuit of holiness, which they personally no longer felt capable of full realization from within what they came to regard as the incomplete doctrinal framework of Evangelicalism. The result was, as Sheridan Gilley maintains, that the "Oxford Movement carried out of the evangelical party the leadership of a whole evangelical generation."[55]

52. Samuel Roffrey Maitland, one-time Librarian of Lambeth Palace, and critic of the accuracy of Foxe's *Book of Martyrs* was at least one exception. See S. R. Maitland, *A Letter to the Rev. Hugh James Rose . . . with Strictures on Milner's "Church History"* (London: J. G. & F. Rivington, 1834).

53. Pereiro, *Cardinal Manning*, 12–16.

54. Mark Pattison, *Memoirs* (London: Macmillan, 1885), 173.

55. Sheridan Gilley, "Edward Irving: Prophet of the Millennium," in *Revival and Religion since 1700. Essays for John Walsh*, eds. Jane Garnett & Colin Matthew (London: Bloomsbury Academic, 1993), 102.

This process was encouraged by the trend towards hyper-Calvinist extremism, anti-establishmentarianism and a "gathered church" ecclesiology among the so-called Oxford seceders of the early-1830s such as Henry Bellenden Bulteel, Benjamin Wills Newton, and J. C. Philpot.[56] Oxford Evangelicalism was weak but had prominent representatives in Exeter College (where Bulteel was Fellow) and Wadham College and St Edmund Hall (whose Principal, John Hill was Oxford Evangelicalism's leader in the 1830s). For a time, Bulteel's preaching at St Ebbe's church was as influential as Newman's was later to be at St Mary's or the moderate Evangelical Charles Simeon's was at Cambridge. As David Newsome, and more recently Grayson Carter, have suggested, the loss to Oxford Evangelicalism of such influential local leaders was a gain to Oxford High Churchmanship. Carter also suggests that Newman's reaction against Evangelicalism was exacerbated by the unattractive face presented by such extremist representatives as Bulteel and his followers.[57] However, former Evangelicals drawn to Tractarianism felt that the pursuit of holiness was still less capable of realization within the arid husks of contemporary "high and dry" churchmanship. The Nonconformist historian, J. Guinness Rogers later made the point crudely: "The 'High and Dry' party had been nothing but churchmen; the Evangelicals had been everything but churchmen. What this new and earnest generation were bent on doing was to retain all the Evangelicalism plus the churchmanship."[58] While this assessment overlooks the real points of doctrinal division that existed, it contains a grain of truth.

Newman's own spiritual journey certainly fits this pattern. There is also an interesting reversal here of a process that had characterized the early Evangelical Revival of a century before. David Bebbington, following John Walsh, has observed that many an early Evangelical of the mid-eighteenth century had previously passed through a high church phase of some type or had commonly been reared in high church or nonjuring households.[59] They

---

56. Timothy C. F. Stunt, *From Awakening to Secession. Radical Evangelicals in Switzerland and Britain 1815-35* (Edinburgh: T & T. Clark, 2000), esp. 194–215.

57. Grayson Carter, *Anglican Evangelicals: Protestant Secessions from the Via Media, c. 1800-1850* (Oxford: Oxford University Press, 2001), 309–11; Gareth Atkins, "Wilberforce and his *milieux*: the worlds of Anglican Evangelicalism, c. 1780–1830," (Ph.D. thesis, University of Cambridge, 2009), 248.

58. J. Guinness Rogers, *The Church Systems of England in the Nineteenth Century For the Sixth Congregational Union Lecture* (London: Hodder and Stoughton, 1881), 172.

59. John D. Walsh, "The Origins of the Evangelical Revival," in Gareth V. Bennett & John D. Walsh, eds. *Essays in Modern English Church History in Memory of Norman Sykes* (London: A & C. Black, 1966), 138–44; Bebbington, *Evangelicalism in Modern Britain*, 36–38.

had abandoned high churchmanship at a time when they perceived that that tradition had lost its earlier spiritual vitality. Nearly a century later, the new high churchmen of the Oxford Movement could have used a similar analogy in relation to their own early Evangelical upbringing, which they now felt was losing its early spiritual vitality, though they might have substituted the word "Church" for "Christ."

Frank Turner was right to emphasize Newman's reaction against Evangelicalism during the hey-day of his leadership of the Oxford Movement. However, it was not so much that this emphasis was more pronounced than or overshadowed Newman's protest against liberalism as Turner suggested, but that liberalism was thereby assailed through his critique of Evangelicalism. At this period, as in his controversial Tract Seventy-Three ("On the Introduction of Rationalistic Principles into Religion") and Tract Eighty-Five ("Lectures on the Scripture Proof of the Doctrine of the Church"), Newman criticized Evangelicalism for over emphasizing mere feeling and for a tendency, albeit unconsciously, to promote rationalism. Evangelicalism was faulted for its apparent subjectivism, individualism, emotionalism, and inadequate ecclesiology. Evangelicalism's very preoccupation with the state of an individual's feelings and relationship with God rendered it peculiarly vulnerable to sliding into the Rationalist mindset of taking as one's spiritual center oneself and not one's Maker, of bringing God to oneself rather than oneself to God. Newman's critique of popular Evangelicalism on these lines was undoubtedly fuelled by the example of the spiritual pilgrimage (in a polar opposite direction to his own) of his younger brother Francis. As such, it found its clearest expression in those two Tracts in his attack on the theology of Thomas Erskine of Linlathen (1788–1870) and Jacob Abbott, designed to show that evangelicalism would not be able to withstand a full-scale rationalistic assault on Biblicism. This was because, according to Newman in relation to Erskine and Abbott, while it was a school of doctrine which intended and professed "peculiar piety," it directed "its attention to the heart itself, not to anything external to us, whether creed, actions, or ritual."[60] Newman's critique is interesting given that some Evangelicals were blamed for the opposite extreme of being too concerned with actions and "activism." However, some commentators have claimed that Newman's critique was prophetic of the challenge to biblical inerrancy mounted in *Essays and Reviews* in 1860, and that Evangelicals were less well equipped as a result to mount an intellectually convincing response to that Broad Church challenge. Moreover, the early and mid-Victorian era of what has

---

60. See *Tract for the Times*, By Members of the University of Oxford. Vol. III for 1835–36. New edition (London: Rivington, 1840), Tract Seventy-Three: "On the Introduction of Rationalistic Principles into Religion," 1–56.

been called "Evangelical disenchantment" witnessed many examples of disillusioned former disciples of the Evangelical tradition following the path to rationalism and Unitarianism, if not outright unbelief. Francis Newman was only one of many examples of the trend.[61]

There was another side to Newman's ambivalent relationship to his Evangelical inheritance—as he abandoned the "Via Media," approached and converted to Roman Catholicism, he appeared to rediscover aspects of his early Evangelicalism.[62] Thomas Mozley observed with keen insight that in the *Apologia* Newman reverted towards his earliest religious impressions and early home in the Evangelical party, increasingly viewing the Church of England as an external affair, out of the sphere of the soul. As Mozley noted, for the Tractarian Newman: "What may be called the hagiology and the traditions of the Low Church still held their ground in his heart and soul, even side by side with Saints, Fathers, and Councils."[63] All this is borne out by the warm and positive references made by Newman to his early Evangelical mentors. Newman singled out not only Walter Mayers who was instrumental in his first Evangelical conversion, but also the influence of Thomas Scott of Aston Sandford (1747–1821): "who made a deeper impression on my mind than any other and to whom (humanly speaking) I almost owe my soul." Newman made his own and "used almost as proverbs" two of Scott's mottos: "holiness before peace," and "Growth is the only evidence of life." He related that while an undergraduate he had intended to make a special visit to his Parsonage "in order to see a man whom I so deeply revered," but Scott's death in 1821 prevented him from fulfilling this aim. He also confided that he had "hung upon the lips of Daniel Wilson [senior], afterwards Bishop of Calcutta," as in two sermons he had delivered on Scott's life and death.[64] Newman's known residual respect for the Calvinist system probably also contributed to the nostalgic hue in which he viewed his early Evangelical masters.

Both Tractarians and Evangelicals taught that conversion and regeneration, however differently interpreted, must result in holiness of life.[65] Yet for all the spiritual affinities, the doctrinal divisions between Evangelicalism and Tractarianism were real and widened over time. The Tractarians ut-

---

61. David Hempton, *Evangelical Disenchantment: 9 portraits of Faith and Doubt* (New Haven: Yale University Press, 2008), 41–69.

62. Gilley, *Newman and his Age*, 90.

63. Mozley, *Reminiscences*, 1:392.

64. Newman, *Apologia*, 60.

65. William Marshall, "The Evangelical and Oxford Movement Compared," in *Scripture, Tradition and Reason: A Selective View of Anglican Theology over Three Centuries* (Dublin: The Columba/S. P. C. K., 2010), 144.

terly rejected the evangelical understanding of the 'new birth' applied in the sense of instantaneous conversion and gave much greater weight to the sacraments and the efficacy of sacramental grace in the whole schema of salvation. Rejecting the idea of "conversionism" as defined by Evangelicalism, the Tractarians tended to apply the evangelical language of conversion such as "creation of a new heart," "new birth," or "supernatural rebirth," specifically to the ordinance of Baptism.

The differences between the two sides as they emerged over the relationship between Scripture and Tradition (Evangelicals holding to *sola scriptura* while Tractarians stressed the co-ordinate role of Apostolical Tradition), and over baptismal regeneration and interpretations of the doctrine of Justification (as played out between Newman and G. S. Faber in 1837-1838, for example) were deep-rooted and deep-seated.[66] Faced with the Tractarian challenge to the principle of *sola scriptura*, Anglican Evangelicals were at the forefront of reaction to Keble's Visitation sermon on *Primitive Tradition Recognised in Holy Scripture* (1837). In the case of Baptism, Evangelical criticism of Pusey's Tracts Sixty-Seven and Sixty-Nine for supposedly advocating an *opus operatum* doctrine of baptismal grace amounted to something of a replay of the baptismal controversy that had divided Evangelical and orthodox churchmen twenty years earlier. In the case of Justification, Newman, following Alexander Knox, was accused of cutting at the root of the Reformation doctrine of Justification by Faith alone. Comparing the Tractarian with the Evangelical view, G. S. Faber asserted:

> The one system grounds our justification upon our own Intrinsic Righteousness, infused into us by God, through our faith in the Lord Jesus Christ. The other System grounds our Justification upon the Extrinsic Righteousness of Christ appropriated and forensically made our own by faith as by an appointed instrument.[67]

Over the doctrine of the Eucharist, however, there was little debate or controversy between the two sides prior to a Tractarian shift of emphasis in sacramental teaching in the 1850s from Baptism to the Eucharist and the emergence of an "objective" doctrine of a Real Presence related to the consecrated Elements.

---

66. Peter B. Nockles, *The Oxford Movement in Context: Anglican High Churchmanship in Britain 1760-1857* (Cambridge: Cambridge University Press, 1994), 236-37.

67. George Stanley Faber, *The Primitive Doctrine of Justification Investigated Relatively to the Definitions of the Church of Rome and the Church of England* (London: R. B. Seeley & W. Burnside, 1837), iv.

Tractarian spirituality may have been at one with Evangelicalism and Methodism in the goal of pursuing holiness[68] but appeared to differ radically over the means of its attainment—they were divided over soteriology. Like John Wesley, Newman urged on his followers the pursuit of Christian Perfection, but unlike Wesley held that perfection was not possible in this life. The Tractarians rejected the Evangelical and Wesleyan assertion that one might be sure of one's salvation or have an assurance of being forgiven. Newman insisted that one could do no more than "fear and hope" of salvation. His and the Tractarian idea of conversion thus seemed to diverge from that of Evangelicalism and Methodism. Newman strongly opposed evangelicals who held that man was "converted to God all at once." Conversion was a gradual process, part of the process of sanctification which was a painful toil of working out one's own salvation with fear and trembling. Yet, as both Sheridan Gilley and Timothy Stunt in different ways have argued, it is easy to caricature the Evangelical position and unfairly restrict it to the idea of instantaneous conversion and a sense of assurance of liberation from sin. On the contrary, as Gilley demonstrates, the moderate Calvinists of the Clapham Sect such as Mayers who so influenced the young Newman, put little stress on intensity of personal feeling and much more on the gradual nature of conversion involving moral effort and self-denial. As Gilley concludes,

> against the radical Evangelical tendency to put all the stress upon conversion, and to make Christ's work for the saved sinner a denial of the need for moral effort—even in extreme cases of the need to obey the moral law—Newman learned from the Evangelical tradition itself the Catholic doctrine of that other need to grow in holiness after conversion, in a better and higher keeping of the moral law which Christ had come not to abolish but to fulfil.[69]

It was for this reason that Newman, as David Newsome has argued, seemed to unite the severer elements of two different systems (the Calvinist and Catholic, both a notion of election and of the necessity and struggle to achieve sanctification).[70] One explanation suggested by Timothy Stunt is that Anglican Evangelicals such as Henry Venn, Thomas Scott, and Henry Martyn, had themselves retained some enduring high church influences of their own youth, notably their reading of William Law's *Serious Call*

---

68. See Trevor Dearing, *Wesleyan and Tractarian Worship: An Ecumenical Study* (London, Epworth/S. P. C. K., 1966).

69. Gilley, *Newman and his Age*, 22.

70. Newsome, *Parting of Friends*, 180–81.

to a Devout and Holy Life, which marked them for life.[71] Here again was common ground between the best in both the Evangelical and high church religious traditions. For while it was said of Hurrell Froude that William Law "was the writer most on his table," and Tractarians admired Law for his assault on Bishop Hoadly in the Bangorian controversy (itself the subject of Henry Rack's scholarly analysis),[72] Law's spiritual influence on the Wesleys and other Evangelicals was such that for Bishop Warburton "he begat Methodism."[73]

How far was the Oxford Movement really a continuation or fulfilment of the Evangelical Revival or at least of the Evangelicalism dominant on the eve of the Movement itself? Robert Wilberforce and William Gladstone were prominent proponents of the Evangelical parentage of the Oxford Movement,[74] with Gladstone famously declaring: "The Evangelical movement filled men so full with the wine of spiritual life that larger and better vessels were required to hold it."[75] Brilioth agreed. As he pithily observed in relation to the three sons of William Wilberforce: "It can be said of those and many others that as they went from Oxford to Rome, so they had already marched from Clapham to Oxford."[76]

It is perhaps noteworthy, however, that most of those who made the direct comparison and link tended to be former Evangelicals who had made the switch to Tractarianism, and sometimes to Rome. They tended to make the comparison at the expense of or detriment to Evangelicalism itself. That creed and religious tradition may have originally inspired them but had been ditched and turned inside out by themselves in favour of what they regarded as fuller "Catholic" teaching and practice. In fact, of those who had embraced the Oxford Movement it was those who had themselves emerged from an Evangelical stable who tended to be the most critical of it. The great medieval historian, William Stubbs, bishop of Oxford, fitted this religious pattern. In later life, he observed that the Evangelical Revival which had carried over into the early part of the century had been "anti-dogmatic and

---

71. Stunt, *From Awakening to Secession*, 192.

72. Henry D. Rack, "'Christ's Kingdom not of this World': the Case of Benjamin Hoadly versus William Law Reconsidered," in D. Baker, ed. *Church, Society, and Politics* (Oxford, Blackwell, 1975), 275–91.

73. Mozley, *Reminiscences of Oriel College and the Oxford Movement*, 1:248.

74. Robert Isaac Wilberforce, *The Evangelical and Tractarian Movements. A Charge Delivered to the Clergy of the Archdeaconry of the East Riding* (London: J. Murray [1851]); W. E. Gladstone, "The Evangelical Movement: Its Parentage, Progress, and Issue," *Gleanings of Past Years*, 7 vols. (London, John Murray, 1879), 7:201–40.

75. Cited in Brilioth, *Anglican Revival*, 43.

76. Ibid., 53.

partial, and contained in itself the element of weakness and narrowness." He felt that the character of Evangelicalism had suffered from gaining popularity too rapidly and that "the very easiness of its formula contributed to make the profession of religion comparatively easy."[77] One thinks of Obadiah Slope of Anthony Trollope's literary imagination. Like Gladstone, Stubbs assumed that Evangelicalism had stood in need of the corrective provided by the Oxford Movement and of being shaken out of its self-complacency.

It is perhaps not surprising that Anglican Evangelicals who did not abandon their tradition were not ready to accept the status of the Evangelical Revival as a mere prelude or transition to a more complete religious revival represented by the Oxford Movement. However, it has been argued that Tractarianism was only one of several responses to the religious crisis of the late-1820s and early-1830s. Timothy Stunt, David Bebbington, John Burnham and others have argued that many of the Oxford Evangelical seceders from the Church of England to Protestant Dissent of the 1820s and early-1830s, such as Henry Bellenden Bulteel, John Nelson Darby, and Benjamin Wills Newton who helped establish the Plymouth Brethren, shared certain attitudes and dissatisfactions about the *status quo* in church and state with the early Tractarians, though they eventually took a very different course from theirs.[78] Bebbington even claims that the radical Evangelicals of the late-1820s were, "not just similar to the Tractarians but were actually an earlier phase of the same movement that in the 1830s proliferated into many strands—including the Brethren and the Catholic Apostolic Church as well as Tractarianism."[79]

This may be overstating the case. Moderate Evangelicals were almost as horrified as were high churchmen by Bulteelite excesses of hyper-Calvinism (bordering on Antinomianism) and opposition to infant baptism. They in turn were castigated by Bulteel and his supporters as deluded supporters of a corrupt establishment. Nonetheless, the affinities were such that John Nelson Darby, one of the founders of the Brethren, later made clear the extent to which he had once felt the same gravitational pull towards ultra-high churchmanship, apostolical succession and high sacramentalism, that was to

---

77. William Stubbs, *A Visitation Charge Delivered to the Clergy and Churchwardens of the Dioceses of Oxford, May–June 1899* (Oxford: Oxford University Press, 1899), 54.

78. Stunt, *From Awakening to Secession*, 214–15.

79. Bebbington, *Evangelicalism in Modern Britain*, 96. See also Peter B. Nockles, "The Oxford Movement and its Historiographers: Brilioth's *Anglican Revival* and *Three Lectures on Evangelicalism and the Oxford Movement* Revisited," in *Tradition and Formation: Claiming the Inheritance. Essays in Honour of Peter C. Erb*, eds. M. Desjardins & H. Remus (Kitchener, Ontario: Pandora, 2007), 179–92 at 187. Sheridan Gilley also compares Edward Irving and Irvingism with Newman and the Oxford Movement. See Gilley, "Edward Irving: Prophet of the Millennium," 95–126 at 102–3.

animate John Henry Newman as leader of the Oxford Movement. Reviewing Newman's *Apologia* (1864), Darby revealingly observed: "I know the system. I knew it and walked in it years before Dr Newman (as I learned from this book) thought on the subject, and when Dr Pusey was not heard of."[80]

In conclusion, one can say that the spiritual character and strength of the Oxford Movement owed much to the earlier Evangelical Revival, and that there were resemblances between Tractarianism and Evangelicalism, just as there were between Tractarianism and Pietism (Pusey's friendship and correspondence with the German Lutheran Pietist Professor Tholuck is an example of the link).[81] Someone like Samuel Wilberforce, bishop of Oxford, linked through background and family to both schools, was in a good position to regard them as parallel attempts to revive "the dormant energies of the spiritual life."[82] There was the same conviction that doctrine must relate to spiritual life and the same emphasis on the quest for holiness. Perhaps the real differences lay over the doctrine of Reserve and Justification as much as that of the sacraments, apostolic succession, *sola scriptura* and role of Tradition, though as Boyd Hilton has demonstrated, one can add the contrast between a Tractarian emphasis on the Incarnation with an Evangelical one on the Atonement.[83] While Frank Turner's contention that Newman and the Movement's main *bête noir* was always Evangelicalism rather than Liberalism is problematic, he persuasively shows the extent of the Movement's repudiation of the terms of expression of Evangelical religiosity, notably its over-familiarity with the sacred.[84] However, Turner's argument lacks nuance and he did not distinguish clearly enough between the radical Evangelicalism of Bulteel and (for a time) John Henry's own brother Francis on the one hand and the more moderate Evangelicalism of the Clapham school. Much of the force of Newman's early Tractarian strictures on Evangelicalism was directed against the former rather the latter.

---

80. Cited in Jonathan D. Burnham, *A Story of Conflict: the Controversial Relationship between Benjamin Wills Newton and John Nelson Darby* (Milton Keynes: Paternoster, 2004), 31.

81. See Peter Erb, "Pietism and Tractarian Oxford: Edward Bouverie Pusey, Evangelicalism, and the Interpretation of German Theology," in *Rezeption und Reform: Festschrift fur Hans Schneider zu seinem, 60 Geburstag*, ed. W. Bruel-Kinkel & L. Vogel (Darmstadt und Kassel: Verlag derr Hessischen Kirchengeschichtlichen Vereinigung, 2001), 399-417.

82. Samuel Wilberfoce, *A Charge delivered to the Diocese of Oxford at his eighth Visitation, November 1869* (Oxford: J. Parker, 1869), 29.

83. See Boyd Hilton, *The Age of Atonement: The Influence of Evangelicalism on Social and Economic Thought* (Oxford: The Clarendon Press, 1988).

84. Turner, *John Henry Newman*, chap 1.

Dieter Voll in his otherwise very persuasive study *Catholic Evangelicalism* (1963), was surely mistaken in his view that the early Tractarians showed no consciousness "of being the bearer of an Evangelical inheritance," and that such a consciousness only emerged in the second generation of the Oxford Movement.[85] The evidence we have adduced demonstrates quite otherwise. Robert Wilberforce, perhaps the Oxford Movement's greatest theologian and of course one of the sons of the notable Evangelical William Wilberforce, made this case very persuasively in a Charge to the clergy of his East Riding archdeaconry in 1851. According to Wilberforce, the Evangelical Revival had produced that essential preliminary renewal of the spiritual life of the Church of England without which the Tractarian message might have fallen on stony ground and captured few hearts. As he put it, in reference to the legislative assault on the Church's position of the years 1828–1833: "God's providence delayed that blow until there was life enough to discern its consequences," and the right men at the right moment to react against them.[86]

In what then did the Oxford Movement's character as a religious revival or spiritual awakening consist? The issue was a source of dispute and some misunderstanding among followers of the rival Anglo-Catholic and Evangelical religious traditions. For the former, when viewing the "Catholic revival" from a retrospect of fifty years or more, it was, as one partisan writing in 1912 put it, "one of the most wonderful revivals in church history," comparable to the religious revival in the "days of Josiah towards the close of the Jewish monarchy."[87] However, like many Anglo-Catholic historiographers of this period, this author focused almost entirely on external matters of liturgy and public worship, notoriously the main concern of the Ritualist movement but almost completely absent from the original Oxford Movement itself. It is clear that what became known as the "Catholic revival" was not co-terminus with the Oxford Movement proper and encompassed something broader and longer in time-span. Later Anglo-Catholics misleadingly tended to conflate the two, but a case can be made for viewing the later ritual and liturgical developments as an outworking of the theological principles of Tractarianism, especially its Eucharistic doctrine.[88]

85. Dieter Voll, *Catholic Evangelicalism: the Acceptance of Evangelical Traditions by the Oxford Movement during the second half of the Nineteenth Century* (London: Faith, 1963), 39.

86. Robert Isaac Wilberforce, *Evangelical and Tractarian Movements*, 10–11.

87. Henry P. Denison, *The Catholic Revival. A Retrospect and a Warning. A Lecture Delivered at the Guildhall, Bath, on Nov 16th, 1911* (Bath: George Gregory, 1912), 11.

88. George Herring, "Tractarianism to Ritualism. A Study of Some Aspects of Tractarianism outside Oxford, from the time of Newman's conversion in 1845 until the

The Oxford Movement was both an intellectual movement and one of spiritual revival; it was concerned with the vindication of theological truth as well as promotion of personal holiness. In fact, one of the criticisms of the Movement was that it was too much directed to the well educated and had less to say to those who lacked learning. It was this intellectual dimension which probably attracted many sons from Evangelical households, such as the Wilberforce brothers, George Dudley Ryder and others, for whom the popular religion of the day was found wanting in practical "reality." For those from this tradition, the "Catholic Revival," unlike its Evangelical precursor, awakened a sense of the independent and corporate life of the Church in relation to the state. It also represented a much needed revival of theological studies and learning, exemplified in the foundation of new theological colleges such as Wells and Cuddesdon, near Oxford (colleges which soon gained a reputation for "Puseyism");[89] a much needed liturgical renewal, stricter attention to the rubrics, architectural improvement, improvement of education, a revival of the Religious life, and also the value of self-denial (fasting being a repeated theme of the early Tracts), a renewed missionary impulse based on a corporate view of the Church rather than freelance zeal, and greater recognition of Christian art and culture. According to Bishop Stubbs, the results were "wonderful" and,

> to be seen in every village church, to be heard in every sermon, to be felt in the administration of every parish. Never since the Reformation had there been such a change, and the influences that wrought it were more intellectual and more spiritual than those which affected the Reformation.[90]

It could hardly be expected that many contemporary Anglican Evangelicals would have agreed with this estimate and they did not. Daniel Wilson was insistent that false doctrine could not accompany or underpin a genuine religious revival. Tractarianism, with its "taste for medieval principles and practices" and its "idolatry of the intellect," was an obstacle to religious revival.[91] In short, the Movement's intellectual character was a

---

First Ritual Commission in 1867," (D. Phil. Thesis, Oxford University, 1984); George Herring, *What was the Oxford Movement?* (London: Continuum, 2002), 94–97.

89. William M. Jacob, "The diffusion of Tractarianism: Wells Theological College, 1840–49," *Southern History* 5 (1983) 189–209. Anglican Evangelicals protested against this trend. See Josiah Bateman, *The Tractarian Tendency of Diocesan Theological Colleges* (London: Seeleys, 1853).

90. William Stubbs, *Visitation Charges Delivered to the Clergy and Churchwardens of the Dioceses of Chester and Oxford* (Oxford: Oxford University Press, 1904), 349.

91. Wilson, *Revival of Spiritual Religion*, 14–15.

stumbling block. Moreover, Evangelical opposition to the central tenets of the Tractarian revival did not diminish with time. On the contrary, as Andrew Atherstone has recently shown, at the time of the centennial celebrations of the Oxford Movement in 1933, most Anglican Evangelicals rebutted determined episcopal attempts to enlist them into joining in a wider and official Church commemoration. Several Anglican Evangelical commentators at that time found the Anglo-Catholic assumption that the Movement was the true fulfilment of the Evangelical Revival to be patronizing as well as untrue, asserting that the Evangelical Revival had awakened the Church of England long before the Oxford Movement was born. On the contrary, they argued that the Oxford Movement amounted to a wholesale radiation of the Church's Evangelical Protestant inheritance. For them, the Oxford Movement had left a baleful legacy of a breach in internal church unity and a subversion of Protestantism. On the other hand, many contemporary Anglo-Catholics took their lead from earlier Tractarian characterizations of Evangelicalism as "an exhausted teaching and a spent enthusiasm."[92] There was not much evidence of consensus building or a healing of past differences here. In spite of the best efforts of the Anglican hierarchy, far from laying to rest old sores and forgotten sources of conflict, the centenary was actually marked by a restatement, if not renewal, of controversy.

Yet even hostile Evangelical critics could not overlook the Oxford Movement's spiritual dimension or deny that this gave it some claim to being a religious revival. Even Daniel Wilson was forced to concede:

> The recent Romanising movement in our own church has been designated by some as a religious revival, and in a certain sense it has been so. The subject of religion has attracted public attention. Its external duties have been more sedulously performed than formerly. There has been more activity among the clergy. Many acts of liberality and self-denial have been exhibited. Much earnestness and zeal for the interests of the Church have been shown.[93]

This was significant testimony from one of the Oxford Movement's most implacable opponents. Moreover, there were many whom while rejecting the Movement's doctrinal teaching, readily embraced and remained indebted to its ethical and spiritual dimension. Evangelicals and even some

---

92. Andrew Atherstone, "Evangelicals and the Oxford Movement Centenary," *Journal of Religious History* 37 no. 1 (2013) 98–134. The quotation is from Dean Church. See Richard.William Church, *The Oxford Movement: Twelve Years, 1833–1845*, rev. ed. (1891; repr., London: Macmillan, 1932), 15.

93. Wilson, *Revival of Spiritual Religion*, 5–6.

Broad Churchmen (such as the elder Archbishop Frederick Temple) could admire its spiritual teaching.[94] Even the hard-line Evangelical Dean Close[95] in a work published in 1866 denouncing the "Catholic Revival" as a "Romanising" programme, was stung by Tractarian claims that the Evangelicals of that day had abandoned the ascetical and self-denying character of the revivalist days of Venn, Grimshaw, Newton, Toplady, and Romaine. Close concluded: "These Ritualists will have done us good service if by their reproofs they excite the Evangelical body to greater zeal, love, holiness and self-denial."[96]

It is fitting to end with a generous encomium on the Movement from another inveterate anti-Tractarian, James Garbett, Bampton lecturer and victor over Isaac Williams for Oxford's Poetry Professorship in 1841. Towards the end of the monumental two-volume edition of his 1842 Bampton Lectures which had challenged Tractarian theological principles at every turn, Garbett had this to say of the *Tracts for the Times*:

> Whatever judgment may be formed of their ultimate tendency ... so wide an influence could never have been exerted, or the approbation, however qualified, of wise and good men have been obtained, unless they had successfully struck some deep chord—had hit on some real wants of the period—and brought out distinctly into light certain substantive principles which, before their appearance, had required an adequate exponent, and had formed none ... they possessed ... occasionally a moving and almost tragic eloquence; and a rich scattering over them of really profound thoughts, which probed unsparingly the religious and political deficiencies of the times.[97]

It was a moving tribute. If it were an epitaph on a movement of religious revival and reform, it would be one of which the leaders of the Oxford Movement could have been proud.

---

94. Peter Hinchliff, *Frederick Temple Archbishop of Canterbury: A Life* (Oxford: Oxford University Press, 1998), 19–22.

95. Francis Close (1797–1882), Rector of Cheltenham, 1826–1856 and Dean of Carlisle, 1856–d. Close was popularly known as the "Pope of Cheltenham" during his incumbency there.

96. Francis Close, *The "Catholic Revival," or Ritualism and Romanism in the Church of England, Illustrated from "The Church and the World": A Paper Read at the Annual Meeting of the Evangelical Union of the Diocese of Carlisle, Printed and Published at their Request* (London: Hatchard, 1866).

97. James Garbett, *Christ as Prophet, Priest and King: Being a Vindication of the Church of England from Theological Novelties. Considered in Eight Sermons Preached before the University of Oxford ... At the Lecture Founded by the late John Bampton M. A.*, 2 vols. (Oxford: T. Combe, 1842), 2:462–63.

12

From *The Soul of Dominic Wildthorne* to the Wesleyan Guild of Divine Service
Some Methodist Responses to Anglo-Catholicism in Victorian and Edwardian England

Martin Wellings

IN AUGUST 1868 *PUNCH* published a cartoon entitled "Rejected Addresses." The cartoon depicted Dr Pusey paying court to a demure Methodist maiden, and the conversation went like this:

> Dr Pusey: And my dear young lady, if I could induce you and your friends to look kindly upon my proposal -
>
> Miss Methodist: But you can't, sir. I don't want to go to church at all, and if I did, I'm sure I wouldn't go with you.[1]

The occasion of the cartoon was an approach by Pusey to the Wesleyan Conference, through a letter to the President, John Bedford, appealing for Wesleyan support to resist J. D. Coleridge's bill to abolish the remaining religious tests at Oxford University.[2] Pusey's proposal for the endowment of Dissenting colleges, so that each denomination could teach according to its own principles, was mocked by *The Times* as an abject surrender and denounced as a "wild expedient" by J. W. Burgon.[3] The approach was rebuffed

---

1. "Rejected Addresses," *Punch, or the London Charivari*, August 29, 1868, 91.

2. H. P. Liddon, *Life of Edward Bouverie Pusey, D. D.*, 2nd ed. (London: Longmans, Green, & Co., 1897), 4:200–02; "Wesleyan Conference at Liverpool," *Guardian*, August 19, 1868, 939–40; W. R. Ward, *Victorian Oxford* (London: Frank Cass & Co., 1965), 252–57.

3. *Times*, August 17, 1868, 6 and August 22, 1868, 6; "Mr Burgon to Dr Pusey,"

by the Conference, and it provoked *Punch* to a mocking adaptation of a popular song, which linked Pusey's unsuccessful overtures to the Methodists with his *Eirenicon* addressed to the Church of Rome:

> You offer one hand to the Papal band
>   And the other to us extend;
> Do you really hope that we and the POPE
>   Can acknowledge a "mutual friend?"
> You tell us our bark is not an Ark;
>   We don't believe that's true.
> We'd trust a raft before your craft:
>   Just paddle your own canoe.
>   For to ourselves we'll keep ourselves,
>   Your Colleges' plan won't do.
>   We shall not drown, if you go down;
>   So paddle your own canoe.[4]

In using this incident to introduce his discussion of "Methodism and the Oxford Movement—Aggressive Anglicanism and Militant Dissent," John Munsey Turner draws attention to the "striking similarities" between Wesleyans and Tractarians, noting that Pusey in the *Punch* cartoon is even dressed, like John Wesley in the portrait behind "Miss Methodist," in cassock, gown, and bands.[5] The similarities have fascinated historians, and have excited the ecumenically minded, but contemporaries were more aware of the differences between Methodism and Anglo-Catholicism. Indeed, the cartoon and the squib hinted at many of the areas of conflict: Pusey's suspicious closeness to Rome; his un-churching of the Wesleyans; Methodism's ambiguity about its relationship to the Church of England; fears of predatory priests making improper approaches to young women; Free Church distrust and truculence in the face of the Establishment; and a sense of the imbalance of power between Anglican privilege and Nonconformist aspirations. This essay will endeavour to map Methodist reactions to Anglo-Catholicism in Victorian and Edwardian England, recognizing that this is a huge topic, and one which remains comparatively neglected in the historiography.[6]

Guardian, August 26, 1868, 949–50.

    4. "Conference to Pusey," *Punch*, August 29, 1868, 87.

    5. John Munsey Turner, *Conflict and Reconciliation: Studies in Methodism and Ecumenism in England 1740–1982* (London: Epworth, 1985), 146.

    6. In addition to Turner, ibid., 146–72, see also Mats Selén, *The Oxford Movement and Wesleyan Methodism in England 1833–1882* (Lund: Lund University Press, 1992) and Gordon S. Wakefield, "'A mystical substitute for the glorious gospel?' A Methodist critique of Tractarianism," in Geoffrey Rowell, ed. *Tradition Renewed. The Oxford Movement Conference Papers* (London: Darton Longman and Todd, 1986), 185–98.

In order to set the scene, some introductory comments about nineteenth-century Methodism may be helpful. Three key features characterized Methodism in the century and a quarter between John Wesley's death and the First World War.[7] The first was considerable numerical growth. In 1791 there were about 70,000 Methodist members in Great Britain and Ireland, supported by three hundred travelling preachers and occupying four hundred chapels or preaching houses. By the time of the religious census of March 1851, Methodism claimed two and a half million attendances at Sunday worship—just over a third of the national total—in more than 10,000 places of worship. There were over a thousand ministers in the Wesleyan Connexion alone, and an army of Local Preachers, Sunday school teachers, and class leaders. Although strongest in Cornwall and Yorkshire, the Potteries and the North East, and comparatively weak in the South and the South East, Methodism was well represented across the whole country and by the end of the nineteenth century the Methodist presence extended from city centers to the new suburbs and from market towns into many villages. Numerical growth was matched by institutional development, so that Methodism had its denominational headquarters, its theological colleges, its schools, newspapers, periodicals, and missionary societies. In the early 1880s Hugh Price Hughes, then the Wesleyan Superintendent in Oxford, clashed with Mark Pattison, Rector of Lincoln College, over the lack of an adequate memorial to John Wesley in the university city. Pattison thought that Methodism was insignificant, and was astonished when Hughes produced statistics to show that the Methodist communion worldwide numbered twenty-five million.[8] Thirty years later the Wesleyans opened the Westminster Central Hall as a visible sign of strength, wealth, and influence at the heart of the Empire.

The second key feature of nineteenth-century Methodism was division. Between 1797 and 1857 the Wesleys' movement split into a series of competing Connexions. The original body continued, holding on to the Wesleyan name, and the Wesleyan Connexion remained by far the largest of the Methodist groups. But gradually, through secession, expulsion and a series of renewal movements, the Wesleyans of the old Connexion were joined by other Methodist denominations: the New Connexion, the Bible Christians, the Primitive Methodists, and the United Methodist Free

---

7. For insightful summaries of this period see Henry D. Rack, *The Future of John Wesley's Methodism* (London: Lutterworth, 1965), 27–38 and "Wesleyan Methodism 1849–1902," in Rupert Davies, A. Raymond George, and Gordon Rupp, eds. *A History of the Methodist Church in Great Britain*, 4 vols. (London: Epworth, 1983), 3:119–66.

8. David Hempton, *Methodism: Empire of the Spirit* (New Haven: Yale University Press, 2005), 1.

Churches, to name but four. Some of these groups extended Methodism into new areas, so that Primitive Methodism, for example, grew strong in the Durham coalfield and in rural East Anglia, while the Bible Christians were concentrated in Devon and Cornwall. In other places, Methodist societies overlapped and chapels competed for adherents.

The third feature of this period which needs to be noted was ecclesiastical realignment. The Wesleys' Methodism was a society within the Church of England, and the expressed intention of John and Charles Wesley was that it should stay there. The brothers differed, however, in assessing the consequences of particular actions for Methodism's ability to remain within the Church. Charles Wesley, supported by a significant body of so-called "Church Methodists," was more sensitive to breaches of ecclesiastical order than was John Wesley. By ordaining preachers on his own authority from 1784, John Wesley took a significant step away from Anglican order, and by bequeathing control of his Connexion and its property to the annual Conference of Methodist Preachers, Wesley gave institutional continuity to his movement. Within five years of his death the Conference had conceded that the Preachers might celebrate the Eucharist for the Methodist people in their own chapels. With the rapid growth of Methodism in the early nineteenth century, the Connexion gradually developed a separate life from that of the Church of England. This was exacerbated both by the rise of new Methodist groups, with fewer residual loyalties to the Established Church, and by pastoral reforms which sought to place an energetic incumbent in every parish. As the parish church was transformed, turning it, in Frances Knight's phrase, into "a resort for the devout rather than a resource for the community," people were forced to choose between Methodism and the Church.[9] The branches of Methodism increasingly moved into the orbit of the Free Churches, sharing in the broader chapel culture of late Victorian and Edwardian England.

Nineteenth-century Methodism, therefore, was an evangelical denomination (or family of denominations) with a particular emphasis on and approach to Christian holiness. It cherished a special relationship with the Church of England: the Wesleyans shied away from referring to their Connexion as a "church" until the 1890s and were careful to distinguish themselves from what they regarded as the dissidence of Dissent. Addressing the

---

9. Frances Knight, *The Nineteenth Century Church and English Society* (Cambridge: Cambridge University Press, 1995), 71. See also Selén, *Oxford Movement and Wesleyan Methodism*, 84, and John C. Bowmer, *Pastor and People* (London: Epworth, 1975), 234, for examples of zealous parish priests challenging Wesleyan influence, and the local study by Edward Royle, "When did Methodists stop attending their parish churches? Some suggestions from mid-nineteenth century Yorkshire," *PWHS* 56 no. 6 (2008) 275–96.

Conference of 1868, Samuel Romilly Hall, the new President, declared that the "*via media* between Anglicanism and Dissent was their proper designation ... Whilst we hold this midway position, we are still prepared to regard ... with respect and affection the state church, so long as she remains faithful to her calling."[10] By the late 1860s, however, Methodists were increasingly doubtful whether the Church of England was indeed remaining faithful to her calling, and the rise and development of Anglo-Catholicism was the most significant cause of anxiety in that regard.[11]

Before turning to some examples of Methodist responses to Anglo-Catholicism, it may be asked how Victorian and Edwardian Methodists encountered Anglo-Catholic life, teaching and practice: what were the likely points of contact?

Methodists might encounter Anglo-Catholicism directly, in their own parish of residence. As already noted, Methodists, especially Wesleyans, continued to attend the local parish church well into the nineteenth century, and even where regular attendance had dropped away or been discouraged, it remained customary in many places to go to church for rites of passage. Although previous generations of scholarship concentrated on a few celebrated centres of Anglo-Catholicism and suggested that ritualism developed slowly among second-generation Tractarians, more recent research by George Herring and Nigel Yates has shown that ritualism was part of the Oxford Movement from the beginning, and that it spread rapidly. Herring estimates that there were over 400 Tractarian parish priests by 1870, and Yates claims that by this time "virtually every diocese in England and Wales had a handful of churches, and some rather more than a handful, that could be described as ritualist." By 1904 the numbers had risen five-fold to 2000 parishes.[12] Moreover, clergy who might disclaim explicit ritualist or Tractarian loyalties might nonetheless adopt liturgical changes which owed something to Anglo-Catholicism, while the climate of public concern about "Puseyism" could generate accusations against traditional High Churchmen who had little sympathy for the Oxford Movement.[13] In other words, Meth-

---

10. Turner, *Conflict and Reconciliation*, 146.

11. See, for example, "Home News," *Guardian*, 5 August 1868, 871, on Hall's address, and "Wesleyan Conference at Liverpool," ibid., August 19, 1868, 939, reporting Thomas Jackson's letter to the Conference on the changes in the Church of England since the 1820s.

12. Nigel Yates, *Anglican Ritualism in Victorian Britain 1830–1910* (Oxford: Oxford University Press, 1999), 83, 278–79.

13. Jeremy Morris, "The Regional Growth of Tractarianism: Some Reflections," in Paul Vaiss, ed. *Newman: From Oxford to the People* (Leominster: Gracewing, 1996), 146. See, for example, the accusation of "Puseyism" levelled against W. C. Risley, vicar of Deddington in Geoffrey Smedley-Stevenson, ed. *Early Victorian Squarson. The*

odists might believe that their local incumbent was an Anglo-Catholic, even when the priest justifiably denied the charge.

Direct contact was probably less likely than vicarious encounters with Anglo-Catholicism, through sermons, lectures and public meetings, and especially through the printed word. In the first half of the nineteenth century every branch of Methodism had its own monthly magazine, and the essays, news items and book reviews afforded opportunities for the Connexional authorities to express their judgements on ecclesiastical developments. The (Wesleyan) *Methodist Magazine* did not begin to notice the "Oxford Tracts" until 1837, but by 1840–1841 there was considerable concern about "Puseyism."[14] Thereafter the course of the ritual controversies was followed in the *Magazine* and in the various weekly newspapers which developed from mid-century to serve the Methodist reading public: the *Watchman* (1835), the *Wesleyan Times* (1849), the *Methodist Recorder* (1861), the *Methodist Times* (1885), the *Free Methodist* (1886), and others. In their reporting and their editorials these publications fostered a negative view of Anglo-Catholicism. Evidence presented to the Royal Commission of 1867, for example, allowed Methodists to be horrified over the wearing of copes, albs, and chasubles, while the Methodist press reported the Bennett (1850–1851), Ridsdale (1868) and Miles Platting (1882) cases with very little sympathy for the respective defendants.[15] Methodists responded to Tractarian criticisms of their ministry, sacraments, and practices in the officially-sponsored *Wesleyan Tracts for the Times* in 1842, as well as in numerous individual publications.[16] In 1843, in its official "Annual Address to the Methodist Societies," the Wesleyan Conference justified its opposition to Graham's factory education proposals in these terms:

> It has been publicly stated, that one ground of our strenuous opposition to the lately-projected measure of public education was, its obvious tendency to give to the Clergy of the Established Church, an unfair and undue control over the religious teaching in the schools which it would have established. We think

---

Diaries of William Cotton Risley, Vicar of Deddington 1845–1848 (Banbury: Banbury Historical Society, 2007), 20.

14. Bowmer, *Pastor and People*, 233.

15. Selén, *Oxford Movement and Wesleyan Methodism*, 96–100. Articles in the *Wesleyan Methodist Magazine* in 1867 included "Ritualism: what is it?" (February), "The teaching and tendencies of Ritualism" (March), "Sacramental confession and absolution" (April and May), "The first report on Ritualism" (November), as well as critical reviews of *The Church and the World* (January), *Sermons on Sin* (December), and lengthy extracts from the anti-ritualist sections of Bishop Waldegrave's Charge (December).

16. Bowmer, *Pastor and People*, 234–47.

> it right to confirm this statement, not out of any hostile feeling towards the Established Church as such, for this has never been the feeling of our Body, but with a view to bear our distinct and solemn testimony against those grievous errors which are now tolerated within her pale ... Opinions ... which can only be distinguished from Popery by an acute and practised observer ... have been revived when they were almost extinct, have spread with fearful rapidity, and are now held by a large number of the Established Clergy ... We deeply condemn and deplore this alarming departure from the truth of the Gospel in doctrine, and from its godly simplicity in divine worship and ecclesiastical observance.[17]

In common with other evangelicals, both Anglican and Nonconformist, Methodists saw Anglo-Catholicism as a distortion of Christian truth, obscuring the doctrine of justification by faith alone and substituting external ceremonial for inner spirituality.[18] They detected what they interpreted as a Romeward drift in Anglo-Catholic theology and practice; and Methodists were among the most sensitive of nineteenth-century British Protestants to the perceived errors of Roman Catholicism.[19] With other Free Churchmen, Methodists resented what they regarded as the intolerant churchmanship of the Tractarians, and claimed that this played out in spiteful persecution in rural communities—in the abuse of power over access to churchyards and parochial charities, in the misuse of influence with employers and landlords, and in the exploitation of control over village schools. Whether experienced directly or mediated through the press (denominational or secular), therefore, Methodists were likely to respond negatively to Anglo-Catholicism.

Turning to four examples of Methodist responses to ritualism and Anglo-Catholicism, it is appropriate to begin with the most influential, prolific, and pugnacious interpreter of the Oxford Movement to Victorian Methodism.[20] James Harrison Rigg (1821–1909) was a prominent Wesleyan minister and a very senior figure in the Connexion for five decades. He entered the ministry in 1845, making a name defending the Connexional establishment

---

17. *Minutes of Conference*, 1843, 557–58.

18. On the Evangelical case against Anglo-Catholicism, see Martin Wellings, *Evangelicals Embattled* (Carlisle: Paternoster, 2003), 9–72 and Peter Toon, "Anglicanism in Popish dress," in Rowell, *Tradition Renewed*, 173–84.

19. Selén, *Oxford Movement and Wesleyan Methodism*, 46–52. David M. Chapman, *In Search of the Catholic Spirit: Methodists and Roman Catholics in Dialogue* (Peterborough: Epworth, 2004), 44–86, gives an overview of nineteenth century Methodist attitudes from the standpoint of an ecumenical enthusiast.

20. Also discussed by Wakefield, "A Methodist critique," 192–94.

and the Wesleyan polity against the "Wesleyan Reform" agitation of the late 1840s and 1850s. Appointed Principal of the Wesleyans' teacher-training college in Horseferry Road in 1868, Rigg escaped the relentless three-year itinerancy of his fellow Wesleyan ministers and was guaranteed an appointment close to the metropolitan centers of power. His place in the esteem of fellow Methodists was marked by his election as President of the Conference on two occasions (1878 and 1892). As editor of the *London Quarterly Review* for thirty years from 1868 Rigg had ready access to a platform for his invariably trenchant opinions.[21]

Rigg was not universally popular. As Principal of Westminster College for thirty-five years, in the words of that institution's historian, "before he retired he came as near to being hated as any man in a College based on a religious foundation could be."[22] He was a vigorous polemicist on a wide range of theological, ecclesiastical, and social topics. He debated Methodist education policy with fellow—Wesleyans, justified Wesleyan ecclesiology against the spokesmen of other Methodist Connexions, and defended the memory of Jabez Bunting, the mid-nineteenth century "Pope of Methodism" as "truly liberal and progressive."[23] Even when trying to be generous to non-Wesleyan Methodists—the groups he had described in the bitter days of the Reform agitation as "rival *Wesleyoid* Societies"—Rigg generally managed to dilute very faint praise with a generous measure of condescending superiority.[24]

When it came to Anglo-Catholicism, however, criticism was not inhibited by any lingering sense of fraternal obligation. Having written on the Broad Church school in the 1850s, from the mid-1860s Rigg turned his attention to the Tractarians, and in 1895, after what he called "many years' study,"[25] he drew together a collection of his essays, many published in the *London Quarterly* over some thirty years, and reworked them into a substantial volume entitled *Oxford High Anglicanism and Its Chief Leaders*.

21. John Telford, *The Life of James Harrison Rigg, D. D., 1821–1909* (London: Robert Culley, 1909).

22. F. C. Pritchard, *The Story of Westminster College 1851–1951* (London: Epworth, 1951), 46.

23. James H. Rigg, *A Comparative View of Church Organisations, Primitive and Protestant*, 2nd ed. (London: Charles H. Kelly, 1891), 255. Wakefield comments that "When [Rigg] set about him, he did so with a bludgeon." Wakefield, "A Methodist critique," 192.

24. James H. Rigg, *The Principles of Wesleyan Methodism* (London: Partridge & Oakey, 1850), 106; Rigg, *Church Organisation*, 297–336.

25. James H. Rigg, *Oxford High Anglicanism and its Chief Leaders* (London: Charles H. Kelly, 1895), v. Rigg's knowledge of Anglo-Catholicism was, not unnaturally, challenged by critical reviewers.

Rigg claimed that his book was "the only attempt to write anything like a history of Oxford High Anglicanism which as yet has been, so far as I know, made by a Nonconformist," and "the only book ... which attempts to trace the history from its early origins ... down to the present time."[26] Thus, while including material on Keble, Newman, the *Tracts for the Times*, and W. G. Ward, Rigg devoted six of his twelve chapters to Pusey's theological development, teaching and influence. In *Oxford High Anglicanism* Rigg argued that "Ritualism is Puseyism adapted to popular acceptance ... Puseyism put on the stage for the public enjoyment" and that "Puseyism ... is essentially Popery."[27] For Rigg, the principal errors of Anglo-Catholic belief and practice—in his words, "the two plague-spots of Puseyism"—were its sacramental theology and its revival of the confessional. In Rigg's mind, Anglo-Catholic teaching turned the sacraments into superstitions, while the practice of confession was "dehumanising" and "revolting." Such beliefs and practices prepared the way for the full Roman system, since "these two roots of error being once accepted, there is no tenet either of Tridentine or modern Popery which may not be received."[28] Moreover, Rigg asserted that the kinship between Puseyism and Popery was more than coincidental: the intention of the leaders of the Oxford Movement from the very beginning had been "amalgamation with the Romish Church."[29] Rigg adopted the conspiracy theory of Anglo-Catholicism in its entirety, with the concomitant accusation of moral dishonesty levelled at those who sought to Romanize a Protestant Church while enjoying its emoluments. This picture of the Anglo-Catholic movement as a Roman Catholic fifth column in the Church of England was strengthened in the second edition of the work, which was published in 1899, in the wake of Walter Walsh's sensational *Secret History of the Oxford Movement* and in the midst of the so-called "crisis in the Church."[30]

Oxford High Anglicanism focussed Rigg's assessment of Anglo-Catholicism into a single contentious volume. It is important to note, however, that it was a distillation of many years' writing on the subject, and therefore that readers of the *London Quarterly Review* and other Methodist publications had been exposed to Rigg's polemical prose since the mid-1860s.[31] More-

26. Ibid., vii.

27. Ibid., 324, 298.

28. Ibid., 298-99.

29. Ibid., 299.

30. Martin Wellings, "The Oxford Movement in Late Nineteenth Century Retrospect: R. W. Church, J. H. Rigg, and Walter Walsh," in Robert N. Swanson, ed. *The Church Retrospective* (Woodbridge: Boydell, 1997), 514.

31. See, for example, "The Catholic Revival," *London Quarterly Review* 57 (1867)

over, Rigg also contributed to the broader context of Methodism's response to Anglo-Catholicism through his interpretation of John Wesley's spiritual development. In *The Living Wesley*, published in 1875 and revised for the centenary of Wesley's death in 1891, and in *The Churchmanship of John Wesley* (1878; revised 1886) Rigg portrayed a Wesley who was a "ritualistic High Churchman," and even "an ascetic ritualist of the strictest and most advanced class" before his evangelical conversion in Aldersgate Street in May 1738.[32] Rigg's engagement in the mid-nineteenth century debates over the interpretation of Wesley's High Churchmanship thus helped to articulate, reinforce, and establish for several generations of Methodists the belief that Wesley was converted *from* an arid High Church piety *to* evangelical Christianity, making Wesley the paradigm of progress from the bondage of ritualism to the liberty of the gospel. This may have been more significant in shaping Methodism's instinctive reaction to Anglo-Catholicism than Rigg's more overtly polemical works because it helped to make a revulsion from High Churchmanship part of the founding myth of the Methodist movement.[33]

James Rigg's close contemporary, Benjamin Gregory (1820–1900), was as robust in his defence of Wesleyan doctrine and polity as Rigg, but arguably a more creative theologian with a more catholic outlook.[34] Gregory entered the Wesleyan ministry in 1840, five years before Rigg, and was less closely associated with the disciples of Jabez Bunting during the fratricidal

---

31–62. Articles in the *LQR* were unsigned until the late 1890s, but this piece is confidently attributed to Rigg by the *Wellesley Index to Victorian Periodicals*. The article-length review of *The Church and the World* and the article on "The first report on ritualism" in the *Wesleyan Methodist Magazine* (January and December 1867 respectively) were signed "J. H. R."

32. James H. Rigg, *The Churchmanship of John Wesley* (London: Wesleyan Methodist Bookroom, 1886), 18; James H. Rigg, *The Living Wesley* (London: Charles H. Kelly, 1891), 89.

33. For the historiography of Wesley biographies, see Richard P. Heitzenrater, *The Elusive Mr Wesley* (Nashville: Abingdon, 1984), with the nineteenth century authors discussed in 2:180–88. The enduring influence of the myth may be seen in debates around the bicentenary of the Wesleys' conversion in 1938, with contributions by Henry Bett, J. E. Rattenbury, and George Jackson. See Martin Wellings, "Discipline in dispute: the origins and early history of the Methodist Sacramental Fellowship," in Kate Cooper and Jeremy Gregory, eds. *Discipline and Diversity* (Woodbridge: Boydell, 2007), 394.

34. Benjamin Gregory, *Autobiographical Recollections, Edited, with Memorials of his Later Life, by his Eldest Son* (London: Hodder and Stoughton, 1903); David J. Carter, "Gregory, Benjamin," in John A. Vickers, ed. *A Dictionary of Methodism in Britain and Ireland* (Peterborough: Epworth, 2000), 141; David Carter, *Love Bade Me Welcome* (Peterborough: Epworth, 2002), 31, 40.

conflicts over "Wesleyan Reform."[35] After a series of circuit appointments, including a gruelling superintendency in the Oxford Circuit (1857–1860),[36] Gregory settled in London in 1868 on appointment as joint Connexional Editor, with responsibility for a range of official Wesleyan publications. Thereafter, like Rigg at Westminster College, Gregory had a permanent base in the metropolis, with access to the levers of Connexional power and time for research and writing. Interestingly it was not until the death of his senior colleague, Benjamin Frankland, in 1876, that Gregory gained control of the *Wesleyan Methodist Magazine* and began to reshape it, broadening the range of contributors beyond the confines of the Wesleyan Connexion. By the time of his retirement in 1893 the *Magazine* had once again become a bastion of Wesleyan conservatism, reflecting Gregory's implacable opposition to the "higher criticism" of the Bible.[37]

In his contribution to a memoir of his father, Arthur Gregory recalled the vigorous ecumenical discussions which took place in Stoke Newington, where the Gregorys resided. The Rector, Prebendary Jackson, was the son and nephew of Wesleyan Presidents of Conference;[38] Dr Belcher, Bunting's grandson-in-law, was Vicar of St Faith's, "the most advanced High Church in the district," where he "used to officiate in garments which amazed his congregation";[39] the Congregationalist Thomas Binney was a near neighbour, and Dean Stanley an occasional visitor. One report of the animated conversations, where "the divergence of opinion was extreme," noted that Father Lockhart remarked: "It's a curious thing, but the only man I always agree with is Mr Gregory."[40] This may indicate that Gregory, while firm in his own opinions, was more open to the views of others, more flexible as a theologian and less preoccupied with polemics than Rigg.[41]

---

35. See the perspective on the nineteenth century controversies in Gregory's *Side Lights on the Conflicts in Methodism 1827-52* (London: Cassell and Company,1898), reflecting the outlook of Joseph Fowler, a senior minister opposed to Bunting.

36. Gregory, *Autobiographical Recollections*, 407.

37. Ibid., 427, 439–41.

38. Ibid., 425. The Rector's father was Thomas Jackson (1783–1873), President in 1838 and 1849, and his uncle was Samuel Jackson (1786–1861), President in 1847.

39. Ibid., 425. Arthur Gregory states that Dr Belcher was Bunting's son-in-law, but the Bunting family tree in Alan Turberfield, *John Scott Lidgett. Archbishop of British Methodism?* (Peterborough: Epworth, 2003), 399–400, indicates that the Revd Dr Belsher of St Faith's was married to Mary Margaretta, daughter of William Maclardie Bunting, and granddaughter of Jabez. Sadly, there is no further description of the garments which "amazed" the congregation.

40. Gregory, *Autobiographical Recollections*, 425.

41. It should be noted that Gregory was quite capable of engaging in a pamphlet controversy with "a very bigoted, narrow-hearted, specious, stealthy Puseyite" while

Two of Gregory's publications may be noted here. His *Handbook of Scriptural Church Principles and of Wesleyan-Methodist Polity and History* (1888), prepared by direction of the Conference as a Wesleyan equivalent to a range of Anglican and Free Church manuals, adopted a catechetical question and answer approach to an array of doctrinal and historical questions.[42] Unsurprisingly, Gregory tackled some of the points at issue between Wesleyans and High Churchmen, including baptism, apostolic succession, ministerial priesthood, the real presence in the Eucharist, and the meaning of schism. Equally unsurprisingly, Gregory defended the importance of baptism while rejecting baptismal regeneration,[43] described "the High Church claim that through the line of bishops only can the Church be kept in existence from age to age, and the grace of the Holy Spirit conveyed to human hearts" as "a transposition and inversion of the Apostles' Creed,"[44] rejected the ascription of priestly functions to the Christian Ministry,[45] argued for a spiritual rather than a bodily real presence in the Eucharist[46] and upheld the legitimacy and duty of withdrawing from a particular Church-organization if remaining within it would break a commandment of God.[47]

Having listed these points of disagreement between Wesleyan Methodists and High Churchmen, it is important to note that Gregory also maintained a high doctrine of the church as "not only an organisation . . . [but] . . . also a living organism of which the Spirit of Christ is the animating principle."[48] He expounded the visibility and historical continuity of the Church, the authority of the ministry and the importance of the sacraments.[49] Unlike Rigg, who was skeptical about the prospects and desirability of visible unity, even among the different Methodist denominations, Gregory answered the question, "Will the Church of Christ ever again be a united Church?" with a confident, "Assuredly," although he interpreted

---

stationed in Barnsley. His opponent, the local vicar, was the son of a Wesleyan minister. Ibid., 406.

42. Benjamin Gregory, *A Handbook of Scriptural Church Principles and of Wesleyan-Methodist Polity and History* (London: Wesleyan Methodist Bookroom, 1888), iii–iv.

43. Ibid., 44–47.

44. Ibid., 103.

45. Ibid., 14.

46. Ibid., 74.

47. Ibid., 114, quoting John Wesley's sermon, "On Schism," in Albert C. Outler, ed. *Sermons III 71–114, BEW* 3:58–69.

48. Gregory, *A Handbook of Scriptural Church Principles*, 6.

49. Ibid., 26, 28, 11–14, 53, 56, 67–78.

this in terms of "one spiritually undivided society," rather than "a universal uniformity of Church government."[50]

The ecclesiology expressed in an abridged form in the *Handbook* of 1888 was expounded in greater detail in the published version of Gregory's Fernley Lecture of 1873, *The Holy Catholic Church, The Communion of Saints*. The lecture, delivered in Newcastle in conjunction with the meeting of the Wesleyan Conference, sought to avoid "a specific Denominational idea of the Church" and to set out instead "the full Divine idea of the Church."[51] Building on a close reading of the New Testament, particularly the Acts of the Apostles, Gregory urged recognition of the Church as the Body of Christ, animated by the Holy Spirit, and therefore in a process of continual development towards the realization of the Divine ideal. He asserted that "the Church is not a thing of rigid definition, and yet is nevertheless a definite community, with a distinct object and reason of existence," its purposes being to continue the mission of Christ, to stand for truth, and to gather into "a glorious society" those rescued from the world and preparing for heaven.[52] Gregory held to an idea of the Church as both spiritual community and mundane institution, emphasizing the community and "mutual vigilance" of fellowship.[53] While deprecating division, Gregory prized "vital unity" in apostolic faith above "visible unity," arguing that there was scope for "denominational distinctions" while working for "outward and visible re-uniting ... by alliance and gradual sound assimilation."[54] Despite a high doctrine of the Church, however, Gregory had no time for High Church theories and Petrine pretensions, devoting an indignant footnote and part of an appendix to Dean Goulburn's *The Holy Catholic Church*, and rebutting the Dean's claims for the visible church and the apostolic succession.[55] Gregory, therefore, was in dialogue with High Church theology, but seeking to uphold a Wesleyan ecclesiology, balancing the importance of the visible Church against the priority of the fundamental spiritual unity of those "who hold the Head."[56]

50. Ibid., 123–4; contrast Rigg, *Church Organisation*, 315–36.

51. Benjamin Gregory, *The Holy Catholic Church, The Communion of Saints: A Discourse* (London: Wesleyan Conference Office, 1873), iii–iv.

52. Ibid., 5–6, 15–16.

53. Ibid., 73–79 and esp. 81. The emphasis on fellowship, as a particular hallmark of Methodism, may be found elsewhere in Gregory's works: see, for instance, *The Thorough Business Man: Memoirs of Walter Powell, Merchant, Melbourne and London* (London: Strahan & Co., 1872), 62–73.

54. Gregory, *Holy Catholic Church*, 165, 201.

55. Ibid., 164, 285–88.

56. Ibid., 159. Compare the definition of catholicity in the Wesleyans' "Liverpool

Gregory's ecclesiology and Rigg's polemics came together in the third example: Joseph Hocking's Protestant potboiler, *The Soul of Dominic Wildthorne*, published in 1908. Joseph Hocking (1860–1937) was a minister of the United Methodist Free Churches, one of the fruits of the agitation for Wesleyan reform in the 1840s and 1850s. Born in Cornwall, the son of a mine-captain and smallholder, Joseph left a career in land surveying to follow his elder brother Silas Kitto Hocking into the UMFC ministry in 1881. After three years in theological college in Manchester, Joseph Hocking served Methodist circuits in Leicester, London, and Lancashire. He also followed Silas into a more lucrative career as a prolific and best-selling novelist, producing almost a hundred novels and innumerable serials and short stories between 1887 and 1936.[57] Although his first novels were written while he was in active ministry, and were published by the UMFC Bookroom, Joseph soon switched to the commercial publisher Ward, Lock, and Company, and retired from the ministry in 1910. A resolution of the United Methodist Conference, accepting Hocking's resignation with regret, expressed the hope that "by the continued exercise of his literary gifts, he may be the means at once of interesting his extensive circle of readers and confirming them in their attachment to the Protestant religion."[58]

Hocking's novels mined several rich seams of contemporary fiction. His first significant success, *Jabez Easterbrook: A Religious Novel* (1890), addressed issues of faith and doubt made fashionable by Mrs Humphrey Ward's *Robert Elsmere* (1888). An unimpressed reviewer summarized the plot thus: "a sturdy young Wesleyan minister encounters a fascinating young lady of agnostic tendencies. They argue throughout the tedious length of the novel."[59] Regardless of such critical disdain, *Jabez Easterbrook* sold well, and Hocking followed it with both "novels of purpose" set in the contemporary era and historical novels, like *And Shall Trelawney Die?* (1897) and *Mistress Nancy Molesworth* (1898). *Lest We Forget* (1901), set in

---

Minutes" of 1820 in William Peirce, *The Ecclesiastical Principles and Polity of the Wesleyan Methodists*, 3rd ed. (London: Wesleyan Conference Office, 1873), 782.

57. R. G. Burnett, "Hocking, Silas Kitto (1850–1935)," in Sayoni Basu, ed. *Oxford Dictionary of National Biography* (Oxford: Oxford University Press, 2004); online ed. May 2006 http://oxforddnb.com/view/article/33912, doi: August 18, 2009; Alan M. Kent, *Pulp Methodism. The Lives and Literature of Silas, Jospeh and Salome Hocking. Three Cornish Novelists* (St Austell: Cornish Hillside, 2002); Martin Wellings, "'Pulp Methodism revisited': the literature and significance of Silas and Joseph Hocking," in Peter Clarke and Charlotte Methuen, eds., *The Church and Literature* (Woodbridge: Boydell, 2012).

58. Kent, *Pulp Methodism*, 109.

59. John Sutherland, *The Longman Companion to Victorian Fiction* (Harlow: Longman, 1988), 301.

the mid-sixteenth century, struck a staunchly Protestant and patriotic note, with a truehearted English hero and a supporting cast of cruel Catholics and villainous Spaniards.

From 1898, when *The Scarlet Woman* began to appear in serial form in *The Temple Magazine*,[60] until 1908 Hocking published four novels drawing on contemporary Protestant polemics. Three—*The Scarlet Woman* (1899), *The Purple Robe* (1900), and *The Woman of Babylon* (1906)—were straightforwardly anti-Catholic, but with *The Soul of Dominic Wildthorne* (1908), Hocking turned his attention explicitly to Anglo-Catholicism. Writing for a Protestant and Nonconformist audience, and in the aftermath of the Royal Commission on Ecclesiastical Discipline of 1904–1906, it is not surprising that Hocking presented Anglo-Catholicism in a thoroughly unflattering light.

The Soul of Dominic Wildthorne begins with an encounter at the gates of the cemetery in the Yorkshire industrial town of Meremeadows. Fletcher Yorke, a local millowner and Nonconformist, and his daughter Maggie, discover an orphaned teenager, Dominic Wildthorne, whose father has just been laid to rest by an unsympathetic Catholic priest. While Yorke is considering offering Dominic a job in his mill or directions to the nearest workhouse, a man "dressed not unlike a medieval monk" appears,[61] and suggests that Dominic might work for the Community of the Incarnation, whose house is nearby. The rest of the novel traces Dominic's struggle for happiness and personal integrity, and this is played out through his relationship with the Yorke family on the one hand, and the Community of the Incarnation on the other. Dominic is educated by the Community, becomes a monk and a priest, and develops into a powerful preacher. There is an authorial undercurrent, however, which portrays the world of the Community as narrow, life-denying and out of touch with modern thought: by the age of twenty four, Dominic is more at home in the twelfth century than the twentieth, and he has become an emaciated ascetic and, in the opinion of Maggie Yorke, a "conceited fanatic."[62] The Community's form of religion appeals to power-hungry ecclesiastics and weak-minded women; no-nonsense Yorkshiremen dismiss it with contempt as "semi-pagan ceremonial," more suited to the Middle Ages, or rural Spain, than industrial England.[63] Moreover, members of the Community are frequently uneasy about the validity of

---

60. Silas Hocking was the co-founder of *The Temple Magazine*. See Kent, *Pulp Methodism*, 74.

61. Joseph Hocking, *The Soul of Dominic Wildthorne* (London: Hodder and Stoughton, 1908), 9.

62. Ibid., 94, 115, 127, 131.

63. Ibid., 10, 30–31, 125, 129–30.

their orders, and are only reassured by surreptitious re-ordination by compliant Roman bishops and by the sense that they are preparing the way for the reconciliation of the Church of England with the Holy See.[64] Hocking loses no opportunity to underline the intellectual weakness and moral dishonesty of this position, speaking through Maggie and her father, through the Nonconformist M. P. Hector Trevelyan, and through the Machiavellian Jesuit Father Ritzoom, who hopes to persuade Dominic to secede to Rome.[65] In typical Hocking fashion, and with the regular end-of-episode cliffhangers inseparable from the genre of magazine serials, Dominic inherits an estate, evades Father Ritzoom, sees the moral bankruptcy of Anglo-Catholicism, and the spiritual tyranny of Rome, and realizes that his true vocation is to marry Maggie and raise a family.

In the author's foreword Hocking claimed that "What I have tried to do is to give in the form of a story a picture of this phase of our English life, without particularizing any Order or person." Thus every statement about usage, ritual or teaching, according to Hocking, could be borne out from one or other of the Orders in the "Catholic branch" of the Church of England. The account of Dominic's vows on joining the Community even received an explanatory footnote: "The above are literal extracts from the office of admission into one of the orders of the Church of England."[66] James Britten, the Roman Catholic controversialist and Secretary of the Catholic Truth Society, was not persuaded, publishing a critical review in *The Month* and reprinting his article as *A School for Slander; or, The Soul of Dominic Wildthorne*.[67] It seems unlikely, however, that Catholic Truth Society refutations would have made much impact on Joseph Hocking's loyal readership, and it may be remembered that two years later the United Methodist Conference celebrated the importance of his literary gifts to the Protestant cause. Moreover, Hocking's fiction, in serial and book form, would have reached a far wider audience than Rigg's *Oxford High Anglicanism* or Gregory's *Holy Catholic Church*.[68]

For the fourth example, attention may turn from authors to an organization, the Wesleyan Methodist Guild of Divine Service. On November 30, 1906, a news item in the *Church Times* picked up a report in a recent issue of the *Manchester Guardian*, in which "a Wesleyan correspondent" had drawn

64. Ibid., 24–25; on 98–99, it is made clear that Father Ritzoom is behind such arrangements.
65. Ibid., 43–51, 140–44, 197–202, 249–58.
66. Ibid., iii–iv, 114.
67. James Britten, "A school for slander," *The Month*, January 1909, 39–53.
68. Kent, 108, suggests that *Dominic Wildthorne* was serialized in the *British Weekly*, the most influential of the Free Church newspapers.

attention to a body called the Wesleyan Guild of Divine Service. According to the *Church Times*, the Guild was first formed at Beccles, and had been in existence for some six years. Among its practices were "kneeling at prayer; reverent administering of Sacraments according to prescribed forms; reading of appointed lessons; offering of alms at the Communion-table; fuller observance of Church seasons; enlarged use of the Church Prayer Book; and frequent Communion; not to mention the endeavour after a more dignified and Churchlike style of building for chapels."[69] This summary echoes the contents of a substantial pamphlet, *Methodist Worship: A Plea for Toleration*, by James Johnson, published in Manchester in 1906. Johnson's pamphlet bore the imprint of the Wesleyan Methodist Guild of Divine Service, and listed as officers of the Guild Johnson, of Manchester, and R. E. Adams, of Beccles. It also listed as supporters nine eminent Wesleyans: five ministers, including four Ex-Presidents of the Conference, and four prominent laymen, and a committee of a further eleven ministers and thirteen laymen.[70]

Although the *Church Times* reported that the Guild "apparently has for its object reunion with the Church," this was not at all apparent from Johnson's pamphlet. Nor did the pamphlet argue for ritual or ceremonial innovation, although, as will be seen later, this accusation was speedily brought against it. Rather, the Guild seems to have represented the outlook of those traditionally minded Wesleyans who valued the liturgical service bequeathed to the Connexion by John Wesley and who wished to defend it against pressure to make all Methodist worship more "simple and free." In his preface to Johnson's pamphlet, Thomas Bowman Stephenson, an ex-President and a revered figure in the Wesleyan Connexion, made clear that the principal aim of the Guild was "liberty for those who prefer a full liturgical service" and respect for "the minority of churches which desire to use on Sunday Mornings the liturgical forms approved for us by John Wesley."[71] Most of the text of the pamphlet comprised quotations from such Methodist authorities as Thomas Coke, Adam Clarke, Jabez Bunting, Robert Newton, Thomas Jackson, and William Arthur supporting the value of the Order of Morning Prayer. Johnson was even able to call that epitome of the Nonconformist Conscience, Hugh Price Hughes, and that hammer of ritualism, James Harrison Rigg, to endorse his argument.[72] The pamphlet made

69. *Church Times*, November 30, 1906.

70. James Johnson, *Methodist Worship: A Plea for Toleration* (Manchester: John Heywood, 1906), endpapers. The ministers were T. B. Stephenson, J. S. Banks, Thomas Allen, W. T. Davison, and J. Agar Beet; among the laymen were Sir Henry Hartley Fowler and Sir George Hayter Chubb.

71. Ibid., 2.

72. Ibid., 18, 20–24.

the case for retaining the option of Morning Prayer, as part of the liberty, comprehensiveness, and catholicity of Methodism.[73] It also gave examples to counter the assertion that liturgical services were less effective in stimulating revivals, citing the 1903 mission at St John's, Manningham, Bradford, where the Connexional Evangelist Thomas Waugh conducted a successful revival with the assistance of a surpliced choir.[74] It may be suggested that the Guild had its principal context within Wesleyanism, formed partly by long-running disputes over the appropriateness of a liturgical service and partly by more recent anxieties over the form of service needed to attract the unchurched.[75]

Not all were reassured by Stephenson's prestige, the authority of the Ex-Presidents and the catena of quotations from eminent Wesleyan divines. Daniel Hone, a sometime Methodist and co-founder with John Kensit of the Protestant Defence Brigade, produced a riposte to Johnson, entitled *Corrupted Methodist Worship*, and dubbed the Guild of Divine Service "the Guild for Corrupting Methodism with Ritualism." Hone saw the Guild as a ritualist stalking-horse, introducing "soul-destroying formalism" into Methodist worship under the pretence of culture and gentility. Hone's sneering dismissal of liturgies, lectionaries, the seasons of the Christian year and most principles of reverence in the conduct of public worship, and his advocacy of a "brief, helpful observance of the ordinance of the Lord's Supper" as a "simple memorial service" probably made the case for the Guild of Divine Service at least as effectively as Johnson's pamphlet.[76]

There is no evidence that this attempt by the "Protestant underworld" to make capital out of the Guild of Divine Service had any success, nor that the Guild represented more than the conservative liturgical instincts of traditional Wesleyans.[77] Two points of wider significance may be made,

73. Ibid., 3.

74. Ibid., 25–26.

75. David M. Chapman, *Born in Song. Methodist Worship in Britain* (Warrington: Church in the Market Place, 2006), 17–23; the report of the Conference Commission appointed to investigate attendance at Methodist places of worship in London opined that "the liturgical form of service is even more unsuitable to the tastes of the people than the [recently built, but poorly maintained and largely Gothic] buildings." See *Minutes of Conference*, 1904, 532. I am grateful to the Revd Dr David Chapman for drawing my attention to the discussion in his book.

76. Daniel Hone, *Corrupted Methodist Worship* (Ipswich: Calver, n.d.), 2, 3, 5. For Hone's biography, and his oscillation between Methodism and militant Protestantism, see *The Churchman's Magazine*, September 1895, 257–58, and *Journal of the Wesley Bible Union*, May 1916, 105.

77. Compare reports of the Guild's first public meeting at the Wesleyan Conference in 1913 in *Methodist Recorder*, July 31, 1913, 20; Also, *British Weekly*, July 31, 1913, 450.

however. First, generations of tension and conflict over ritualism had made the discussion of liturgy increasingly difficult within Methodism: just as the development of Tractarianism made Methodists like Thomas Jackson re-evaluate their appreciation of the Church of England, so ritualism left Wesleyans who prized John Wesley's Order of Morning Prayer feeling vulnerable to Protestant pressure to abandon the liturgy. The Wesleyans revised their Book of Offices in the 1880s to remove elements which might lend colour to Anglo-Catholic teaching;[78] twenty years later, the use of the liturgy itself was seen to be at risk.

Second, despite the ritual controversies, some Wesleyans still valued the liturgical tradition. Others, moreover, were being drawn to greater order, more structured devotions and an appreciation of Catholic spirituality.[79] Rigg had argued as long ago as 1868—against Orby Shipley's *Tracts for the Day*—that Gothic architecture, chanted psalms and "a liturgical element in public worship" were "simply aesthetical" and did not "express the slightest tendency to Sacerdotalism" in the Nonconformist churches.[80] For most, that was true. For some, however, there was a temptation to flirt with ritualism, and for others, a progression to Anglo- or Roman Catholicism.[81]

Modern historical and ecumenical studies have done much to recover points of similarity and continuity between the Evangelical and Oxford Movements, and to identify common ground and shared emphases between Anglicans and Methodists. To some extent, as in the history of Methodist-Roman Catholic dialogue, it has become evident that protagonists could only see one another through polemical lenses, magnifying differences and obscuring agreement. It is important, however, not to exaggerate the degree of convergence or to impose a late-twentieth century agenda on the nineteenth century. Victorian and Edwardian Methodists had plenty of reasons—theological, ecclesiological, cultural, and socio-political—for drawing away from the Church of England. Ritualism sharpened the points of difference, added more, and set the denominations on paths of separate development which the ecumenical endeavours of recent generations have yet fully to overcome. Despite the work around the "Conversations" of the 1960s and the

---

78. Chapman, *Born in Song*, 24. Even this revision provoked opposition because all liturgy had become suspect in some quarters.

79. Wellings, "Discipline in Dispute," 390.

80. Rigg, "Catholic Revival," 48.

81. Wellings, "Discipline in dispute," 391–94. E. J. B. Kirtlan, a member of the Guild committee in 1906 was a prominent and controversial figure in the Methodist Sacramental Fellowship in the 1930s; S. B. Gregory, another committee member, was the uncle of T. S. Gregory, driving force behind the MSF and convert to Roman Catholicism in 1935.

Anglican-Methodist Covenant of 2003, there are still plenty of vexed issues prompting some Methodists to echo *Punch*'s maiden of 1868: "I don't want to go to church at all, and if I did, I'm sure I wouldn't go with you."

13

Bibliography
The Principal Published Writings of Henry Denman Rack

Clive D. Field

THIS IS A LISTING of the principal published writings of Henry Rack. It was prepared in consultation with him, to minimize errors and omissions, and his assistance in this regard is readily acknowledged. The only genre excluded (on the grounds of space) is reviews of individual books, of which Dr Rack has written several hundred, over almost five decades.

Publications have been grouped into four main categories: books and booklets; journal articles; chapters in edited books; and contributions to encylopedias. In each section references appear in ascending chronological order of the cover date of the publication concerned, even if the actual year of publication is known to have been later.

For journals, part numbers are only given where the relevant volume was not paginated continuously. The following abbreviations have been used: *BJRULM* = *Bulletin of the John Rylands University Library of Manchester*; *ER* = *Epworth Review*; *JEH* = *Journal of Ecclesiastical History*; *MH* = *Methodist History*; *PWHS* = *Proceedings of the Wesley Historical Society*; and *WMS* = *Wesley and Methodist Studies*; *WTJ* = *Wesleyan Theological Journal*.

Books and Booklets

The Future of John Wesley's Methodism. London: Lutterworth Press and Richmond, VA: John Knox Press, 1965, 80p.
20th Century Spirituality. London: Epworth, 1969, x + 172p.

Wesleyanism and "the World" in the Later Nineteenth Century. Wesley Historical Society Lectures 43. Chester: the Society, 1979, 21p.
Reasonable Enthusiast: John Wesley and the Rise of Methodism. London: Epworth and Philadelphia, PA: Trinity Press International, 1989, xvi + 656p. Second edition, London: Epworth, 1992 and Nashville, TN: Abingdon Press, 1993, xiv + 658p. Third edition, London: Epworth, 2002, xxi + 662p. Korean translation, Seoul: Kamnigyo Sinhak Taehakkyo, 2001, 720p.
The Swiss Connection: Manchester Essays on Religious Connections between England and Switzerland between the 16th and 20th Centuries. Edited with an introduction by HDR. [Manchester: University of Manchester, 1994], 101p.
How Primitive was Primitive Methodism? An Examination of Some Characters and Characteristics. Sixth Chapel Aid Lecture, 1996. York: printed by Quacks for the Englesea Brook Primitive Methodist Museum Committee, 1996, 32p.
Early Methodist Experience: Some Prototypical Accounts. Religious Experience Research Centre, Westminster College, Oxford, Occasional Paper, second series 4. Oxford: the Centre, 1997, 14p.
John Wesley and Early Methodist Conversion. Position Paper 28, Currents in World Christianity, University of Cambridge. Cambridge: North Atlantic Missiology Project, 1997, 31p.
The Works of John Wesley, Volume 10: The Methodist Societies – The Minutes of Conference. Edited by HDR. Nashville, TN: Abingdon Press, 2011, xxi + 1,046p.

Journal Articles

"The Decline of the Class-Meeting and the Problem of Church-Membership in Nineteenth-Century Wesleyanism." *PWHS* 39 (1973) 12–21.
"Domestic Visitation: a Chapter in Early Nineteenth Century Evangelism." *JEH* 24 (1973) 357–76.
"The Church and the Uses of History." *ER* 1:2 (1974) 75–81.
"What Must we Believe?" *ER* 2:2 (1975) 13–19.
"The Church's Mission to Society." *ER* 3:3 (1976) 57–64.
"Methodism and Revolution: a Problem in Relating Religion to Politics." *University of Manchester Papers in Religion and Politics* 2 (1977) 5–8.
"Wesleyanism and 'the World' in the Later Nineteenth Century." *PWHS* 42 (1979) 35–54.
"Recent Books on Methodism." *ER* 7:1 (1980) 82–8.
"Theology and Personality." *ER* 9:3 (1982) 43–8.
"Wesley and Romanticism [review of Richard Brantley, *Locke, Wesley and the Method of English Romanticism*]." *PWHS* 45 (1985) 63–5.
"Early Methodist Visions of the Trinity." *PWHS* 46 (1987) 38–44, 57–69.
"Religious Societies and the Origins of Methodism." *JEH* 38 (1987) 582–95.
"The Manchester Corporation Project of 1763: Legend or History?" *Transactions of the Lancashire & Cheshire Antiquarian Society* 84 (1987) 118–42.
"Establishments, Evangelicals and Enthusiasm in Eighteenth-Century Manchester." *Shaker Quarterly* 17 (1989) 35–53, 75–93.
"Starting with Oneself: Spiritual Confessions, 6 – John Wesley's *Journal*." *Expository Times* 101 (1990) 228–31.

"A Descriptive and Plaintive Elegy on the Death of the Late Reverend John Wesley, 1791." By Thomas Olivers, abridged by HDR. *ER* 18:2 (1991) 35–40.

"The Providential Moment: Church Building, Methodism and Evangelical Entryism in Manchester, 1788–1825." *Transactions of the Historic Society of Lancashire and Cheshire* 141 (1991) 235–60.

"Wesley and his Biographers." *Wesley Historical Society North East Branch Bulletin* 57 (1992) 3–8.

"Evangelical Endings: Death-Beds in Evangelical Biography." *BJRULM* 74:1 (1992) 39–56.

"Wesley Observed: an Unpublished Character Sketch by John Pawson." *PWHS* 49 (1993) 11–17.

"Young Mr Wesley, Old Mr Wesley: the Making of an Evangelist." *Journal of the Lincolnshire Methodist History Society* 4 (1993) 107–14.

"Methodist Classics Reconsidered, 1: Simon's life of Wesley." *PWHS* 50 (1995) 15–18.

"John Wesley and his Early Biographers." *Wesley Historical Society Cumbria Branch Journal* 39 (1997) 2–15.

"Between Church and Sect: the Origins of Methodism in Manchester." *BJRULM* 80:1 (1998) 65–87.

"John Wesley as Theologian." *ER* 27:1 (2000) 43–7.

"The Man the Church of England couldn't Contain [John Wesley]." *Church Times*, February 18, 2000, 14–15.

"'But, Lord, Let it be Betsy!' Love and Marriage in Early Methodism." *PWHS* 53 (2001) 1–13.

"Charles Wesley and the Irish Inheritance Tradition." *PWHS* 53 (2002) 117–26.

"The Rise of Evangelical Independency in Manchester." *Journal of the United Reformed Church History Society* 6 (2002) 724–42.

"The Wesleys and Manchester." *Proceedings of the Charles Wesley Society* 8 (2002) 6–23.

"John Wesley's 1770 Will." Transcript by Wanda Willard Smith, notes by Page Thomas, John Lenton, and HDR. *PWHS* 54 (2003) 29–38.

"Profile: John Newton." *ER* 31:2 (2004) 8–16.

"A. S. Peake, Liberal Evangelical." *ER* 31:3 (2004) 48–53.

"Wesley Portrayed: Character and Criticism in Some Early Biographies." *MH* 43 (2005) 90–114.

"John Wesley and Ireland." *Bulletin of the Wesley Historical Society in Ireland* 10 (2005) 3–13.

"An Acquisition and a Rediscovery." *PWHS* 55 (2006) 197–8.

"Some Recent Trends in Wesley Scholarship." *WTJ* 41:2 (2006) 182–99.

"Charles Wesley and the Supernatural." *BJRULM* 88: 2 (2006) 59–79.

"John Wesley: Ecumenical Pioneer." *Wesley Historical Society (Yorkshire Branch) Bulletin* 92 (2007) 11–24.

"A Man of Reason and Religion? John Wesley and the Enlightenment." *WMS* 1 (2009) 2–17.

"John Wesley and Overseas Missions: Principles and Practice." *WMS* 5 (2013) 30–55.

Chapters in Edited Books

"'Christ's Kingdom not of this World': the Case of Benjamin Hoadly Versus William Law Reconsidered." In *Church, Society and Politics*, edited by Derek Baker, 275-91. Studies in Church History 12. Oxford: Basil Blackwell, 1975.

"Doctors, Demons and Early Methodist Healing." In *The Church and Healing*, edited by William Sheils, 137-52. Studies in Church History 19. Oxford: Basil Blackwell, 1982.

"Wesleyan Methodism, 1849-1902." In *A History of the Methodist Church in Great Britain, Volume Three*, general editors: Rupert Davies, Raymond George and Gordon Rupp, 119-66. London: Epworth, 1983.

"Evangelicalism in Manchester in the 18th Century." In *Regional Studies in the History of Religion in Britain since the Later Middle Ages*, edited by Edward Royle, 116-25. [Hull]: Humberside College of Higher Education, [1986].

"Survival and Revival: John Bennet, Methodism and the Old Dissent." In *Protestant Evangelicalism: Britain, Ireland, Germany and America, c. 1750-c. 1950 - Essays in Honour of W. R. Ward*, edited by Keith Robbins, 1-23. Studies in Church History, Subsidia 7. Oxford: Basil Blackwell, 1990.

"The Religion of Matthew Arnold." In *Modern Religious Rebels: Presented to John Kent*, edited by Stuart Mews, 97-122. London: Epworth, 1993.

"The Man the Church of England couldn't Contain [John Wesley]." In *Not Angels, but Anglicans: a History of Christianity in the British Isles*, consulting editor: Henry Chadwick, commissioning editor: Allison Ward, 187-93. Norwich: Canterbury Press, 2000. New edition, Norwich: Canterbury Press, 2010.

"James Crawfoot and the Magic Methodists." In *James Crawfoot and the Magic Methodists*, 1-13. [Englesea Brook: Englesea Brook Chapel and Museum], 2003.

"Charles Wesley and Early Methodism." In *Charles Wesley: Life, Literature and Legacy*, edited by Kenneth Newport and Ted Campbell, 40-57. Peterborough: Epworth, 2007.

"John Newton: a Life." In *A Thankful Heart and a Discerning Mind: Essays in Honour of John Newton*, edited by Mervyn Davies, 15-26. [Dursley]: Lonely Scribe, 2010.

"John Wesley and Eighteenth-Century Dissent." In *A Thankful Heart and a Discerning Mind: Essays in Honour of John Newton*, edited by Mervyn Davies, 40-56. [Dursley]: Lonely Scribe, 2010.

"In Memoriam: William Reginald Ward (1925-2010)." In John Virgoe, *Thomas Eccleston (1752-1809): A Progressive Lancastrian Agriculturalist*, 241-2. Remains, Historical and Literary, Connected with the Palatine Counties of Lancaster and Chester, third series 49. Manchester: Chetham Society, 2012.

"Using John Wesley Today: Some Suggested Principles," In *The Path of Holiness: Perspectives in Wesleyan Thought in Honor of Herbert B. McGonigle*, edited by Joseph Cunningham and David Rainey, 7-25. Lexington, KY: Emeth, 2014.

Contributions to Encyclopedias

The Encyclopedia of World Methodism, Nolan Harmon, general editor. Nashville, TN: United Methodist Publishing House, 1974, 2 vol. [13 articles by HDR on Richard Alleine, Samuel Annesley, John Atlay, Beckly Trust, Johann Albrecht Bengel,

Joseph Butler, Herrnhut, Anthony Horneck, George Lavington, William Law, religious societies, Edward Stillingfleet, and George Whitefield].

Theologische Realenzyklopädie, Band VII. Berlin: Walter de Gruyter, 1981 [two articles by HDR on Robert Boyle and Thomas Chalmers].

The Penguin Dictionary of Religions, edited by John Hinnells. London: Allen Lane, 1984. Revised edition, *A New Dictionary of Religions,* edited by John Hinnells. Oxford: Blackwell, 1995 [83 articles by HDR on – within the context of Christianity – Africa, afterlife, Anabaptists, Anglicanism, architecture, Arminianism, Asia, Australasia, authority, Baptists, Britain, Calvinism, Canada, Catholic, China, Christadelphians, Christian Science, Christianity, Christology, church discipline, church organization, conciliar movement, Congregationalism, cosmology, councils of the Church, Counter-Reformation, creeds, crusades, drama, ecumenical movement, Eucharist, Europe, Evangelical, evil, Friends (Religious Society of), God, grail, heresy, humanity, iconography, India, Jansenism, Jehovah's Witnesses, liturgical movement, Lutheranism, marriage, mass, Methodism, millenarianism, missions, Moral Re-Armament, moral theology, Moravian Brethren, Mormons, Papacy, penance, Pentecostalism, Pietism, pilgrimages, Plymouth Brethren, Presbyterianism, Protestantism, Puritanism, Reformation, revivalism, Roman Catholicism, sacraments, saints, salvation, Salvation Army, sects, sexuality, Shakers, sin, social morality, Southcottians, State, theodicy, Trinity, Turin Shroud, Unitarianism, and West Indies. Four articles co-authored by HDR on Church music, Mary (Virgin), ministry, and worship].

The Blackwell Dictionary of Evangelical Biography, 1730–1860, edited by Donald Lewis. Oxford: Blackwell, 1995, 2 vol. [six articles by HDR on John Crosse, William Darney, William Roby, James Scott, Edward Smyth, and David Taylor].

The Dictionary of Eighteenth-Century British Philosophers, general editors: John Yolton, John Valdimir Price and John Stephens. Bristol: Thoemmes Press, 1999, 2 vol. [article by HDR on John Wesley].

The Dictionary of Historical Theology, general editor, Trevor Hart. Carlisle: Paternoster Press/Grand Rapids, MI: William B. Eerdmans Publishing Company, 2000 [article by HDR on John Wesley].

Fifty Major Thinkers on Education: from Confucius to Dewey, edited by Joy Palmer. London: Routledge, 2001 [article by HDR on John Wesley].

Oxford Dictionary of National Biography, edited by Colin Matthew and Brian Harrison. Oxford: Oxford University Press, 2004, 60 vol. and http://www.oxforddnb.com/ [24 articles by HDR on John Bennet, Samuel Bradburn, William Bramwell, Joshua Brookes, John Clayton, Samuel Francis Collier, James Crawfoot, James Creighton, Ann Cutler, John Glover, William Hulme, Matthew Mayer, Robert Newton, Elizabeth Rhodes, James Harrison Rigg, Nicholas Stratford, David Taylor, Richard Watson, Charles Wesley, John Wesley, Samuel Wesley, Sarah Wesley, John Whitehead, and Richard Wroe; reference group theme essay on Holy Club].

The Oxford Dictionary of the Christian Church. Third edition, edited by Elizabeth Livingstone. Oxford: Oxford University Press, 1997. Third edition, revised, 2005 [unsigned revision by HDR of various articles, including Methodism, Methodist Church, Methodist New Connexion, Primitive Methodism, revivalism, Shakers, Joanna Southcott, Charles Wesley, and John Wesley].

Index

Adam's sin, 24, 133–34
    as *reatus* and *privation*, 24
Advice with Respect to Health (John Wesley's Extract of Tissot's *L'Avis*), 137
Aeneid (Virgil), 130
Aepinus, John, 47, 55
African Methodist Episcopal Zion Church [AMEZC], 204, 223
Aldersgate, 67, 83, 85, 134, 141, 179, 269
American Revolution, 176–78, 187
Anabaptists, 10, 15, 45
Angels, 72, 147
Anglican, 148–49, 152, 163, 193, 236, 239–40, 243, 257–58, 261, 266, 271, 278
    and Anglican Evangelicals, 233, 236, 244–47, 254, 257–58
    and Evangelicals, 236, 257–58
Anglican Revival: Studies in the Oxford Movement (Yngve Brilioth), 7, 235
Anglo-Catholic, 236–37, 256, 258, 261, 264, 266, 268–69, 278
Annual Conference, 62–63, 78
Antinomianism, 87, 120, 254
Apologia Pro Vita Sua (John Henry Newman), 242–43, 246, 255
Apostolic Faith, The, 212, 224
Aquinas, Thomas, 72

Arians of the Fourth Century (John Henry Newman), 240–41
Arminian Magazine, The, 4, 8, 83, 103, 130, 144, 154, 158–65, 172
    and *The Methodist Magazine*, 103, 165, 169, 265
    and *Wesleyan-Methodist Magazine*, 166, 170
Arminianism, 2, 8n2, 9, 17, 20–24, 26, 28, 90
    and political and religious boundaries, 10–17
    and human freedom, 20–28
Arminians, 11–12, 14–15, 19–20, 22–23, 27–28
Arminus, Johann, 2, 9–11, 14, 16–19, 21n31, 23–28
    on grace, 27–28
    on justification, 21–22
    on sin, 23
Arnobius, 229
Arthur, William, 276
articulus stantis et cadentis ecclesiae, 231–32
Asbury, Elizabeth, 174, 176
Asbury, Francis, 5, 173–76, 178–87, 191–92
    and the American Revolution, 5
    and camp meetings, 183
    and emotionalism, 183
    and ordination, 185–87

Asbury, Joseph, 174–76
Asbury, Sarah, 174
Assertio Septem Sacramentorum (Martin Luther), 33–34
assurance, 66, 68, 194, 201–2, 207
atheism, 157
Atonement, 194–95, 240, 255
  limited, 194–95
Augsburg Confession, 34, 41, 48–49, 54
  and good works, 49
Augustine, 23, 243
Augustinian, 14, 24, 26
autobiography, 105–6, 115, 117, 126, 128, 201–2, 243
Autobiography (William Stevenson), 5, 189–90, 192–93, 195, 197–98, 200, 205–8
Autobiography (Isaac Williams), 241

Babylonian Captivity of the Church, The, 33–34, 41n48
Balch, Hezekiah, 191, 195
Bancroft, Richard, 161
Bangs, Carl, 20
Bangs, Nathan, 186
Baptism, 75–77, 195–96, 251, 271
  infant, 196, 254
  and *opus operatum*, 251
  and regeneration, 271
Baptism of the Holy Spirit, 3, 77, 211–12, 221–25
Baptists, 148, 189, 193, 195–98
Baring-Gould, Sabine, 236–37
Barnes, Robert, 2, 29–31, 35, 37–47, 50–51, 53–57, 59
Bartleman, Frank, 215, 223, 232
Baxter, Richard, 156, 160
Beaufort, Margaret, 34–35
Bebbington, David, 233–34, 248, 254
Bedford, John, 260
Bell, George, 154, 219–20
Benson, John, 118
Benson, Joseph, 165
Bertius, Peter, 14, 19–23, 25
  on justification, 20–23
Bible Arminians, 87
Bible Calvinists, 87
biblicae sortes, 232

biblicalism, 226, 249
Black, John, 109, 111, 117
Boehm, Henry, 181
Boleyn, Ann, 48n75, 50
Bolton, Ann, 141
Bond, John Wesley, 181–82
Bosanquet, Mary, 92, 220
Bourne, Hugh, 171
Boyle, Robert, 160
Brackenbury, Robert Carr, 143
Brilioth, Yngve, 7, 235, 238, 253
British Critic, 239
Britten, James, 275
Brontë, Charlotte, 159
Bucer, Martin, 50
Bugenhagen, Johann, 40–41
Bullinger, Heinrich, 52
Bulteel, Henry Bellenden, 248, 254–55
Bunting, Jabez, 269, 276
Bunyan, John, 243
Burgon, J. W., 260
Butler, Joseph, 227

Calm Address to Our American Colonies, A (John Wesley), 177
Calvin, John, 25, 66
Calvinist, 16, 60, 86–87, 90–92, 252
Calvinists, 9–11, 15
Cambridge University, 30–31, 34–35, 37–38, 227–28, 248
  Augustinan Friars at, 35
  St John's College, 34
  Queen's College, 35
  Trinity College, 37
Camp Meeting Methodists, 171, 191
Campbell, Ted, A., 5–6
Carter, Grayson, 248
Catholic, 149, 166, 253, 274, 278
Catholic Evangelicalism (Dieter Voll), 256
Certainty of the Worlds of Spirits, The (Richard Baxter), 156, 160
Cessationism, 227
Charismatic movement, 210, 212, 216, 222, 224, 230
Checks to Antinomianism (John Fletcher), 87–89, 92
Cheyne, George, 136, 138

Christian conference, 2, 61–62, 64, 68, 77
Christian Faith, 61, 193, 196
Christian Library (John Wesley), 101, 108
Christian Prudence (John Norris), 75
Church, 9, 14–15, 17–18, 28, 38–39, 42, 45, 49, 56, 58, 67, 75, 79, 206, 226, 234, 236, 243, 271–72
    Early, 67
Church of England, 6, 29, 32, 57, 86, 151, 159, 173, 175, 182, 186, 235–38, 240, 250, 254, 256, 264, 258, 261, 263, 268, 275, 278
Church and State, 15–16, 243–44, 254, 257
Church, Thomas, 213–14
Church Times, 276
Churchmanship of John Wesley, The (James Harrison Rigg), 269
Civil War (England), 178
Clapham Sect, 252
Clarke, Adam, 115, 143, 276
Cloister Church (*Kloosterkerk*), 13, 19
Close, Francis, 236, 259
Coke, Thomas, 122, 157, 173, 186, 190, 207, 276
    and ordination, 185–86
Coleridge, J. D., 260
Collection of Modern Relations of Matter of Fact Concerning Witches & Witchcraft, A (Matthew Hales), 160
Collins, Kenneth, 85, 86n21, 105n16
Compassion, 70
Concise Ecclesiastical History (John Wesley), 246
Confessions (Augustine), 243
Contra-Remonstrants, 9, 11–13, 18, 20, 28
Conversation, 62–63,
    and inclination of human heart, 63
Conversion, 105–6, 109–16, 128, 179, 196–97, 201–3, 207, 214, 233, 238, 250, 252, 269
    as instantaneous, 252
Conviction, 197, 200
Cooper, Ezekiel, 180, 187

Corrupted Methodist Worship (John Kensit), 277
Council of Trent, 95
Covenant services, 112
Coverdale, Miles, 41
Cox, Harvey, 216, 217n28, 224
    and Pentecostal expansion, 216n25, 217
Cranmer, Thomas, 29–30, 51–53, 59
Crawfoot, James, 171
Credulity, Superstition, and Fanaticism (William Hogarth), 150–51, 155
Cromwell, Thomas, 45–46, 48, 51–54, 56
Crosby, Sarah, 220
Cyprian, 229

damnation, 200
Darby, John Nelson, 254
Davies, Owen, 4–5, 148n4
De Vera Obedentia (Stephen Gardiner), 50–51
Declaration of Sentiments (Johann Arminus), 9, 14, 16
Defensor Fidei, 33, 41n54
Deificatio, 67
    and Eastern Christianity, 67
Deists, 94, 149, 241
Demon Expelled: Or, The Influence of Satan, and the Power of Christ, The (John Heaton), 168–69
    Copy found in Lewis Carroll's library, 169
Demonic Possession. *See* Supernatural
Demons. *See* Supernatural
Demonology. *See* Supernatural
Devils. *See* Supernatural
Diary (John Wesley), 63, 144–45
Dickens, A. G., 32n12, 35n27, 40n44, 47
Disease, 139, 145
disciplina arcanae, 241
Dissenters, 149, 163, 173
divine presence, 70–73, 115, 117
Dover, Thomas, 136
Dugdale, Richard (Surrey Demoniac). *See* Supernatural

Earthquakes, 199–200, 215

New Madrid, 199
Lisbon, 199, 215
Easterbrook, Joseph, 163
Ecclesiastical Injunctions (Thomas Cromwell), 51
Ecclesiology, 58, 104, 267, 272
Edgecomb, Elizabeth, 220
Edwardian era, 261, 263, 278
Edwards, Jonathan, 233
Election, doctrine of, 194–95
Electrical therapy, 137
Ellis, Mark A., 24
Empirical approach, 136–37, 160, 163, 214, 229
Enlightenment, 4, 6, 132, 139, 148, 165, 213, 217, 226, 230, 241
Enthusiasm, 117, 124–25, 139, 149, 153–54, 185, 213, 227, 245
    of George Bell, 154
    and sexual licentiousness, 149–50
Enthusiasm Delineated (William Hogarth), 150–51
Enthusiasm of Methodists and Papists Compared, The (George Lavington), 245
entire Sanctification. *See* Sanctification
Episcopalian, 193
Episcopius, Simon, 14, 19, 23–26
Epworth, 172–75, 199
    Epworth fire, 199, 206
Erasmus, 32, 35, 45n63
Erastianism, 15–16, 28
    and anti-Erastian, 244
Erskine, Thomas, 249
Essay of Health and Long Life (George Cheyne), 136
Eucharist, 75, 194, 251, 256, 263, 271
    and real presence, 251, 271
Evangelical Conversion Narrative, The (D. Bruce Hindmarsh), 104
Evangelicalism, 233, 235–42, 246–47, 249–50, 252, 254
    and emotional excess, 240–41
    and journal keeping, 242–43
Evangelicals, 2, 36, 131, 214, 226, 234–35, 237–38, 241–44, 247, 251, 253, 256–58, 263, 266
    and Evangelical religion, 244
    and High Church, 238
Evangelism, 4, 103, 165, 175
Exorcism, 4, 158, 161, 166–70, 214, 219, 224, 230
Explanatory Notes Upon the New Testament (John Wesley), 66n15
Extraordinary Affliction and Gracious Relief of a Little Boy: Supposed to be the Effects of Spiritual Agency, The (John Heaton), 168–69

Faber, G. S., 251
Faith, 30, 41, 43, 55, 66, 68, 77, 85–86, 89, 93, 102, 105, 132–33, 146, 213, 218, 226,
    and justification, 134
    and revelation, 132–33
    as a spiritual sense, 229
    and works, 43, 55, 66, 89
faith-healing, 144
Fall. *See* Original Sin
Fasting, 75, 141, 144, 158, 257
Faussett, Godfrey, 245
Field, Clive, D., 7
First Great Awakening, 195
Fisher, John, 43, 48, 51
Five Points of Calvinism, 11
Five Points of Remonstrance, 11
Fletcher, John, 3, 82, 86–98, 101, 178
    and American Methodists, 87
    and Sanctification, 3
    and the second blessing, 93–98
Foote, Julia A. J., 204
Forest Methodists. *See* Magic Methodists
forgiveness, 64, 113
Foundry, 141
Foxe, John, 31, 37–38, 40, 52, 55, 57
Frederick, John, 48, 53
Freedom (human), 9, 19, 24, 27, 88–89
French Prophets, 229
Froude, Hurrell, 235, 240, 243, 245, 253
Furley, Dorothy, 219, 220
Furz, John, 109

Garbett, James, 259
Gardiner, Stephen, 35–36, 45, 48–51, 50, 54, 56

Gentleman's Magazine, The, 158
Georgia, 141, 173
Ghosts, 147–49, 171
    and the Cock Lane Ghost, 151–53
    and ghost of Julius Caesar, 151
Gibson, William, 246n51
Gifts of the Holy Spirit (*Charismata*), 211, 222–24, 227–28, 230
    and healings, 224
    and miracles, 224
    and tongues (*Glossalia*), 211, 222–24, 228, 230
Gilley, Sheridan, 247, 252
Gladstone, William, 253–54
Glanvill, Joseph, 156–57, 160
Gomarus, Franciscus, 9, 14, 15–21, 23
Grace, 2–3, 19, 21, 23, 26–27, 56, 59, 62, 64, 67, 69–71, 73–74, 78, 88, 90, 96–97, 99, 115, 119, 145–46, 197
    as convincing grace, 99, 121
    and election, 238
    as judging grace, 73
    as justification, 67, 73, 85, 99, 107, 134
    as prevenient, 26, 56, 59, 73, 85, 99, 110–11, 121
    as a relational concept, 70–71
    as sanctification, 67, 73, 85, 99, 107
    and works, 21, 66
Grace Abounding (John Bunyan), 243
Gregory, Arthur, 270
Gregory, Benjamin, 269, 271–73
Grimshaw, William, 259
Grotius, Hugo, 16, 28, 238
Gutiérrez, Gustavo, 217
Gunter, W. Stephen, 1–2, 11

Haime, John, 126
Hales, Matthew, 160
Hales, William, 157
Hall, Samuel Romilly, 264
Hamilton, Walter Kerr, 247
Hampson, John, Jr., 159
Hanby, Thomas, 113
Harris, Howell, 233
Harrison, Henry, 170
Haweis, Thomas, 246
Heaton, John, 166–69

Heitzenrater, Richard P., 2, 64n10, 84
Hempton, David, 6, 209
Herring, George, 264
Heygate, William Edward, 242
Henry VIII, 32–34, 39, 41, 43, 45–48, 50–54, 56–57
Hindmarsh, D. Bruce, 104–6
Historical Essay Concerning Witchcraft (Francis Hutchinson), 149
historiography, 4, 139, 233, 256, 261
History of the Church of Christ (Joseph Milner), 246
History of England (John Wesley), 246
Hoadly, Benjamin, 253
    and Bangorian controversy, 253
Hocking, Joseph, 273–75
Hogarth, William, 150–51
holiness, 64–68, 85, 97–99, 103, 105–8, 110, 116–17, 120, 145, 215, 248, 252, 255, 257
    and discipline, 145
Holiness Movement, 175, 187, 207, 210, 214, 263
Holland, Thomas, 161
Hollenweger, Walter J., 223n49
Holy Catholic Church, The Communion of Saints, The (Benjamin Gregory), 272
Holy Club, 179
Holy Conferencing, 2, 61, 67, 78–79
Holy Spirit, 2–3, 59, 71, 73, 85, 110–11, 113, 117, 123, 221, 223, 271–72
    witness of, 59, 65–66, 85
Holy Spirit baptism. *See* Baptism of the Holy Spirit
Homilies of the Church of England, 2, 29
Hopper, Christopher, 113–14, 122–23, 26
Howitt, William, 160, 169
Hughes, Hugh Price, 262, 276
Hughes, Lewis, 161
    and Exorcism of Mary Glover, 61
Humane Society, 89
Huss, John, 50
Hutchinson, Francis, 149
Huxham, John, 136, 145
imatatio Christi, 134, 138, 141–42
Irenaeus, 229

Institution of a Christian Man, The (Bishops' Book) 51, 54, 56
invisible world, 4, 147–50, 155–58, 164–67, 170, 172, 212, 229, 242
Irish Methodist Church, 157
Irving, Edward, 254n79

Jabez Easterbrook: A Religious Novel (Joseph Hocking), 273
Jackson, Elizabeth, 161–61
Jackson, Thomas, 103, 276, 278
Jebb, John, 237–38, 246
Jefferson, Thomas, 186
Jeffrey David Lyle, 103
Jenkins, Philip, 209
Jerome, William, 54
Johnson, Samuel, 152, 177
Jollie, Thomas, 149
Journal (John Wesley), 29, 63, 71, 80, 88–89, 131, 144–45, 151, 153–57, 159, 190, 200, 206–7, 211, 218
Journals and Letters (Francis Asbury), 5, 175
Joyce, Matthias, 119, 123–24
Julius Caesar (William Shakespeare), 151
justification, 2, 19–23, 29–30, 42–43, 49, 54, 56–57, 60, 66–67, 85–86, 89, 91, 97, 106, 194, 196–97, 201, 218, 251, 255
    Falling Away from, 196–97
Justin, the Martyr, 229

Keble, John, 251, 268
Kingswood School, 164
Knight, Francis, 263
Knight, Henry H., III, 226
knowledge, 108
    and revelation, 132
Knox, Alexander, 237–38, 246

Lactantius, 229
L'Avis au Peuple sur sa Sante (Samuel Tissot), 137
Large Minutes (John Wesley), 2, 61–63, 65, 77–79
Latimer, Hugh, 36, 52–53

Latitudinarianism, 239
Lavington, George, 245
Law, William, 245, 252–53
Lectures on Types of Prophecies (Edward Bouverie Pusey), 242
Lee, Thomas, 112, 126
Liddon, Henry Perry, 246
Life of the Reverend John Wesley, The (Thomas Coke and Henry Moore), 190, 207
Limborch, Philipp van, 238
Lives of Early Methodist Preachers, The, 103, 105, 107
Living Wesley, The (James Harrison Rigg), 269
Locke, John, 134, 241
London Quarterly Review, 267–68
Lopez, Gregory, 93
Lord's Supper. See Eucharist
love, 30, 66–67, 70, 85, 91, 96–99, 102, 109, 111, 113, 116–18, 120–22, 129, 218, 220
love feast, 76, 109, 112, 123
Lubbertus, Sibrandus, 20–23
    on justification, 21–22
Lukins, George. See Yatton Demoniac.
Luther, Martin, 33–36, 41, 46, 49–50, 53, 66
Lutheran, 31, 33–34, 41–42, 46–47, 51, 54, 56, 60

Macchia, Frank D., 221
MacDonald, James, 141
McGeary, Thomas, 164
McGee, Gary, 232
Mack, Phyllis, 213
McKendree, William, 191–92
Madden, Deborah, 4
Maddox, Randy, 84
Magic Methodists, 171
Maleficium, 153, 158
Manning, Henry Edward, 244, 247
Martyn, Henry, 243, 252
Maskew, Jonathan, 127
Mason, John, 122
Mather, Alexander, 114–16, 118–19, 122, 127
Mather, Cotton, 157

INDEX

Maurits, Prince, 13, 19
Maxfield, Thomas, 219–20
Mayers, Walter, 250, 252
Meadows, Philip, 3–4
means of grace, 2–3, 61–62, 68, 73–77, 79, 106, 129, 187
    and general means of grace, 75, 77, 79
    and instituted means of grace, 75–76, 79
    and prudential means of grace, 75–76, 79
    and spiritual reading, 108
mechanical philosophy, 4
Melanchthon, Philipp, 47, 49–50, 52–53
Memoirs of the Late Rev. John Wesley (John Hampton, Jr.), 159
Methodism, 6, 79, 81, 83, 86, 92, 97, 103, 140, 148–50, 152–53, 165–66, 175, 183, 188–90, 206–7, 209–10, 214–15, 238, 252, 262, 269, 277
    and Pentecostalism, 214
    and sanctification, 211
Methodism: Empire of Spirit (David Hempton), 6
Methodist culture, 197, 199, 279
    and the miraculous, 199
    and ritual controversies, 265
Methodist Magazine. See The Arminian Magazine
Methodist Episcopal Church [MEC], 173, 192–93, 214, 222
Methodist Preachers, 3–4, 191, 221, 263
    and autobiographies, 3, 202
    and deathbeds, 4, 115, 127
    and spiritual warfare, 4
    and violence, 4
Methodist Recorder, 265
Methodist Societies, 29, 59, 88, 92, 111–13, 124, 127, 183, 185, 191–93, 196, 205, 211, 213, 219, 263
    and bands, 113, 116, 119
    and class meetings, 112–14, 123–24, 183, 185, 191, 196, 203–4, 213
Methodist Times, 265
Methodist and Wesleyan movement, 1, 28, 125, 153, 163, 189, 193, 200, 203, 205, 209–10, 233, 235, 238–39, 252, 260–62, 264, 266, 271–72, 277–78
    and Anglo-Catholics, 264
    the Bible Christians, 262–63
    and the New Connexion, 262
    and the Primitive Methodists, 262–63
    and the United Methodist Free churches, 262–63
Methodists, 76, 85, 87, 110–11, 117, 124–25, 128, 138, 141, 152–54, 163, 169, 184, 195–96, 206, 211, 213–17, 219–20, 224, 226–27, 232, 261, 264, 269
    and High Churchmen, 271
    and London debating societies, 164, 176
Middleton, Conyers, 227–31
Milner, Joseph, 246
Milner, John, 127
Minutes of the Methodist Conference, 1
Miracles. See Supernatural
Missio Dei, 121
Mission spirituality, 107–9, 120, 128–29
    and the Second Blessing, 115
Missionaries, 105
Moltmann, Jürgen, 216–17
Monro, Sr., James, 150
    and Bethlam hospital, 150
Moore, Henry, 190, 207
Moore, John, 152
Moravians, 66–67, 89
Moore, Henry, 140
More, Thomas, 45n63, 48, 51
Morgan, James, 106, 108–9, 114, 123

Natural Method of Curing Most Diseases (George Cheyne), 136
Nelson, John, 120
Neo-Anglicanism, 238
Neo-Charismatics, 216
new birth, 85, 91, 97, 106, 115, 132
New Orleans Christian Advocate, 5, 189, 193
Newman, Francis, 236, 250, 255
Newman, John Henry, 236, 238–243, 246, 248–52, 255, 268

and abandonment of
Evangelicalism, 241–42
and Joseph Milner, 246
News from the Invisible World, 159–60
Newsome, David, 248, 252
Newton, John, 259
Newton, Benjamin Wills, 248, 254
Newton, Robert, 276
Ninty-five Theses, 33
Nobbs, Douglas, 9n3, 16
Nockles, Peter B., 6–7
Nonconformity, 148, 236, 261, 266, 274, 278
Norris, John, 72n27, 75
Notes and Queries, 169

Oldenbarneveldt, General, 12–15
ordo salutis (Way of Salvation), 198, 220–21
Original Sin, 133. 135, 138, 141
Ott, Phillip W., 133
Otto, Rudolf, 67n21
Outler, Albert C., 81, 83, 100n65
Oxford High Anglicanism and Its Chief Leaders (James Harrison Rigg), 267–68
Oxford Movement, 233–35, 240, 243–44, 246–47, 249, 253–59, 264, 266, 278
Oxford Movement and Wesleyan Methodism in England 1833–1882: A Study in Religious Conflict, The (Mats Selen), 236n10
Oxford University, 34, 71, 173, 176, 178–79, 186, 260, 262
and Christ Church, 175
and Exeter College, 248
and Lincoln College, 175, 262
and Wadham College, 248
Ozman, Agnes, 222

Paget, Francis, 242
Paley, William, 241–42
Palmer, Phoebe, 221n44
Parham, Charles, 222–23
Parker, Samuel, 192
Pattison, Mark, 247, 262

Pawson, John, 108, 114–15, 118, 122, 124, 127–29
Pentecostals, 175, 187, 210–14, 216, 218, 222, 224–26, 231–32
Pentecostalism, 6, 209–10, 215–16, 221–22, 230
and come-outism, 215, 222
essentials of, 230n75
Perfection, 85, 87–88, 97–99, 105–6, 115–17, 119–21, 141, 175, 203, 211, 218–19, 252
and discipline, 123–24, 128
and perfectionism, 220
as sinlessness, 119, 141
Perfectionist Controversy, 3, 93–98, 211
Pereiro, James, 244n41, 247
Perronet, Vincent, 137
Philosophical Considerations Touching the Being of Witches and Witchcraft (Joseph Glanvill), 156
Philpot, J. C., 248
Pietism, 255
piety, 108, 141, 179–80, 186
Pilgrimage of Grace, 50–51
Pilmore, Joseph, 183
poltergeist phenomena, 147
Popery, Superstition, Ignorance and Knavery (Zachary Taylor), 149
Prayer, 62, 69, 75, 112–13, 116–17, 119, 139, 145, 158, 163, 167,170, 179, 196, 204, 223
Preachers, 31, 62, 76, 103–4, 107, 111, 115, 117–25, 127, 129, 157,
and exhorters, 115
and mission spirituality, 103
and perfection, 115
preaching, 57, 81, 85, 91, 113–14, 116–17, 124, 198, 217
and women preachers, 92, 165
Predestination, 9, 15, 87, 91, 197
Presbyterianism, 194
Presbyterians, 148, 189–90, 193, 196
Primitive Christianity, 137, 141
Primitive Methodism, 170, 172
Primitive Methodist Magazine, 171
Primitive Physic (John Wesley), 4, 133, 136–38, 142, 145–46

Primitive Tradition Recognised in Holy Scripture (John Keble), 251
Principles of a Methodist, The, 31
Proby, H. L., 236
Protestant, 2, 10, 39–41, 45–46, 49–52, 54, 58, 95, 166, 175, 189, 203, 236–37, 241, 266, 268, 274–75
Providence, 106, 117, 123, 125, 138, 149, 153, 165, 172
Punch, or the London Charivari, 260–61, 279
Pusey, Edward Bouverie, 242, 246, 251, 255, 260–61
Puseyism, 257, 268

Quakers (Society of Friends), 148–49

Rack, Henry D., 1, 82, 105–6, 112–13, 116n63, 136, 139, 141, 154, 174–75, 179, 187–89, 233, 234n5, 246, 253, 280
   and Class Meetings, 1
   and Death Bed Experiences, 1, 127–28
   and Religious Enthusiasm, 1
   and Women, 1
Rankin, Thomas, 116–17, 123, 183, 184n29, 185
realpolitik, 46
reason, 134, 139, 182, 206, 213
Reasonable Enthusiast: John Wesley and the Rise of Methodism (Henry D. Rack), 1, 82, 139, 189
Reformation, 2, 29, 31–32, 34, 40–41, 238
religious conversation, 62–64, 79
religious experience, 179, 198, 207
Remains (Hurrell Froude), 243, 245
Remonstrants, 9, 11–13, 16, 20, 23, 25–26, 28
Renaissance, 34
de Renty, Monsieur, 93
repentance, 85–86, 105
Resolution for Peace, The, 11–12
Revival of Primitive Doctrine, The (Samuel Francis Wood), 235
Revivalism, 6, 124, 170, 234

Revivals, 85–86, 89, 93, 95, 98, 102, 111, 125, 141, 165, 183, 198, 201, 205, 218, 233–34, 257–59
   Azusa Street Revival, 212, 215, 225
   and Catholic revival, 256–57
   and Evangelical revival, 233, 244, 248, 253–56, 258
   and Great Awakening, 233
   at Everton, 218
   at Weardale, 218
Rhetoric, 5–6, 80, 101, 237
   of the supernatural, 5–6, 212, 214, 226n58, 230
Rigg, James Harrison, 266–69, 273, 276, 278
Righteousness of Christ, 21–22, 30, 43
   as imputed, 43
Ritualism, 7, 256, 264, 266, 278
Robinson, Jasper, 119
Rodda, Richard, 112, 117
Rogers, J. Guinness, 248
Rogers, James, 118–20, 125
Rogers, John, 41, 124
Roman Catholics, 95, 266, 268, 278
Rowland, Daniel, 233
Royal Divorce, 46, 49, 53
   and Queen Caroline, 47
   and Martin Luther, 46
Royal Society of Science, 157
Runyon, Theodore, 84
Ryan, Sarah, 220
Ryder, George Dudly, 257
Ryle, J. C., 236–37

Sacraments, 75, 240–41, 251, 254, 268
Sadducismus Triumphatus, or Full and Plain Evidence Concerning Witches and Apparitions (Joseph Glanvill), 156, 160
Salkeld, Jane, 218–19
saluus, 132, 146
Sanctification, 65, 68, 85–86, 120, 194, 197, 203–5, 207, 211, 219, 221–22, 224, 252
   and Entire Sanctification, 115, 203–5, 207, 222
Satan. *See* Supernatural
Scherpe Resolutie (Sharp Resolution), 13

Schmalkaldic League, 48, 51
Schmidt, Darren, 246n49
School for Slander; or, The Soul of Dominic Wildthorne, A (James Britten), 275
second blessing, 6, 93–99, 116, 119, 218–22
    instantaneous or gradual, 98–100, 220
    losing the second blessing, 220–21
Secret History of the Oxford Movement, The (Walter Walsh), 236, 241, 268
Selen, Mats, 236n10
Selina, Countess of Huntingdon, 239
Sententiae ex doctoribus collectae, quas papistae valde impudenter hodie damnant, 41, 45
Serious Call to a Devout and Holy Life (William Law), 252–53
Serious Thoughts occasioned by the late Earthquake at Lisbon (John Wesley), 199
Sermons, 81–83, 85–86, 88–91, 93, 95–96, 98, 102, 131, 138–40, 154, 188, 195, 197
Sermons On Several Occasions (John Wesley), 82
Seymour, William, 222–23
Shadford, George, 112, 118, 184
Shirley (Charlotte Brontë), 159
signs and wonders, 47–48
Simeon, Charles, 248
sin, 19, 23–24, 27, 65, 85, 98, 218, 220, 252
    as actual, 220
    as inbred, 220
sins, 64, 202
Smith, Timothy L., 218
Society for Pentecostal Studies, 216
sola fide, 43, 56
sola scriptura, 251
Soteriology, 8, 23, 25, 26–28, 59, 73, 252
Soul of Dominic Wildthorne, The (Joseph Hocking), 273–74
Southern California Holiness Association, 223
Southey, Robert, 159

Specimen controversarium Beligarum, 14
Spirit. *See* Holy Spirit
Spiritual Magazine, The, 172
spiritual senses, 134
spiritual warfare, 112, 118, 125
    and mobs, 125
Spiritualism, 172
Spiritualist (newspaper), 172
Standard Sermons (John Wesley), 81, 83–84, 97, 101, 190
Staniforth, Sampson, 110
Stephenson, Thomas Bowman, 276
Stevens, Able, 154, 172, 206n78
Stevenson, James, 190–92
Stevenson, William, 5, 189–93, 195–98, 200–207
Storey, George, 111, 119
Streiff, Patrick, 3
Stubbs, William, 253–54
Stunt, Timothy, 252, 254
Supernatural, 5, 144, 151, 153, 155, 158, 213–14, 220, 226–30, 232
    and apparitions, 148, 151, 155, 160, 164
    and demonic possession, 153, 160, 163–64, 166–68
    of William Dove, 170
    of John Evens, 167
    of Mary Glover, 167
    and Surrey Demoniac (Richard Dugdale), 149
    and demonologists, 148, 154
    and demonology, 148, 169–70
    as mesmeric illness, 169
    and demons, 147, 171
    and debilitating illnesses, 154
    and Devil, 147, 151, 164–65, 170
    and divine communications, 160
    and dreams, 153, 160, 163, 218, 224
    and Hell, 160, 170
    and magic, 153
    and miracles, 158, 172, 198–200, 207, 213, 224, 227–29
    and miraculous protection, 125, 199, 206
    and preternatural, 148, 153–54, 159–160, 171
    and resurrection of the dead, 219

and Satan, 112, 116, 129, 165,
    170–71
and spiritual healing, 145, 153, 160,
    199, 212, 214, 216, 224, 231
and trances, 171
and visions, 171, 218, 224
and witchcraft, 4, 147–48, 154–55,
    157, 160–61, 164–65, 167–68,
    172
    and bewitchment, 160–63, 165
    and Witch trials, 147–48,
        165–66
    and Witches, 147–48, 151,
        153–54, 163–64, 171
        and Witchcraft Act, 147–48,
            153
    and Witchcraft and
        Conjuration Act, 147
Supernatural consciousness, 6
Supplication to Henry VIII, 42, 45–46
Surrey Demoniac, 149
Survey of the Wisdom of God, A (John
    Wesley), 157
Synan, Vinson, 214
Synod of Dort, 2, 8–10, 15–16, 26, 28

Taylor, Thomas, 108, 111, 124, 126
Taylor, Zachary, 149
Taxation No Tyranny (Samuel Johnson),
    177
Temple, Frederick, 259
Temple Magazine, The, 274
Tertullian, 229
testimony, 106–07, 115, 123, 127, 145,
    155–57, 229
Theists, 149
Theophilus, 229
Thoughts Upon Slavery (John Wesley),
    177
Tissor, Samuel, 136
Toft, Mary, 151
Toplady, Augustus Montague, 259
Tory Party, 173
Tractarian Movement (Oxford
    Movement), 6–7, 234–35,
    237–38, 240, 246, 250–51, 253,
    254–57, 264–65, 266–67
    and Evangelicalism, 240, 242

and piety, 246
and revivalism, 7
and Tractarian *ethos*, 240–42, 244,
    247
Tracts for the Times, 7, 240, 242–43,
    259, 268
Transubstantiation, 40, 52
Trapp, Joseph, 245
Trollope, Anthony, 254
Trussler, John, 151, 155
Tudors, 32, 34–35, 40
Turner, Frank, 239, 244, 255
Turner, Frank, 236, 249
Turner, John Munsey, 261
Tyndale, Matthew, 40, 50

Union of Utrecht, 10
United Methodist Church, 61
Uytenbogaert, Johannes, 10, 12, 16–18,
    20

Valton, John, 108, 118–19
Venn, Henry, 252, 259
Vernon, Walter N., 189n2, 201, 206
via media, 30
Victorian era, 242, 261, 263, 266, 278
    and Methodism, 266, 278
Victorian Religious Revivals (David
    Bebbington), 233
View of the Evidences of Christianity, A
    (William Paley), 241
Virgil, 130–31
Voll, Dieter, 256

Walpole, Horace, 152
Walsh, John, 220
Walsh, John (eighteenth century), 233–
    34, 246n48, 248
Walsh, Thomas, 108–10, 120–21, 123,
    126, 221
Walsh, Walter, 236–37, 241, 268
Ware, Thomas, 184–85
Washington, George, 186
Watch Nights, 76
Watson, David Lowes, 1–2
Wealth, 180, 182
Webster, Robert, 1–7, 125n105, 210n7,
    214n20, 226n58

Wednesbury, 174
Welling, Martin, 6–7
Wenham, Jane, 147
Wesley, Charles, 5, 59, 83n6, 90, 92, 98, 134, 157, 177–79, 207, 213, 226, 233, 263
Wesley, John, 1–4, 29–31, 57, 59–68, 75, 77, 80–103, 106–8, 111, 114, 116, 121–23, 127, 130–31, 133, 136–38, 141, 143–48, 150–51, 153–54, 156–57, 159–60, 163–65, 173–79, 183–85, 187, 189, 193, 195, 197–203, 206–07, 213, 217, 219, 226, 228–29, 232–34, 238–39, 245, 252, 262–263, 269, 278
  and the American Revolution, 176–79
  and appointments, 122–23
  and *Arminian Magazine*, 4
  and Asbury, Francis, 5
  and conversion, 179
  as cultural mediator, 136
  and demonic possession, 164, 227
  and early morning preaching, 140–42
  and the Enlightenment, 139
  and Epworth fire, 199
  and exorcism, 4, 227
  and faith, 3
  and Fletcher, John, 3
  and Georgia, 63
  and ghosts, 148
  and Holy conferencing, 2, 217–18
  and justification, 2, 29–30, 201–2, 218
  and means of grace, 2
  and medicine, 4, 133–46
  and miracles, 198–200
  and natural healing, 4
  and new birth, 59
  and open-air preaching, 143–44
  and Order of Morning Prayer, 278
  and ordination 173, 185–87
  and perceptible inspiration, 198
  and preachers, 111
  and preaching, 60, 114
  and preaching tours, 130, 228
  and prisoners in Oxford, 2
  as reasonable enthusiast, 154
  and religious conversation, 2, 63–64
  as revivalist, 234
  and salvation, 4
  and sanctification, 3, 202–5, 217–18, 221
  and sin, 4, 218
  and spiritual economics, 180–82
  and supernatural, 5, 226
  and supernatural healing, 4
  and witchcraft, 4, 148, 164–65
  and women, 186
Wesley, Samuel, 166, 173–75
Wesley, Sarah, 145–46
Wesley, Susanna, 173–74
Wesley and the People Called Methodists, 64n10, 84
Wesleyans, 278
Wesleyan Methodist Guild of Divine Service, 275, 277
Wesleyan Methodist Magazine, 270
Wesleyan Times, 265
Wesleyan Tracts for the Times, 265
Wesleyan/Arminian tradition, 8, 27n54, 28, 105, 110, 160, 187, 206–7
Wesleyan-Methodist Magazine. See *The Arminian Magazine*
Westminister Central Hall, 262
Westminister College, 267, 269
Whatcoat, Richard, 191
Whig Party, 243–44
White Horse circle, 35–37, 39
  and new theology, 36–37
Whitefield, George, 90–91, 150–51, 233–34, 239, 245
Whitehead, John, 140
Wigger, John, 5
Wilberforce, Henry, 247
Wilberforce, Robert, 247, 253, 256–57
Wilberforce, Samuel, 244, 255, 257
Wilberforce, William, 256
Williams, Isaac, 240–41, 259
Wilson, Daniel, 236, 257
Witchcraft. See Supernatural
Wittenberg Articles, 49
Wolsey, Thomas, 33, 37–39, 41
Wood, Samuel Francis, 235

Woodfield, Gabriel, 191, 200
Works of John Wesley, The (John Wesley), 82–83, 88
Wycliff, John, 40

Yates, Nigel, 264

Yatton Demoniac, 4, 163–64
Yong, Amos, 216, 221
    and Baptism of the Holy Spirit, 221n45
Young, David, 192
Younger, Daniel (the younger), 234

297